DIGITAL MEDIA AND CHILD AND ADOLESCENT MENTAL HEALTH

The NSPCC

The authors are pleased to support the National Society for the Prevention of Cruelty to Children (NSPCC) through donating all author royalties from the purchase of this book to the charity. The authors are especially pleased to have a contribution of expertise from Kirsty Donnelly who works for the NSPCC as the Childline Community Manager.

DIGITAL MEDIA AND CHILD AND ADOLESCENT MENTAL HEALTH

A PRACTICAL GUIDE TO UNDERSTANDING THE EVIDENCE

MICHELLE O'REILLY

NISHA DOGRA

DIANE LEVINE

VERÓNICA DONOSO

Los Angeles | London | New Delhi
Singapore | Washington DC | Melbourne

Los Angeles | London | New Delhi
Singapore | Washington DC | Melbourne

SAGE Publications Ltd
1 Oliver's Yard
55 City Road
London EC1Y 1SP

SAGE Publications Inc.
2455 Teller Road
Thousand Oaks, California 91320

SAGE Publications India Pvt Ltd
B 1/I 1 Mohan Cooperative Industrial Area
Mathura Road
New Delhi 110 044

SAGE Publications Asia-Pacific Pte Ltd
3 Church Street
#10-04 Samsung Hub
Singapore 049483

Editor: Donna Goddard
Editorial assistant: Esmé Carter
Production editor: Rachel Burrows
Copyeditor: Solveig Gardner Servian
Proofreader: Brian McDowell
Indexer: Adam Pozner
Marketing manager: Camille Richmond
Cover design: Wendy Scott
Typeset by: C&M Digitals (P) Ltd, Chennai, India
Printed in the UK

Library of Congress Control Number: 2020949999

British Library Cataloguing in Publication data

A catalogue record for this book is available from the British Library

ISBN 978-1-5297-0939-1
ISBN 978-1-5297-0938-4 (pbk)

At SAGE we take sustainability seriously. Most of our products are printed in the UK using responsibly sourced papers and boards. When we print overseas we ensure sustainable papers are used as measured by the PREPS grading system. We undertake an annual audit to monitor our sustainability.

CONTENTS

ABOUT THE AUTHORS

Michelle O'Reilly (BSc [hons], MSc, MA, PhD, PGCAPHE) is an Associate Professor of Communication in Mental Health at the University of Leicester and a Research Consultant for Leicestershire Partnership NHS Trust. Michelle is also a Chartered Psychologist in Health. Michelle has specific interest in child and adolescent mental health and has been investigating the relationship between mental health and social media as part of that work. Michelle has made several media contributions about the research with adolescents, educationalists, and parents, as funded by the Wellcome Trust. Additional to her research interests in mental health and social media, Michelle also undertakes research in self-harm and suicidal behaviour, neurodevelopmental conditions, and child mental health services, such as mental health assessments and family therapy. Michelle recently won the Anselm Strauss Award for Qualitative Family Research for her co-authored contribution on discursive psychology in this area. Michelle has expertise in qualitative methodologies and specialises in discursive psychology and conversation analysis.

Nisha Dogra (BM DCH FRCPsych MA [Socio-legal studies, children], Postgraduate Certificate in Systemic Practice, PhD) is Emeritus Professor of Psychiatry Education at the Greenwood Institute of Child Health, University of Leicester. She is an external lecturer on the MMedSci Medical Education Master's at the University of Nottingham. She was, until her retirement, working as a generic child and adolescent psychiatrist. Currently, her work in child mental health is focused on how young people see the relationship between mental health and social media. Throughout her career Nisha has been involved in the development and delivery of a wide variety of teaching and training events in undergraduate and postgraduate education, locally, nationally, and internationally in both psychiatry and diversity. She has published widely, including peer reviewed publications, edited and written books as well as contributing chapters to edited books related to psychiatry and education.

Diane Thembekile Levine (BA [QTS], MRes, MA, PhD) is Deputy Director of the Leicester Institute for Advanced Studies, University of Leicester. She began her career as a primary school teacher, before spending many years working in public service as a commissioner, translator and senior manager of an evidence function in national government. Di's research interests focus on interdisciplinary approaches to understanding the ways – including digitally-mediated ways – children and young people develop their resilience pathways. In particular, she works with collaborators in South Africa, Guyana and Kenya to raise the voices of under-represented young people in majority world contexts in research and practice. Di has published both in academic journals and is co-author of Oxford University Press's best-selling textbooks on computing for 4–14 year olds.

Verónica Donoso (PhD in Social Sciences [KU Leuven, Belgium], MA in education and BA in linguistics [Universidad de Chile]) is a Research Associate at the Institute for Media Studies (IMS), University of Leuven (KU Leuven) and an independent consultant specialising in digital literacy, online safety and education. Verónica has more than 18 years of experience on research and policy work and has written several pieces which have served to inform practitioners, researchers, and policymakers both in the EU and worldwide. She provides advice and works with organisations committed to empowering and protecting children and young people so that they can navigate the digital world knowledgably, safely and creatively. Through her career Verónica has advised several organisations, including the United Nations, the European Commission, The European Advertising Standards Alliance, The World Federation of Advertisers, London School of Economics, University of Leicester and European Schoolnet, among others. Before becoming an independent consultant, Verónica was INHOPE's Executive Director. INHOPE is the leading global network combating online Child Sexual Abuse Material.

ACKNOWLEDGEMENTS

The writing of this book was made possible thanks to many who helped. We are grateful to the editors at SAGE: Donna Goddard, Marc Bernard, Esmé Carter, Rachel Burrows, and Katie Rabot, as well as others behind the scenes.

We have included a range of artistic images throughout the book, and appreciate our artist, Tom Cleaver of Mr Cleaver's Monsters. Tom also created our emoji icons associated with the boxes.

The book benefits significantly from different experts who made valued contributions in the form of short expert voices, or longer expert contributions. Our expert voices represent a range of disciplines as well as more personal experiential accounts. *For the sake of clarity, the authors note that these are independent views and do not necessarily reflect the views of the authors.*

In alphabetical order by surname, we thank the following:

Najwa Albeladi – PhD student, University of Leicester (UK) and researcher (Saudi Arabia)

Dr Mark Bowler – Educational Psychologist, Staffordshire (UK)

Zoe Chapman – Secondary School Teacher, Leicestershire (UK)

Darren Doherty – Parent (UK)

Amber Dumbleton-Thomas – Parent (UK)

Dr Seyda Eruyar – Assistant Professor of Psychology, Necmettin University (Turkey)

Juliana Fleury – Volunteer CEO, ASEC Brazil |Movimento Saber Lidar and Partnership for children/UK network parter (Brazil)

Simon Genders – Safeguarding Development Officer, Leicestershire County Council (UK)

Laura Higgins – Director of Community Safety and Digital Civility, Roblox (UK)

Madalyn Heaton-Ward – Secondary School student (17 years old), Leicestershire (UK)

Dr Sajida Hassan – Child and Adolescent Development Programme (CADP) Hussaini Foundation, Karachi (Pakistan)

Professor Athina Karatzogianni – Professor of Media and Communication, University of Leicester (UK)

Dr Nikki Kiyimba – Clinical Psychologist and Senior Educator, Bethlehem Tertiary Institute (New Zealand)

Patrick Krens – Executive Director, Child Helpline International, Amsterdam (Netherlands)

Dr Daria J. Kuss – Associate Professor in Psychology, Nottingham Trent University (UK)

Professor Effie Lai-Chong Law – Professor of Human-Computer Interaction, University of Leicester (UK)

Caitlin McReynolds – Parent (UK)

Annie Mullins, OBE – Yubo Safety Officer (France)

Dr Lindsay O'Dell – Senior Lecturer in Children and Young People, Open University (UK)

Dr Amy Orben – College Research Fellow, University of Cambridge (UK)

Caroline Palmer – Digital Development Clinical Lead, ChatHealth, Leicestershire Partnership NHS Trust (UK)

Nina Puttini – ASEC Brazil Movimento Saber Lidar Team Member (Brazil)

Professor Tom Strong – Professor Emeritus of Counselling Psychology, University of Calgary (Canada)

Dr Tom van Daele – Head of the Expertise Unit Psychology, Technology & Society, Thomas More University of Applied Sciences (Belgium)

Isabella Maria Valério – Secondary School student (16 years old) (Brazil)

Dr Christine Wekerle – Associate Professor in Pediatrics, McMaster University (Canada)

Angharad Wells – Programmes, Operations and Communications Officer, Child Helpline International, Amsterdam (Netherlands)

Luke Whitney – Head Teacher, Mayflower Primary School, Leicester (UK)

Rowena Wilding – Parent (UK)

Ryan Zappelline – Secondary School student (16 years old) (Brazil)

Many children and young people in the UK also contributed to this book, either through consultation groups, research participation or writing letters or contributions on sticky notes. We do not include surnames, but are grateful to: Lily, Mia, Theo, Oliver, Sam, Joseph, and Hannah for their letters. We thank, Blaine, Sam, Madalyn, Madi, George, Dylan, Libby, Rose, Lily, Rhiannon, Will, Tristan, for their sticky notes and consultation comments. Further we thank all our anonymous research participants from London and Leicester who participated in our research projects.

We also have longer expert contributions at the end of each chapter. In alphabetical order by surname, we thank the following:

Sarah Adams – Lecturer in Education, University of Leicester (UK)

Dr Sharon Cooper – President & CEO Developmental & Forensic Pediatrics, PA (USA)

Kirsty Donnelly – Childline Community Manager, NSPCC (UK)

Professor Tamsin Ford – Professor of Child and Adolescent Psychiatry, University of Cambridge (UK)

Professor Gordon Harold – Professor of the Psychology of Education and Mental Health, University of Cambridge (UK)

Dr Jessica Lester – Associate Professor of Inquiry Methodology, Indiana University (USA)

Professor Sonia Livingstone, OBE – Professor of Social Psychology, London School of Economics and Political Science (UK)

Dr Megan A. Moreno – Professor of Pediatrics, University of Wisconsin Madison (USA)

Tink Palmer – CEO Marie Collins Foundation (UK)

Vicki Shotbolt – CEO Parentzone (UK)

Professor Linda Theron – Professor of Educational Psychology, University of Pretoria (South Africa)

Professor Patti Valkenburg – Distinguished Professor, University of Amsterdam (Netherlands)

Valerie Verdoodt – Fellow in Law at the London School of Economics, affiliated postdoctoral researcher at Ghent University and KU Leuven (Belgium)

ABBREVIATIONS

ACEs – Adverse Childhood Experiences

ADHD – Attention Deficit Hyperactivity Disorder

AMER – Automatic Multimodal Emotion Recognition

ASD – Autism Spectrum Disorder

AI – Artificial Intelligence

APA – American Psychiatric Association

CAMHS – Child and Adolescent Mental Health Services

CAP – Child and Adolescent Psychiatry

CBT – Cognitive Behavioural Therapy

CT – Complex Trauma

CYP – Children and Young People

DfE – Department for Education (UK)

DSM – Diagnostic and Statistical Manual of Mental Disorders

DSMM – Differential Susceptibility to Media-effects Model

EU – European Union

FOMO – Fear of Missing Out

fMRI – Functional Magnetic Resonance Imaging

ICD – International Classification of Diseases

iGen – Internet Generation

IoT – Internet of Things

ICT – Internet and Communication Technology

LAD – Language Acquisition Device

LGBTQ – Lesbian, Gay, Bisexual, Transgender and Questioning

MIL – Media and Information Literacy

ML – Machine Learning

MRI – Magnetic Resonance Imaging

NGO – Non-Governmental Organisation

NHS – National Health Service

NICE – National Institute for Health and Care Excellence

NSPCC – National Society for the Prevention of Cruelty to Children

NSSI – Non-Suicidal Self-Injury

OCD – Obsessive Compulsive Disorder

OECD – Organisation for Economic Co-operation and Development

ONS – Office of National Statistics

PFC – Prefrontal Cortex

PHE – Public Health England

PV – Polyvictimisation

SMS – Short Messaging Service

SNS – Social Networking Sites

SSNPs – Safer Social Networking Principles (for the EU)

UNCRC – United Nations Convention on the Rights of the Child

UNESCO – United Nations Educational, Scientific and Cultural Organization

WHO – World Health Organization

A NOTE ON COVID-19

During our writing, the world experienced an unprecedented health crisis in the form of the severe acute respiratory syndrome coronavirus 2 (SARS-CoV-2), which is the virus that causes COVID-19. In a very short timeframe, the world responded variably and in ways that saw technologies rise to the forefront of managing the issues arising, including testing treatments, creating vaccines, helping patients, and communicating news (both genuine and fake). Perhaps unsurprisingly the global rise of community and individual anxiety as well as the underpinning issues that were created by the pandemic have important implications for the relationship between children and young people's (CYP) mental health and the use of digital media in positive and negative ways.

There is no doubt that COVID-19 is leading to mental health challenges and a rise in demand for mental health support, including on- and off-line resources. It is expected that a demand for mental health care will continue to rise (Blumenstyk, 2020) as levels of anxiety increase through direct causes, such as fear of contamination, stress, grief and depression because of exposure to the virus, and through social consequences of the societal and economic mayhem that is likely (Wind, Rijkeboer et al., 2020). This is a 'black swan' moment (Blumenstyk, 2020); that is, an unforeseen event that changes everything and will lead to shifts in mental health care demand and service provision in the future (Wind et al., 2020). It is crucial that societies and health services are aware of the role of psychological processes and fear that could cause additional harm on top of the pandemic (Asmundson and Taylor, 2020).

The challenges of mental health that are being seen during the height of the outbreak could have long-term consequences far into the future (Holmes, O'Connor et al., 2020). The prevalence rates of child and adolescent mental health conditions have been rising (Bor, Dean et al., 2014) and the social, economic and individual impacts of COVID-19 are likely to see rates rise further. This is because the aetiology (causes) of mental health conditions is multifactorial, with issues like poverty, adverse childhood experiences (like abuse or domestic violence), parental mental health, stress, poor sleep and so on will influence the overall picture. Unfortunately, COVID-19 is increasing poverty, impacting sleep, affecting parental mental health, increasing stress, and exacerbating experiences such as violence. Furthermore, it has been suggested that the virus may 'trigger immune responses that have additional adverse effects on brain function and mental health in patients with COVID-19' (Holmes et al., 2020, n.p). Holmes et al. noted that it is important that we deploy research funds to better understand the social, psychological and neuroscientific impact of this pandemic.

There is also a risk that we may see rises in suicide rates. This is not inevitable, especially where there are national mitigation efforts (Gunnell, Appleby et al., 2020). Anecdotally, however, technology companies are reporting an increased flow of traffic to sites about self-harm, suicide and eating disorders and we need to find ways to promote coping and not encourage maladaptive behaviour. Of course, at the point of our writing this book we do not know what the acute or longer-term issues might be. Many countries across the globe are locking down their societies and this may have implications for CYP mental health. The loss of social contact, bereavement due to COVID-19, loss of educational routine, freedoms and usual support systems could have a huge effect, especially on CYP with potential vulnerabilities or in vulnerable situations, like those with existing mental health conditions (Holmes et al., 2020). The political and community discourse is certainly that this pandemic is exacerbating inequalities on a range of levels.

We would point out at this juncture, however, that there are some potential positives. In 1918 the world was plagued by a flu pandemic (so-called Spanish flu) which lasted two years and infected 500 million people, with estimated deaths of 17–50 million people. But the world was a very different place in 1918. During this 2020 crisis, many CYP have found myriad ways to manage the isolation, the anxiety and the impact of the virus. Technology has enabled them to stay connected to their schools, peers and families. While they have not been able to visit elderly grandparents or vulnerable family members, many have been able to call, text and video conference. They have been able to continue with their schoolwork by checking in on their school's website, asking questions and watching educational videos that have been created across the world. People have been able to order essentials online, so parents who can afford to so do have provided creative tools, educational materials and toys, as well as food for their children. Many parents in some countries have been able to work from home, so they are connected to their children and able to support them through the challenges that isolation and social distancing bring. Furthermore, services have responded, changing their modes of delivery, creating new ways of communicating with children and families, and finding creative ways to offer support. We provide an example, in the box below, where one practitioner working in Brazil, Nina Puttini, reflects on the sudden changes they needed to make to help children during the pandemic.

Expert voice: Nina Puttini

Lockdown mental health response in Brazil

ASEC Brazil team members worked to design nine weeks of activities adapted to be delivered by virtual-environment trained volunteers and psychologists having sessions with three children at a time during COVID-19 pandemic lockdown in Brazil.

(Continued)

The project called 'Light, Mind and Heart' was created to give emotional support to children from 6 to 13 years old during this pandemic. Knowing that children are not going to school and are being kept at home as much as possible, it was expected that they were experiencing lots of difficulties, feelings and loss.

We created nine lessons for groups of maximum three children. Each lesson had a specific feeling as the main topic. We talked about how they were feeling since they stopped going to school, about sadness, anger, fear, what and who they are missing, always with much respect and care.

All the lessons were thought to be fun, even though we were talking about difficult feelings. We added activities and games that are simple and possible to play virtually and with no material, or just paper and pencil. For example, relaxation exercises, small videos, pictures and stories, simple origami. We also talked about the good things we are experiencing on this same context, like having more time to spend with family; we talked about empathy and solidarity, love and gratitude.

I felt like each time we met was like a party, like an opportunity to spend good time with friends. And it was surprising how the children got involved, talked about themselves, showed their home, always with a smile on their faces, always interested and paying attention.

We had some challenges with technology sometimes, like audios and videos interrupted, links that did not work, virtual rooms that just closed out of the blue. It was beautiful to see all of them committed to coming back, asking for help, and discovering ways to return to the meeting. Everyone willing to help those who could not participate for some personal reason.

I saw family members helping the children many times, but the children were the protagonists! It was moving to see how they trusted and opened themselves, so quickly!

As the meetings gave them opportunities to share their feelings and focused on the children's wellbeing, I believe the project reached a special meaning for them.

For me it was an amazing experience, a gift in the middle of the COVID-19 crisis, and reinforced my hope and certainty that we need to take care of children, to promote resilience for a better world.

Nina Puttini

ASEC Brazil Team Member

Of course, while all this technology has been hugely positive, influential and helpful, it is not all good news. We have seen the disparities between social groups, and the gaps of affluence have never been so starkly obvious. CYP with limited or no internet access at home, or those with basic or no equipment to connect are likely feeling the loss of peers and loss of education more greatly. Those living in densely populated cities in small apartments with no gardens and limited funds to purchase necessities online will also struggle more. As food banks and charities find it increasingly difficult to continue, the CYP who rely on these will be suffering the effects. Those CYP living in households where substance abuse, domestic violence, child abuse or other challenging issues are common, the impact on their mental health will be significantly greater, and if they have lost their usual support stream through education or peers, this will be more significantly felt. Early evidence is showing that these challenges are rising, with COVID-19 exacerbating domestic violence in households where it was already present (see Home Office, 2020). Many of these issues will be addressed further in the book as we provide details about the relationship between digital media in mental health as well as clear definitions of these concepts in our Introduction.

We hope that as you read this book, we will have come through the worst of the COVID-19 pandemic. We hope you are well and safe. It is likely that the issues we raise are more pertinent than ever before, and, as we move through these challenging times, the practical aspects of this book should be useful.

INTRODUCTION

Learning points

After reading this chapter, you will be able to:

- Contextualise the core definitions used in the book
- Understand the importance of digital media and mental health
- Appreciate the challenges that COVID-19 has posed

Introduction

The focus of this book is on the complex relationships between digital media and child and adolescent mental health. In this chapter we outline our core aims and objectives to give you some context of what to expect, and we overview the scope by describing the three main parts that the book divides into. The book contains many practical aspects and, as part of this, we recognise the reflection skills that practitioners have when they work with children and young people (henceforth CYP) and thus there is a reflective element to the chapters with related activities for you to consider. As we build the book, we recognise that there are many different challenges in everyday practice that we hope to help you with.

Definitions

In the first part of our book, we spend some time exploring and critically assessing core definitions from interdisciplinary perspectives as these are important to how we understand evidence and present arguments. As we move on, we recognise that different disciplinary professionals have an institutional vocabulary that is congruent with their field, and this means there are different languages used in research and practice, different perspectives, different terms and concepts and so forth. We navigate through these, but we do not detail the academic tensions and controversies, and instead move to provide explanations, encourage reflection and critical thinking, and promote further reading.

So, there are four broad areas of concepts to which we pay attention:

1. Those relating to children and childhood, parenthood, and society.
2. Those relating to mental health, mental health conditions and wellbeing.
3. Those relating to parts of the globe.
4. Those relating to digital media.

In this introduction, we do not detail definitions as we develop these in appropriate later chapters. For simplicity, however, we consider these concepts by way of an introduction:

Children and childhood: Books need a simple conceptualisation to capture a population and this is our preferred grouping. Throughout the book we refer to CYP as two broad categories of childhood: *children* and *young people* – to distinguish those children before adolescence and adolescents. We use the United Nations Convention on the Rights of the Child (UNCRC) (United Nations, 1989) definition as outlined in Article 1: 'a child means every human being below the age of eighteen years unless under the law applicable to the child, majority is attained earlier.' We recognise in Chapter 1 that there are many different categories and conceptualisations associated with childhood, but for simplicity we use the abbreviation CYP.

Parents and parenthood: When we refer to *parents*, we recognise that there are many ways in which legal guardianship of children can be expressed, such as legal guardian, primary caregiver, parent, biological parent, foster or adoptive parent, carer and so forth, and again we cannot use the long list of terms each time we refer to those who take parental responsibility, so we use 'parents' to capture the group.

International countries: We use the terms *majority world* and *minority world* throughout this book. Naming things is difficult, and it is especially difficult to know what to call different parts of the world. 'First/second/third/fourth world' refer to blocs during the Cold War era and are lacking in nuance as well as being outdated. 'Developing' countries has been heavily criticised for again lacking in nuance, and implying a standard and linear hierarchy of countries in which some places are ideal and others are ignorant or irresponsible. 'Global North and South' have been criticised for being inaccurate – Haiti, for example, is globally North but experiences extreme poverty. 'Low-and-middle-income countries' offered some semblance of objectivity, but in shortening to LMIC and MIC has led to offensive abbreviations and jargon. As a result of decades of debate, we have chosen to adopt a more contemporary framing that has been increasing in popularity in development terms. By 'majority world' we speak to the fact that most of the world's population lives in parts of the world that have been historically termed 'developing' economically. 'Minority world' means the countries where a minority of the world lives, that has historically been economically richer.

Mental health and mental health conditions: Later we provide more depth and consider the medical, clinical, social and critical ideologies around these concepts. In a broad and simplistic sense, we talk about *mental health* to refer to positive mental health and positive emotional states, and we refer to *mental health conditions* when we consider those CYP who have been given a clinical diagnosis of a condition as consistent with medical criteria.

Digital media: Typically, in the literature, media are divided into traditional media and new or *digital media*. Traditional media tend to refer to communication portals, like newspapers, television, radio and film, and cover institutionalised structures, formats and interfaces for the dissemination of content (Couldry, 2012). Couldry noted that almost all content is now digital and includes both mass-produced content and interpersonal communication, blurring boundaries between mass media and general communication. Our focus in this book is on digital media. We recognise that this is a challenging concept to define, digital media devices range from very large home theatres to very small, mobile or wearable devices such as smartphones or smart watches able to connect CYP to each other and to the world around them (Calvert, 2015). As Calvert (2015, p. 407) notes 'increasingly media are seamlessly integrated across both real and virtual life experiences'. Consequently, it is hard 'to keep pace with this rapidly shifting array of platforms, allowing various affordances to content access, creation, and distribution' (Calvert, 2015, p. 407). In this book we define digital media in broad terms, to refer to a range of technology like smartphone applications (apps), social media platforms, wearable devices, video gaming platforms, and so on. Because of the wide volume of literature and the general public concern, there are areas within our book where we focus more specifically on social media, which are those online platforms designed to allow the sharing of content and communication via digital devices, including social networking sites (SNS) and video gaming.

Our project/our study: Throughout the book we refer to our own research project (funded by the Wellcome Trust) on social media and adolescent mental health. In that work during our focus groups (i.e. group discussions) with young people aged 11–18 years from London and Leicester (UK), we asked for definitions of social media and of mental health, as well as their thoughts on the relationship between the two. This was an open discussion that was led by the young people. In total we conducted six of these groups with 54 young people in age clusters (11–12, 12–13, 13–14, 14–15, 15–16, 17–18 years) as this reflects the English education year-group system. We also refer to our consultation groups, which comprised adolescents in Leicestershire who helped us in our planning and thinking and created sticky notes which are represented in the book, and primary school children from the Midlands who wrote down their ideas in letters.

Aims and objectives

The main aim of this book is to present the evidence that explores the relationship between child/adolescent mental health and digital media, with attention paid to social media. In doing so we will also identify the gaps in our knowledge to propose possible future research areas and important aspects of need. We can learn lessons from the existing evidence, even when the findings are mixed and sometimes contradictory. It is important that, in your practice, your decisions and understandings are based on empirical work. The book provides practical guidance for those working with or living with CYP to better understand the core issues in terms of the relationship between digital media and mental health. The relationship is a complex one, that has caused and continues to cause much controversy reflecting a broad range of opinion and evidence in the area. In developing this book, we engage with research evidence and expert opinion to navigate the complex mass of information about digital media, with a strong focus on social media, and the connection to mental health and mental health conditions in CYP. We offer practical and accessible perspectives on a range of different issues pertinent to the field.

The importance of looking at technology

We can safely say that quickly evolving digital technologies are here to stay and have become embedded in the lives of many CYP. Societies have become increasingly reliant on technologies to perform daily activity in all areas of life. In terms of social media specifically, by 2015 over two billion people globally had active social media accounts (Kempt, 2015). With the connectivity that digital interaction brings, there is greater concern about CYP's safety, wellbeing, and their rights (Livingstone, 2013). Livingstone noted that in economically wealthy countries, children tend to use the Internet at home, school and on the go, and as families, schools and communities become ever more reliant on Internet-enabled technologies, researchers are having to work harder to grasp the significance of these socio-technical changes in the conditions for communication, learning, socialisation and participation. Because technology, social media and other-related phenomena are advancing so rapidly, it is challenging for research to match the pace, and work in this area is relatively new (Allen, Ryan et al., 2014). This makes it difficult for societies to recognise the considerable opportunities that using digital media affords, as well as the challenge of managing the diverse array of risks (Livingstone, 2013).

The importance of looking at mental health

The world is changing and globally there has been growing attention paid to mental health, in terms of promoting and maintaining positive mental health and diagnosing and treating mental health conditions. Mental health is incredibly complex, and there are many factors that contribute to maintaining well-being, and to poor mental health. It is especially important to look at mental health in CYP, particularly as many of the mental health conditions in adulthood were first present before the age of 15 years old and become sustained into adulthood (Kessler, Amminger et al., 2005). Across the world, CYP are facing threats to their mental health, and these can only be adequately addressed when researchers, service providers, practitioners and communities share knowledge and resources, and if we transcend traditional disciplinary boundaries to mobilise the full potential of evidence and practice-based knowledge (Zinck, McGrath et al., 2013).

Scope of the book

This book is divided into three sections to reflect the main areas of evidence associated with digital media and mental health. The book opens with section I Digital Media and Child Mental Health, addressing the key concepts that are relevant to the text. This is necessary as many of the terms and ideas used in the field are in themselves contentious or ill-defined. This section of the book is necessarily more academic in style than sections II and III, and the contributions from experts are also more academically framed. In this section there are four chapters, each addressing one of the focus concepts of this book, namely children and childhood, mental health, digital media and risk, resilience and vulnerability. In these chapters we deal with these issues individually in turn, and, while there is some orientation to the overlap, these chapters are foundational knowledge chapters and stand alone, and the rest of the book is devoted to the connections across them.

Secton II of the book, The Impact of Digital Media, relates to contentious arguments about the different kinds of risks, content and impacts digital media use may have on child and adolescent mental health. There are a broad range of reported negative impacts, including eating disorders, depression, low self-esteem, self-harm, and even suicide, to name just a few. However, there are also positive effects that promote good mental health, and these have been less well publicised. Synthesising the evidence across the chapters in this section, we make sense of what the evidence means in practice, accounting for both positive and negative discourses, impacts and perspectives.

Section III, Practical Ideas for Families and Professionals, distils the messages of the book for practice. The chapters offer practical tips, advice and interpretations of the issues to help individuals communicate with CYP about matters of digital media, to build their resilience pathways and ecologies and online safety skills, and to raise awareness of possible risk and benefit. This section of the book will help those individuals to constructively engage in discussions about issues that matter to CYP and which are related to their mental health and their use of digital media, especially social media.

The scope of the book is interdisciplinary, both in terms of the nature of the evidence presented and in terms of the practical advice offered. The book benefits from the diverse but complementary authors' backgrounds and training as well as the input of experts from different disciplines and professions. This is in two forms: first, shorter expert voice boxes to illuminate personalised accounts of experience; and second, longer expert contributions at the ends of chapters. We note that as the authors of the book we are not endorsing these opinions/contributions, and neither are we agreeing or disagreeing with them. We present them as real-world views on these contemporary issues.

The book makes an important academic and practice-based contribution to the growing field and will be a useful platform for more specialised and focused reading, adding to the debates that are pertinent in the field. Throughout the book we draw upon a range of evidence that is grounded in research in the field and reflects a range of different methodological traditions. The World Health Organization (WHO) recognised that best practice should be founded on evidence, but that evidence should be relevant and fit for purpose and there should not be *a priori* assumptions about superiority of evidence (Bonnefoy, Morgan et al., 2007). We therefore include a wide scope of different types of evidence generated in different ways from different fields and using different methods to generate knowledge.

Intended audience

This book is a practical text designed for those working with CYP in many fields, including health, social care and education, but also of benefit to parents. This interdisciplinary text addresses and assesses research evidence and provides a critical debate of interest to related academic fields including Health, Sociology, Psychology, Social Work, Childhood Studies, Media, Forensic Science, Social Policy, Counselling, Education and Criminology to name the most obvious disciplines. We therefore expect this book to be useful for professionals working with and doing research with CYP, as well as students undertaking courses related to these fields. The book has predominantly been written for practising professionals, and as a useful resource to vocational courses for those training to work with CYP.

The value of reflection

As we expect most of our audience to be practising professionals, we focus our language and ideas in that direction. As a practitioner you are likely to be well-versed in the art of reflecting as this is now considered as an essential professional skill. Many professional disciplines in their training are encouraged to reflect on practice and think about their own beliefs, values, attitudes and practices. Other readers, however, may be less familiar with the practice, and therefore we provide some context.

According to Yip (2006), being reflective is a process of the individual practitioner being aware of the influence of ideological and societal assumptions, especially moral and ethical beliefs that underpin professional practice. We outline this in Box 0.1 below.

Box 0.1: What this means

There are two key points being made by Yip (2006):

1. Being reflective is a process – in other words, it takes time, effort and action for the individual to genuinely reflect and think about something that is important in their practice.
2. Professional practice is underpinned by guidelines, training, codes of conduct, ethics and so on, and the way in which individual practitioners implement those is influenced by their personal belief system.

As you read this book, we would strongly encourage you to engage with the material and reflect on how what we present relates to your practice. You may have heard of the famous distinction between reflection-in-action and reflection-on-action as presented by Schön (1983):

- *Reflection-in-action* is when the practitioner reflects at the time it occurs and reacting to that in situ.

- *Reflection-on-action* is when the practitioner reflects after the event or incident.

Embedded in the chapters are a series of reflective activities designed to help you recognise, reflect, and maybe even challenge your preconceptions, ideas and beliefs. If you work with CYP, or are training to do so, these reflections will help you to think about the kind of practitioner you are and/or want to be.

In the spirit of reflection, we provide our own expert voice reflections on the issue to open our dialogue and introduce you to our own views on this issue. As authors of this book we come from different disciplinary backgrounds. In author order we provide a personal reflection on our own views on the broad issue of the relationship between digital technology and mental health and give you a little insight into who we are and how we got here. These are found in Box 0.2, 0.3, 0.4 and 0.5, respectively.

Box 0.2: Expert voice: Dr Michelle O'Reilly

Michelle's reflection

My interest in child mental health began before my career as an academic, and long before I became qualified in psychology and completed my PhD. I was 11 years old when I first started volunteering for charities that did work with CYP who had 'special educational needs' and I became fascinated by the different practitioners that seemed to be involved in the lives of those families, such as clinical psychologists, specialist teachers, social workers and psychiatrists.

As I battled through my honours degree, Master's qualification and PhD, I learned more and more about children, childhood and mental health, and began my academic career formally in 2003 at the University of Leicester and Leicestershire Partnership NHS Trust. My joint role in Child and Adolescent Mental Health Services (CAMHS) and the academic role in psychology and sociology provided me with the opportunities to establish a truly interdisciplinary focus on mental health, and to develop working partnerships with clinical practitioners.

During this time I have seen services cut, the challenges for professionals working with minimal resources, and yet we are all united in working toward a better future for CYP. We are inspired to help navigate the minefield that is mental health and the huge range of factors that can threaten wellbeing. I want governments to prioritise mental health and mental health conditions as it is the foundation of wellness, including physical wellness. We need more research, more understanding, more resources and more awareness. In an ever-more complex environment CYP are facing new challenges, and technology has contributed in so many ways to the new social landscape.

It was relatively recently that my interest in digital media and its relationship to mental health became piqued as I started working with colleagues with specialist skills in informatics and education. I was successfully awarded a research grant to explore the relationship between social media and adolescent mental health from the perspectives of educationalists, young people, and mental health professionals. It was through this project that I was exposed to a huge and conflicting evidence base, many personal narratives and stories, and professional ideas and creativity.

While there are undeniably some negative aspects of social media in terms of mental health in childhood, I believe that the positive impacts are important and less well recognised. I also believe that society, researchers, policies, parents, teachers, governments and CYP can do so much more to create opportunities, promote mental health and build the positive effects of digital and social media on CYP's mental health, and we need more financial resources, research and commitment to achieve it.

Dr Michelle O'Reilly

Associate Professor of Communication in Mental Health and Chartered Psychologist in Health (University of Leicester)

Research Consultant and Quality Improvement Advisor (Leicestershire Partnership NHS Trust)

Box 0.3: Expert voice: Professor Nisha Dogra

Nisha's reflection

My interest in child mental health was sparked by watching a family therapy session when I was a third-year medical student. I didn't especially enjoy medical school as I found it highly competitive and perhaps less appreciative of areas that interested me – paediatrics and psychiatry. It is perhaps then no surprise that I ended up in child psychiatry. The people side of medicine was always fascinating to me. I retired a couple of years ago but could not have asked for a more rewarding career. I remain involved in some teaching and research.

I have long been an advocate for high-quality training in child mental health and mental health promotion. I consider it important for schools to talk to children about their mental health as part of their overall health (and that teachers need to be supported). I strongly believe we need to be proactive in supporting children as they develop their skills and identities.

I am pragmatic and probably a touch cynical, so it is hard for me to believe claims that technology is either all good or all bad. As with most things, the answer is that it has some benefits if it is used wisely, and there are potential

(Continued)

disadvantages we need to be aware of. It is too simplistic to blame digital technology for children's increasing mental health problems. We already know that children's mental health problems are caused by a range of factors, and technology is now another factor we need to include. I am not convinced that as adults we are setting good examples to young people of how we manage digital advances. I have watched my youngest nephews develop familiarity with mobile phones, iPads and so on – there is no denying it is an everyday part of their lives. I think we need to undertake better research to help us identify how we can help all children to use digital media well so that it is not detrimental to their mental health, and make them aware that help is available should they develop mental health problems.

Professor Nisha Dogra

Emeritus Professor of Psychiatry Education and retired Consultant in Child and Adolescent Psychiatry (University of Leicester)

Visiting Lecturer (University of Nottingham)

Box 0.4: Expert voice: Dr Diane Thembekile Levine

Diane's reflection

I have spent more years than I care to admit working in education and technology practice, policy and research. When I started teaching, computer rooms, ranks of computers and walled gardens were increasingly common in the UK. Even as a music specialist, I found it challenging to avoid seeing the impact that this exposure to what we now see as very simple technologies was having on some ways of teaching and learning.

Consequently, when I moved into public service, educational technology policy became a natural evidence home. I did not see myself as an advocate, but rather as an intermediary between the best evidence available and both policy and practice. During this time, I had the privilege of being a member of certain groups, including the Expert Advisory Group for the UK Council for Child Internet Safety. In that forum I had listened and contributed to a range of issues relating to child and adolescent safety, mental health and wellbeing, and the online lives of young people. As time went on, for me the questions only grew in number, complexity and difficulty, and, as a result, I grabbed the opportunity to do a PhD exploring the ways in which adolescents understood themselves and the worlds around them through the lens of digital technologies: their social cognition.

I wish I could say I had all the answers. I don't. What I do have is a strong belief that we aren't going to be able to address the big questions surrounding adolescence, digital technologies and mental health without working together across disciplines and sectors.

Since 2010 my research work has been committed to raising the profile of majority world CYP in research relating to pathways of resilience, including where these are digitally mediated. By 2050, the African continent's population could have increased from about 1.2 billion people to 2.2 billion people. Around 42% of people on the continent are under 15 years old, and another 20% are between 15–24 years old, sometimes called the 'demographic dividend'. Currently, 90% of the research published about teenagers is from Western world contexts – the USA, UK, Europe, Canada, Australia in the main. We barely know anything systematic about the lives of what will likely become the largest population of young people in the world. In a digital world, full of turbulence, we need to work together – urgently – to ensure that these voices are also heard and considered. My contributions to this book are therefore an expression of my commitment to taking global perspectives on these issues, and to facilitate happy, productive lives for CYP everywhere.

Dr Diane Thembekile Levine

Deputy Director, Leicester Institute for Advanced Studies

University of Leicester

Box 0.5: Expert voice: Dr Verónica Donoso

Verónica's reflection

My interest in children and digital technologies began way before social media became popular. In 2002, I started my PhD entitled 'Adolescents and the Internet: Implications for Home, School and Social life', and since then I have been involved in several projects and initiatives which have given me the opportunity to better understand how digital technologies impact CYP's lives and how they appropriate and contribute to shape emerging digital technologies.

Compared to a couple of decades ago, research about CYP and digital technologies has skyrocketed worldwide. We have not only witnessed an increasing amount of research in more countries and regions, but also increasing interest from different disciplines on a wider range of related topics such as children's rights in the digital age or mental health and digital wellbeing). Despite the increasing amount of research, evidence is usually inconclusive or even contradictory. Moreover, research is not always easily accessible to people outside academia. Therefore, much of what is popularly known about CYP's online experiences is based on personal accounts or news which are usually tragic

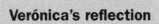

(Continued)

and not always trustworthy. Hardly ever is this knowledge based on solid evidence. This is exactly why books such as this are needed.

Another common problem is that research on CYP does not always inform nor accompany the development of digital technologies and so we continue seeing the proliferation of apps, social media platforms and digital services which target CYP but which are not designed to cater for their specific needs, vulnerabilities and their rights. Providing safe and stimulating digital services that support children's development and wellbeing remains a big challenge for tech companies, governments and regulators alike. Achieving this is difficult because to make a real difference in CYP's lives, and open and honest dialogue and cooperation must exist among many players who do not necessarily share similar values or interests. Despite the imminent difficulties, governments, industry, academia, civil society, professionals working with CYP, educators, families and CYP themselves must work more closely together. For instance, educators and other professionals working with CYP are key to supporting efforts to foster media and digital literacy as well as CYP's healthy engagement with digital services, but if families do not commit to these efforts, the impact of schools and youth organisations remains limited. Similarly, even if schools, families and governments align their efforts, little can be achieved if design decisions are driven by commercial or other less transparent purposes without (much) consideration of children's best interests. Therefore, although education remains crucial to enjoying the benefits of a healthy and balanced relationship with digital technologies, it is not enough. Tech developers, policymakers and regulators must also embrace their responsibility to ensure that CYP's safety and wellbeing is safeguarded and that their rights are fully respected, protected and realised offline and online.

Dr Verónica Donoso

Independent consultant specialised in digital literacy, online safety and education

Conclusion

In this chapter we have introduced you to the main concepts you will find in the book. We have provided our positions on the core issues at stake for digital media and mental health in childhood and have summarised the chapters you will read. We hope you find the book useful and practical. Enjoy the read!

PART I

DIGITAL MEDIA AND CHILD MENTAL HEALTH

DEFINING TERMS AND IDENTIFYING RELEVANT ISSUES

1

CHILDREN, CHILDHOOD AND CHILD DEVELOPMENT

Learning points

After reading this chapter, you will be able to:

- Explain the constructions of children and childhood and paradigm shifts
- Appreciate what rights children have
- Understand child development

Introduction

The relationship between mental health and digital media is a controversial one, with tensions, disagreements, contradictory evidence and different viewpoints. To address the specific issues of the relationship between mental health and digital media, it is first important to contextualise some relevant issues of children and childhood. Our first three chapters introduce important areas that are relevant to the relationship, without making many connections across them at this point. This chapter focuses on the definitions of children and childhood to illustrate changes in thinking over time, and outlines some of the basics of child development. We briefly outline how the ways in which children are viewed have changed and how this influences concepts such as children's rights and child-centred practice. Most of this chapter is dedicated to the basic developmental theories proposed. We caution here though, that in presenting those theories, different categories and groupings of children are used which are ostensibly inconsistent. However, when we report those theories and ideas, we are reporting the work of other scholars, and exactly because these differences in categorising reflect the tensions and differences in thinking, we do not try to modify them. Therefore, in our boxes and descriptions *different age groupings are used deliberately*, and this illustrates some of the challenges of defining CYP into categories.

Constructions of children and childhood

There are many views of children and childhood, and over time different ways of thinking about these topics have emerged. There are also variations in how the terms are understood between differing cultures. Even today, differences of opinion of what constitutes children and childhood remain. The history of the child is complex, and we cannot cover the entire spectrum of ideas nor the centuries of history and global cultures. We will, however, draw your attention to some key relevant points and encourage you to reflect on your own ideas about children and childhood as these might influence the way you practise, and how they might shape your ideas about digital media and its relationship with mental health which we focus on later. We invite you to consider the following question:

What is the child?

This may seem a little simplistic and initially you may feel that the answer is obvious. Yet we would encourage you to think a little more deeply and really consider what this concept means to you. Try the reflective activity in Box 1.1.

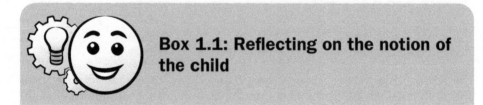

Box 1.1: Reflecting on the notion of the child

What is the child to you?

- Note three things that characterise a child and try to explain why.
- Think about the kind of words that you associate with children. Make a list of those terms and reflect on why they are important.

We are sure that different readers will have come up with a wide range of words to describe the child, and the ease with which you will have been able to respond will be as varied. A key point we want to highlight here is that children are not mini adults, they are unique, developing, creative young populations, with different levels of maturity, with rights to be involved in aspects of their lives, and a lot to say about their lives. We encourage you to hold your three words in mind as you read through the rest of the chapter.

Children and childhood

The notion of *childhood* being a distinct part of the lifespan was first raised by the French historian Ariès whose work challenged the idea of a universal childhood for all societies (Kellet, 2014). Ariès (1962) distinguished the child from the adult but since then there have been significant efforts to conceptualise the different phases within childhood itself, and these have become more varied over time. The distinct period known as 'childhood' has expanded with various stages or phases identified and some of these are illustrated in Figure 1.1, which represents a White male developing through different iterations of childhood.

Figure 1.1 Child development

Consider these groupings (noting that there is some overlap and different theories, and not all countries have this whole spectrum, or the ages might differ):

- Neonate (new-born baby)
- Infant (baby – some theories say child under one year, others say under two years)
- Toddler (young child, two–three years)

- Pre-school child (young child, pre-school age (UK) four years; however, note that different countries have children start school at different ages, not all have this category, e.g. Belgian children start school at two-and-a-half years, and other countries start older)
- Young child (school-age, five–ten years)
- Pre-teen (before adolescence, typically 10–11 years, although some say 10–13 years)
- Tween (early puberty and just before adolescence, 11–12 years)
- Adolescent (tends to be 13–16 years)
- Older adolescent (typically 17–18 years, although others consider 17–24 years)
- Young adult (little agreement on this and can include as young as 19 and as old as 30)
- Adult (the legal age of majority in many, not all, countries is 18 years, but as you can see from the above descriptions, the age at which a person is considered a fully-fledged adult varies depending on the theory and context, although the UNCRC states that childhood ends at 18 years).

Consequently, CYP, particularly in minority world economies, are constructed (at least academically) as passing through many more phases of childhood than they did historically (see Corsaro, 2011 for discussion). Each conceptual category of childhood is associated with different developmental abilities and societal expectations, and there is disagreement as to what age a child should be to fit into the category.

As noted, the ways we conceptualise children have expanded over the last century. These categories are often grouped together under chronological age and so we offer a brief description. Each of these categories will help you understand the child development section, which we turn to shortly. Note that we stop our description at the point the child turns 18 years, which is the legal age identified by the UNCRC, but recognise that many theories and scholars extend childhood beyond this age. We note that there is no simple or agreed way of grouping childhood categories, and therefore encourage you to be reflective.

Birth–four years

This category of childhood generally encompasses four main categories: neonate; infant; toddler; and pre-school children (see the challenge of this category in our earlier list). Children in this age group develop rapidly as they move from new-born baby through to young child. School starting age varies from country to country, but in many countries typically happens at approximately four or five years.

Five–seven years

By the time the child has reached five years they will have normatively acquired language skills, and can walk, climb and run, and are developing their social and cognitive skills. The child during this age-range often starts formal education and begins to build their academic abilities. At this age they are now able to think more abstractly and rapidly progress their intellectual and cognitive development.

Eight–ten years

The child is learning new skills and working through academic demands in settings where this is facilitated by socio-economic and geographic structures. They are learning to relate to peers, learning new social rules and continue developing physically.

11–12 years

This age category is relatively new and has been conceptualised as the 'tween' years. We include it here as some researchers separate this age group and the evidence sometimes refers to tweens. Tweens transition from being considered developmentally a child to developmentally an adolescent. While tweens used to be considered pre-teens, the pre-teen category was added to with tweens. Some children of this age will start to go through puberty. It is typically during this age stage (often 11 years) that the child moves out of primary (elementary) school and goes into secondary (high) school.

13–15 years

This age category is now considered adolescence (although some use the term 'early adolescence'). The category of adolescence was first introduced by G. Stanley Hall (1904) at the start of the 20th century, and he marked this as an age whereby the individual moved toward adulthood but without the full responsibilities of adulthood. This is typically when the young person goes through puberty (although that can happen earlier).

16–18 years

While still constituting adolescence, this category is generally demarcated as older adolescent, noting they are developmentally different from their younger adolescent counterparts. They are often afforded rights that younger adolescents are not; for example, in some countries they can drive, have consensual sex, get married, vote, legally purchase cigarettes or alcohol, and can consent to participate in health care without parents (this varies depending on the activity and on the country). Also, in many countries they can leave school, go to college, or stay on for more education, can go into employment and so on.

There are various ways in which scholars, governments, practitioners and others break down different age categories of CYP, and we have already presented two slightly different lists so far in this chapter. However, this more detailed conceptualisation tends to reflect the school years system in many countries and is one of the common ways in which they are conceptualised. We invite you to consider the following question:

> In what ways might these categories be useful in my practice?

We would encourage you to think about the ways in which these categories resonate for you in your practice and why they might matter in terms of the work you do. Try the reflective activity in Box 1.2.

 **Box 1.2: Reflecting on your practice**

What do these different categories mean to you?
   Think about your own practice and how these different categories of children and childhood fit in. Are these various categories ones that you use and had thought about before, or did you think in terms of child, adolescent, adult? Think about why you conceptualise children and childhood the way you do.

The way you conceptualise the child in terms of age categories will be helpful later in the book when thinking about what CYP are capable of in terms of digital engagement. This is also important in terms of how you think about children's agency and the ages at which they should have freedom to make decisions. We turn your attention now to this issue by considering the current debates in terms of children's rights.

Children's rights

One endeavour influencing the way society views CYP is the establishment of children's rights. This was achieved through the treaty of the UNCRC (United Nations, 1989), as well as the European Convention on Human Rights. While the UNCRC contains 54 Articles, four of these are regularly cited as important and UNICEF (1989) highlighted these as:

Article 2 – non-discrimination of CYP.

Article 3 – to act in the best interests of the CYP.

Article 6 – the rights to life, survival and development.

Article 12 – respect for the views and voice of the CYP.

Highlighted point!

Although the UNCRC is the most widely ratified human rights treaty in history, the gap between the ideology of the child holding rights and the reality of those being implemented remains, often due to lack of economic and practical resources (Wall, 2008).

This treaty has changed the way CYP are regarded in society. The Convention went on to become the most ratified human rights treaty in history and has certainly helped societies to transform children's lives (UNICEF, n.d.). Indeed, drawing on the UNCRC (United Nations, 1989), Livingstone and Third (2017) specified many important human and children's rights in relation to the digital and encourage a rethinking about children's rights in terms of digital media (see Figure 1.2).

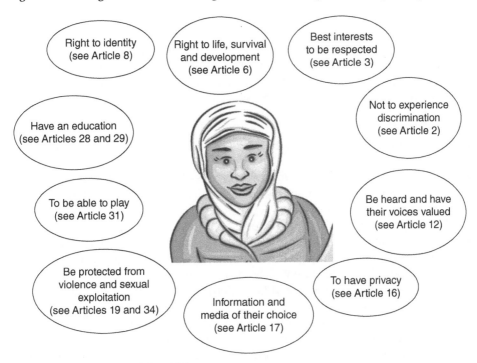

Figure 1.2   The rights of the child

We invite you to review the UNCRC and to reflect on how this could directly or indirectly impact your work with/for children, by working through the reflective activity in Box 1.3.

What role do you think you have in facilitating children's rights?

 **Box 1.3: Reflecting on the notion of children's rights**

- What can you, as practitioner working with CYP, do to ensure that children's rights are realised?
- As a practitioner, what children's rights are the most relevant to your day-to-day work? Write down what you currently do to ensure that children's rights are put into practice?
- Are there things that could be improved in your profession to ensure that children's rights are realised? Think about what the limits of those might be and how your views in one context might conflict with or be different in another.

It is necessary to think critically when looking at policies, legislations, research evidence and professional viewpoints, and we will continually encourage you to do so. While the UNCRC has certainly made a difference, some problems remain with the principles. Here we list some criticisms that were put forward by Freeman (2000):

- It is important to recognise that the UNCRC had no input from children and is adult-centric.
- Although disabled children are recognised via non-discrimination it focuses on non-discrimination and not inclusion and thus emphasises welfare rather than rights.
- Furthermore, inequality and poverty are not fully accounted for.
- The Convention does little to enhance the status of girls; for example, it fails to set a minimum age for marriage. However, we recognise that the Convention does refer to equality of the sexes.
- The Convention utilises an outdated definition of refugees and ensures no duty to provide asylum.
- Article 5 is important recognising the need to promote children's rights but places the burden predominantly on their parents.
- While the Convention gives children the right to health care it does not fully acknowledge the child who might choose to refuse treatment.

While the UNCRC proposed that public bodies should always act in ways consistent with the best interests of CYP (remembering the best interests of children will be interpreted differently in different cultures and contexts), this has only recently begun to account for the implications of digital technology in terms of how practitioners (or society generally) can achieve this in terms of protecting children or promoting their rights (United Nations Convention on the Rights of the Child, 2021) and we explain this in Box 1.4. For this reason, the Committee on the Rights of the Child (2019, n.p.) decided to develop a General Comment on children's rights in relation to the digital environment that aims at clarifying:

> how this rapidly evolving environment impacts on the full range of children's rights in positive and negative ways. The purpose of the General Comment will be to strengthen the case for greater action and elaborate what measures are required by States to meet their obligations to promote and protect children's rights in and through the digital environment, and to ensure that other actors, including business enterprises, meet their responsibilities.

In relation to the digital environment, the General Comment is a game-changer because it clarifies 'what the digital environment means for children's civil rights and freedoms, their rights to privacy, non-discrimination, protection, education, play and more. It also explains why States and other duty bearers must act and how they should act.' (Livingstone, 2021).

Box 1.4: What this means

Despite limitations, the UNCRC made an effort to consult CYP, and the approach has changed the way we work and think. This treaty has also changed the way we do research with CYP and this has impacted on the kind of evidence produced that informs practice. It is therefore a crucial and seminal change in thinking about CYP.

The new guidance from Comment 25 (UNCRC, 2021) shows how important digital media are in the lives of CYP and that their rights are equally important in a digital environment.

The importance of agency

We now see children and childhood differently, and this has been widely conceptualised in research as a 'new sociology of childhood' (e.g. Corsaro, 2011; James and Prout, 2015). In this paradigm, childhood is seen as a period whereby individuals have agency in their own lives, and therefore children's social relationships and cultures are worthy of attention as they are actively involved in the construction of their own social worlds (James and Prout, 2015). This viewpoint reflects a tension of positioning children as innocent and lacking competence or maturity, against positions where children are decision makers and competent to oversee their lives.

We argue that for children's rights to be realised, practising professionals need to believe in the importance of those rights. Earlier we encouraged you to reflect on your own beliefs about this and to think about how that might shape the way you work with CYP. Of course, different disciplines and training backgrounds can influence how decision making by CYP is viewed and the extent to which they are actively engaged in decisions. Arguably one of the most influential ways that practice has been influenced by these changes is in relation to the notion of child-centred practice, that is, the encouragement to listen and consult with CYP in your work.

Children's agency, then, is evidently important in these arguments about children's rights, especially as this has important implications for their health (and mental health). Like many of the concepts we have introduced you to so far, 'agency' is another one that has caused some tension in the literature and one with different points of view. For example, a literature review showed that in older literature, it agency tended to be defined in terms of children's abilities that developed with age, but in more contemporary literature tends to refer to the capacity of children to influence decisions and as children being active agents who reflect and construct their social world (Montreuil and Carnevale, 2016).

We encourage you to reflect on these meanings of agency, and critically question the often-made assumption that adult-imposed structures or adult power over children is negative, as this is not necessarily the case (Punch, 2016). Some difference in position between adults and children is positive; it is helpful to balance children's rights to agency with their developmental and chronological state as children, where they likely need different degrees of protection (Hudson, 2012). It is essential that adults working with children listen to their voices carefully to maximise opportunities to support their sense of personal agency, especially as children's agency tends to be largely structured and limited by adults (Sirkko, Kyrönlampi & Puroila, 2019). Notably, in doing so, it is helpful to remember that children's agency is interconnective with moral and political ideas about what kinds of agency might be appropriate in specific social and cultural contexts (Bordonaro, 2012). In this way, it is necessary to take a critical, nuanced, complex and dynamic conception of children's agency, whereby we consider the structural, moral, contextual and political aspects of it (Sirkko et al., 2019).

Being child-centred

A child-centred approach is one in which the child and their needs are central to the process under consideration whether it be within a parenting, health, social care or educational arena. Child-centeredness recognises that whatever age the child, they have a right to a voice and for that to be considered when decisions are made about them. However the interpretation of this right will vary in practice because the extent to which adults commit to a child-centred approach will depend on how they view children and their rights. To some extent it may also be influenced by the chronological age of the child they are working with, and the developmental maturity of that child. Child development therefore is an important area of focus and we now turn to some of the key elements of this, although we note that this is simply a *brief introduction* and not a full account.

Child development

In introducing development, we want to be clear that as well as different perspectives, there have been critical narratives around many of the core premises, including criticism of the idea that children develop through linear, demarcated stages. Ideologies of what children 'should do' (such as going to school, having secure and happy home lives) are often framed as a 'worldview of childhood'. As adults working and living with CYP in a globalized world, we need to remember that this worldview may not be an accurate representation of the realities – and the lived experiences – of children in our homes and classes coming from majority world contexts (see Abebe & Ofosu-Kusi, 2016).

There are clearly limitations to the frameworks we present, but they do remain useful. In our discussion of child development, we provide the traditional developmental psychology perspective to help you understand the developmental trajectory in different domains and, to help you consider how the 'normal' child matures, we take each domain in turn. As we do, we encourage you to bear in mind that none of these domains develops in isolation. Development also needs to be considered within a range as opposed to an arbitrary concrete age, so, whilst for example most children will be walking by 18 months, some will walk earlier and others later. Significant deviation from the range may be cause for concern. If you want to know more about alternative perspectives to this more traditional perspective, you may be interested in, for example, finding out more about the growing African-centred psychology movement (Ratele, Cornell et al., 2018) or critical psychology/sociology perspectives (Burman, 2008). As we mentioned earlier, different theories categorise the ages in different ways and so there is not a consistent conceptualisation of those categories in this chapter as we report those theories as they were framed by the authors. This means that for each area of development we cover, we are using *different* groupings of children's ages and this reflects the field of research.

Physical development

Physical development is usually divided into gross motor (large movement) and fine motor skills. As mentioned above, children develop at different rates but key motor developmental milestones as outlined by Oswalt (n.d) include:

Infant – birth to one year

- Able to drink from a cup.
- Able to sit, without support.
- Pulls self to standing position.
- Rolls over by self.
- Walks while holding on to furniture or other support.

Toddler – one to three years

- Able to feed self neatly, with minimal spilling.
- Able to draw a line (when shown one).
- Able to run, pivot and walk backwards.
- Able to walk up and down stairs.
- Dresses self with some help.
- Masters walking.

Pre-schooler – three to five years

- Able to draw a circle and square.
- Able to draw stick figures with two to three features for people.
- Balances better, may begin to ride a bicycle.
- Begins to recognise written words, reading skills start.
- Catches a bounced ball.
- Hops on one foot.

School-age child years – 6–11 years

- Begins to lose 'baby' teeth and get permanent teeth.
- Girls begin to show growth of armpit and pubic hair, breast development.
- Menarche (first menstrual period) may occur in girls.

Adolescent – 12–18 years

- During this period children begin to reach an adult height, weight, and develop sexual maturity.
- Boys show growth of armpit, chest, and pubic hair; voice changes; and testicles/penis enlarge.
- Girls show growth of armpit and pubic hair; breasts develop; menstrual periods start.

During childhood and throughout adolescence there are a broad range of physical changes and growth periods that the child goes through.

Brain development

An important aspect of development is that of the brain. From birth to five years, a child's brain develops more than at any other time in life, and early brain development has a lasting impact on a child's ability to learn and succeed in school and life. The positive or negative quality of a child's experiences in the first few years of life helps shape how their brain develops, and this in turn influences their overall development. The strongly negative experiences have been referred to as 'adverse childhood experiences' (ACEs), originally investigated in the Kaiser Permanente study, 1995–1997 (Center for Disease Control and Prevention, 2019), although this phrase, what 'counts' as an ACE, and what we do with that classification as professionals is contested.

Highlighted point!

Understanding the brain and its development is important for the study of mental health and mental health conditions, as the brain plays a crucial role.

Understanding the brain and how it works has been a central task in the field of mental health, as medical models of mental health conditions (mental illness in that language), have attempted to attribute the aetiology as located within biological pathways, including genetics, the brain and chromosomes. While this idea has received a lot of criticism, many scholars accept that the interplay between biological factors, social factors and psychological factors is important (Keenan, Evans & Crowley, 2016), and we turn to this in Chapter 2. Furthermore, brain development is also important in terms of digital media use, which we examine in Chapter 3. Our intention in this section is not to provide you with a lecture on neuroscience but we do provide a brief introduction to this issue as a way of bringing your attention to its importance.

So, here is the science. The brain is complex. The adult brain has about 100 billion cells referred to as *neurons*, and each neuron consists of a *cell body* connected by *dendrites* and an *axon* (Howard-Jones, 2009). The axon ends in presynaptic terminals that form connections (i.e. synapses) with the dendrites of other neurons, and the terminals at the end of an axon contact with the dendrites of other neurons and allow connections to form between neurons so that complex neural networks can be created, and so signals flow down the axons of one neuron and cross the synapse to other neurons, allowing neuron communication (ibid.). In simple terms this means that the brain sends signals between the neurons so that they communicate.

You have probably heard that the brain is described as having two hemi-spheres, a left and right, which are joined by a mass of fibres referred to as the *corpus callosum* (Howard-Jones, 2009). Howard-Jones highlights that the brain is divided into four lobes – the frontal, parietal, occipital and temporal – and each of these is responsible for different functions. The frontal lobe is responsible for reasoning and movement, with the temporal lobe being associated with some aspects of memory and auditory skills. The parietal lobes are necessary for inte-grating information from different sources, and the occipital lobes are important for visual processing. Howard-Jones (2009) cautioned, however, not to view a single component of the brain as solely involved in one task as any task requires a large and broadly distributed range of neural networks that communicate with each other, with the cortex playing a crucial role – described by Howard-Jones as the 'wrinkled surface' of the lobes. Other structures crucial for learning include the *hippocampus*, as this is responsible for consolidating new memories, and the *amygdala*, which plays a role in emotional responses (Blakemore, 2018a).

As CYP grow, so do their brains. It is the developing brain that has been a source of both support and concern in terms of the relationship between dig-ital media and mental health of CYP. This is because when considering this relationship, it is necessary to think about the biological and physiological make-up of the human body and brain, the psychological and emotional pro-file of the CYP, and the social circumstances in which they live. In research terms, academics call this the 'biopsychosocial approach' to understanding CYP, because this accounts for all these aspects that are relevant.

Language development

Communication and social interaction are important human skills, and these invar-iably rely on language. Humans can communicate with each other and to do so we need to be able to do at least four things, as proposed by Keenan et al. (2016):

1. Produce sounds that make up language and convey meanings to others.
2. Know what the words of a language mean.
3. Construct words together in grammatically appropriate ways so oth-ers can understand.
4. Know how to use language effectively to communicate with others.

Keenan et al. highlighted the point that scholars who study language tend to do so from one of four domains:

Phonology: the study of how humans produce meaningful sounds.

Semantics: the study of word meanings.

Grammar: the study of how humans combine words into meaningful sentences.

Pragmatics: the study of how we use language to achieve communication.

Linguistics, and its subdomains of psycholinguistics, sociolinguistics, neuro-linguistics, and ethnolinguistics, are helping us to develop a much deeper and more nuanced understanding of the ways in which we acquire and use language. In relation to digitally mediated lives, sociolinguistics and ethno-linguistics are particularly interesting: *sociolinguistics* gives us a framework to understand the use of language in 'social' lives (including those online); and *ethnolinguistics* helps us to understand the cultural contexts (including digital cultures) in which language is used. Heyd (2016), for example, exam-ined digitally mediated use of a Nigerian contact language (sometimes unhelpfully called 'Pidgin'), and found that 'small words' were crucial to communicating significant meanings.

This field is complex, so we summarise in Box 1.5 the general language skills that children tend to acquire at different points in childhood to give you an overview of language development.

Box 1.5: Key research evidence

Language development stages (adapted from Keenan et al., 2016 and Oswalt, n.d.)

Infant – birth to one year

- Babbles.
- Displays social smile.
- Using terms appropriately to identify the mother and father.
- Understands 'NO' and will stop activity in response.

Toddler – two to three years

- Able to say first and last name.
- Can name pictures of common objects and point to body parts.
- Imitates speech of others, 'echoes' word back.
- Recognises and labels colours appropriately.
- Uses more words and understands simple commands.

Pre-schooler – four to six years

- Begins to recognise written words, reading skills start.
- Enjoys rhymes and word play.
- Language starts to develop and evolves from short phrases to full sentences.
- The child can tell stories, and develops their imagination.

(Continued)

School-age child – 7–12 years

- Reading skills develop further.
- Understands and can follow several directions in a row.
- Language becomes more creative and active.
- Some theoretical and abstract thinking begins as the child moves through this stage.

Adolescent – 13–18 years

- Understands abstract concepts in that they have capacity for abstract thinking and reasoning.

There are many theories of language development and these were helpfully summarised by Keenan et al. (2016) as follows.

Learning theory

Key learning theorists were Skinner and Bandura. Skinner focused on operant conditioning, arguing that the development of language occurs because of parental reinforcement (1966). Bandura focused on observational learning, arguing that children observe and imitate others (1977).

Nativist theory

The key theorist was Chomsky who argued that children have innate mental structures that are responsible for language and referred to the Language Acquisition Device (LAD) (1971). This contains the common grammar concepts allowing its operation. Thus, Chomsky distinguished between learning and acquisition. Children are argued to be biologically predisposed to acquiring language.

Interactionist theory

The key theorist was Bruner who argued that the social support and social context of instruction was crucial for learning language and these aligned with biological factors (1960). Bruner claimed that scaffolding, motherese (known as 'baby talk', where pitch and intonation are raised and is infant directed) and expansion, all facilitate the operation of the biological predisposition of language.

Cognitive development

There are two famous psychologists who have made a significant contribution to our understanding of cognitive development – Piaget and Vygotsky.

Piaget (1936) argued that all normally developing children go through a series of four stages as they mature; these are outlined in Box 1.6.

Box 1.6: Key research evidence

Cognitive development stages (Piaget, 1936)

Sensory motor phase (0–2 years): This is when the child gains motor mastery and their understanding of the world is through perception and action. The child experiences the world through sensory motor activity occurring before the acquisition of language.

Concrete pre-operational phase (two–six years): This is when the child can make mental representations of objects and is able to imagine the actions related to them. At this age, the child is still egocentric and unable to distinguish others' views from their own.

Concrete operational (7–11 years): This is when the child can think in logical ways, but this is in concrete terms. Thought is flexible, logical and organised, but still tied to concrete information.

Formal operational (12+ years): This is when the child moves beyond concrete experiences and starts to think in logical and abstract ways. The adolescent can represent and manipulate thought processes as they are able to combine ideas logically and use deductive reasoning, solve problems through scientific reasoning, and think about possibilities by thinking abstractly and considering consequences, and this makes longer-term planning possible.

Vygotsky (1978) described the dependence of cognitive development (including thinking, memory and attention) upon external factors, such as the social environment, which includes the context of guiding adults who 'scaffold' the child's development. This approach recognises the close links between cognitive, social and language development. Cognitive development depends on the child making active use of social interactions and internalising these. Thus, 'internal' (cognitive) development depends on 'external' (social) interaction, not the other way around – in contrast with the ideas of Piaget and information processing theory.

Vygotsky concluded that cognitive development depends on the social environment and context of guiding adults or older peers. Specifically, a child's cognitive development is enhanced by encouraging the child to complete tasks with assistance that would be beyond the child's potential to complete without assistance.

The *zone of proximal development* is the range of potential each person has for learning, and the learning is shaped by the social environment in which it takes place. When someone with greater expertise or in collaboration facilitates the learning with more capable peers, the potential ability is greater than the actual ability of an individual. An example of this may be when young people work in groups and together may achieve more than they might individually. Children may be guided to solve problems through cues and prompts rather than just being given answers. We explain the evidence in Box 1.7.

Box 1.7: Key research evidence

Valsiner (1997) built on Vygotsky's work by proposing activity in three 'zones' (see Levine, 2019).

The *zone of free movement* defines opportunities as the realm of what is safely available to a child or young person in a specific time or place. For example, age restrictions on a social media site could be providing a zone of free movement for young people within the appropriate age range.

The *zone of promoted action* 'promotes' development through actions or objects from others. No one can be forced to act within this zone unless it becomes another type of zone: for example, a coding dojo where young people learn to code, or common enthusiasm for a social media 'influencer' in a group of young people.

The *zone of proximal development* lays out possible future states for a child or young person in a context and importantly together with others. For example, a teacher, parent, or peer could work with the young cyberbully to co-develop approaches to manage personal relationships and behaviours.

Social development

Human beings are inherently social; they form groups and relationships at different levels, which serve different functions for the individual. In his early work Piaget (1932) argued that children's relationships with adults were qualitatively different from their relationships with their peers, as relationships with adults are vertical containing a dimension of power, but with peers are horizontal and more balanced. Please look at Box 1.8 for an overview of the proposed stages of social development as outlined by Keenan et al. (2016).

Box 1.8: Key research evidence

Social development stages

Keenan et al. (2016) outlined nine stages of social development:

0–6 months: This is when the infant becomes aware of and takes an interest in other infants.

6–12 months: This is when the infant shows a clear interest in peers and starts to display emotional expressions toward them.

12–36 months: This is when the child predominantly engages in parallel play and their social interactions begin to increase in length and complexity and start to understand the roles of social exchange.

3 years: This is when the child starts to engage in cooperative play and dominance hierarchies can be observed in their peer groups.

4 years: This is when associative play can be observed, and the child has acquired a representational theory of mind. Conflict can be observed in their relationships.

6 years: This is when the child increases the amount of time they spend with their peers, and their peer groups increase in size. Peer interactions take place over a wider range of settings and the goal of children's friendships are typically defined by shared interests and coordinated play.

7–9 years: This is when the goal of friendships is peer acceptance.

Early adolescence: This is when friendships are centred around self-disclosure and intimacy. Peer groups are generally organised around crowds and cliques and adolescent egocentrism appears.

Late adolescence: This is when friends become a source of emotional and social support, and adolescent egocentrism begins to decline.

It is nonetheless important to be aware that factors within the child, such as if they have a certain mental health condition or factors present in the environment can significantly influence how children develop. Furthermore, gender can play an important role in social development, and this has implications for peer relationships. Social development is particularly important in adolescence as peer relations play a crucial role in their lives, decisions, interactions and choices. There are a range of important messages to consider about peer relationships in adolescence. These were outlined by Bradford and Larson (2009) and we describe this in Table 1.1.

Table 1.1 Peer relations in adolescence (Bradford and Larson, 2009)

Message	Outline
Peer relations become more salient during adolescence	As young people transition through childhood and into adolescence, there are changes to the social context and social norms that function in a way to elevate the importance of peers, which is juxtaposed with changes in the individual. It is during adolescence that young people are more likely to spend time with peers of the same age and they put greater emphasis on the expectations and opinions of their peers.
Peer relations become more complex during the transition into adolescence	It is during adolescence that new kinds of relationships start to emerge, and romantic relationships develop. There is a stronger emphasis on youth culture. Adolescents select friendship groups and become more sensitive to the impact of certain relations for their social status or reputation.
Friendships are characterised by similarity	As children grow into adolescence their friendship selections are based on similar characteristics. Existing friendships may diminish if attitudes and interests diverge.
Status becomes a central aspect of friendship	During adolescence the notion of peer relation infers equal partners, but equality is confined to those who share the same life stage. Adolescents negotiate their relationships and they become more sensitive to status.
Social adjustment becomes important as do social skills	Those adolescents with good social skills are more likely to be better adjusted than individuals with poor social skills.
Social acceptance is a central feature of social skill	An indicator of adjustment is social acceptance. Young people range themselves in terms of their sociometric status and their power within the peer group. Sociometric status predicts emotional and behaviour outcomes but is also predicted by them.
Self-perceptions of peer relations are unreliable	During adolescence, individuals tend to overestimate the congruence between themselves and their peers and exaggerate the degree of peer influence.
Peer reputations and affiliations are only moderately stable	Peer relations are transient and fluid, but as they move through adolescence friendships become more stable.
Peer influence is reciprocal as they are influenced by one another	It is during adolescence that individuals have greater influence on one another. The relations become reciprocal and transactional in nature.
The characteristics of the influencing agent become important	During adolescence the characteristics of the individual peer become important, as well as the target of that influence, and the relationship with that individual. There is variability in the individual's self-confidence and competence and this impacts on the degree to which they are affected by others.

Emotional development

Emotions underpin behaviour and the two are intrinsically linked. In childhood it has been argued that individuals go through a series of stages as their emotional regulation, emotional literacy and emotional states develop; see Box 1.9 for a description.

Box 1.9: Key research evidence

Emotional development

As outlined by Saarni (2011), there are a series of stages of emotional development:

Birth to 12 months: The child is learning to self-sooth and regulate attention. There is an increasing ability to discriminate others' expressions and the use of socially instrumental signal use (e.g. crying to seek attention).

12 months to 2½ years: There is an emergence of self-awareness and self-evaluation. Irritability because of constraints. Some expressive behaviour. Anticipation of differing feelings toward different people.

Two to five years: There is symbolic access to facilitate emotion and pretend expressive play. Some sympathetic emotions toward peers and an increasing insight into the emotions of others.

Five to seven years: There are now self-conscious emotions and increased coordination of social skills with their own and others' emotions. They still seek support from parents/caregivers for coping strategies.

7–10 years: There is now an appreciation of norms for expressive behaviour, and an awareness of multiple emotions toward the same person. Problem solving is the preferred coping strategy.

10–13 years: There is an increased accuracy of appraisal of realist control in stressful circumstances and a distinction made between genuine emotional expression with close friends and managed displays with other peers. There is increasing social sensitivity and awareness of emotion related to social roles.

13+ years: There is an awareness of one's own emotion cycles, and of mutual and reciprocal communication of emotions that impact the quality of relationships. There is some skilful adoption of self-presentation for the management of impressions.

When considering emotional development this is an important area of development for mental health and wellbeing. This is because the ability to regulate one's emotions is important for positive emotional health. Emotional regulation is the process through which the individual's emotional arousal is aligned with their ability to cope and refers to both the intrinsic and extrinsic processes that are responsible for the individual to be able to monitor, evaluate and modify any emotional reactions (Thompson, 1991). In terms of understanding mental health therefore, Thompson claimed that it is necessary to study emotional regulation as this understanding of emotional development helps us to understand the child's personality and social functioning, as well as how that child makes decisions about how to act in response to stress. Thus, to understand this, five domains of emotional intelligence were proposed by Mayer and Salovey (1993):

1. Knowing one's own feelings.
2. The ability to use and manage feelings in ways appropriate to the situation.
3. The ability to self-motivate through decisions about one's own goals and acting in ways consistent with achieving them.
4. Being able to recognise the emotions of others.
5. Capability to build and maintain positive relationships with others.

Being emotionally intelligent facilitates the child in staying mentally healthy.

As a note of caution, however, we would point out that the notion of intelligence is a contested term and what we have talked about in this section is *emotional intelligence*. There are of course many different types of intelligence and different ways of marking that intelligence.

Highlighted point!

There is no common language across disciplines when talking about intelligence, or even when talking about emotional intelligence, and some refer to this as 'emotional literacy'.

Erikson's 'eight stages of man'

It is important to recognise that social and emotional development have a lot of overlap, and these were conceptualised by Erikson. Erikson (1968) described the 'eight stages of man', a model for socio-emotional development in humans (we do not describe those relevant to adulthood). We acknowledge the problematic gender focus. Longitudinal cohort studies of up to 80 years have demonstrated the validity of these concepts in minority world societies. The five stages relevant to childhood are detailed below.

Basic trust vs. mistrust (first year)

The child will develop trust in the world if their needs are predictably met. Otherwise, the child may develop a perception of the world as a hostile and unpredictable place. Gross deprivation at this stage may lead to emotional detachment in childhood and throughout life, with difficulties forming deep and lasting relationships in adulthood.

Autonomy vs. shame and doubt (one to three years)

The child acquires confidence in their own ability as opposed to self-doubt. The child begins to recognise their own will, and ability to be independent, and may feel guilty if they do not conform to expected behaviours. This stage is about learning to balance one's own wishes against those of others. Failing to exert oneself may lead to reduced confidence and initiative, but failure to account for others' wishes may make it difficult to integrate into society fully.

Initiative vs. guilt (three to five years)

The child acquires more social skills and assumes greater responsibility for self. A sense of time begins to develop. The child builds on the tasks accomplished in the previous stage. Successful resolution at this stage results in a confident and outgoing child. Others may develop fears or problems with nightmares as they struggle to resolve the conflict.

Industry vs. inferiority (5–11 years)

The challenge here is to achieve and overcome feelings of failure. The child will be industrious in schoolwork, sport and social relationships. If these are not achieved, then the child may feel a sense of failure and inferiority. He/she may also become isolated from the peer group.

Identity vs. confusion (11+ years)

In this stage, the child acquires a firm sense of who they are (separate from the family), what they want from life and where they are going. This is further discussed in adolescent development.

The three remaining stages for completeness are: intimacy vs. isolation (young adulthood); generativity vs. stagnation (middle adulthood); and integrity vs. despair (old age).

Moral development

Morality reflects the child's cognitive and emotional state and their behaviour. It is argued that an individual's morality is dependent on their emotions and their ability to feel empathy (Cimbora and McIntosh, 2005). As children grow, they learn right from wrong and they adopt their personal moral standards. There are different theories of moral development. The most prominent are those grounded in cognitive development from Piaget (1936) and Kohlberg (1969), and those grounded in social learning theories, focusing on external influences.

Social learning theory has been influential over many areas of children's development, but in terms of morality it sees their moral code developing through operant conditioning, reinforcement, punishment, observation, modelling and imitation. Bandura (1977) argued that modelling is a powerful tool to teach children morality. Social learning theory is an early theory that in simple terms argues that children learn by observation and imitation, and by association. Social learning theory emphasises rewards and punishment as central to that learning.

Other theories of moral development focus more on cognition. For example, Piaget (1932) argued that in early childhood children are at a pre-moral stage as they do not understand rules, and thus the first real stage of moral development happens at five to nine years, where the child views rules as important but as inflexible and imposed by adults. The next stage is moral relativism, where at 8–12 years they start to understand that social rules can be flexible and change with agreement. At this age they also differentiate intention from the accidental.

Perhaps the most influential theory of moral development was put forward by Kohlberg (1969). Informed by Piaget, Kohlberg argued that children's understanding of morality progresses through stages and is directly related to their cognitive development. To test the theory and identify the stages, Kohlberg used the stories of a man called 'Heinz' and presented dilemmas to children. The dilemmas centred round the idea that Heinz's wife was dying from cancer, but a life-saving drug could be purchased at a price he could not afford. He tried to borrow money but could not, so he could break into the pharmacy and steal the drug. Children were asked if he should or should not do so. Based on responses Kohlberg developed his theory and this is presented in Box 1.10.

Box 1.10: Key research evidence

Kohlberg's theory of moral development

Kohlberg (1969) argued that there are three levels of moral development, with each consisting of two substages:

Level 1 – Preconventional morality

Punishment and obedience orientation: The child follows rules set by their parents without question and obeys these to prevent punishment.

Instrumental orientation: The child can recognise that people have different points of view but see that correct behaviour comes from self-interest.

Level 2 – Conventional morality

Good boy–good girl morality: The individual sees morality as more than an exchange as people are required to live up to the expectations of family and society. Here the individual is concerned to do good and this is generally driven by a desire for approval rather than fear of parental power.

Maintenance of social order: The individual accounts for the larger social law perspective where rules are considered crucial for natural order. Kohlberg argues that most people do not get beyond this level of morality.

Level 3 – Post-conventional morality

This is characterised by the individual moving beyond simply conforming to rules and instead they actively question the laws of society which requires a level of thinking in terms of abstract moral principles.

Social-contact orientation: The individual sees rules as flexible with a function of promoting human wellbeing. Laws are seen as modifiable in cases where a culture believes it to be to the advantage of society.

Universal ethical principle orientation: Morality is seen as involving social standards and internalised ideals and decisions are grounded in principles like equality, compassion and justice. Here, morality is based on respect for others and these may conflict with rules.

Although Kohlberg's theory has remained dominant in our understanding of CYP's moral development, it has been subject to criticism. For example, Gilligan (1982) argued that it was a male-centric theory and therefore not gender neutral, and Kahn (1997) argued that it fails to account for different cultural understanding of rules as it is focused on individual rights rather than collectivist ideas pertinent in some cultures. We return to morality and digital media later in the book.

Conclusions

In this chapter we have set the context for why we need to reflect on how we view the concepts of children and childhood. In completing this chapter, we provide an academic viewpoint on child development from an expert and here we make links between child development, mental health and digital media. In Box 1.11 we present the perspective of Professor Gordon Harold, who has been undertaking research in child development for many years.

Box 1.11: Expert contribution: Professor Gordon Harold

Role: Professor of the Psychology of Education and Mental Health

Organisation: University of Cambridge

Brief bio: Professor Gordon Harold recently joined the University of Cambridge as the inaugural Professor of the Psychology of Education and Mental Health. He specialises in research on the role of the family for understanding children's mental health and development. He is a consultant and advisor to several UK government departments.

Understanding child development in a digital world

The digital world: rethinking our understanding of socialisation influences on children

Children's development occurs through a complex interplay between biological, social and wider contextual influences. Understanding development from conception through infancy, childhood and adolescence has moved on from early stage-based developmental theories (Thomas, 2000), to recognising that typical versus atypical cognitive, emotional, physical, social and psychological development occurs through a complex cascade of bidirectional and reciprocal biological and social influences that enhance or disrupt health, mental health and development during childhood, adolescence, adulthood and older ages (Drabick & Kendall, 2010). While much is known about the biological (e.g. genetic) and early environmental (e.g. parental caregiving) underpinnings of typical versus atypical mental health and development (e.g. Harold, Leve & Sellers, 2017), new knowledge is emerging about the role of wider social environmental influences and how these factors work together with biological factors across the lifespan to explain differences in developmental outcomes for CYP (Thapar & Harold, 2014). This commentary focuses on new knowledge, challenges and opportunities in this area with a focus on how the digital world is increasingly shaping the social environments that CYP experience.

Three historical dimensions (pillars) of socialisation influences on children's development

Three primary areas of social environmental influence on CYP's mental health have dominated past research and practice.

> **Family socialisation processes** (e.g. inter-parental and parent–child relationship quality) are widely recognised as a substantive influence on children's mental health and development. Children living in households marked by

high levels of inter-parental conflict, poor parenting, economic deprivation, family breakdown and poor parent mental health are at elevated risk for multiple negative mental health outcomes, including academic failure (Harold & Sellers, 2018).

Peer influences are recognised as an important influence on CYP's mental health and development. Disruptive behaviour in peer play and deviant peer actions (e.g. bullying) are associated with poor developmental outcomes, including reduced early learning and motivation, reduced social competence and social interaction skills, reduced academic attainment, antisocial and criminal behaviour, as well as elevated anxiety, depression, self-harm and substance misuse (Arseneault, 2018).

School-based factors are recognised as an important contributor to overall socialisation influences on CYP's mental health and development (Ford, Edwards et al., 2012). Promoting effective interventions that target family, peer and school influences on youth mental health continues to represent an area of high priority for researchers, practitioners and policy makers (Harold, Acquah et al., 2016).

One priority for researchers and policymakers is to engage in careful analysis of associations between digital world influences and CYP's mental health. Importantly, this question should be examined across different stages of development and across different social, contextual, sociodemographic, cultural and educational domains in order to more usefully and constructively illuminate public debate and inform professional practice (Odgers and Jensen, 2020), as well as inform the development of the next generation of effective interventions that harness the huge potential that the digital world offers in this area. However, given that digital risks and opportunities are likely to be correlated, future interventions and innovations must be responsive to the nature and consequences of the so-called digital revolution and its potentially profound implications for childhood socialisation, mental health and development, and the professional practice disciplines that work to improve outcomes for children. New technologies and an array of other digital resources now intersect with traditional (offline) family, peer and school influences on CYP, increasingly providing the underpinning infrastructure for the social environments that children, families, schools, peers, educators, health and social care professionals now occupy and must understand (Fazel, Hoagwood et al., 2014). This fundamentally changes the reality of children's social worlds and the development of practice models required to promote effective interventions and positive mental health trajectories for young people.

The digital environment: Understanding risks and harnessing opportunities

The digital world permeates every part of modern life, with one recent estimate suggesting that there are now more connected digital devices than people on Earth (Wang and Degol, 2016). Indeed, it is next to impossible to completely disengage from the digital world and yet engage effectively in the modern social world; this is especially the case for CYP who are often the first to embrace and

(Continued)

experiment with new technologies. Recent and upcoming developments represent significant opportunity as well as substantive risk for CYP when considered relative to family, peer and school contexts. How do we harness this new knowledge to promote effective family, school and peer-based programmes to help protect and support youth mental health? The transformative power of the digital world to 'harm and/or help' derives from a subtle and complex combination of its accessibility, intimacy, immediacy, potential anonymity and sheer reach in terms of content, scale and power to interconnect across traditional social and cultural boundaries. This makes it difficult for parents (families) and teachers (schools) to regulate both in terms of the amount of access to digital technology (e.g. screen time), but also in terms of content accessed and social connections made. Positive parental involvement plays a key role in reducing online risk. Lack of parental involvement is associated with vulnerability to being groomed online for sexual abuse (Future of Privacy Forum & Family Online Safety Institute, 2016) and with increased risk for bullying, including cyberbullying (Smahelova, Juhová et al., 2017). Peer factors also play a significant role relative to digital impacts on CYP (Arseneault, 2018).

Digital world influences and child development: The need for a new developmental perspective

What is clear is that the current generation of CYP have been 'born digital', that is, they do not recognise a social world without digital connectivity (George & Odgers, 2015), a factor that singularly separates them experientially from the social worlds that most of their parents, educators and relevant practice professionals grew up in. This disparity of lived-experience knowledge is a source of substantial anxiety and concern for parents, educators and policy makers who consistently ask the question and seek guidance regarding the possible link between digital world influences and CYP's mental health and development. It is time to re-write our developmental textbooks in order to update our knowledge base as to the three 'pillars' of traditional family, school and peer influences on children's typical and atypical development and to acknowledge not only a new 'pillar' of primary socialisation influences on children, the 'digital' environment, but how the digital environment infuses these other historical socialisation influences for children and what this means for their long-term development and future intergenerational transmission processes. Recognising and better understanding the risks and opportunities that the digital world represents for CYP's healthy development through careful research that is effectively translated to policy and practice applications is essential if we are to protect the mental health of the present generation, while also promoting improved understanding for future generations of parents and CYP.

2

CHILD AND ADOLESCENT MENTAL HEALTH

Learning points

After reading this chapter, you will be able to:

- Critically assess the notion of the normal child
- Understand the relevance of mental health
- Identify the challenges of help-seeking

Introduction

Mental health is a complex area attracting global attention. While the focus of this book is on the relationship between mental health and digital media, this chapter attends to mental health for context, and only has some reference to the overlap with digital media. In this chapter we discuss mental health in terms of positive mental states, (psychological functioning and normal emotions), and mental health conditions, those who have a clinically diagnosable condition. Before we consider the clinically diagnosed conditions, we must first think about what constitutes the 'normal' child and what it means to be mentally healthy. We deliberately put the word normal in inverted commas as it is itself a controversial concept, and one that has sometimes been taken for granted. In Chapter 1 we introduced you to the traditional theories of child development, but here we provide some of the more critical discourses that have questioned some of those ideas.

In this chapter we differentiate mental health from mental health conditions. It is important to note that the traditional concepts of 'mental health' and 'mental illness' are not without their critics and the very language we use in the book is underpinned by tensions around vocabulary and arguments about culture and terminology. In medical disciplines, there is a language of mental illness or mental disorder, yet critics have argued that this orients to deficit, impairment and negative ideas around psychiatric disability. Social sciences and political advocates have tended to favour more neutral notions, such as mental health condition or mental health difficulty, but even these concepts invoke tensions. Our multi-disciplinary authorship reflects some of these arguments in the use of terms also, but we have settled on *mental health condition* to refer to those who are diagnosed with a label consistent with the psychiatric classification system, to be as neutral as possible. When we are writing in a more medical context, we use the notion of *mental illness*.

Practitioners in different disciplines play an important role, and this can be in relation to mental health promotion and awareness, mental ill health prevention and mental health condition intervention. While these are different, there is some overlap, and we describe what they mean. To understand some of these issues we consider the different explanations of what may cause CYP to develop mental health conditions, or what factors put them at risk. We finish the chapter by considering the importance of the language you use in practice and think about the issue of stigma as related to help-seeking.

Developmental psychology, child psychiatry and demarcating the 'normal child'

We begin this chapter by connecting back to Chapter 1 and the developmental trajectory of children and childhood. However, here we relate that discussion from Chapter 1 more specifically to mental health and mental health conditions and consider some of the more critical ideas that have been put forward in the literature.

One discipline that developed during the early 20th century was that of child and adolescent psychiatry (CAP). It is still a relatively young speciality and, in many ways, continues to be a developing one, especially in the majority world. In some countries CAP has well-established roots as a separate specialty, whereas in others the work is carried out by general psychiatrists or paediatricians (Dogra, 2015). Training in CAP varies widely across international contexts and there is a large disparity of standards and practice in CAP in the UK. It was promoted through some of the work undertaken by psychotherapists and further cemented by epidemiological studies indicating the level of unmet need for children with mental health conditions (Dogra, 2015).

The changing views of children and the notion that children had specific rights may also have played a part in promoting a need to target CYP in medicine (O'Reilly, Ronzoni and Dogra, 2013). By the 1960s and 1970s, we saw the emergence of treatments in psychology and psychiatry that were specifically designed to treat children (Karim, 2015), and socially we saw a spotlight on exploring how families play a role in children's mental health with the rise of family therapy (Dallos and Draper, 2010). These different disciplines and approaches had different ideas about normality and different training backgrounds for practitioners, but all focused on treating and helping the child that deviates from the standardised norms of society.

It is, however, important to think about what this means in practice and for you to critically appraise the evidence we present. We have given you a brief overview of some of the most common developmental theories as this is important for understanding the 'normal' child, and often those traditional theories serve as important benchmarks for those working with CYP. However, as we noted, it is not the case that these developmental trajectories in the different domains are universally accepted, as they have been subject to some criticism and indeed, even within a traditional way of thinking there are differences of opinion on how children develop. Underpinning those criticisms are two main issues: first is that not all scholars accept the premise that children go through stages or in the linear manner suggested by developmental theory; and second, some argue the notion of the 'normal' child is inappropriate as some question the boundaries, language and criteria that define normality. We encourage you to think about this by undertaking the reflective activity in Box 2.1.

What is the normal child?

Box 2.1: Reflecting on 'normality'

What does the phrase 'normal child' mean to you?
   Write in your reflective diary your personal views of the concept normality and what this term means to you.

In thinking about the 'normal' child you may recall our discussion earlier in the chapter where we considered the history of the child. It is only quite recently in the Western world that a universal education system was introduced for CYP. In the UK, this was in the late 19th century (Karim, 2015).

This formalisation of education in Europe and North America required a codification and distribution of standards that defined normality (Nadesan, 2008). This grouping of large numbers of children together in one environment and the establishment of norms by which to measure children's behaviour and ability allowed adults to recognise when children deviated from those standards and this led to establishing disciplines such as social care, educational psychology and developmental psychology (Karim, 2015). Psychiatry came under the branch of medicine, especially with the rise of pharmacological treatments.

Highlighted point!

For a long time during the 20th century, the notion of the 'normal' child was heavily influenced by psychoanalytic theory, which shaped how we think about children. Over time, there have been changes in our thinking, which reflects the challenges of defining normality.

There has been a large body of work critiquing the traditional developmental idea of standardised norms for CYP and concerns expressed about the language of the normal child. In society, what constitutes normal behaviour, normal emotions and normal reactions is measured via statistics, as representing a person against the average person in a specific sociocultural context (Davis, 1995). This is mostly because the notion of normality always involves a level of contrast to something else (Lester and Paulus, 2012). In this way children were argued to be measurable against developmental milestones. However, while these developmental trajectories can be useful in practice, the issues arise in viewing the 'normal' child by creating comparative scores on an age-graded basis, and yet no real child lies at that baseline (Burman, 2008). Of course, developmental psychology does not operate in isolation from other disciplines, and the idea of measurable standardised norms is well supported in other areas such as psychiatry, nursing, education and social care.

We bring your attention to some of these critical positions to show you that measuring the normal child is complex and challenging and, equally, understanding mental health conditions in CYP is difficult, something we attend to in the next section. We would encourage you to think about how your disciplinary training has influenced your view of the 'normal' child, and whether you believe that those standards are useful markers to help us understand when CYP need help, or if you think this has created artificial demarcations between stages of development that fail to reflect real children. We ourselves are an interdisciplinary team of authors, and we are not passing judgement on either side of this debate. Rather we encourage you to have your own opinions and engage in some additional reading to understand some of the wider criticisms levied at both sides. We encourage you to think about any potential unconscious bias you might have about the 'normal' child in relation to protected characteristics such as race, ethnicity, gender or disability. This can be uncomfortable work – you may wish to do it together with a colleague or friend and try to find evidence for your self-awareness in your everyday practices.

This is an area that has received a lot of attention and there are some authors who take a critical position on the idea of a 'normal' child. We have therefore consulted an expert in this field and present her opinion in Box 2.2.

Box 2.2: Expert voice: Dr Lindsay O'Dell

The 'normal' child

Ideas about who, and what, is a 'normal' child are evident in public discourse as well as in clinical and developmental psychology and related fields of practice. There are several ways in which 'normal' childhood is understood. Developmental psychologists have produced theories that articulate normal development. However, 'normal' childhood is also understood through articulating what is considered not 'normal', such as through classification systems including the DSM (*Diagnostic and statistical manual of mental disorders* – APA, 2013) and ICD (*International Classification of Disease* – WHO, 2018b) that are used by clinicians to diagnose disorders. Ideas of what is a 'normal' childhood and developing appropriately are also widely assumed within everyday discourse. There is a great deal of controversy about the use of diagnostic categories for understanding (some) children who differ from the norm. For some, a diagnosis can bring much needed resources and support. For others, it can be seen as pathologising and stigmatising.

Critical social scientists have argued that everyday understandings of the normal child and clinical categorisation of childhood disorders articulate wider ideas of normality and culturally valued attributes. For example, in Western societies there is an implicit expectation that as we develop, children move from a state of dependency (on their parents, families etc.) to independency. Hence being independent is understood as the most developed and valued state. However, this assumption has been widely critiqued for its assumptions about families, devaluing dependency and the mutual benefits of being part of a reciprocal arrangement of care.

In my research I have worked with CYP and families who are often seen to be outside of the 'norm'. Along with others, I have argued that one implication of assuming normal childhood is children that are seen for whatever reason to be outside the norm, are often devalued. For example, it is common in research

(Continued)

into the reactions of parents of disabled children that initially their reactions involve a mourning of the loss of the child they were expecting – a normal child. My research has focused on arguing that there needs to be a widening of developmental descriptions to enable a much wider understanding of normal childhood. CYP are often very aware that their experiences differ to a 'norm'. In my research their reactions to this include articulating their differences as a loss to themselves and their family, being proud of their differences or seeing their (and their family's) situation as just normal life.

Dr Lindsay O'Dell

Senior Lecturer in the Children and Young people research group in the Faculty of Wellbeing, Education and Language Studies; Open University.

Until recently Dr O'Dell was the Editor of the journal *Children & Society*.

Mental health and mental health conditions

There is no one definition of mental health and there is a wide range of terminology used including mental wellbeing, emotional wellbeing or psychological wellbeing, as well as mental health. There can be a tendency to avoid the term 'mental health' as it is still considered to have stigmatising connotations and can sometimes be thought to imply negativity or the notion of illness. The WHO definition (2014a) seems to be aligned to the concept of mental health as a dynamic state, within which the individual can develop their own potential and build positive relationships with others, defining mental health as:

> Positive mental health is essential if children are to flourish and lead rich and fulfilling lives. It provides a solid foundation for all aspects of development. Many things can contribute to a child or young person being mentally well. These aspects are relevant to all children and young people, not just those with difficulties or vulnerabilities, and include physical health and well-being, nutrition and exercise, as well as family, relationships, education, leisure time and social life, as well as a sense of confidence and self-esteem. Understanding what a mentally healthy child looks like can help professionals to sustain it and to focus on areas that can be strengthened: it can also help to identify areas where there may be difficulties and to think about interventions that might help.

As Dogra, Parkin et al. (2017) discussed, there are a few commonly used definitions to describe mental health in CYP. The Health Advisory Service (1995) suggested the following definition:

- A capacity to enter and sustain mutually satisfying personal relationships.
- Continuing progression of psychological development.
- An ability to play and learn so that attainments are appropriate for age and intellectual level.
- A developing moral sense of right and wrong.
- The degree of psychological distress and maladaptive behaviour is within normal limits given a child's age or context.

This definition implies that there is an ideal state of mental health that all strive to reach. As raised above, the 'normal state' will depend on the socio-cultural context.

A similar and commonly used definition was offered by the Mental Health Foundation (1999) and states that children who are mentally healthy will have the ability to:

- Develop psychologically, emotionally, creatively, intellectually and spiritually.
- Initiate, develop and sustain mutually satisfying personal relationships.
- Face problems and setbacks, and resolve them and learn from them in ways appropriate for their age.
- Be confident and assertive.
- Use and enjoy solitude.
- Become aware of others and empathise with them.
- Play and learn.
- Develop a sense of right and wrong.

This definition may also be criticised for presenting an idealised and simplified view of mental health and may be from a minority world perspective. It also perhaps fails to acknowledge the diversity of human responses to different experiences and the diversity of human individuality and ability.

However, we recognise that both definitions focus on trying to define what mentally healthy CYP should be able to do – should they so wish. This is impor-tant as these definitions begin to provide some clarity about when CYP are not mentally healthy and perhaps might be considered as not being within the 'nor-mal range'. Such definitions are therefore important for recognising when CYP might need some additional support or help, or in some cases formal treatment.

Mental health as a continuum

It is important to emphasise that there is a continuum between mental wellbe-ing and mental health condition. At one end is complete mental health and at the other severe mental disorder. The continuum between the range of 'normal' human experience and most mental health conditions means that the cut-off between what is normal and abnormal can be hard to define. Mental health characteristics can emerge along the continuum and may or may not culminate in a clinical diagnosis. Mental health changes over time in response to different stresses and experiences. There are many factors, both internal and external, that affect where someone generally sits on the continuum, and where they sit at any given point in time. We represent this visually in Figure 2.1.

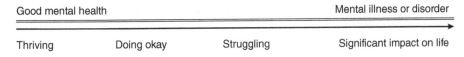

Figure 2.1   A continuum of mental health

There are behaviours that in certain contexts may indicate a mental health condition. These can include erratic behaviour, mood lability (changeable mood), agitation, disinhibition, paranoia, incoherent speech, unusual or inappropriate behaviours, repetitive actions, hearing voices, and holding fixed irrational beliefs that are not culturally contextual. However, it is important to note that these behaviours may be indicating other problems not associated with mental health, such as confusional states due to infection or intoxication. In relation to mental health conditions, it is not just the presence of symptoms that defines a 'disorder' but also its impact on the individual's functioning. For example, feelings of anxiety before big events are perceived as a normal response. However, for some, the levels of anxiety may prevent functioning and warrant attention. In others, the characteristics may be severe but manageable and not seen as limiting.

For CYP it is important to consider their age, as emotions and behaviours will differ at different stages of development. It is also important to consider context and what is going on in their life. Strong emotional and behavioural reactions are understandable and expected when someone is faced with difficult circumstances and should not necessarily be considered signs of a mental health condition. Thoughts, emotions and behaviours are also influenced by many other factors that need to be considered, such as temperament, cultural background, and the presence of learning and developmental disabilities. Determining whether a change in a CYP can be explained by age and context or whether it is the early signs that a mental health condition is developing, can be hard and may only become clear over time. We also note that connected to mental health are other types of wellbeing, which are across three domains as defined by Adi, Killoran et al. (2007):

1. Emotional wellbeing, including happiness and confidence.
2. Psychological wellbeing, including resilience, problem solving and autonomy (see Chapter 4).
3. Social wellbeing, including good relationships, and issues of interpersonal violence and bullying.

It must be recognised that there can be an inability or unwillingness by some CYP's parents and professionals to recognise that distress is a component of human experience and not necessarily a mental health condition. If this is recognised, it can be appropriately addressed rather than labelled and passed on to specialists for management. It is also important to empower individuals to take responsibility for their own health, including mental health, in appropriate ways. That requires greater openness and willingness to talk about mental health and making it everyone's business. All professionals working with CYP have a responsibility to consider their psychological health as well as to pay attention to their physical health (Dogra et al., 2017; Tamburrino, Getanda et al., 2020).

Furthermore, the absence of a mental health condition does not necessarily mean the presence of positive mental health, and neither does the recovery from mental health conditions guarantee a mentally healthy society (Keyes, 2007). We would also encourage you to think about an initiative that is currently being promoted in the field of health: that is, *parity of esteem* (see Morton and O'Reilly, 2019). It has been noted that the division between mental health and physical health is an artificial one promoted in the minority world, whereas many other traditional cultures closely align physical, social, emotional and spiritual health (Swartz, 1998). At the very least, parity of esteem is an initiative whereby governments set out to treat mental health on an equal footing with physical health, in terms of commitment of resources, attitudes and treatment pathways. It is argued that a meaningful understanding of parity of esteem is one where there is an equal aspiration, hope, respect and effort afforded to mental health as there is in physical health, and efforts to address the concrete factors to reduce mortality and stigma (Millard and Wessely, 2014).

The role of clinical manuals

Central to mental health conditions is the practice of diagnosis. Diagnosis is the action of confirming the presence of a cluster of characteristics that meet criteria for a specific condition. Diagnosis is conducted by mental health professionals and this process provides the basis for supporting the individual through treatment, but also support from other services like education, social care and welfare. In practice, diagnosis relies on clinical judgement and skills, but also reference to the standardised manuals that outline the criteria necessary for an individual to meet the threshold of a condition.

As already stated above, there are two main diagnostic manuals available, the ICD and DSM. We explain what these mean in Box 2.3. Again, there are criticisms that these, especially the DSM, medicalise 'normal' human experiences.

Highlighted point!

The ICD is used for both physical and mental illnesses, but the DSM focuses only on mental health conditions.

Box 2.3: What this means

The role of clinical manuals is important for mental health practitioners in three ways:

1. The way we conceptualise what constitutes a mental health condition is now different from earlier decades as manuals and views change over time.
2. The manuals provide criteria and a standard against which individuals' mental health is assessed, and this is used by diagnosing practitioners to help their decision making.
3. The demarcation of what constitutes a condition, and the boundaries of normality are constructed, rather than fixed, and therefore what is believed to be normal or abnormal changes over time.

It is important to recognise that while the manuals provide the standards, clinical judgement, clinical expertise and experience, diagnostic tools and observation also form an important part of the process and a diagnosis of a mental health condition should be undertaken by a professional.

Prevalence and the mental health crisis

Mental health conditions (along with substance use disorders) account for 7.4% of the global burden of disease (Whiteford, Degenhardt et al., 2013). In majority world countries, the economic impact is significant, as in 2010 it was estimated to be $870 billion, and is set to double by 2030 (Bloom, Cafiero et al. 2011). However, we have encouraged you to be critical of evidence and these costs only reveal a partial picture. It is not clear if it has greater economic impact because there is greater prevalence of conditions, or if because treatments are more expensive, or because the lack of services means that conditions worsen and become more expensive. Evidence tells us that most adult mental health conditions begin in childhood or adolescence (Kessler, Amminger et al., 2007). This is especially noteworthy as 40% of the world's population is under the age of 24 years, with most of these living in the majority world (The Academy of Medical Sciences, 2018). However, in those countries there are few mental health services designed for them (ibid.) and we outline what this means in Box 2.4.

We live in a time where the world media talks about a mental health crisis for CYP. In the UK, it has been argued that government cuts and austerity (Allan, 2018), and limited access to specialist care and treatment (Young Minds, 2018),

Box 2.4: What this means

Good mental health is integral to human health and many of the common mental health conditions are shaped by social, economic and physical context, with social inequality increasing risk (WHO and the Calouste Gulbenkian Foundation, 2014). There are too many CYP not receiving the help or services they would benefit from, and this is especially the case in low income families or children with disadvantaged backgrounds. This is the case all over the world and social inequality clearly impacts on access to mental health support. This is arguably worsened in countries with extreme poverty, war conflict and other adversities. Furthermore, the quality of any available mental health support varies significantly from country to country, and is especially concerning in countries with greater levels of socio-economic inequality. This is problematic as without support and/or treatment the mental health condition is likely to worsen and, depending on the nature/characteristics of that condition, could lead to adverse outcomes including (but not limited to) those related to employment, social functioning, emotional regulation and/or physical health issues.

have created a situation that should be characterised as a crisis. Not only does society have to grapple with cuts to funding, and issues with access to support, but there also seems to be a rising demand in need. Synthesising sources from studies around the world, a systematic review showed that the burden of mental health is increasing in CYP (Bor et al., 2014) and mental health need is high in this group (Dogra et al., 2017). The WHO (2019) reported that demand is high, and resources are low across the globe, and that this is concerning. In a recent UK survey by NHS Digital (2018) it was shown that all areas of mental health are increasing in prevalence and this has important implications for practitioners working with CYP. It is important to note that the criteria for mental health conditions were based on ICD classifications (which tend to be more restrictive) and not DSM (which tends to be broader), and therefore prevalence could be even higher. We outline the key findings from that survey in Box 2.5.

There are some gender differences in terms of the types of conditions experienced more by girls than boys, and vice versa, and the way in which those conditions are visible socially. For example, girls in the UK consistently show higher rates of emotional problems and boys have higher rates of conduct problems – although what we might define as 'emotional' versus 'conduct' is contested and perhaps reflects problematic societal norms and expectations. The NHS Digital survey showed that young women aged 17–19 years were at high risk, especially as this group showed higher rates

Box 2.5: Key research evidence

NHS Digital survey 2018 results

Overall, the results of the NHS Digital survey 2018 showed that 12.8% of children aged 5–19 years had at least one mental health condition (referred to as 'disorders'), and 5% met the criteria for two or more conditions. In the report, disorders were grouped according to four types:

1. **Emotional disorders**: such as anxiety disorders, depressive disorders, mania, and bipolar disorders. Results showed that 8.1% of 5–19 year olds had an emotional disorder. Rates were higher in girls (10%) than boys (6.2%). Anxiety disorders (7.2%) were more common than depressive disorders (2.1%).
2. **Behavioural disorders** (sometimes referred to as conduct disorders): which are disorders characterised by repetitive and persistent patterns of disruptive or violent behaviour where social norms or rules are violated. Results showed 4.6% had a behavioural disorder, which was higher in boys (5.8%) than girls (3.4%).
3. **Hyperactivity disorders**: which included those conditions characterised by inattention, impulsivity and hyperactivity. The number of children with hyperactivity disorder is lower as defined by the ICD-11 than those with attention deficit hyperactivity disorder (ADHD) as defined by DSM-5. Results showed that 1.6% had a hyperactivity disorder and this was higher in boys 2.6% than girls (0.6%).
4. **Other less common disorders**: these included autism spectrum disorder (ASD), eating disorders, tics, and some other very low-prevalence conditions. Results showed that 2.1% had one of these conditions, with 1.2% ASD, 0.4% eating disorder and 0.8% tics.

of emotional disorders and self-harm than all other groups. In this age group rates of body dysmorphic disorder (where the child is highly focused on body flaws and becomes anxious and ashamed) were high (5.6%), and 1.6% had an eating disorder. This suggests that young women in this age category are especially at risk from factors that may lead to emotional health conditions. Interestingly, the EU Kids Online report (Smahel, Machackova et al., 2020) showed that most children aged 12–16 in most of the surveyed countries had not seen ways of physically harming or hurting themselves and had not seen ways to be very thin on the Internet in the past year. The report identified that although about one-fifth of respondents did report being upset after seeing harmful material online, one fifth experienced no harm, and girls were more likely to report feeling harmed than boys. However, the report also indicates that in some countries, the most potentially harmful effect was through exposure to hate content.

Emerging evidence suggests that this pattern may not be restricted to one culture; a study with Asian, Latina and White university students in the USA found that there were only small effects of ethnicity on negative body talk, with women's ethnic-racial identity linked to less frequent such talk, and men's ethnic-racial identity linked with more frequent negative body talk (Sladek, Salk, & Engeln, 2018). However, most of the research about child and adolescent mental health is from minority world contexts; we can have little confidence that what we understand about developed economies will apply to other cultural contexts or regions such as the majority world.

We would encourage you to think about what this means for you as a practitioner. Have a look at the reflective activity in Box 2.6. The answer to the following question will depend on the nature of your position, the role you have, and the type of work you do:

> ## How might the rising rates of mental health conditions impact you and your work?

Box 2.6: Reflecting on your role

How might the increased prevalence of mental health conditions affect you in your role?

Write in your reflective diary your experience of CYP with mental health conditions or mental health need. In your view, do you think the number of CYP you are working with have increasing levels of mental health need (even if that is not at a level that requires a formal diagnosis)? If so, why do you think that might be?

It is crucial that societies do more to promote positive mental health and help individuals to stay mentally healthy, do more to prevent CYP who are at risk from developing mental health conditions, and spend more money on interventions, treatments and services to support those with significant mental health need.

Promotion, prevention, and intervention

As we have shown, tackling the growing global mental health problem in relation to CYP is economically challenging and pragmatically difficult. Responding to the growing need is going to require a commitment in terms of financial resources, but also in terms of organisational assurance, training, skills, time and knowledge, amongst other things. The challenge is typically conceptualised under the three broad categories of promotion, prevention and intervention. We consider what this means in Box 2.7.

 **Box 2.7: What this means**

This means that there are three major ways in which governments, society, communities, organisations and families can work to address mental health and need with CYP. The WHO (2016) described these as:

1. By promoting positive mental health in children by raising awareness, increasing knowledge, finding ways to help them relax and cope with stressors, supporting need and building resilience.
2. By actively putting in strategies to prevent the onset of mental health conditions by targeting groups that are likely at risk from development.
3. By ensuring that those children who have a diagnosable mental health condition obtain timely diagnosis, access to treatment and relevant interventions to help support them, and, where possible, recover or at least improve quality of life.

Mental health promotion and prevention strategies that are effective, and interventions that improve mental health outcomes are essential. We separate these but note that they overlap in practice.

Promotion

It is globally evident that many CYP are not especially well-informed about mental health and mental health conditions (Dogra, Omigbodun et al., 2012; Pinfold, Toulmin et al., 2003) and although there have been efforts to raise awareness about mental health, the very idea of mental health is frequently conflated with the idea of mental illness. Mental health promotion is one way in which societies learn about mental health and provides strategies to protect and safeguard wellbeing. Clearly then, mental health promotion should be an integral aspect of all health promotion activity (Sturgeon, 2007).

Mental health promotion is important at both the individual level of the child/young person, and the community level. The WHO published their first report on mental health promotion in 2004, where they highlighted (as we did earlier) that mental health is not simply the absence of a mental health condition. In that report, the WHO argued that individuals need to reach a state of wellbeing where they can cope with life, contribute to society, and achieve to the best of their abilities. This report proposed the need for mental health promotion, arguing that this has the potential to increase positive mental health, and that is an important way of protecting against the onset of mental health conditions.

Mental health promotion was defined by the WHO (2016) as the actions needed to create the environment and conditions where individuals have the skills needed to maintain healthy lifestyles, and are afforded their civil, cultural, political and socio-economic rights. There are generally three types of mental health promotion utilised for child and adolescent mental health and these were described by Humphrey and Wigglesworth (2016):

Universal:those programmes designed to address the whole population.

Targeted: those programmes designed to target specific groups who have certain risk factors, including those at high risk.

Specialist: this is mental health provision designed to support children with identified conditions and these programmes are usually designed in collaboration with specialist services like CAMHS or paediatric experts.

There are several ways to promote mental health, such as via support programmes for CYP, improving socio-economic empowerment for women, programme delivery for underserved groups, promotion activity through schools, poverty reduction, community development programmes, anti-discrimination strategies, and promotion of human rights (Dogra et al., 2017). For this group, it has often been the case that school settings provide a sensible place to implement programmes as children spend so much of their time in education, both in terms of the number of weeks in any given year, as well as the number of years before they leave. It is probably unsurprising therefore that across the globe (particularly in the minority world), there have been a growing number of mental health promotion programmes delivered through schools, that is, school mental health promotion. This has been described as a continuum of strategies, programmes and services delivered through education, enhancing the school environment, and promoting emotional and social learning to help promote positive mental health in CYP (Weist and Murray, 2008). Weist and Murray argued that there are eight principles that are necessary for school mental health promotion:

1. The ethos and environment.
2. Curriculum, teaching and learning.

3. Enabling students to influence decisions.
4. Staff development and staff mental health.
5. Identifying needs and monitoring the impact of interventions.
6. Working with parents.
7. Targeted support.
8. Leadership and management support.

There have been many school mental health promotion programmes around the world. Subsequently various evidence reviews have examined how useful such approaches are. Crucially, some interventions and programmes in less developed economies have been less extensively evaluated, and certainly have benefited from much less financial resource. They may, however, still be very worthy of consideration for other settings.

We summarise some of these reviews in Box 2.8 to give you an overview of the decades of research in this area.

Box 2.8: Key research evidence

Reviews of mental health promotion

There have been several reviews of evidence over the decades and we report on three post-millennium reviews here:

First, Green, Howes et al. conducted a review in 2005. In their narrative synthesis they found that there was a lack of good-quality evaluations in mental health promotion. They reported that the most common limitation of the pro-grammes was that the evaluations of them tended to be short-term and lacked a long-term follow-up. They also reported that the research articles they reviewed lacked detail about the intervention, with limited specification of goals and outcomes or the process factors that contributed to programme success.

Second, in a review by Weare and Nind in 2011, research was examined focusing on school mental health promotion from the previous 25 years. They reported that there exists repeated evidence that mental health promotion in schools has positive impact. The promotion programmes reviewed were univer-sal and targeted programmes that focused on CYP and they reported that such universal approaches in isolation were not as effective as those that had a robust targeted component. They argued that the combined approach is most effective and felt that those with a targeted component had a more dramatic effect on high-risk children.

Third, in a recent review we conducted (O'Reilly, Svirydzenka et al., 2018) we focused on 10 years of universal mental health promotion programmes for CYP. We examined universal interventions in schools including relevant articles from UK, Australia, the USA, Sweden, Denmark, Germany and Ireland. The review recognised that terminology across educational and health sectors differs (Rowling, 2009), and this can make reviews complex and challenging. The key finding of the review was that very little had changed over the decades and there had been limited advancement in the field. The authors reported that terminology remains variable and there is little work looking at the longer-term impacts of universal mental health promotion programmes. The methods used were of variable quality, with some studies being vague about their description of the intervention. The key finding was that there was a lack of digital interventions, such as promotion work that used artificial intelligence (AI), robotics, social media or other internet-enabled approaches.

We argue that a key part of mental health promotion for CYP is raising awareness, building knowledge, and increasing skills in coping with stress. It is especially important that these groups understand what mental health is and what mental health conditions are, as well as having the competencies to recognise when their psychological state is threatened or when they might need support. Younger populations do not always understand what mental health is or understand how it is different from mental health conditions. Although many children are turning to the Internet to learn about mental health, adults need to help educate CYP on the difference between being mentally healthy and being mentally ill. This varies significantly across cultures. In some parts of southern Africa, for example, the characteristics clinical experts might define as a mental health condition are considered a 'call from the ancestors'. The CYP in your care may be hearing a range of messages about mental health and wellbeing across school, home and the Internet.

Research studies have shown that CYP rarely think about mental health as part of their healthy living, as when asked about health, 97% of 218 young people aged 13 years talked about being physically healthy and only 8% raised their mental health as part of that bigger picture (Singletary, Bartle et al., 2015). Furthermore, research suggests that CYP find it challenging to define mental health, often conflating mental health with mental illness, or defining it in terms of specific conditions (Bone, Dugard et al., 2015; O'Reilly, Dogra et al., 2018). Clearly this population needs an education about mental health as this can help them to better understand their own wellbeing, reduce stigma and help them better understand when their peers experience difficulties. However, this can be challenging to deliver. Research suggests that CYP want to be educated about mental health, that they are motivated to receive this knowledge, but that their preference is to learn about this in school (Bone et al., 2015; O'Reilly, Adams et al., 2018).

Mental health promotion using digital media

In this contemporary world of new technologies, it is perhaps surprising that using digital media, or social media more specifically, for mental health promotion is only just emerging. Yet, it is known that CYP use the Internet and social media to seek out information about their own wellbeing, health, symptoms and so on, but this of course raises issues of trustworthiness and credibility.

For example, in the UK recent work showed that 63% of young people found social media a useful source of information about their health (Royal Society for Public Health, 2019). Mental health is especially important to many adolescents and they tend to look on the Internet for this information, especially for sensitive information (Wartella, Rideout et al., 2016). However, while the use of social media in health care is widely advocated, there is relatively little in the way of evidence about the current state of the science and how those tools might be used to benefit patient populations (Hamm, Chisholm et al., 2013) (and CYP populations specifically), especially as the Internet is not restrained by the geographical location of the information-seekers. Ziebland and Wyke (2012) suggested that there are seven main domains through which health can be impacted by sharing experiences online:

1. Finding information.
2. Feeling supported.
3. Maintaining relationships with others.
4. Affecting behaviour.
5. Experiencing health.
6. Learning to tell the story.
7. Visualising disease.

What is especially interesting in the case of CYP, however, is that while they frequently use digital sources for information about their health, they seek out trusted sources and have concerns about the validity of that information (Fergie, Hunt & Hilton, 2013). In our own work on this issue, we found that adolescents liked to find health information using internet search engines and asking friends via digital messaging services, but they wanted to bring that information into schools for teachers to verify (O'Reilly, Adams et al., 2018).

An advantage of online modalities is that they can be used anonymously, which can reduce stigma associated with seeking help (Boydell, Hodgins et al., 2014). Cotton (2019) reports on Headspace programmes run in Australia and commented that the work by Headspace is seen as important by both staff and clients for mental health promotion and for raising community awareness. In this way she argues that these kind of promotion programmes seem to have some positive impact to reduce the stigma that is frequently associated with those who experience mental health conditions and, furthermore, they can encourage CYP to seek help when it is needed.

Cotton (2019) reported that mental health promotion programmes like Headspace undertake various activities for CYP at risk, and this includes mental health service support such as access to a psychiatrist online. The work of Headspace has now expanded in Australia and the USA to being available digitally as 'e-Headspace'. This reflects much of the context of the report. However, mental health promotion and reducing stigma associated with mental health does not feature heavily in the literature. Cotton's (2019) review of these kinds of services in Australia and the USA highlights that to date the emphasis has largely been on using technological advances to better deliver services for those who need them. It may be that these fall under general wellbeing and avoid mental health terminology.

Prevention

Mental health condition prevention overlaps with mental health promotion, and the two are often undertaken together. That is, some targeted mental health promotion programmes also have a prevention component. However, promotion and prevention are different and therefore we discuss them separately. Many negative outcomes we are seeing in society due to the increased prevalence of mental health conditions in CYP could be reduced or possibly avoided (at least for some) if there was earlier recognition and treatment, as well as support for the child and their families.

The WHO (2016) reports that the prevention of mental health conditions requires strategies designed to reduce the incidence, prevalence or recurrence of mental health conditions. Like targeted mental health promotion programmes, prevention strategies tend to target specific groups of CYP who are considered at risk. It is reported that there are three themes of prevention described by Herrman (2001), outlined in Table 2.1.

Table 2.1 Three themes of prevention (Herrman, 2001)

Theme	Description
Development and maintenance of a healthy community	To ensure that CYP are provided a safe and secure environment, a positive educational experience, good housing, a supportive political infrastructure, some autonomy and control over their lives, self-determination, minimising conflict or violence, provision of social support, positive role models and ensuring that their basic needs are met.
Abilities to cope with the social world	To provide CYP with the skills and competencies to cope and deal with their social world, and this includes skills like tolerating diversity, participation and mutual responsibility. This is underpinned by the importance of attachment, positive relationships, positive communication and feelings of being accepted.
Abilities to manage thoughts and feelings	To ensure that CYP are equipped with the skills and competencies to deal with their thoughts and feelings, and to manage their life. They need to be equipped with skills to build emotional resilience, build positive self-esteem, promote their physical health, manage conflict, and the ability to learn.

Intervention

For those CYP who experience a mental health condition, whether emotional, behavioural or neurodevelopmental, they should have access to mental health support and treatment. In most minority world countries this requires the family (or school) to request a referral to a specialist mental health service where the child/young person can be assessed, diagnosed and treated.

These initial assessments are important as they determine whether there is mental health need and an assessment for risk (Sands, 2004), and during these, families are asked many questions about the child, family and the 'problem' being attended to (O'Reilly, Karim & Kiyimba, 2015; Stafford, Hutchby et al., 2016).

Once it has been determined that the child has a condition, and this is diagnosed formally, the specialist service will determine the most appropriate form of treatment. One option sometimes considered necessary is pharmacology. Although this has been controversial in some circles, there is some good evidence that medication can be helpful for *some* children with *some* conditions. There are a range of medications that may be offered (see Dogra et al., 2017).

For some CYP, it is more appropriate to be offered talking-based therapy. Mental health professionals are trained in different types of therapeutic approaches, and these differ based on the approach, the framework and the delivery. While these different therapies represent different disciplinary thinking, the mainstay of treatment is talking. Some of the more common therapies offered to children include those founded in the psychodynamic traditions, (like psychotherapy), the cognitive behavioural therapies (CBT), and the systemic therapies. Thus, some therapies, like psychodynamic psychotherapy, focus on childhood experiences, talking through past issues and considering the wider impact; others, like CBT, are more present-focused and problem solving, while those like systemic therapies tend to involve families and consider the dynamics of family members (Kiyimba & O'Reilly, 2016).

Aetiology and the multi-factorial profile of mental health

To provide stronger frameworks for promotion, prevention and intervention it is important that we have a good understanding of the underlying issues. The aetiology of mental health conditions in CYP is complex. By 'aetiology' we mean the cause of a condition. It is multi-factorial and multi-dimensional, and different conditions have a different profile and cause or causes, which sometimes remain unknown or lack good quality evidence. For mental health conditions, it is argued that there are different risk factors that can increase the likelihood of difficulties occurring. A well-established framework is that of the four Ps as summarised by Weerasekera (1996):

1. **Predisposing**: those are the factors that are more likely to make a child vulnerable to developing a mental health condition.
2. **Precipitating**: those are the factors that may trigger the onset of a condition.
3. **Perpetuating**: those are the factors that increase the likelihood of a mental health condition occurring and maintain the symptoms or characteristics.
4. **Protective**: those are the factors that can reduce the likelihood of a condition developing.

Thus, these four categories may be biological, psychological or environmental. We provide examples of each of these in turn (see Adams, O'Reilly, and Karim, 2019). The mental health problems of childhood and adolescence (and adulthood) usually have a multifactorial aetiology. Mental health conditions tend to have a combination of biological (e.g. genetic), psychological (e.g. individual factors such as personality type, temperament) and social factors (e.g. family, school, community etc.).

Biological

Predisposing – may include medical conditions, issues in pregnancy or genetic factors.

Precipitating – may include effects of infection or illness or side effects of medication.

Perpetuating – may include a chronic illness or disability.

Protective – may include good physical health, regular exercise, diet and genetics.

Psychological

Predisposing – may include learned behaviours, learned helplessness and low self-esteem.

Precipitating – may include low academic achievement, and pressure at school.

Perpetuating – may include a repeated sense of failure, and unrealistic personal expectations.

Protective – may include positive self-esteem and self-confidence, academic attainment, and good coping strategies.

Environmental

Predisposing – may include poor family relationships and social deprivation.

Precipitating – may include conflict with others, bullying.

Perpetuating – may include an ongoing conflict, unresolved long-term bullying, and abuse and/or neglect or domestic violence.

Protective – may include positive relationships, positive social relationships and strong sense of community.

There are many factors that might influence a CYP's state of mind, and often these are thought of as overwhelming and are typically represented in negative ways as Figure 2.2 highlights.

Figure 2.2   Feeling overwhelmed

In simple terms, understanding the contributing factors has been character-ised as the *nature* versus *nurture* debate, as professionals have grappled with the extent to which mental health conditions might be explained by biological and genetic factors and/or environmental, cultural and social factors. There is much overlap and most professional groups now accept that most mental health conditions are caused by a blend of these.

In recent discussions we are seeing more attention directed toward digital media, screen time and specifically social media as being a possible factor that contributes to the development of mental health conditions. We are not, how-ever, going to talk about that here in this section, as the rest of the book is devoted to this complex relationship. Instead, we turn our attention to four key areas that have received a lot of attention. We only offer a cursory over-view of each of these four issues by way of an introduction.

Bronfenbrenner's (1979) ecological model is useful to understand the mul-tiple layers in the development of children's problems: the microsystem, mesosystem, exosystem, macrosystem and chronosystem.

- The *microsystem* is at the level of the relationships in which the child is actively involved, for example, with parents, siblings and peers. These interactions inevitably depend on the sociocultural context and the child's characteristics or personality.

- The *mesosystem* describes how the different components of the microsystem come together, such as clubs and schools.
- The *exosystem* is the wider local community, such as the neighbourhood.
- The *macrosystem* is usually more remote but may still be a major social influence, for example, through socio-economic policy on child rearing, education and health policies, and wider sociocultural contexts.
- The *chronosystem* is wider still, such as the country's political framework like communism or democracy.

It is worth noting that different factors may be important at various stages of the child's life. Two clear factors that are known to play a significant role are socio-economic factors and family factors.

Socio-economic factors and mental health

Despite the demand for support for mental health, there is a high level of unmet need across the globe. For example, in England, of the 338,000 children referred to CAMHS, only 31% received treatment within one year, and 37% were not accepted into treatment, with 32% still on waiting lists after a year (Lennon, 2018). In some countries this is even worse, with some countries in the majority world spending less than 1 US$ per capita on mental health (WHO, 2018c). In England, an average of 14% of the health budget was spent on mental health, but only 0.9% on child mental health, comparatively spending £55 per child on mental health services against £800 on physical health (Lennon, 2018). Economically this insufficient attention and spending on child and adolescent mental health is failing a generation, and furthermore failing society. Research has shown that when mental health conditions in children and/or young people remain untreated it can have longstanding social and economic consequences in adulthood, leading to increased likelihood for contact with the criminal justice system, reduced levels of employment, lower salaries and difficulties in personal relationships (Chen, Cohen et al., 2006).

Evidently, there is a clear and strong association between poverty and mental health (Boardman, Dogra, and Hindley 2015). Adults in contact with mental health services are likely to be on welfare benefits and may not receive their full benefit entitlement. Children living in households where an adult is in receipt of benefit payments are 2.5 times more likely to have a mental health problem than the average child (Meltzer, Gatward et al., 2000). Again, we encourage you to think critically about these types of associations, as this is correlational and not causal. It is important we think about the reasons why and how families on lower incomes may experience greater prevalence of mental health need. For example, one connection may be parental education level.

Family factors and mental health

Parental mental ill health can be a predisposing and precipitating aetiological factor for CYP's mental health conditions, working through the biological and social spheres. Family adversity, domestic violence, parental hostility may all be relevant aetiological factors, as may parenting styles (Dogra, 2010a). Family relationships and a mismatch between the parental and child perspectives may be relevant factors. We discuss the role of family in more detail in Chapter 9 and so simply draw your attention to it here.

The role of culture

Culture influences how mental health conditions are conceptualised, who is approached to help and what treatments are deemed acceptable. Prevalence rates may vary across different cultures, but this may relate to how conditions are identified and whether the impact and characteristics prompt help-seeking and diagnosis. Culture strongly influences the role of parents and of CYP. Whilst traditional domestic routines may continue to be of great importance to CYP of British minority ethnic groups growing up in the UK, this is not seen as the only way to do things and they are increasingly exposed to other cultures. Ethnically Indian adolescents had lower rates of all types of mental health condition except for eating disorders, compared with their White counterparts (Dogra, Svirydzenka et al., 2013). South Asian CYP may be brought up with a strong sense of family responsibility implicit in certain relationships. However, outside the family and in their communities, they are exposed to different expectations. Where there is a tendency for the family to have a central role, the needs of the family and the needs of the individual may conflict. Asian girls, and especially those who find their choices restricted because of cultural expectations, can experience considerable distress (Husain, Waheed & Husain, 2006). This can be compounded by the unwillingness of some minority groups to discuss this openly. However, culture can also provide CYP with a sense of belonging and some appreciation of their role. Thus, there are many ways in which culture influences mental health and we outline these in Box 2.9.

 **Box 2.9: What this means**

Culture influences mental health in the following ways:

- The way that people think about mental health and mental health problems.
- The way that they make sense of certain symptoms and behaviours.

- Their view of potential services and the services they choose to accept (e.g. seeing traditional healers or religious advisers before medical professionals).
- The treatment and management strategies they find acceptable.

(Dogra, Vostanis & Karnik, 2018; Glover, Karnik et al., 2018)

Stigma and help-seeking

To be able to support CYP with their mental health needs, whether they meet the threshold for diagnosis or not, relies heavily on identification of those needs. This means that professionals and families need to spot the signs and come forward and seek help. However, CYP and their families do not always identify those issues, and one major contributing factor (not the only one) is stigma. Stigma is an area related to mental health that has received considerable research attention, in terms of the different types of stigma, the impact and effect of stigma, and possible strategies and campaigns to reduce and eliminate the prejudice and discrimination that can arise from stigma. Indeed, there are whole books devoted to this subject. Inevitably then, what we provide here is merely a brief introduction.

The language associated with mental health tends to have a negative valence, and the way individuals with mental health conditions are represented through various media also tends to be negative. It is often the case that when people are asked to describe mental health, they conflate it with mental illness, and so mental health as well as illness tend to invoke negative descriptions. We would encourage you to reflect on the words you think of when prompted, usually by the words 'mental illness' which alongside 'mental disorder' tends to be the language of medicine. Think about this question and try the reflective activity in Box 2.10.

What does the term 'mental illness' mean to you?

Box 2.10: Reflecting on language

What does the term mental illness mean to you?

We have deliberately used the term 'mental illness' for this reflective activity rather than our preferred concept of mental health condition, as this is the term

(Continued)

that tends to be used in lay discourse and is a term that tends to invoke different opinions.

In your reflective diary write down the first five words that come to mind when
thinking about mental illness. Do not over-think it and be honest; what did initially come to mind when presented with the words?

There is a large body of work that shows that people tend to think about mental
health conditions and those who experience them in negative ways. In a study
of adolescents, Rose, Thornicroft et al. (2007) were given 250 words associated
with mental health conditions, and most of these were negative. Of the 44 concepts most frequently used by adolescents, 33 were negative, seven were neutral
and only four were positive. This seems to be the case even for those who are
diagnosed with mental health conditions themselves, as they also provide a
negative language around mental illness (O'Reilly, Taylor and Vostanis, 2009).
From these two studies we illustrate some concepts in Figure 2.3.

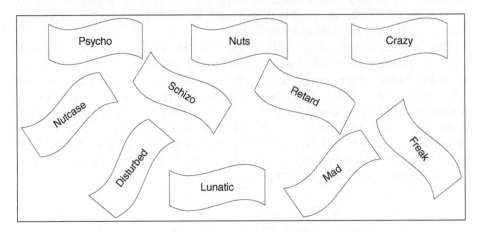

Figure 2.3   Negative concepts (O'Reilly et al., 2009: Rose et al., 2007)

This negative language is important when thinking about stigma. Stigma
is one of those concepts that has varied definitions and while there is some
difference of opinion regarding the specifics, there is agreement on certain
elements including:

- There is a negative impact on the individual belonging to the stigmatised
  group.
- There is typically a social cognitive reference to prejudice, stereotyping
  and discrimination.

Different definitions have been put forward and these have similarities
(although generally in an adult context). We offer some in Table 2.2.

Table 2.2   Definitions of stigma

Authors	Definition
Susman (1994)	Stigma is an adverse reaction to perceptions of negatively evaluated difference.
Link, Struening et al. (2001)	Stigma is a process that results in a reduction of status and in discrimination.
Link and Phelan (2001)	Stigma is the process of labelling, stereotype awareness, stereotype endorsement, prejudice and discrimination to the detriment of the stigmatised social group.
Hatzenbuehler, Phelan & Link (2013)	Stigma is a co-occurrence of labelling, stereotyping, separation, discrimination and loss of status.

Stigma therefore is an amalgamation of three related social cognitive problems as proposed by Thornicroft (2006):

1. Lack of knowledge – *ignorance*.
2. Negative attitudes – *prejudice*.
3. Excluding or avoiding behaviours – *discrimination*.

Furthermore, there are different types of stigma, and these have been described by Clement, Schauman et al. (2015) as:

•   *Anticipated stigma* is when the individual anticipates that they will be treated unfairly.
•   *Experienced stigma* is when the individual actually experiences a personal stigma by being unfairly treated.
•   *Internalised stigma* is when the individual has a stigmatised view of themselves.
•   *Perceived stigma* is when the individual has perceptions about the extent to which others might hold stigmatising attitudes and behaviours toward them.
•   *Stigma endorsement* is when individuals hold and express their own stigmatising behaviour and attitudes toward others who have mental health conditions.
•   *Treatment stigma* is when an individual experiences stigma associated with seeking or receiving help from mental health services.

Goffman (1963) also referred to *courtesy stigma*, which is when individuals linked to the individual with mental health conditions, like their family members, also experience stigma in the form of prejudice or discrimination. Stigma can be one of the issues that impacts on help-seeking.

As noted, it can take parents time before seeking help and the reasons for this are multifaceted. Research indicated that on average it takes about 3.1 years for parents to receive help from the point of their initial concerns, and children are an average of 7.5 years old when they receive it (Shanley, Reid & Evans, 2008), although for some conditions, like autism this can occur slightly younger, but it still takes an average of 3.5 years to receive help (Crane, Chester et al., 2016). We are not suggesting it is only because of stigma that it takes so long for parents to seek help or acquire it. Of course, that is not the case! It may relate to a lack of awareness or education around mental health, fear or concerns about medicine, cultural beliefs, concerns that they will be judged as being an over-anxious parent, denial and so on. However, research has shown that stigma can be a contributory factor, as families struggle to manage some of the negative discourses that exist. In a recent systematic review of many research studies from across the globe, Clement et al. (2015) found that there were several stigma-related barriers to help-seeking, including shame, embarrassment, fear of negative social judgement, disclosure concerns and fear of discrimination.

Stigma is pervasive and problematic as society grapples with ways to challenge negative attitudes, language and thinking. As a practitioner you play an important role in this. Interestingly, research has shown that practitioners, even mental health practitioners, can hold negative attitudes about mental health; for example, Accident and Emergency staff (Clarke, Usick et al., 2014), social workers (Kotera, Green, and Sheffield 2019), doctors (Wallace, 2010), nurses (Shaw, Sandy & Gesondheid, 2016) and teachers (Gur, Sener et al., 2012), as well as some mental health professionals (Hansson, Jormfeldt et al., 2011). However, for context we would note that these attitudes relate to a wide range of issues, and it is often the case that training and increased knowledge often improves attitudes, whereby some of the negative attitudes reflect frustrations about systems and policies, lack of support, time and resources and concerns about not knowing what to do rather than a negative attitude about individuals with conditions. We therefore encourage you to think about the following question and attempt the reflective activity in Box 2.11.

What can you do to challenge stigma?

 **Box 2.11: Reflecting on stigma**

What can you do as an individual to challenge stigma?

Think about your own attitude. Does the nature of the mental health condition make a difference? For example, do you think differently about teenagers with schizophrenia, differently to autism or depression?

In your reflective diary write your initial thoughts and see if you can think of three ways in which you might be able to challenge stigma in your job.

Although we recognise that organisational policy and strategy is important in managing stigma, there are things that you can do, and we provide practical tips in Box 2.12.

Box 2.12: Practical tips for managing stigma

We encourage you to:

- Be mindful of your language.
- Reflect on your views about CYP with mental health conditions and how they have been formed.
- Challenge people when they use derogatory terms for those with mental health conditions.
- Challenge stereotypes.
- In your workplace, encourage openness in talking about mental health.

Conclusions

In this chapter we have discussed the challenge of defining 'normality' and the terms used when individuals deviate from that 'norm'. We have discussed definitions and meanings of mental health and mental health conditions and the aetiological factors. In completing this chapter, we provide a viewpoint on mental health from an expert in this field. In Box 2.13, we present the perspective of Professor Tamsin Ford, who is a practising clinical and academic psychiatrist.

Box 2.13: Expert contribution: Professor Tamsin Ford

Role: Professor of Child and Adolescent Psychiatry

Organisation: University of Cambridge

(Continued)

Brief bio: Professor Tamsin Ford is known internationally for her work in child psychiatric epidemiology and her work on the organisation, delivery and effectiveness of services and intervention in child mental health. Her work is translational and cross-disciplinary.

Are we really amid a child and adolescent mental health crisis?

I have spent the last two decades studying how many CYP have impairing mental health conditions and how best to organise services (Ford, Vizard et al., 2020), but struggle to answer this question. It is much harder than you might think to be clear about whether the mental health of CYP is deteriorating. I would qualify my answer, which is 'almost certainly', with 'it depends what you mean by "mental health" and "crisis"'.

Like the authors of the book, I use the term 'mental health condition' to describe poor mental health of a severity that impairs a child's ability to function or develop, and focus my discussion on this clinically relevant group. Precision of language is essential, particularly in conceptually challenging areas, and even more so in terms of measurement. Despite the authors' excellent deconstruction of the concept of wellbeing, we are less certain in our definitions and measurements of the former than mental health (Mehta, Croudace & Davies, 2014). Besides, if the object is to improve health, then the adoption of a health model seems logical and the setting irrelevant.

As mental health is a continuum, the accumulated scores of large samples of CYP on questionnaires about mental health difficulties when plotted on a graph produce the familiar bell-shaped curve seen with similar plots of height and weight. Relatively few will be thriving or struggling, while most scores cluster in the middle (Ford & Parker, 2016). The threshold for those whom a mental health practitioner would assess as having a mental health condition is often taken as a cut-point on a scale, but is much less precise in practice. This is why not all CYP who score above a cut-point would have significant mental health needs if assessed (a major problem for screening programmes), with errors occurring in both directions. In clinical practice, the impairment of function is key to the decision about whether a child requires intervention. Functional impairment will be influenced by biological, psychological and social influences on all four 'Ps' described in this chapter: predisposing, precipitating, perpetuating and protective factors.

This is not unique to mental health conditions. High blood pressure, asthma and diabetes are among the many physical health conditions diagnosed when values fall above or below a somewhat arbitrary cut-point. Often the risks to health and wellbeing are not confined to those with clinical levels of impairment (Patel, Saxena et al., 2018), while social and psychological influences on physical conditions are also common if less regularly considered. Just think of the three conditions listed above, in which lifestyle, social circumstances and mental state can profoundly influence clinical outcomes.

The number and types of difficulties commonly experienced vary by gender, cultural background and age groups so that differences in the age range studied, the mental health conditions assessed and how the sample generalises to the reference population will influence how many CYP appear to have difficulties. For example, given the consistent relationship between poor childhood mental health and poverty, samples drawn from schools or populations in deprived areas will produce much higher estimates than those that reflect the general population (Ford & McManus, 2020).

Even small changes to standardised questionnaires can lead to large and important differences in how people respond and thus how many appear to be struggling (Goodman, Iervolino et al., 2007). Yet our understanding of mental health in CYP as well as how we measure it has changed, leading to difficulties in comparing studies completed at different times. To complicate matters further, the salience and attributions of some psychosocial risk factors vary with time and place; for example, parental separation, corporal punishment, sexuality and gender identity. Sometimes questions asked differ between studies, which leaves us trying to compare apples and pears, while in other cases, those responding may understand or respond to the questions differently even if they are the same (Collishaw, 2015). For example, a study that compared large population surveys in different but comparable samples over two decades did not consistently demonstrate increased psychological distress on the questionnaires used, but did demonstrate a significant trend for parents and young people to state that they thought that they had a mental health problem (Pitchforth, Viner & Hargreaves, 2016).

There are also differences in how different informants respond about the same child (Ford and Parker, 2016). Teachers and parents have different frames of reference and relate to the child in different environments, while children are the best informants on their internal world. The most accurate method of assessment when measuring population mental health (and in clinical practice) is standardised diagnostic assessments with specified diagnostic criteria that combine information from several informants: commonly young people, parents and teachers (Goodman, Ford et al., 2000). In summary, what you measure and how you measure it matters a great deal in terms of accurately counting how many CYP are struggling with poor mental health.

However, most recent high-quality research does suggest evidence for deterioration in young people's mental health in high-income countries in recent years, with increased anxiety, depression and self-harm that seems particularly prevalent among older teenage girls and young women (Collishaw, 2015; Sadler, Vizard et al., 2018). If we could provide timely and effective intervention, increased demands on services would be a good thing, but we know that only a small proportion (25% in the UK) of those with mental health conditions reach mental health services (Patel et al., 2018; Mandalia, Ford et al., 2018). Administrative data from services suggests a massive increase in referrals to CAMHS and presentations of self-harm to Accident and Emergency (Frith, 2017a). Contact with services may reflect changes in reporting, help-seeking, professional recognition, diagnostic practice or service-provision, as well as the underlying mental health of the population (Collishaw, 2015). Increased demand on services does not accurately reflect population mental health, but we have documented cuts to CAMHS provision as well as to the mental health support provided by schools, children's centres and the voluntary sector at a time of demonstrably increased demand (Frith, 2017a; Humphrey, 2018).

(Continued)

CAMHS currently reject 25% or more of referrals as having problems below their threshold (Frith, 2017a). Given that mental health is a continuum, several other CYP will also be struggling for each one who meets diagnostic criteria, albeit to a lesser extent. While we should be proud that in the UK, the impact on the child predicted access to services for all conditions (Ford, Hamilton et al., 2008), marked variation in levels of service use and costs suggest inequalities in the way that services are responding to children's mental health needs (Knapp, Snell et al., 2015). The gap between provision and need does represent a mental health crisis, and is why the universal, targeted and indicated approach to mental health promotion, prevention and intervention discussed by the authors is so important. Access to evidence-based mental health interventions and services clearly needs expansion, and we should not expect teachers and social workers to become expert therapists. But we should strive to develop and implement mental health promotion, prevention and intervention across all services that work with CYP.

3

AN INTRODUCTION TO DIGITAL MEDIA

Learning points

After reading this chapter, you will be able to:

- Critically assess the changes in the use of digital media
- Identify core concepts
- Appreciate the controversial issue of screen time
- Understand CYP perspectives

Introduction

This foundational understanding of child development and mental health has been presented as context for the book. The focus of this chapter is on digital media and we introduce you to the key issues, but do not fully consider the relationship with mental health until later chapters. All over the world, more CYP are going online, more frequently, via more devices and platforms, at ever-younger ages. Although internet and mobile phone access vary, it is known that one-in-three users of the Internet worldwide is under the age of 18

(Keeley & Little, 2017). The Internet and accompanying technological developments offer huge opportunities, but also pose challenges to children's safety, mental health, and their rights. To be able to critically appraise the evidence that connects digital media with mental health and mental health conditions, along with the entire spectrum of mental health in between (as introduced in Chapter 2), it is helpful to understand the key terms in the language of digital media. There is an entire related vocabulary, and here we consider what some of these terms mean. Some of these concepts have become rather controversial and we therefore encourage you to reflect on these tensions.

The connected society – a paradigmatic shift

Digital technology is and will continue to be an increasingly important part of the daily lives of CYP and their families. The portability of mobile devices has greatly contributed to the intensity with which digital technologies are being used to perform everyday activities such as shopping, banking or even practising sports. They are present in the physical infrastructure of many homes through internet-enabled televisions, smart-heating, lighting and security systems. *Smart* devices are built into existing infrastructures, like toys or refrigerators, and have additional enhanced interfaces, sensors and controls. *Connected* devices, as their name indicates, connect to the Internet and may or may not have a physical form. Smart and connected are not exclusive terms. On the contrary, many devices can be both 'smart' and 'connected', as is the case of the many AI-enabled 'smart-home' devices available nowadays (Blum-Ross, Donoso et al., 2018).

These connected or smart devices – also sometimes known as the Internet of Things (IoT) – have a presence in spaces which were traditionally confined to intimate family or peer relationships. In the privacy of their homes, CYP are not only interacting with their parents, siblings, relatives and friends, but also increasingly exchanging experiences with a much broader virtual audience which sometimes includes people they may not know in person, and transmitting their data with no conscious knowledge of that act. Moreover, CYP are not only interacting with other human beings but also with a wide range of devices and toys, able to process children's instructions and even to follow simple commands such as reading a fairy tale, playing a favourite song or answering common questions. As Blum-Ross, Donoso et al. (2018) reflect, these new possibilities raise important questions about privacy, safety and commercial risks, but also about media and information literacy (MIL). We invite you to think about them, too. For instance:

> When unaware of how and why search results are produced, will younger children simply believe 'answers from smart devices' are always true?

How might the use of smart devices impact on family relationships, and will this impact on children's intellectual growth?

What if a consequence of their searching leads CYP to be confronted with unwanted or inappropriate content with no adult close by to supervise?

Undoubtedly, technological developments offer a wide range of conveniences for CYP, their families and communities in general. However, in some cases, these opportunities may also be accompanied by greater risks. For this reason, throughout this book, we focus on the many dimensions of digital media and the range of their potential impact. Given the rapid development and changes of digital media, it is not surprising that parents, educators and the wide range of professionals working with CYP start to question the impact of these developments. For example, we question how CYP interact with and understand the media itself, and we reflect on what types of security and privacy risks interacting online poses. To better understand the debates that exist, and for us to go forward in providing guidance about the relationship between digital media and mental health, it is important to better understand some of the core concepts, and we now move on to describing these.

Understanding digital media and related concepts

Society has seen many changes in how people are living their lives and socially interacting, as much of this is now mediated using digital devices. During the early rise of digital and social media, it was thought that CYP lived separate lives, one online and the other offline. Thus, it was common to hear discourses of *real* life and *virtual* life. This is a rhetoric that is still drawn upon in some circumstances today. However, there has been a shift in thinking more recently, as scholars are recognising that children's lives are an integration of what goes on online and offline, and the intertwining of the virtual and the real makes them less distinguishable. In that way the *two lives* perspective has been mostly replaced with the *one life* perspective (Ohler, 2011). This is worth thinking about as CYP compartmentalise their lives in different ways to adults; digital media tend to be embedded in various parts of their lives and are not necessarily treated as a separate aspect of it.

In practice this means that you are likely to be seeing evidence of CYP negotiating their development of knowledge and identity as they search for autonomy in much the same way as they have always done, and yet in contemporary society, much of this is also done online (Ito, Baumer et al., 2010). Ito et al. argued therefore that in terms of communication, friendship, self-expression and play, such developments are now reconfigured through their engagement with digital technology and social media. Interestingly, even the distinctions between types of digital media and social media are becoming increasingly blurred (Betton & Woollard, 2019).

When discussing the relationship between digital media and mental health in CYP there are many relevant concepts, and while we briefly outlined these in our introduction, we provide more depth here. As we noted, sometimes the boundaries between some of these terms is becoming blurred or integrated, and language evolves over time, as does meaning. We argue that it is crucial to pay attention to language and meaning, both in terms of critically assessing how concepts are used in the evidence base in this area, but also in terms of how CYP define and give meaning to different concepts themselves. We start with a fundamental concept for this book and encourage you to ask yourself what digital media means to you by answering this question and engaging with the reflective activity in Box 3.1.

What constitutes digital media?

 **Box 3.1: Reflecting on what digital media are**

Create your own working definition of digital media and technologies.

In your reflective diary note what you think the key characteristics are of digital media and start your own working definition of this concept. Reflect on how challenging (or easy) you find that activity, and think about what you have read on this before.

Many of the core concepts in the field overlap and therefore any definitions of those concepts inevitably overlap too. For simplicity we work our way through some of these key terms and give you a brief introduction to each of these.

Digital media, the Internet and social media

Digital media are defined by the dictionary as an overarching term to describe all forms of electronic data, including text, images, databases, audio and video. The term also refers to the electronic devices that store the data and to the communication methods that transmit it, like email, instant messaging, text messages and video-calls. Thus, we use the term in a broad way to include a range of technological devices, apps, social media platforms, social gaming and so forth.

The Internet can be described as a huge global network (e.g. Granic and Lamey, 2000) linking millions of computers through various telecommunication media mediated through different hardware and software tools. The Internet comprises millions of people with different backgrounds and it is through the complex inter-relations among these users and the machines by which they are linked that the Internet self-organises (Granic & Lamey, 2000; Qvortrup, 2006). Granic and Lamey (2000) explain that some components of the Net, such as the graphics and text on Web pages and the number of existing Web pages, mutate and reconfigure daily, while others, such as the Transfer Control Protocol (TCP)/Internet Protocol (IP), remain stable for years. Continuously changing technologies and day-to-day interactions among users keep the Net in constant flux. The continuous input of information creates the conditions under which adaptive patterns develop and stabilise. A clear illustration are popular search engines like Google, which develop and stabilise as an adaptation to the enormous amount of information constantly being inputted into the Net. The Internet is, therefore, a vast, coherent system because of the mass of millions of users who electronically interact daily, and not only because of its complex technological infrastructure.

Social media, traditionally known as social networking sites (SNS), are commonly understood as 'web-based services that allow individuals to (1) construct a public or semi-public profile within a bounded system; (2) articulate a list of other users with whom they share a connection; and (3) view and traverse their list of connections and those made by others within the system' (boyd & Ellison, 2007). One important affordance of social media is allowing users to affiliate with a group and strengthening or affirming these relationships in a public context (Ellison, Steinfield & Lampe, 2007). In that sense, social media refer to websites and apps that are specifically designed in ways that provide mechanisms for people to share content with one another. There are a range of different types of social media like SNS, wikis and microblogging, and of these there is great diversity, like Twitter, Facebook, Skype, Instagram, WeChat, Weibo, WhatsApp and many, many more.

Highlighted point!

We argue then, that the distinctive characteristic of social media is its social function; that is, social media allow for interaction to take place on digital platforms, but also for the dissemination of information and community development.

Information and communication technologies (ICT) refer to:

> all technical means used to handle information and facilitate communication, including computer and network hardware, as well as necessary software. ICT includes telephony, broadcast media, and all types of audio and video processing and transmission. It stresses the role of communications (telephone lines and wireless signals) in modern information technology. (UNESCO, 2013: 149)

Digital skills and citizenship

UNESCO (2013: 147) defines *digital citizenship* as 'having the ICT equipment and skills to participate in a digital society, for example to access government information online, to use social networking sites, and to use a mobile phone.' When employed within the literature, the concept of digital citizenship usually refers to the individual acting in ways that are safe and responsible online. In other words, it refers to the person behaving in ways that respect the rights of others and being secure (Ribble & Bailey, 2007). It has been argued that to be a digital citizen requires CYP to understand how to safely and appropriately participate online and understand how to navigate the Internet with an understanding of the rules of a digital world alongside the consequences if those norms are violated (Young, 2014).

Apart from digital citizenship, terms such as digital competences or digital skills are also abundant in academic research, policy reports and on the media. The International Telecommunication Union (ITU) defines digital skills as 'the ability to use ICTs in ways that help individuals to achieve beneficial, high-quality outcomes in everyday life for themselves and others' and to 'reduce potential harm associated with more negative aspects of digital engagement' (2018, p. 23). As we can see, there is a plethora of definitions in use to refer to different aspects of CYP's engagement with the digital environment. These definitions are not much discussed, making it difficult for the field to come to a consensus. Moreover, these definitions and conceptualisations inevitably evolve. This is why throughout our book we emphasise the importance of being critical even about the definitions we provide here. We need these definitions to provide a basic understanding of key concepts and tensions in the field and for you to reflect about these issues, but we are aware that definitions are not a perfect representation of reality.

Online risks and safety

Digital media are now available on portable devices and CYP are increasingly more likely to access the Internet and social media via their smartphone, tablet or laptop. Such portability has led to concerns that CYP are 'disproportionately affected by the risks of the digital world, given both their developmental vulnerabilities and their status as "early adopters" of emerging technologies' (5Rights Foundation, n.d.). *Online safety* is referred to with a range of terms like 'digital safety', 'Internet safety', 'cyber safety', 'media safety', amongst others. However, what these concepts refer to is how individuals can stay safe from harm when they are online. This includes protecting the self from a wide range of evolving online risks such as privacy risks, risks on health and wellbeing, hateful, harmful and illegal content or disinformation. It is arguable then, that adults in various settings, both practitioners and parents, help CYP to use digital tools in productive and safe ways. Nevertheless, despite the fact that *online safety has gained* considerable importance, parental or adult mediation is made more challenging by the changing nature of the digital environment (Livingstone, Haddon et al., 2014).

In the last decades, online safety has received hightened attention from policymakers and the general public due partly to the unbalanced negative representation of social media and digital technologies in the media. While we acknowledge the importance of informing the public about potential risks of digital technologies, the media has tended to one-sidedly concentrate its reporting on negative effects, failing to provide a nuanced view demonstrating also the opportunities of technical innovations or highlighting the importance of media literacy and digital skills education (Donoso, Retzmann et al., 2020). Online safety is important but fostering media and digital literacy is also necessary to ensure that children engage creatively, knowingly and safely in the digital environment. This is why we discuss these concepts below.

Media & information literacy (MIL) and digital literacy

Over the past 30 years numerous efforts have been made to define the scope of concepts such as media literacy, information literacy and, more recently, MIL and digital literacy. Even though these terms are closely interrelated, they emerged from different disciplines and, hence, their focus was different, and they are sometimes confused or used interchangeably. For instance, UNESCO (2013) defined some of these concepts in the following ways:

- *Information literacy* is a term that emerged from the field of library and information and is used to refer to 'the importance of access to information, the evaluation, creation and sharing of information and knowledge, using various tools, formats and channels' (UNESCO, 2013: 29).
- In contrast, *media literacy* usually refers to the education for individuals about their use of screen-based materials that underscores the importance of being able to understand, evaluate and use media 'as a leading purveyor and processor, if not producer, of information' (UNESCO, 2013: 29).
- *Digital literacy* is the person's ability to engage with digital technology, networks or communication tools so that they can locate, use and create information. 'It also refers to the ability to understand and use information in multiple formats from a wide range of sources when presented via computers, or to a person's ability to perform tasks effectively in a

digital environment' (UNESCO, 2013: 147). Digital literacy is essential for governance, citizenship and development in the digital-based knowledge economy.

Given this conceptual diversity as well as the greater accessibility, convergence and distribution of information and media content, in various formats and via diverse digital tools, UNESCO (2013: 151) decided to introduce the concept of media and information literacy (MIL), that is, 'The essential competencies (knowledge, skills and attitudes) that allow citizens to engage effectively with media and other information providers and develop critical thinking and life-long learning skills for socializing and becoming active citizens.' We explain this in Box 3.2.

 **Box 3.2: What this means**

This means that a person who is media and information literate, is not merely a consumer of information or content from that media, but also takes some responsibility as an information-seeker, as a person creating knowledge and innovating, and as one who makes use of the diversity of information and communication tools and media (UNESCO, 2013).

MIL demands a new and combined set of competencies and collaborative mechanisms which can help people to participate more easily in the knowledge societies. Similarly, Hobbs (2010) defined digital and media literacy as the collection of skills required so that the individual might participate fully in the 'media-saturated' and information filled society. These skills include the ability to:

- Make responsible choices and access information by locating and sharing materials and comprehending information and ideas.
- Analyse messages in a variety of forms by identifying the author, purpose and point of view, and evaluating the quality and credibility of the content.
- Create content in a variety of forms, making use of language, images, sound, and new digital tools and technologies.
- Reflect on one's own conduct and communication behaviour by applying social responsibility and ethical principles.
- Take social action by working individually and collaboratively to share knowledge and solve problems in the family, workplace and community, and by participating as a member of a community.

Highlighted point!

Although most CYP in full-time education have received some lessons on using the Internet, it is not the case for all (Livingstone, Bober, & Helsper, 2005), and research with over 300,000 15–24 year olds showed that they are not as digitally literate as one might expect (Nominet Trust, 2017). The impact of COVID-19 in 2020 may well have a significant impact on these figures.

Digital native and digital immigrant

You may have come across the idea of a *digital native* before as this is one that has been a concept that has become embedded in a range of fields. Again, this is a concept that has attracted a lot of criticism and so we encourage you to be critically reflective. The concept of digital native derived from work by Prensky (2001), who described a generation of young people (those born after 1980) in this way as they had an innate confidence in technology. Prensky argued that the near ubiquitous engagement with technology means that young people now think and process in different ways to previous generations, making them 'native speakers' of the digital language. Conversely, Prensky referred to older generations as *digital immigrants*, as they must adapt and flex with technology. Arguably though, this distinction is an oversimplification (Buckingham, 2008; Betton & Woollard, 2019).

The criticism is that we should be cautious to engage in making assumptions and it is inappropriate to assume that millions of people born from a certain date are all like one another in a meaningful way (Hoover, 2009). The phrase 'digital native' tends to overlook the nuances and subtleties and diversities of online behaviours (Betton and Woollard, 2019). Furthermore, CYP do not acquire their digital literacy automatically (Helsper and Eynon, 2010). Thus, the idea that young people are qualitatively different from previous generations in terms of their technical aptitude and ability should cause some 'alarm', especially as this divide has been highly influential in popular and political discourse (Selwyn, 2009). This also assumes that all children born after a certain date have similar access to digital technology, which is not the case, and assumes that they are able to meaningfully engage with content, when it may be that they merely know how to operate the device.

Related to the concept of a digital native, a series of terms have been coined to refer to the idea that an entire generation can be characterised by its use of technology. However, the use of terms such as iGen (internet generation), Google-generation, Net-Gen and others can be problematic. For example,

Poore (2016) argues that these concepts overlap and there is no agreed-upon date for the start of these different generations, while authors like Buckingham (2008) are critical about the discourse of the 'digital generation' and warns us that these types of 'marketing rhetoric' represent not what CYP really are, but instead offers imperatives about what they should be. Furthermore, he argues that generations are not simply produced by technology but are a result of cultural, historical and social forces. Buckingham (2008: 5) claims that

> The invention and use of a category like 'Generation X' (and its subsequent muta-tions) reflects both the importance and the complexity of age-based distinctions in contemporary consumer culture. As this implies, 'youth' is essentially a social and historical construct, rather than a universal state of being.

Digital capital and digital inequality

A concept that has also been used mostly in the social sciences is that of *digital capital*; that is, 'the accumulation of digital competencies (information, com-munication, safety, content-creation and problem-solving), and digital technol-ogy' (Ragnedda, 2018: 2367). This refers to the capital that is used to negotiate daily life, and is a concept used to describe people's wealth in relation to the resources, networks, knowledge, connections and skills that are valued by society and viewed as valuable (Grant, 2007). Even though the concept of dig-ital capital is common in the literature, there is still a lack of clear definition of this concept.

From a more critical perspective, digital capital is understood as 'a set of internalized ability and aptitude' (digital competencies) as well as 'external-ized resources (digital technology)' that can be historically accumulated and transferred from one arena to another (Ragnedda, 2018: 2367). Ragnedda argues that the level of digital capital that an individual has might influence the quality of their experience on the Internet, and this may be 'converted' into different types of capital, like personal, economic, cultural or political in the social sphere.

Through digital capital, activities such as time spent online, information and knowledge found, or resources and skills acquired, become externally observable social resources (e.g. better job, better salary, bigger social network etc.). Indeed, Buckingham (2008) claims that CYP who actively use technology for creative purposes, or for social or educational purposes, tend also to be privileged in other areas of their lives and in this way using technology sup-ports their access to other forms of cultural and social capital. We ask you to consider this question:

> What happens to those who lack access to this social and cultural capital?

Thus, it is argued that there are *digital inequalities*. Not so long ago, deterministic views suggested that, provided access, disadvantaged groups would make equivalent use of ICT (Compaine, 2001). However, these views have been criticised for failing to recognise that access on its own does not result in use, and that other factors such as attitudes toward technology, skills level, usage patterns, cultural aspects and even lifestyles are also important to consider (Van Dijk, 2006). Indeed, several authors have suggested that inequalities in use are more persistent and difficult to resolve than simply giving access to digital technologies (e.g. Selwyn, 2009). These differences in use amplify risks for CYP who are already vulnerable or in vulnerable situations and do not have the necessary skills to successfully manage all their online experiences (Odgers & Jensen, 2020). As Odgers and Jensen (2020: 345) argued,

> The introduction and broad reach of digital technologies offers the promise of reducing health and educational disparities, but the fear is that if adequate supports are not provided, or technologies are not tailored, inequalities will be further amplified.

These arguments make us reflect on the importance of education, and particularly media education (and we return to the role of schools later in the book).

The controversial issue of screen time

A fundamental argument entrenched in discussions about digital media and mental health for CYP relates to the amount of time the individual spends on different devices, referred to as *screen time*. Although the evidence regarding screen time varies across studies, most contemporary research in Europe and beyond consistently shows that CYP are spending considerably more time online than a few years ago. For example, The PISA 2015 results (OECD, 2017) show that on average across OECD countries, 15 year old students spend about 2 hours and 26 minutes per day online after school on a typical weekday, and more than 3 hours online on a typical weekend day. The study also shows that there are large differences between countries and economies with children in countries like Brazil, Bulgaria, Chile, Costa Rica, Sweden, the UK and Uruguay where students spend more than 3 hours online per typical weekday, and countries such as China and Korea where children spend less than 1 hour online after school. The report highlights that on average across OECD countries, 26% of students could be considered 'extreme internet users' during weekend days, as they spend more than 6 hours on line during those days as compared to 16% of students who can be classified as extreme internet users during weekdays. In almost all countries and economies, the time spent online outside of school increased, on average, around 40 minutes between 2012 and 2015 on both weekdays and weekends. Similarly, in South Africa, just over 70% of 9–17 year olds had access to the Internet, and of these 90% used the Internet weekly, daily for 39%, and 28% several times a day (Phyfer, Burton & Leoschut, 2016). There are evidently a broad range of statistics available about the time spent across devices and although these numbers vary slightly from study to study, they all tend to agree that CYP are spending more time in front of screens than ever before.

In contemporary society, the concern of screen time is shifting from time spent on a variety of screens like television and computers, and is more and more about portable devices like smartphones, tablets and laptops. This steady increase in the amount of time children spend online coincides with the greater access to mobile, portable technologies and more content being available on these mediums. According to the Global Kids Online project (Byrne et al., 2016), most 9–17 year olds access the Internet at home (e.g. between 62% in the Philippines, 98% in Argentina and 97% in South Africa), although many fewer children have school internet access. They also found that internet access is becoming more personal and private and smartphones are the most common devices used by CYP to get online in the 10 countries they studied. Indeed, in 2010, most European children aged 9–16 used fixed computers and laptops as compared with over one-quarter (c. 28%) of 9–12 year olds and three-fifths (c. 60%) of 13–16 year olds accessing the Internet via a smartphone in 2013 (Stald, Green et al., 2014). In the USA, a survey by Anderson and Jiang (2018b) found that internet access is almost ubiquitous among teens in the USA, with 95% of American 13–17 year olds reporting that they have a smartphone or access to one. These mobile connections are fuelling more persistent online activities: 45% of respondents report using the internet 'almost constantly,' and 44% say they go online several times a day. This means that roughly nine in ten adolescents go online multiple times per day.

There are some gender differences in the study of Anderson and Jiang (2018b) though, suggesting that girls are more often online than boys. The survey showed that half of adolescent girls (50%) are near-constant online users, compared with 39% of adolescent boys, and Hispanic adolescents are more likely than White adolescents to report using the Internet almost constantly (54% vs. 41%). According to the report, social media use is nearly universal among American teens, and YouTube, Instagram and Snapchat are the most used online platforms among America's youth. Of these online platforms, Snapchat (35%) and YouTube (32%) are the ones that they use most often. Adolescents especially value social media for helping to build stronger friendships and exposing them to a more diverse world. However, they also express several concerns, including that these sites lead to drama and social pressure. The reasons for these differences are not entirely clear and could, for example, be related to cultural differences, parenting styles, or socio-economic factors.

Different ages and screen time

It is also interesting to observe that children are not only using digital media more often and more intensively, but they are also starting to use these technologies at increasingly younger ages (e.g. Holloway, Green & Livingstone, 2013; Chaudron, Beutel et al., 2015, Marsh, Plowman et al., 2015). Marsh et al. (2015) reported that children under five in the UK spent on average 1 hour and 21 minutes a day using tablets, which included some television and gaming in many cases.

While we have acknowledged through this book that grouping children's ages in developmental categories is challenging and varies across countries and disciplines, when working with CYP it can be helpful to group them into developmental areas, even if this is a loose conceptualisation of ability and skills. We now try to provide more specific areas, and we use the conceptual categories that are broadly found in developmental psychology textbooks and reflecting the age grouping in education in the UK. We do this for no other reason than simplicity of writing. However, we note that research on children's digital lives has been disproportionately located in the minority world (Livingstone, Lemish et al., 2017). We cannot draw on a robust evidence base for most majority world countries because there are still only pockets of insight (e.g. through the work of Global Kids Online). The risk is that, given the significant inequalities that are experienced by those living marginalised lives in challenging circumstances, going forward we need to ensure there is access to technology – the available techno-spaces – and to make sure these do not become sites where inequality is reproduced or reinforced. Thus, the age groupings that appear here are simply to give a sense of how young children are increasing their screen time and engagement with digital media and how that increases with age.

Modern use, Birth to three years

Children are using digital media from younger and younger ages, from clapping their hands to turn on lights or activate toys, voice command functions on home devices, to using screens for entertainment and learning. It is becoming more common that toddlers and pre-schoolers are using the Internet and are doing so through touch-screen tablets and smartphones (Holloway et al., 2013). Indeed, Figure 3.1 caricatures the issue nicely.

Figure 3.1 Children using digital devices have got younger

Contemporary use, three to five years

Children in this age group are increasingly going online and spending more time on the Internet. Research from the UK shows that 27.6% of children were younger than 6 years old when they first used the Internet (OECD, 2017). Indeed, statistics show that children aged 3–4 years are also increasingly owning smartphones and tablets. For example, research shows that 1% of them have a smartphone, with 21% owning a tablet, and 53% going online for about eight hours each week (Ofcom, 2017). This Ofcom survey also showed that 48% of children aged 3–4 years are watching videos on YouTube and 40% are playing games. According to the Zero-to-eight report (Holloway, Green, & Livingstone, 2013), in Belgium (Flanders) 70% of pre-schoolers were online, usually from the age of 3–4 onwards. Similarly, in Sweden 70% of 3–4 year olds were online at least sometimes, and in the Netherlands 5% of babies under the age of 1 were going online.

Contemporary use, 5–11 years

From the age of 5 years onward internet use, screen time and digital device variety increases, as the child progresses from child, to pre-teen to tween (see Chapter 1 for definitions). As a matter of fact, Stald et al. (2014: 4) found that 'even if the "age effect" has become less pronounced as smartphones and associated services are taken up throughout the community, 13–16 year olds are still more likely to go online from a smartphone (62%) than 9–12 year olds (31%).' This is mirrored in South Africa, Argentina and the Philippines, although not at the same rate or with such a trend towards ubiquity. The global picture presented to us, however, is that regardless of where children come from, they need support to develop the kinds of digital skills that will keep them safe across their life course (Byrne, Kardefelt-Winther et al., 2016).

Contemporary use, 12–18 years

Research confirms that adolescents, older adolescents and young adults are using digital media frequently and for considerable hours per week, and this is the case across Europe. By the ages of 12–15 years, 83% of UK adolescents have a smartphone, 55% have a tablet, 77% play games for approximately 12 hours per week, and 99% are going online for approximately 21 hours per week (Ofcom, 2017). Furthermore, Ofcom showed that 90% used YouTube and 74% have a social media profile, with these young people owning multiple devices. Social networking is especially prevalent for adolescents, with 82.1% having a social media account for at least one year and 92.9% having at least one social media account, with 68.1% checking those accounts at least once every day (Barry, Sidoti et al., 2017). In other countries statistics are similar, although the age conceptual categories used in research tend to be slightly different (focusing on 9–17 year-olds, rather than 12–18 year olds).

In the USA figures were also high, and the research from the Pew Research Center (Anderson, 2018a) focused on 13–17 year olds. This survey demonstrated that social media use was nearly universal amongst American adolescents as 24% were online 'almost constantly' because of high access to smartphones (95% had access to one), and 81% of 15–17 year olds and 68% of 13–14 year olds use SNS. This survey showed that girls were online more than boys. Girls are more likely than boys to say Snapchat is the site they use most often (42% vs. 29%), while boys are more inclined than girls to identify YouTube as their most frequented platform (39% vs. 25%). In addition, White teens (41%) are more likely than Hispanic (29%) or Black (23%) teens to say Snapchat is the online platform they use most often, while Black teens are more likely than Whites to identify Facebook as their most used site (26% vs. 7%). In Australia, the figures are similar again as 96% of households with a child under 15 years had the Internet at home (Australian Bureau of Statistics, 2014). On average, children aged 12–13 years spent three hours on a weekday and four hours at a weekend on screens (Yu & Baxter, 2016).

Highlighted point!

Remember that statistics are a mere snapshot of how much digital media CYP are using and for how long. Statistics change, they vary from country to country and differ among age, gender and ethnicity.

Screen time and mental health

Part of the difficulty is that screen use and screen time have not been especially well defined in the mainstream press or in scientific research (House of Commons Science and Technology Committee, 2019). Nonetheless, what is concerning is work that associates screen time with mental ill health. It has, for example, been claimed that CYP who spend in excess of 6 hours online outside of the school environment are more likely to be dissatisfied with their life, and the suggestion is therefore that internet use should be balanced with other activities to protect mental health (OECD, 2017). In the UK, the Office for National Statistics (2015) survey suggested that those who spent more than 3 hours per day on social websites on a typical school night were twice as likely to have characteristics consistent with a mental health condition than those who spent less time on it. Other related work conducted by NHS Digital (2018) showed that in 11–19 year olds, those diagnosed with a mental health condition were more likely to use social media every day compared to CYP without a diagnosis and were more likely to use these media for longer, with those with emotional conditions using social media most. Of course, the direction of travel is difficult to know and so you should always think critically about these kinds of claims.

Highlighted point!

We cannot be sure if children who have existing mental health conditions are more likely to use social media because of their condition, or if the use of social media has led to negative impact on their mental wellbeing.

Interestingly, CYP themselves are aware of the possible relationship between screen time and their mental health. It is typically assumed that CYP are enthusiastic about digital media, and yet research has demonstrated that some are sceptical about the convenience of online interaction and others worry about possible negative impacts on themselves and their peers, such as spending too much time in front of screens, less-healthy lifestyles or demanding social expectations and peer pressure (Anderson & Jiang, 2018a; Anderson & Jiang, 2018b; Blum-Ross et al., 2018; O'Reilly et al., 2018). Of course, it is this potential impact that we are seeing reported through different news channels, concerning the relationship between digital media (especially social media and interactive gaming), on the mental health of CYP. For some this is argued to relate to screen time, but research shows a mixed picture with many different factors affecting this relationship. Although the evidence is mixed, screen time remains a 'hot issue' that deserves further attention. See Box 3.3 for examples.

Box 3.3: Key research evidence

Time online and mental health

There have been core concerns raised about digital media focusing on screen time; that is, the amount of time a person spends interacting with screens within a certain period of time (Orben, 2020). In a recent study, composed of three nationally representative large-scale data sets from

Ireland, the USA and the UK (N = 17,247 after data exclusions), researchers found that 'there is little clear-cut evidence that screen time decreases adolescent wellbeing' (Orben and Przybylski, 2019a: 687).

In another study, results showed that both those CYP who spent little time online compared to those who spent comparatively excessive amounts of time online had the worst mental health. This is what the researchers called the Goldilocks Hypothesis, which 'postulates that there are empirically derivable balance points, moderate levels, that are "just right" for optimally connected young people' (Przybylski & Weinstein, 2017: 205). In other words, they argued that a balance must be struck between too much and too little time spent online, and this is likely to vary from child to child.

It is problematic that much research on CYP and digital media uses screen time as 'an index of engagement' with digital media and is usually measured in terms of the number of hours or minutes they spend on devices (Odgers & Jensen, 2020, p. 339). It is perhaps unsurprising that reviews of evidence relating to screen time highlight inconsistency in research and conflicting evidence about screen time and mental health (Orben, 2020). Relying on screen time in research is arguably unhelpful as not all screen time is equal in terms of risk and benefit (Odgers & Jensen, 2020).

Notably, then, authors such as Orben and Przybylski (2019a: 1) argue that 'there is still little consensus as to whether and, if so, how digital-screen engagement affects psychological wellbeing; results of studies have been mixed and inconclusive, and associations – when found – are often small'.

The evidence regarding screen time and negative impact on mental wellbeing is clearly controversial. We encourage you to give this some thought before you continue with the chapter and consider your own view on this. Think about what you believe to be an appropriate number of hours for CYP of different ages to spend on digital media and on what basis have you decided on those times. Think about the types of activities they perform online. Do they deserve the same amount of time? Think, for example, about watching online tutorials to learn how to play a musical instrument or to do homework versus playing video games or watching YouTube videos for fun. We outline the activity in the reflective activity in Box 3.4.

How much time per week is acceptable to spend on digital media?

We ask you to reflect on your own views here as it is quite easy to assume positions based on instinctive gut reactions rather than on the evidence available. It is worth critically reflecting on your perspective and how it was reached. For example, in our study, the mental health professionals and teachers, when asked more specifically about social media, made comments like those shown in Figure 3.2.

Box 3.4: Reflecting on views of screen time

Thinking of the CYP you work with, what would you recommend in terms of hours per day to spend on digital media? Why?

Beyond time recommendations or restrictions, what else is important to take into consideration when making these recommendations (e.g. personality, contexts of use etc.)?

In your reflective diary we encourage you to reflect on your own beliefs about this controversial issue.

I don't have anything good to say about social media for anybody under the age of 18 years.

(Teacher)

One of the scariest things is, I think, as a culture in terms of working as clinicians, we'd like it to go away.

(Mental health professional)

Figure 3.2 Comments on social media

Although these comments were about social media, our respondents did talk more broadly about digital media and the Internet and had more mixed views on these. During the discussions they were also able to find positive uses of social media, and digital media more broadly, and with reflection started to develop a more balanced perspective.

How children and young people use digital media

For a long time, screen time debate focused on quantitative measures and ways to 'correctly' measure time and paid less attention to *how* CYP spend their time in front of screens. More recent debates highlight the importance of looking at what CYP are doing on/with these screens (e.g. Livingstone, 2019a;

Orben and Przybylski, 2019a; Przybylski & Weinstein, 2017). After all, it is not the same if a child spends two hours watching seemingly frivolous videos on YouTube, or if that child spends two hours learning about history or how to play a musical instrument. Furthermore, even seemingly frivolous videos may have an educational value if, for instance, a child watches them in a foreign language he/she is trying to learn. Therefore, it is arguably more important to understand and reflect on how different CYP are engaging with the various technological affordances available to them and how this is impacting on other areas of their lives. This knowledge, rather than mere measurements of screen time, can help us to better grasp how CYP's interactions with digital media may impact on their wellbeing.

Highlighted point!

We note that current debates centre less around time and more on actual media use, so while parents and professionals still report concerns about the amount of time spent, there are also issues about how and when technology is used and in what ways.

We asked Dr Amy Orben for her thoughts on CYP and screen time and we present those in Box 3.5.

Box 3.5: Expert voice: Dr Amy Orben

Screen time debates

The debate about whether time spent on digital technologies (i.e. so called 'screen time') negatively affects adolescents is fierce and has been of growing importance to parents, practitioners and policymakers. It is therefore surprising how little clear-cut academic evidence there is about these purported links (Odgers & Jensen, 2020). In reviews of the literature it becomes clear that there exists a small negative correlation between screen time and adolescent wellbeing in cross-sectional data (Hancock, Liu et al., 2019); however, the correlation is extremely small, and it is still not well understood if it should

(Continued)

engender concern and policy change (Orben and Przyblski, 2019b). In longitudinal samples the directional links between wellbeing and activities like social media use seem to go both ways, with a recent study showing that decreases in life satisfaction precede a small increase in personal social media use one year later, while increases in social media use predict a decrease in life satisfaction during that same time period (Orben, Dienlin & Przybylski, 2019). However, many results are conflicting and there is still no clear picture emerging of whether screen time is actually harmful or not (Hawkes, 2019).

This lack of consensus could be traced back to the low quality of research available in the area. Self-reported time spent on screens is very likely a bad measure of actual digital technology effects. First, because teenagers are inherently bad at estimating the amount of time they spend with digital technologies throughout the day (Ellis, Davidson et al. 2019). And second, because time spent on screens does not take into account the nuances of the content teenagers see, the motivations they have and the different usage patterns, which will all impact the effect that technologies have on them (Orben, Etchells & Przybylski, 2018). In the next year academic, public and policy debate will need to move away from using the defunct idea of 'screen time' to understand adolescent digital technology use to make real progress.

Dr Amy Orben

College Research Fellow, Emmanuel College, University of Cambridge

Research Fellow, MRC Cognition and Brain Sciences Unit, University of Cambridge

Although the number of hours CYP spend on various screens is quite important to parents and professionals, new ideas and research are showing that the issues are more complex than this, and focusing solely on time is not necessarily the way forward. For example, Livingstone (2019a) argued that parents do not need generic rules which focus on time spent, but instead need constructive guidance that helps them to see the advantages of technology and the skills to avoid any harms. Livingstone argues that we need to pay more attention to reports that weigh evidence and not focus on 'panicky media reporting'.

Perspectives of social media

In understanding the relationship between digital media and mental health, and more specifically in understanding social media, we argue that it is helpful to listen to CYP. We noted earlier that they were mostly able to define social media, but conflated that with the Internet, search engines and other forms of digital media. We now turn our attention to look at what CYP think of social media specifically. However, before we look at what they think, what do you think? We encourage you to reflect on your opinion of social media, what you believe about it, and to think about your own experiences of social media, by answering this question and engaging with the reflective activity in Box 3.6.

What are your views of social media?

Box 3.6: Reflecting on your view of social media

When linking the words 'social media' and 'children/young people', what do you think of?

In your reflective diary write down the first few things you think of when we put social media and CYP together. Go with your instincts and write down your first thoughts. This is for your own learning experience so try not to censor your ideas.

This is an interesting thing to do as practitioners have some quite strong reactions to these two terms. For example, in Figure 3.3 we highlight from our project some secondary school (those who teach 11–19 year olds) teachers' (this included head teachers and teaching assistants) from London and Leicester (UK) initial thoughts about social media and young people.

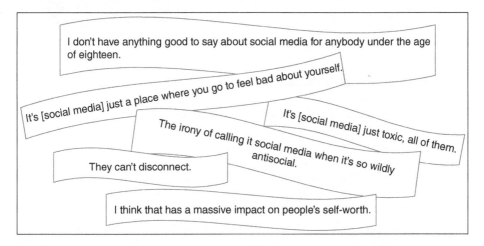

Figure 3.3 Secondary school teachers' initial thoughts

You will see that the secondary school teachers when asked about young people and their social media use reported quite negative thoughts about it. They said things like it is 'toxic', and 'widely antisocial'.

Have a look back at what you wrote in your reflective diary. Think about whether your reflections mirrored those of the teachers we spoke to or whether you had some different initial reactions to the concepts. It is important to also reflect on CYP's views of social media and the kind of things they say when asked to think about social media. Consider, for example, Hannah's thoughts when asked to describe her view of social media (Figure 3.4).

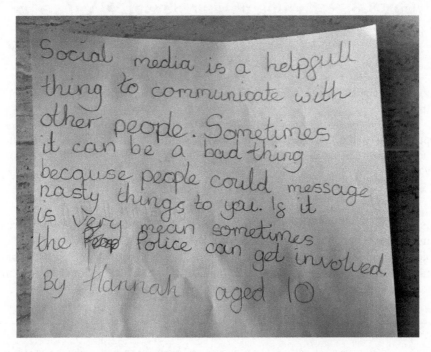

Figure 3.4 Hannah – aged 10 from Tamworth

What is interesting from this perspective is the sense of balance in her viewpoint. She points out that in her opinion social media can be a good thing as it is a communication platform, but also notes that it provides a way for children to post 'nasty things' about others. Most interestingly, Hannah recognises that in some cases these 'nasty things' can lead to police involvement. Theo had a similar balance in his viewpoint, recognising the risk that strangers bring (Figure 3.5). Theo also recognises the value in communicating with others through social media platforms, but he expresses some concern that 'strangers' can see the things posted.

The evidence on CYP's views and perspectives on social media is quite limited. While there is extensive research on areas like how much social media is being used and for what reasons, there is less on what they think about it. Our own research in this area shows that young people (aged 11–18 years) have mixed views about social media (see O'Reilly, Dogra et al., 2018). What was especially interesting about this research was that the young people did two things:

1. They reported that they believed that social media was a negative type of media for their generation, that it caused all sorts of harms to *other* teenagers.
2. They reported that social media was positive and beneficial for them as an individual because they took steps to protect themselves online and used it for relaxation and coping with stressors in their lives.

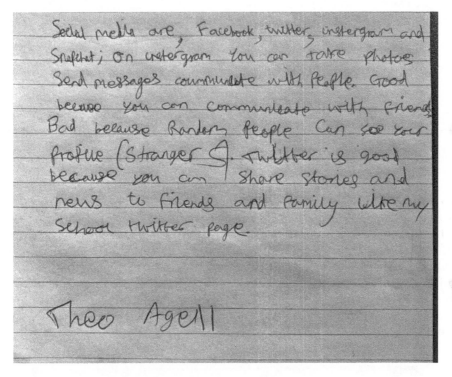

Figure 3.5   Theo – aged 11 years from Leicester

In this way the generic overview of social media was viewed in negative terms, and yet personal and individual use was positively viewed. It is now argued that, as technology advances, the lines between different types of digital media have become increasingly blurred and the division between 'internet use' and 'social media use' is not as differentiated as it once was (Frith, 2017b). In our focus group discussions, we found that young people, like most in their age group, conflated a range of concepts in defining social media, arguing that social media consisted of communication platforms, search engines (like Google), and the Internet more broadly. They did not differentiate digital media from social media from the Internet, and treated all these online modalities as 'social media'. See Figure 3.6 for some examples of the kinds of things they said.

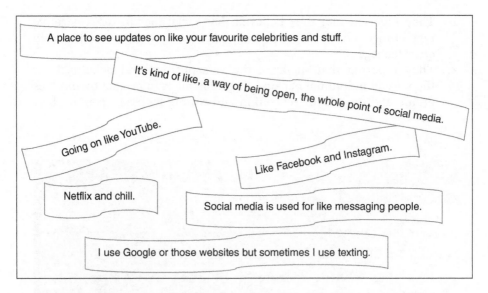

A place to see updates on like your favourite celebrities and stuff.

It's kind of like, a way of being open, the whole point of social media.

Going on like YouTube.

Like Facebook and Instagram.

Netflix and chill.

Social media is used for like messaging people.

I use Google or those websites but sometimes I use texting.

Figure 3.6   Young people's definitions of social media

In a related activity, we asked younger children (aged 6–11 years) from different regions from the Midlands (in the UK) to also define social media. The activity required them to write down a basic definition of social media from what they knew and had learned. Interestingly, most of the children recognised the social interaction function of social media, talking about communication, although we did have one child who did not know what it was (this is not surprising because the child in question was only 7 years old and it is common that at that age children are not yet acquainted with social media platforms). We include their writing in Figures 3.7–3.11 (with their and their parents' consent, we photographed their written contributions).

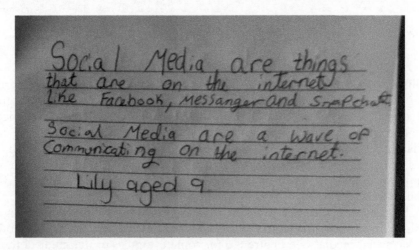

Figure 3.7   Lily – aged 9 from Walsall

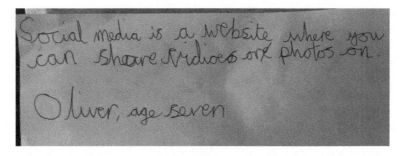

Figure 3.8   Oliver – Aged 7 from Measham

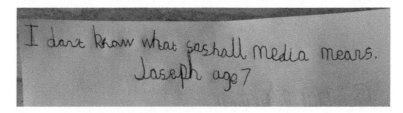

Figure 3.9   Joseph – aged 7 from Tamworth

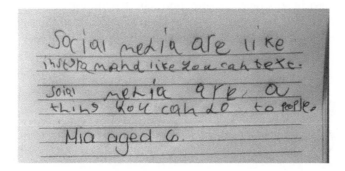

Figure 3.10   Mia – aged 6 from Walsall

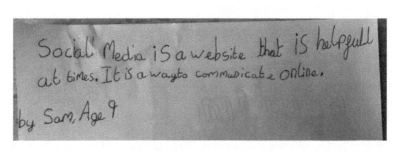

Figure 3.11   Sam – aged 9 from Measham

Evident from these younger children and from our adolescent descriptions of social media is that this has become pervasive in their lives. Apart from one young child (aged 7) who did not know the term 'social media' (but did know the platforms YouTube, Facebook and Instagram in discussion), the children we consulted all knew what social media were in some form or other, they understood the relevance of communicating in digital ways. This is important for you as a practitioner, as the CYP you work with are likely to understand the relevance of socially interacting online and will likely have variable levels of education around this. This is important for digital education and safety, and for the role you might play in helping correct misconceptions, raising awareness about potential risks and adequate strategies to mitigate them, and facilitating an understanding about what it means to communicate and actively engage via digital platforms. It is important not to make assumptions about their understanding or use.

Conclusions

In this chapter we have focused on digital media, providing definitions of some of the core concepts. It became apparent that terms like 'digital and social media', 'the Internet/Web', digital skills and literacy although relatively distinctive in the scientific literature, are often used interchangeably in practice. In completing this chapter, we provide a viewpoint on digital media from a leading expert in this field, as someone who has undertaken research across the globe. In Box 3.7, we present the perspective of Professor Sonia Livingstone, who has been leading research in digital media and CYP for many years.

 **Box 3.7: Expert contribution: Professor Sonia Livingstone, OBE, FBA**

Role: Professor of Social Psychology

Organisation: London School of Economics and Political Science

Brief bio: Professor Sonia Livingstone takes a comparative, critical and contextualised approach, she examines how the changing conditions of mediation reshape everyday practices and possibilities for action. She has published 20 books on media audiences, especially CYP's risks and opportunities, media literacy and rights in the digital environment. She leads the Global Kids Online project together with UNICEF, and recently published *Parenting for a Digital Future: How hopes and fears about technology shape children's lives* (with Alicia Blum-Ross, 2020).

How can evidence about children's online lives guide policy and practice?

Many of the consequences of our digital age are exciting for CYP, and CYP themselves very often embrace digital technologies and even believe it is their right to have access to them. Global Kids Online findings from 11 very different countries so far show that whether they live in Brazil or the Philippines, in Bulgaria or Ghana, CYP are gaining valuable digital skills and enjoying new opportunities to participate in socialising, education and entertainment online. This is the case despite huge differences in how much they can access the Internet or a mobile phone. Especially in lower-income countries, and households, most CYP are 'mobile-first' internet users. As a 12-year-old Serbian girl put it, 'The phone is somehow simpler. We can carry it anywhere, it's smaller and it's easier to work on it. I like it better in this way [demonstrating it] by fingers and not with the keyboard.'

Some CYP also report that the Internet is important for their expression of identity and to find recognition from peers. A 15-year-old boy from the Philippines told us, 'Online, I can show my true self'. This is partly because the Internet fosters the joy of creating, and much of the online content that CYP find and value has been produced by other CYP. Typically, in the 11 countries surveyed, 10–30% of CYP aged 9–17 create and upload their own video or music each week, or write a blog, story or create web pages on a weekly basis. A young girl (9–11) in Ghana explained: 'You can share music. You can also share pictures, ideas, games.'

Adults often underestimate CYP's considerable appetite for information. Between one- and two-fifths of Internet users told us in the Global Kids Online survey that they carry out multiple information searches online each week – to learn something new, to find out about work or study opportunities, to look for news, to source health information or to find events in their neighbourhood. But the potential to become active citizens in a digital world remains unrealised for many CYP, so far at least: Global Kids Online findings suggest that relatively few CYP are taking advantage of the civic engagement opportunities online. Interestingly, some of the online activities that adults tend to denigrate, or consider 'just entertainment', such as game playing or watching videos or chatting and posting content, may act as a gateway to gaining the confidence and skills to undertake more creative or civic activities. It is also a problem that societies around the world tend to consider CYP as 'just children', neglecting their 'right to be heard' as stated in the UNCRC. Perhaps many children do not participate in civil or political activities online because they are unconvinced that the adults are really listening?

While the promise of digital opportunities is still exciting, there is plenty to worry about in terms of the content, contact, conduct and commercial risks to children's safety and wellbeing. Of most concern to parents, educators and policy makers, the Internet is also an environment in which CYP are exposed to risks of many kinds. Here our research shows why it is important to ask CYP directly about their experiences; for example, adults worry a lot about sexual risks online, but often CYP are more concerned about encountering violent or hateful content online.

(Continued)

Whether online risks result in actual harm depends partly on the nature of the risk, and partly on whether a child's circumstances have helped to make them resilient. When we present these findings to policy makers and practitioners working to make the Internet a safer place for CYP, we emphasise how important it is to target interventions particularly towards those who might be more vulnerable, keeping in mind that many CYP live in poverty or alternative institutions or on the move or have disabilities or belong to discriminated-against or marginalised communities. Engaging the professionals who work to support CYP in diverse and often difficult situations, and ensuring that they have access to the latest evidence and expertise, is important.

What kinds of interventions are needed? There is a lot of attention to how governments can regulate the Internet to reduce CYP's exposure to risk, and to eliminate the worst risks. It's going to be vital to get this right, in the coming few years, empowering CYP rather than overprotecting them at the cost of their civil rights and freedoms, for example to access information and to express themselves. It is also important for governments to support the everyday processes of technology adoption so that technology becomes meaningful and valuable in CYP's lives. The state support required to optimise digital opportunities includes teacher training, curriculum revisions focused on digital literacy, parental awareness-raising, and policies to help disadvantaged families gain internet access. Without such interventions, it is very likely that existing (and long-familiar) forms of socio-economic inequality will have consequences in the digital environment, and that digital inequalities will exacerbate the inequalities in CYP's physical lives.

Also important are policies and practices which encourage CYP to express themselves online in diverse ways. For example, the government could promote online participation tools, give awards to digital services which engage their creativity, train peer mentors, appoint digital youth champions, and ensure that state-supported online deliberation spaces are welcoming to CYP.

Today we are moving from a world of living with screen media, often chosen by CYP and more or less under their and their parents' control, to a world of embedded media, of smart cities and smart homes. Policy and practice so far have focused on how to guide CYP and parents to make wise choices – media literacy, and parental mediation, respectively. But as the digital technologies become less visible, more environmental, we will need a new approach. Media literacy and parental mediation will still be important, but the role of the state in regulating the invisible and increasingly invasive role of businesses in our children's lives, and influencing the realisation of their rights, will be crucial.

For more, see Livingstone, S. (2019c)

4

RISK, RESILIENCE AND VULNERABILITY

Learning points

After reading this chapter, you will be able to:

- Explain the importance of risk, vulnerability, and resilience
- Understand the importance of safeguarding
- Contextualise risk factors in terms of digital media and mental health

Introduction

The law and most policy in relation to CYP, especially in terms of digital media and mental health, positions them as a vulnerable population and proposes a protectionist position to manage this. The focus of this chapter is to highlight and critically assess the tensions and differing opinions about CYP. In so doing, we consider the notions of digital risk and resiliency. Central to CYP's use of digital media, especially social media, and the Internet, are the concepts of risk and opportunities online, as Professor Livingstone discussed in Chapter 3. Although online risks can potentially bring harm to CYP, it is argued that limiting risks can also limit CYP's online opportunities and, consequently, impact their ability to effectively cope with risks. Thus, actively supporting CYP with their online activities can increase competencies, but restrictive approaches could lead to fewer skills (Duerager and Livingstone, 2012). Rather than simply limiting internet use, it is important that CYP learn to develop resilience, that is, the ability to deal with negative experiences online or offline (d'Haenens, Vandoninck and Donoso, 2013). As a practitioner you have a role to play in facilitating CYP's pathways of resilience.

In your work, you are likely to have heard practitioners speak about the importance of helping CYP develop resilience. However, there are different types of resilience and different theories. It is argued that the exposure to risk online can leave some CYP vulnerable to negative impact and, furthermore, those CYP deemed vulnerable are at greater risk. This issue is one, therefore, that is especially important for considering their use of digital media, as some argue that they require greater protections online because of their chronological and developmental maturity. However, such a protectionist position does not necessarily account for the different types of vulnerability and in some ways can conflict with the ideology of child-centred approaches and children's rights (see Chapter 1). Furthermore, a protectionist perspective is not mutually exclusive, and we argue that it is possible to protect children online while accepting the positives of digital media and promoting children's rights. In this chapter, we lead you through some of these different perspectives and encourage you to reflect on where you position yourself. This is especially important as there are opposing assumptions made of CYP using digital media and the Internet. For instance, as outlined in Table 4.1, CYP tend to be viewed either as intrinsically vulnerable or as competent and creative agents in their own lives, although this is a continuum and children are usually positioned somewhere in between (Livingstone, Bober and Helsper, 2005).

Table 4.1 Livingstone, Bober and Helsper's (2005) proposal of two opposing assumptions

Two opposing assumptions of digital media and Internet use	
Position of vulnerability	**Position of empowerment**
Younger populations are positioned as vulnerable because they are in the process of developing their social and cognitive skills. Digital media and internet use can pose risks by introducing potential harms to them and because of this risk of harm it is necessary for adults to implement protective strategies. This is seen as important to keep CYP safe.	The alternative position has a different assumption. From this position, there is an assumption that CYP are both competent and creative agents in their own lives. It is argued that this translates online as children competently navigate the online world and creatively engage with it as they have necessary media skills.
From this perspective, there are questions raised about internet literacy that argue that CYP may be naïve in their risky access to online content and thus parents and other adults need to be equipped to control the meanings and networks in which they participate. In this way adults can step in and protect them online.	From this perspective, adults are argued to underestimate the abilities of CYP, and they fail to recognise the benefits to them of going online. In this way online communication is a core skill they develop and exposure to digital media allows them to build skills and ability to evaluate their online resources.

We would encourage you to return to Chapter 1 and consider how children of different ages are at different points in their development, and have different cognitive, social, moral and physical competencies which will influence and shape the way in which they interact online, use their digital devices and the extent of their skills to stay safe online. Similarly, think about how CYP live in hugely variable contexts around the world; different CYP need different types of support at different times of their lives. Seeing young people as only vulnerable, or only competent, is an oversimplification which does not allow us to capture the diversity or the individual differences and specific needs of children coming from different backgrounds and living in different cultures and contexts. This simplified view does not make it possible to provide the right kind of support, both technology and non-technology enabled, when they need it most.

Risk

We begin our discussion with the notion of risk. In simple terms the Oxford Dictionary defines risk in this way:

A situation involving exposure to danger.

A more useful definition was arguably proposed by Aven and Renn (2009) who argued that risk relates to uncertainty regarding the severity of consequences or outcomes of an event or action in terms of something that is valued by people.

In the context in which we are writing we need to consider risk in relation to health, especially mental health and wellbeing. While there are some slightly different frameworks, what is consistent is the idea that each person has an integrated health profile, and any risk taken can impact some or all these dimensions in different ways. We outline the eight dimensions of health and wellbeing as described by Stoewen (2017) in Table 4.2. We encourage you to bear these in mind as you read the discussion of risk and think about how some of these could be relevant to digital media use.

Table 4.2 The eight dimensions of health and wellbeing (Stoewen, 2017)

Dimension	Description
Physical dimension	Taking care of the physical, biological and physiological aspects of the body and brain.
Intellectual/cognitive dimension	This is intellectual health and growth, as individuals develop and learn they respond to intellectual challenges. To grow intellectually the person expands their knowledge and skills.
Emotional and mental dimension	This refers to feelings, values and attitudes and the appreciation of the feelings of others. As children grow older, they learn to manage their emotions in a constructive way. To stay mentally healthy the individual needs to feel positive and enthusiastic about life.

(Continued)

Table 4.2 (Continued)

Dimension	Description
Social dimension	This is the ability to maintain healthy relationships, develop friendships and engage in intimate relations. Having good social health means the ability to care about others and allow others to care about them. Social health also means contributing to the community.
Spiritual dimension	To maintain spiritual health requires the individual to find a purpose in life, a value and meaning in life, and to participate in activities consistent with beliefs and values.
Vocational dimension	Relates to the ability to participate fully in employment and to gain a personal satisfaction and life enrichment from it that are consistent with goals and lifestyle. To maintain vocational health requires the individual to contribute skills and talents to work in ways that are personally meaningful and rewarding.
Financial dimension	This refers to the individual's ability to manage resources, to live within means and make informed financial decisions and set realistic financial goals.
Environmental dimension	This is the ability of the individual to recognise how the social, natural and built environments impact health and wellbeing, and how daily habits affect one's physical environment and contribute to a healthy planet.

As you can see, these different dimensions of health intersect and overlap, and this is important when considering CYP and the risks they may pose to their health when engaging with digital media, but also when considering how they protect their health by engaging with digital media. We encourage you to look back at Chapter 2 where we outlined the four Ps and revisit the importance of the risk (predisposing, precipitating, protective and perpetuating) factors that might be important when considering the mental health of CYP.

The notion of risk is embedded in society as communities grapple with trying to find strategies to protect and mitigate risk for CYP. This has been characterised as the *risk society*, where risk is thought about as a systematic way to manage hazards introduced by modern society (Beck, 1992) and we describe what this means in Box 4.1.

 **Box 4.1: What this means**

There are three key points being made by Beck (1992) in his proposal of the risk society:

1. Historically society was concerned with natural hazards like floods and plagues, which were uncontrollable and difficult to manage.

2. However, social, civic and community living has changed because of globalisation and human relationships are now fragile and arguably superficial.
3. We now live in a period of greater uncertainty and changes in society mean that individuals face more and greater risk.

Child and adolescent risk

It may not be entirely clear what this means for CYP, but if you work with them you will know that they sometimes take risks, and these are taken in different ways and for different reasons. Indeed, it is by managing risk and engaging in behaviours that are risky that CYP achieve their identity as members of cultural groups (Green, 1997). It is important to contextualise this in relation to cognitive, social and moral development, as they require a certain level of cognitive skill, have a level of moral understanding, and are building their social skills for risks to be taken and for adults to provide a framework of understanding. So, it is at about the age of eight to nine years that the safe conduct can be taught, and at this age children believe that their parents know best and tend to be rule-driven (Pickhardt, 2014). In the pre-teen and tween years this advances quite considerably. Thus, Pickhardt noted that from approximately 9–13 years, there is more of a personal disorganisation seen, a more negative attitude can develop, and there is more active and passive resistance as the individual starts to push boundaries. It is, however, during adolescence that risk-taking becomes much more prominent, and it is during this developmental period that the individual takes more risks than any other age group (Steinberg, 2010). During adolescence more risk-taking happens as young people begin exploring and experimenting as they start to increase their autonomy and freedom (Pickhardt, 2014).

Highlighted point!

Remember that adolescence is a developmental period characterised by biological, psychological and social changes, including physical and hormonal transformations of puberty (Patton, Sawyer et al., 2016). Consider how this might influence risk-taking behaviour.

Increased risk-taking behaviour during adolescence links to the ability to self-regulate and this gradually improves over time (Steinberg, Icenogle et al., 2017). It is therefore important to think about your own beliefs regarding adolescent risk-taking. Stereotypically, adolescents are impulsive and engage in dangerous behaviours and they need protection and surveillance to prevent certain consequences. However, it has also been argued that risky behaviours could be rational and adaptive actions are simply part of the adolescent profile for them to fulfil their developmental goals and navigate the period to reach independence (Romer, Reyna & Satterthwhaite, 2017). Thus, we ask you the following question, and encourage you to look at the reflective activity in Box 4.2.

Do you think adolescents need to be protected from their risk-taking?

 **Box 4.2: Reflecting on risk**

To what extent should adolescents take risks to naturally work through the developmental period?

In your reflective diary we encourage you to consider the tension between allowing young people to take risks, experiment and explore to build their identity, and to what extent they need protecting to avoid negative consequences of those risks.

Adolescent risk-taking has the potential to impact on all eight dimensions of health and wellbeing (as outlined earlier). Indeed, in Public Health, there has been significant effort made to reduce adolescent engagement in risky behaviour that could result in poor health outcomes, as well as building research to better understand the susceptibility of adolescents to the influence of their peers (Blakemore, 2018b). A good example of this is the anti-smoking campaigns in UK schools designed to reduce tobacco use by this age group because of the physical health risks associated with smoking (Campbell, Starkey et al., 2008), and sex education to reduce teenage pregnancy and sexually transmitted diseases (Perry, Kayekjian et al., 2012).

CYP do not develop in a vaccum; freedom and autonomy can be gendered in complex and intersecting ways across many cultures and societies. CYP are very likely to continue to engage with digital media and continue to go online for a range of reasons. There has been significant effort to educate them about the possible consequences of risky behaviours, and yet research shows that despite

Highlighted point!

For adolescents growing up in an environment where they are gradually afforded more freedom and autonomy, interventions designed to promote positive health and reduce risky behaviour could focus on showing how adolescents might engage in risky behaviour whilst minimising the potential for negative outcomes (Blakemore, 2018b).

this, adolescents continue to behave this way (Kann, Kinchen et al., 2014). You may be curious as to why this is the case. Economically, millions have been invested in research and campaigns to reduce adolescent risk-taking and to promote more positive outcomes for CYP both online and offline. Concerns have been proposed about a broad range of different aspects of child and adolescent health and so it stands to reason that practitioners want to know why education rarely impacts in the way it is designed to and why young people continue to take risks generation after generation (see Jones, Mitchell & Walsh, 2014a, 2014b).

Relevance of the brain

It has been argued that neuroscience and brain research can contribute to our understanding of the relationship between digital media and mental health, and we introduced you to how the brain works in Chapter 1. It was traditionally believed that the reason why young people engage in risky behaviour was because they lacked the cognitive, social and moral skills needed to be able to fully evaluate the risks they are taking, and yet this idea has been largely discredited (Magliano and Grippo, 2015). Even early developmental work showed that adolescents are just as competent as adults in evaluating the risk associated with their behaviour (Beyth-Marom, Austin et al., 1993). Advancements in digital technology and increased availability of magnetic resonance imaging (MRI) and of functional magnetic resonance imaging (fMRI) means that there has been an increase in research using these tools to look at the brain in puberty (e.g. Blakemore, 2012). Interestingly, these brain studies have shown that several areas of the brain are important as they make the adolescent more sensitive to the rewards associated with peer relationships, much more so than adults (Albert, Chein & Steinberg 2013). This is especially important as we know from the social development theories that it is during adolescence that peer relationships become more intense and so susceptibility to peer influence increases during this period, peaking at about aged 14 years (Berndt, 1979). Notably then, these peer relationships and sensitivity to those relationships could play a strong role in situations involving risky behaviour (Magliano and Grippo, 2015). We outline what this means in Box 4.3.

Box 4.3: What this means

There are four key points being made by this evidence:

1. Adolescent brains are flexible, developing and changing, which is important for how they engage in risk.
2. Different parts of the brain are responsible for different behaviour and different responses.
3. For adolescents it may be the case that being rejected by their peers is more of a risk to them than not engaging in a certain behaviour and this outweighs any risk to health for them.
4. Research into brain development during adolescence could be important in helping us understand the kinds of risks, responses and outcomes in adolescents who engage in risky behaviour online.

There is little research on how technology or social media impact on CYP's brains. An important issue therefore is understanding any changes that might occur in the brain when they engage with digital or social media or the Internet. This is especially pertinent during adolescence as the brain undergoes so much change in this developmental period. As Betton and Woollard (2019: 85) put it:

> The prefrontal cortex is the part of the brain that contains those self-control systems. It is also referred to as the seat of executive function because it helps us evaluate situations, judge risks, plan opinions based on potential outcomes, and make decisions, whilst inhibiting impulses from our brain's emotion and reward centres. During adolescence, the prefrontal cortex undergoes significant change, resulting in it containing a smaller number of neurons that have greater and more selective connectivity with each other. This increases its power at controlling the impulses from our social reward and emotion centres, such that as young people reach late adolescence, they are able to make more considered decisions.

There are some things about brain development that are important. Children of different ages will be at different points in their brain development, and in terms of their cognitive and intellectual development. It is important to recognise that CYP's brains are different from adults' brains. Throughout life humans continue to produce neurons in areas of the brain like the hippocampus, and the birth of new neurons is connected to learning as the key process to learning is thought to be related to changes in the connectivity between neurons (Howard-Jones, 2009). The development of these connections (i.e. synapses) in technical terms is called *synaptogenesis* and in children this occurs much more rapidly than in adults, and childhood is therefore a good time to learn as they are more sensitive to external influences (ibid.).

The period of adolescence may be especially relevant in terms of the influence of digital media. There are certain changes in brain development that happen during puberty. For example, during puberty a process called *myelination* occurs, which is when the axons carrying messages to and from neurons are insulated by myelin and this improves the efficiency through which information is communicated, and because the myelination increases in adolescence in the frontal and parietal lobes it increases the speed of neural communication (Sowell, Peterson et al., 2003). This development and learning process is relevant to adolescents' engagement with digital and social media. For example, in the brain is the limbic system that contains the emotion and reward centres, and during adolescence this becomes more sensitive (Betton & Woollard, 2019) and it is reasonable to suggest then, that this part of the brain becomes active when young people are engaging with digital technology.

Neuroimaging techniques have been instrumental here. Such techniques have shown that there is enhanced activity in the brain's reward system in adolescents (Howard-Jones, 2009). Thus, it is possible that the heightened risk-taking in this developmental period could be due to unequal competition between increased activity in the reward system and top-down control from the cortex, which is of course still developing at this age (Blakemore, 2008). It is reported that adolescents' cognitive self-control systems are not mature enough to balance their reward pathways and this increases their likelihood of making poor decisions for immediate social reward (Gabriel, 2014), and to some extent this may explain some of the poor decision making made by some young people online. Indeed, some research using MRI scans found that when young people viewed images on social media platforms, they were more likely to 'like' something seen if it already had a high number of 'likes' and that centres in the brain (such as the nucleus accumbens) became activated, which is linked to reward systems (Sherman, Greenfield et al., 2018). Notably, though, risk taking is also connected to the presence of peers and thus is highly dependent upon the social context (Steinberg, 2008).

Online risks

It could be argued that the types of risks that CYP are taking online are different, albeit related, to the offline risks that they take, and that the consequences are potentially different. Understanding the nature of risk and consequences of risks as mediated through digital media is important to better understanding the relationship between digital media and mental health. Various authors have contributed to conceptualising these risks and different ways of categorising online risks have been proposed. One of these classification models is the four Cs (Livingstone & Stoilova, 2021) outlined in Table 4.3.

Table 4.3 Four Cs, tabulated from Livingstone & Stoilova (2021)

	Content (child as receiver of mass communications)	Contact (child as participant of adult-initiated activity)	Conduct (child as actor – perpetrator/victim)	Contract (child as consumer)
Aggressive	Violent or gory content	Harassment or stalking	Bullying or hostile peer activity	Fraud, identity theft, phishing scams and security risk
Sexual	Pornographic content	Grooming, sexual abuse on meeting strangers	Sexual harassment or sexting	Streaming child abuse, sextortion
Values	Racist or hateful content	Ideological persuasion	Potentially harmful user-generated content	Polarisation, profiling bias
Cross-cutting	Privacy and data protection abuse, mental health risk and different types of discrimination			

Although existing classifications of risks are useful to capture trends, raise awareness, plan interventions, and ultimately to provide greater insight into online safety (Livingstone et al., 2015), it is important to understand their limitations. For instance, emerging risks may not easily fit into predefined categories or certain risks may fit across several ones. Even more important is to understand that what is risky for someone might not pose a risk to someone else and, thus, even if different children are exposed to the same risks, the outcomes for different CYP might be different. Therefore, it is necessary to distinguish between online risk and *harm* (Livingstone, 2013).This is particularly important in the context of digital risk, as taking risks online does not always result in harm (d'Haenens et al., 2013). Evidently, we need to think about what we mean by harm, and three dimensions of harm were proposed by Livingstone (2013):

The type of harm: such as physical, psychological and social harm.

The severity of the harm: in terms of the impact it has on the individual.

The longevity of the harm: how long the impact influences the individual.

In digital environments there are three problems to account for and these were proposed by Livingstone (2013) as being:

1. Assessing, evaluating and managing risk do not focus on the possible benefits of Internet use and so adults might fail to balance opportunity against risk. If not carefully approached, avoiding online risk altogether might be equated with needing to prevent CYP from engaging with digital media, which may stop them developing digital skills and resilience.
2. There are certain sensitivities over risk evaluation for CYP as society seems to adopt a 'zero tolerance' attitude. In this way we see a gap between a rational balancing of possibilities and the unacceptability of harm that *may* be experienced by the child or young person.

3. It is not sensible to strive for a world or society without risks. It is crucial that CYP learn to take calculated risks and develop resilience. Harm is inevitable to some extent in the 'real world' and the Internet is simply one new source of risk in children's lives and indeed, 'the history of harm is as old as childhood' (p. 25).

Although as a practising professional you will be concerned with the type, nature, extent and frequency of risks that the CYP you are working with are taking in the digital space, it may be the case that it is necessary to accept that risks will be taken. Because risks may be inevitable, it is important to support CYP to develop resilience as they are faced with harms. Although research suggests that most children know how to cope with common online risks (Smahel, Machackova et al., 2020), practitioners and professionals working with CYP should remain alert, responsive and supportive because even if the chances are reduced, for some CYP – especially those in more vulnerable situations – some of the risks they take may be so extensive that the harms they experience could become profound or life-threatening.

Highlighted point!

Just as crossing a road poses a risk that may or may not result in a traffic accident, so, too, does using the internet expose a child to a range of risks that may or may not result in harm. More contentiously perhaps, exposure to a hostile message or pornographic image might also not result in harm on all occasions or for all children. (Livingstone, Mascheroni and Staksrud, 2015: 3)

We provide you with some practical recommendations in Box 4.4, as outlined by d'Haenens et al. (2013) in their report on digital media and CYP based on the EU Kids Online research study.

Box 4.4: Practical tips from d'Haenens et al. (2013)

Several recommendations were made in the report and you might find these helpful in your professional role:

(Continued)

- It can be very helpful if adults encourage an open dialogue. This is important for practitioners and parents alike, to talk to CYP at home and in school as well as other environments. Encourage open communication about digital experiences and emotional health, as this can be an important first step in noticing if the individual has been affected by something online.
- Help teach CYP proactive coping strategies online, such as how to delete inappropriate messages and block contacts who are unhelpful. It is important to start teaching children these skills from an early age.
- These age groups will benefit from building their self-confidence, so it is important to recognise those children or young people who may have low self-efficacy, including those with existing mental health conditions.
- It can be helpful to promote internet access and use among adults. Parents and practitioners who use the Internet frequently tend to be more confident with technology and are generally more confident in guiding their children or the children they work with.
- It is important to promote a positive attitude toward online safety and proactive coping strategies amongst peer groups. Peers are an important influence and so this is relevant to how they cope with online risks.
- Although the study showed that levels of teacher mediation are generally high, many children are not reached by this teacher guidance. Schools, and specifically teachers, need to be equipped to provide active support in relation to digital safety. Teachers need to be mindful that this is not limited to technical help or rule-setting, but in helping CYP to develop proactive problem-solving strategies that are relevant on- and offline. This does mean that teachers need digital skills themselves.
- Some parents simply restrict their child's use of the Internet, but this does not really prevent CYP from having negative experiences, engaging in risky behaviour or encountering harm. A more beneficial approach is to help the child develop resilience and coping strategies, and thus a communication mediating approach could be more beneficial (we return to this later in the book).
- Parents and other significant adults may also want to remember that children model and observe adult behaviour, and so an adult who is over-reliant on screens is being seen.

Vulnerability

In Chapter 1 we encouraged you to reflect on your own position on CYP in terms of how you view them and how that might shape the way in which you work with them, and one concept you may have thought of is *vulnerability*, as CYP are often positioned in this way. We encourage you to think more about this, especially in relation to the notion of vulnerability, so try the reflective activity in Box 4.5.

To what extent do you think CYP constitute a vulnerable group?

Box 4.5: Reflecting on vulnerability

Are CYP naturally vulnerable by virtue of being children?

In your reflective diary we encourage you to think about the tension between positioning CYP as vulnerable by virtue of their developmental maturity and positioning them as autonomous and capable of making their own digital decisions.

It has long been the case that certain groups in society are constructed as being vulnerable and greater care has been taken to protect their interests. This is because it is argued that these groups are not able to protect their own best interests in the same way as fully competent adults. It is probably unsurprising that definitions of vulnerability are difficult to create, and there has been little consensus on what constitutes a vulnerable group (Ruof, 2004). This is because the concept of vulnerability is not static; it is contextual and not absolute (Nordentoft & Kappel, 2011). If we turn to the dictionary definition, vulnerability is argued to be:

> The quality or state of being exposed to the possibility of being attacked or harmed, either physically or emotionally.

Thus, tied up with the notion of vulnerability are the issues of risk and harm, as we have discussed. It is argued that individuals who are vulnerable are those whose freedoms of capacity to protect themselves from these possible harms and risks are decreased in some way and their ability to make informed choices are impaired (Shivayogi, 2013). As Nickel (2006: 247) eloquently put it:

> Ordinarily, we expect people to safeguard their own rational interests. Some people, however, cannot do this adequately; because of this, their rational interests must be safeguarded institutionally and procedurally.

It is necessary to think about vulnerability more broadly and think about how these thoughts and feelings impact on your work with CYP. Vulnerability is more than simply a risk from harm, and as we pointed out earlier, exposure to some risks can help some CYP to build resilience, and risk does not necessarily lead to harm for all children or in all circumstances. However, although CYP tend to belong to a category that is assumed to be 'vulnerable' because of a lesser capacity associated with developmental maturity, some CYP may be more vulnerable than others or some may be in situations that exacerbate vulnerability.

However, as already stated, defining what constitutes a vulnerable group is challenging, and deciding what constitutes risk can be difficult. One argument proposed by Nickel (2006) is that we should define vulnerability by two criteria, as a vulnerable person is not defined merely by vulnerability characteristics that define the population (e.g. simply belonging to the group 'children' does not automatically mean you are vulnerable), but how those vulnerability characteristics interact with health matters:

Consent-based vulnerability: This is vulnerability based on the capacity to provide informed consent and express autonomy. Individuals who have reduced capacity to safeguard their own interests are more vulnerable to exploitation and coercion.

Fairness-based vulnerability: This vulnerability relates to the lack of opportunity and/or freedom rather than reduced capacity. For example, these are groups affected by economic disadvantage, or who do not speak the native language of a country. These individuals are susceptible to being unduly persuaded or coerced.

CYP are not a homogenous group, and some have social competencies to make informed decisions. Furthermore, the context in which that decision making takes place and what is at stake in that decision making all have a bearing on the extent to which the individual is 'vulnerable'. Indeed, it is arguable that the entire human race is vulnerable in some circumstances and contexts and it is therefore important to think about the source of the vulnerability (consider the COVID-19 context, where children are less vulnerable than adults to dying from the virus, and there are different levels of vulnerability to the illness in different populations). Rogers, Mackenzie and Dodds (2012) posed that there are three sources of vulnerability, outlined in Table 4.4.

Table 4.4   Sources of vulnerability (Rogers et al., 2012)

Source of vulnerability	Description
Inherent vulnerability	The human species is inherently vulnerable due to the humanness of individuals. In other words, the affective and social nature of individuals as related to being human means that all individuals are vulnerable to injury, illness, psychological conditions and emotional impact, and all could face risk of death. Therefore, individuals are always vulnerable physically, emotionally and psychology merely by being human.
Situational vulnerability	All humans are part of a social, economic and political context, and these vary across groups but can influence their vulnerability. This means that the social, economic and political environment varies across populations and individuals who can influence how vulnerable a person is.
Pathogenic vulnerability	This relates to situational vulnerabilities that arise because of adverse social issues. These are vulnerabilities caused by oppression or injustice, such as a vulnerability to stigma and discrimination.

Thus, when thinking about sources of vulnerability, those sources may be dispositional to the individual or external to them (Rogers and Lange, 2013). It is clearly inappropriate then, to label an entire group as vulnerable and make a sweeping conceptualisation that they all need the same level of protection just because they share certain characteristics with others in that group. Treating CYP as a homogenous group risks denying them the rights to decision making in their lives, underestimating their digital competence and denying their autonomy. This is not to suggest that CYP should not be protected and safeguarded (of course they should!), but as practising professionals it is important to balance protection against harm with promotion of rights and safeguarding against inappropriately homogenising vulnerability.

Vulnerability online

As you read through this section of the chapter, we would encourage you to hold in mind some of those tensions about vulnerability and what they mean in relation to CYP. We also encourage you to think about the reflective activity you completed to consider your own personal view about the extent to which they are vulnerable because of the shared developmental characteristics. The debate pertinent to the relationship between mental health and digital media is whether children are developmentally capable of coping with the online environment and all that goes with it, and younger children may find this more challenging. Consider the study in Box 4.6. below.

Box 4.6: Key research evidence

Examining the evidence

An Australian research study by Ey and Cupit (2011) that included children aged five to eight years concluded that these younger children are more vulnerable when interacting online than children who were older than nine years. What this research showed was that these younger children did have some understanding of the risks they might face online, and that these were learned mostly from parents and other family members. So, these children could identify content risks like sexual or violent content and contact risks like meeting strangers on the Internet, but because of their developmental immaturity they were somewhat naïve in assessing these risks and often failed to identify inappropriate communication, unreliable information, commercialism or other risks that were associated with revealing personal information about themselves.

While the age of the child is an important characteristic, as research has highlighted that negative online experiences increase with age, as do taking risks (Smahel et al., 2020), age is not the only characteristic that may position them as more vulnerable than others. It is helpful to recognise that children who may be more vulnerable than others are generally not just more vulnerable in a digital space. Therefore, those existing vulnerabilities offline are significant predictors of risk and impact online (Asam & Katz, 2018; Katz & Asam, 2019). It can sometimes be misunderstood by adults that children are vulnerable online just because they are children. The evidence, however, demonstrates that CYP tend to be quite capable online and are aware of ways to stay safe (Asam and Katz, 2018; O'Reilly et al., 2018). Yet this is not the case for all CYP, and evidence suggests that certain groups of CYP are more vulnerable than others. It seems to be the case that some who are vulnerable in other areas of their life are also vulnerable when interacting online. Thus, research indicates that CYP who are raised in difficult family circumstances (including looked-after children), those with disabilities or special educational needs, those with mental health conditions or emotional difficulties, and those who experience exclusion (such as traveller children or asylum seekers) are more likely to be vulnerable and thus encounter harms and to a greater extent than their peers (Asam and Katz, 2018). Further, those children who do not have secure family support can lack parental advice and guidance which can be essential in helping them stay safe, and children or young people who have experiences of adversity may be isolated, which might motivate them to seek compensatory relationships online (Livingstone et al., 2005).

Resilience

Resilience research relating to CYP has been growing since the 1970s, when researchers noticed the variability surrounding the ways in which some young people experiencing significant adversities seem to cope. Resilience research has since aimed to reveal why some children survive and thrive in very challenging conditions, and others less so. Early resilience theory emerged out of studies of adversity, and how difficult life experiences impact on people. Emmy Werner's work on Hawaiian children born into challenging socio-economic circumstances in the 1970s and 1980s is a good example of this pre-generation of resilience research (Werner, 2001). Werner's and similar work showed that childhood 'vulnerability' contributed to problematic outcomes later in life. The evidence soon began to show that the link between vulnerability and poor outcomes did not apply to every individual, all the time. Some people seemed to be impacted only minimally. Some seemed to recover. Some seemed to emerge even stronger than might be expected. Resilience research aims to understand this variation.

In mental health work, resilience has become a core concept and often refers to the child's ability to 'bounce back' from adverse circumstances

(Turner, 2001). However, these individualistic ideas about resilience have been critiqued for oversimplifying the complexity of the reality of adversity (Ungar, 2005). Contemporary research defines resilience as 'the capacity of a system to adapt successfully to challenges that threaten the function, survival, or future development of the system' (Masten & Barnes, 2018: 98). In other words, there are larger contextual concerns in terms of how individuals interact with the environment, and how the developmental pathways and trajectories lead to resilience (Ungar & Liebenberg, 2011; Zinck et al., 2013). This definition has three important implications for those of us aiming to build pathways to resilience in practice:

1. Most importantly, an individual young person's resilience is not completely defined inside the brain and body of that person. Resilience is not a trait, although the differences we see in people can contribute to their adaptive capacity. Rather, resilience is more appropriately considered a process that depends on their relationships and attachments (Chiang, Chen & Miller, 2018), heritage-based and cultural influences (Theron, Liebenberg & Ungar, 2015) and capacity for evolution.
2. This definition can be applied at an individual, group or system level. It frames resilience as an adaptive process that we could consider for individuals, a family, a school, or a wider ecosystem.
3. We can apply this definition across many disciplines. The processes of resilience are dynamic and shaped by complex interacting systems. If we want to understand how children's physical, biological, natural and psychological environments intersect, we must work together across disciplines.

What we do not yet know are exactly which protective factors matter most in different situations, sometimes termed the 'differential impact' (Didkowsky and Ungar, 2016). But those working with CYP are sometimes expected to make judgements about a child's capacity to adapt to trauma or other challenge, based on incomplete information. It is at these times that we should remember that resilience is a process, rather than a trait. However, resilience research has been subject to criticism from many quarters. Despite the best of intentions, research focusing on personal, individual factors such as self-efficacy (Bandura, 1982) or 'grit' (Duckworth, Peterson et al., 2007) have stored up problems for practitioners in contemporary times.

Now, you might feel under pressure to place the full responsibility for improving a life at the foot of the individual, a family, or even yourself. This focus on individual factors disregards the fundamental importance of social systems, structures and dynamics. Van Breda (2018) has reflected on the responsibilities placed on individuals for 'being resilient' that should, in practice, lie with collective structures and systems (such as social welfare or education). Individuals demonstrating resilient outcomes are valorised – when, in reality, risk and protective factors acting with them are not limitless – and those struggling to bounce back in the face of significant challenge are criti-cised. We therefore provide some practical guidance based on van Breda's (2017) PIE approach in Box 4.7.

Box 4.7: Practical tips – PIE (van Breda, 2017)

Take the PIE approach to building resilience processes (Van Breda, 2017):

- **P** – Personal processes, such as optimism or reflectiveness, or develop-mental stages such as onset of adolescence.
- **I** – Interactional processes that link an individual and their environment, such as group working or cultural practices.
- **E** – Environment, such as social environments and relationships, or broader definitions of environment such as financial security or exposure to natural or man-made hazards.

Now reflect on strategies you can build with your colleagues and service users that will strengthen and enhance resilience processes for everyone.

Fortunately, resilience theory and the science of resilience has progressed, and the evidence now squarely places resilience processes within mutual net-works, groups, social and cultural structures (Theron, 2016). Ungar's (2011) social ecologies of resilience place enormous emphasis on the I of the PIE approach. In social ecologies of resilience, resilient outcomes depend as much as – or even more – on the capacity of an individual to 'potentiate' positive outcomes than their personal agency to recover from exposure to risk. The responsibility moves from the individual to the wider environment and mech-anisms for interacting with it. Similarly, the 'fourth wave' of resilience research accounts for biological, neurological, behavioural and contextual data (Wright, Masten & Narayan, 2013). This investigation at the micro and nano level is mirrored by work on system-level impacts, in which social justice and resistance are placed at the heart of both explicit and 'hidden' resilience process growth (Ungar, 2011).

We asked an expert, Christine Wekerle, about her work in Canada on this issue and report her perspective in Box 4.8. Doctor Wekerle's work has recently focused on developing an evidence-based app that supports mental health and resilience. The app arose out of her work on the interplays between mental health in the context of gender-based violence and indigeneity, important because we know that mental health challenges can often be intersectional.

Box 4.8: Expert voice: Dr Christine Wekerle

Using digital technologies for resilience

Gender-based analysis reflects inequities related to gender and the social determinants of health. It includes the systemic impacts of colonialism, racism, discrimination and oppression. For youth at higher risk for mental health and violence victimisation, systemic resource discrimination compounds individual trauma (Andersen & Blosnich, 2013). For Indigenous and two-spirit youth – an Indigenous term for the inclusion of both feminine and masculine components within one individual (Walters, Evans-Campbell et al., 2006) – additional burdens include unsafe, unstable housing, food/water insecurity, and fewer health resources (Sethi, 2007; Stettler & Katz, 2017); yet, youth remain resilient. For on-reserve Indigenous youth, resilience has been shown to moderate the relationship between violence exposure and re-experiencing of trauma (Zahradnik, Stewart et al., 2009).

Emotion dysregulation has received much attention as a mediator of lasting trauma impacts, as it impairs metabolism, immunity and mental health (De Bellis, Hooper et al., 2010). Among child welfare system-involved youth, self-compassion is linked to less psychological distress, less problem alcohol use and fewer suicide attempts (Tanaka, Wekerle et al., 2011). A recent meta analysis concluded a large effect size for linkages between low self-compassion and adolescent distress (especially depression, anxiety, and stress) (Marsh, Chan & MacBeth, 2018).

In response to access needs, mental health apps may be a cost-effective, familiar format. An example of this is the JoyPop™ app, which (see youthresilience.net) was developed to support resilience by: (1) being trauma-informed and (2) focusing on emotion regulation, to help counter trauma reactions (i.e. emotional avoidance, re-living, dissociation, cognitive distortions and challenges to focused attention). One salient trauma impact is the over-learning of negative emotionality and under-learning of positive emotionality (e.g. inability to experience happiness). From focus groups with two-spirit, Indigenous youth and LGBTQ+ youth, the value of support from those with lived experiences was identified, and these resources reflect that diversity.

We therefore aim to incorporate holistic health teachings, bringing together emotional, mental, physical and spiritual health.

Dr Christine Wekerle, PhD

Associate Professor, Pediatrics

McMaster University, Hamilton, Ontario, Canada

Digital resilience

A concept in contemporary discourse is that of digital resilience. Simply, this means providing CYP with the skills to be resilient in the online environment and manage their own safety when interacting through the Internet so that they have 'the ability to deal with negative experiences online or offline' (d'Haenens et al., 2013: 1). Childnet (2018) refers to resilience as CYP having the ability to recognise when their online interactions might have a negative impact on them and learning the strategies to recover from such impact. Childnet argues that children who have digital resilience are those who feel supported by important adults and peers, are empowered in digital spaces, and have a range of techniques to use for managing their online interactions.

For CYP to be resilient, they need to be able to deal with negative experiences in all areas of their lives. To be resilient online CYP need to be able to transpose negative emotions into more neutral or positive ones (d'Haenens et al., 2013). d'Haenens et al. argued that CYP learn how to cope with adversities online and develop their digital resilience, using coping strategies like deleting messages and blocking senders when confronted with risks. Glazzard and Mitchell (2018) differentiated two forms of resilience that are important in digital spaces:

Emotional resilience: refers to the individual's ability to control their emotion when faced with adversities online. Younger populations need to be empowered to recognise and regulate their emotions and manage their responses to online adversity. With support they can take positive action.

Social resilience: refers to the ability to create and maintain social relationships with others. Younger populations need to develop strong and lasting social networks in their offline worlds as this helps them manage negative experiences online.

Central to digital resilience then, are the social and contextual conditions in which the CYP find themselves, and their ability to cope with stress and adversity. Coping strategies are those thoughts and behaviours that are used to adapt to stressors in ways that protect them from psychological harm (d'Haenens et al., 2013). Some coping strategies are stronger than others and d'Haenens et al. differentiated three forms of coping:

Passive coping: Characterised by hope that the problem will go away, and children or young people tend to stop using the Internet for a short while.

Communicative coping: Characterised by communication strategies, where the child or young person talks to someone about the adverse experience.

Proactive coping: This is an active form of coping where the child or young person tries to fix the problem. They may do this by deleting the messages or blocking the sender.

Highlighted point!

Some CYP demonstrate less digitally resilient pathways because of their age and cognitive maturity, and those children who appear to be less resilient tend to be more distressed when things go wrong or if their online profiles are misused (Holloway, 2013).

As practitioners working with CYP there are some things you can do to help promote digital resilience in those you work with. Young Minds (2016) outlined some of these strategies which we describe in Box 4.9.

Box 4.9: Practical tips for promoting digital resilience (Young Minds, 2016)

There are several ways in which you might be able to promote digital resilience:

- Being proactive and open about the potential issues: that is, not simply to hope that the issues will simply resolve themselves, as unresolved issues will contribute negatively to a CYP's mental health.
- Working with schools to think about how online safety can be embedded in the wider curriculum, so that they can learn to protect their mental health from negative things on the Internet.
- Find ways to ensure that CYP have engaging, accessible and age-appropriate information about mental health and related to the kinds of sites and apps that they are using.
- Practitioners can direct CYP to credible, supportive sites and apps that support positive mental health.
- Practitioners can undertake additional training where it is offered to upskill themselves in digital technology and social media, to have a better understanding of the issues that are faced by CYP that may impact their mental health.
- As offline vulnerability is closely related to online vulnerability, additional attention and protections may be needed for those groups.

(Continued)

- Actively create opportunities for open dialogue, debate and discussion between adults and CYP and foster an environment where they feel they can discuss openly, as talking about emotions is important for mental health.
- Talk to families about the emotional and social aspects of the digital world to help raise awareness for parents.
- Ensure that CYP are involved in the development and creation of any rules, procedures or guidelines related to digital media use so that they do not engage in activities that impact negatively on their mental health.
- Remember that most CYP are quite competent online.
- Encourage them to use digital media in positive ways and communicate when affected by an adverse experience.
- Be aware of the sociocultural origins of each child. Work with them to create maps of the protective factors they can draw on in their everyday lives.

Safeguarding

One of the central discourses through this chapter has been that it is necessary to balance protecting CYP in digital spaces and empowering them. One way to empower them online and to ensure that they have the digital resilience to cope in digital spaces is to make certain that they have the necessary skills to do so. In this way, safeguarding becomes a central mechanism for ensuring that CYP are protected, and *safeguarding* refers to the process of protecting children (NSPCC, 2016). This is, of course, important in an online context, given issues of grooming, trolling and so forth (which we discuss later). It also relates to more general safety online, usually referred to as *online safety* and we introduced this in Chapter 3. It is in the safeguarding space that our understandings of vulnerability, risk, protection and resilience converge. Different social, cultural and temporal locations view these concepts in different ways, placing some as more important in certain contexts. A young person with strong protective factors using social media to connect with others sharing their political or religious views in one context, might need a different approach to a young person with strong protective factors using social media to follow a celebrity in another.

For example, Mlambo-Ngcuka (2013) carried out a study with four resource-constrained schools in South Africa. They used simple messaging facilities on the social network Mxit and the Chat Call Centre online (C3TO) platform to deliver and support Life Orientation and Life Skills (similar in nature to Personal, Social and Health Education) tutorials outside school. The study found that although the lack of technology-enhanced learning policies in the schools restricted the contribution made to poverty and inequality reduction, the security offered by the platforms and ease of use meant that both the teachers and the students were able to advance their knowledge and skills and developed mentoring relationships that extended beyond the subject-specific context. This study and others like it teach us that there are ways in which we can all work together to develop best practice in the converging space. We outline these in Box 4.10:

Box 4.10: Practical tips for developing best practice on safeguarding

We can:

- Lobby for policy and legislation that adapts to emerging social media trends and the ways in which these can manifest in young people's lives.
- Take multi-agency and coordinated approaches to safeguarding young people's mental health online by working together across organisations.
- Develop digital safeguarding policies and training that speak to the socio-cultural context in which young people live their daily lives and be cautious of applying 'what works' approaches without sensitivity to regional and environmental variation.
- Use consistent language to describe online risks and mental health protective factors.
- Focus on children's rights to provision, and participation in a digital age, rather than solely on protection.
- Facilitate conversations between young people, families, community elders and technology developers to support CYP in their goals and in becoming more resilient.
- Develop recording mechanisms for schools and youth services that detail online risks and incidents so that it is possible to create a deeper understanding of safeguarding in our own local setting.

Consider peer-to-peer mentoring as well as education to address topics such as responsible and appropriate online behaviour, protecting data, personal and mutual responsibilities as well as mental health education. Safeguarding CYP has been an important concern of professionals in most countries and organisations' (both statutory and voluntary) work together to support these objectives. However, as we have noted, when the challenges occur online this presents new problems, and we encourage you to think about this by undertaking the reflective activity in Box 4.11.

Why is online safeguarding important for mental health?

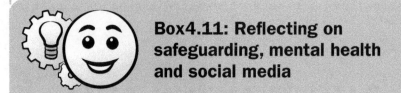

Box4.11: Reflecting on safeguarding, mental health and social media

Is there a relationship between safeguarding, mental health and using social media? And if so, what is that relationship?

In your reflective diary we encourage you to consider two contrasting cases of social media use of which you are aware. Observe your case study participants using social media. Think about:

- How do adults surrounding the child or young person use social media?
- How could we encourage CYP to talk more openly with adults and each other about how they feel during and after social media use?

Accounting for vulnerability in safeguarding and online safety

Research suggests some groups of CYP tend to be more upset or distressed by certain content online than others, and there remains a gender gap in this regard as girls seem to be more affected than boys (Livingstone, Haddon et al., 2014). Online safety education, however, tends to provide generic rules and strategies, but does not always consider differences between children, their emotional need or motivation, and neither does it tend to recognise that some groups of CYP are more likely to engage in risky online behaviour than others (Katz & Asam, 2019). In the UK for example, an issue in the delivery of online safety programmes was the quality of staff training in online safety. Not all staff received systematic programmes of support in this field (Ofsted, 2014). It is reasonable to advocate that some CYP need greater attention, more considerable protection and further levels of online safety support than others.

Katz and Asam (2019) noted that more vulnerable children will often miss out on online safety education, as they may feel it is irrelevant to them. They give an example of the group 'young carers' whose parents may not play an active role in their child's online safety, and the child may also miss out in school due to high levels of absence and therefore miss input about online safety in the classroom. Katz and Asam also reported that looked-after children may be another group who do not receiving the level of online safety education they need. In managing online safety, therefore, many recommendations have been made for schools (and parents), especially relating to vulnerable CYP. These were outlined by Asam and Katz (2018) and are described in Box 4.12.

Box 4.12: Practical tips for online safety (Asam & Katz, 2018)

There are several things schools and parents can do:

- It is important not to react to the media panic. Instead, schools and parents should develop their own critical appraisal skills and not just impose a digital media ban that risks leaving CYP ill-prepared for the digital world beyond the school gates. If they are not well-prepared then they are more likely to be impacted by negative experiences and this will have a more detrimental impact on their mental health.
- Actively encourage CYP to develop healthy peer relationships and have interests offline. This is good for their mental health as strong peer relationships benefit them psychologically, as do hobbies and physical exercise.
- Try to avoid banning social media completely as it is likely young people will find a way to circumnavigate those rules. Instead, find appropriate ways to communicate with CYP about their online behaviour. This means that they will be able to speak to an adult about things that upset them, which will help them build resilience and cope with negative experiences.
- Encourage an open dialogue and help them to develop digital skills and be mindful of online safety. This is because adverse experiences online threaten their mental health.
- It is important to tailor safety education so that it accounts for the diversity within the student body. This is because some CYP are more vulnerable than others or are living in situations that create a vulnerability.
- Promote strategies for the development of problem-solving skills to help CYP cope with adversity online. Promoting and building a sense of autonomy through dialogue can help this, which benefits their mental health.
- Do not be afraid to discuss more challenging issues, for example self-harm, as this can be important for some CYP. Limiting discussions or avoiding these topics can lead to inhibition and leave those children unsupported. However, we do caution that it is not always appropriate and special care should be taken with younger or more vulnerable children.
- Implement strategies to evaluate the effectiveness of the online safety programmes you deliver.

Conclusions

This chapter represents our first moves toward integrating CYP, digital media and mental health. In completing this chapter, we provide an expert viewpoint on resilience and vulnerability from an expert in this area, especially in majority world countries whereby some of the vulnerabilities and issues faced are different from in wealthier parts of the world. In Box 4.13 we present the perspective of Professor Linda Theron, who has been leading research in this area.

Box 4.13: Expert contribution: Professor Linda Theron

Role: Professor of Educational Psychology

Organisation: University of Pretoria, South Africa

Brief bio: Professor Linda Theron, DEd, is an educational psychologist by training. She is a full professor in the Department of Educational Psychology/Centre for the Study of Resilience, Faculty of Education, University of Pretoria, South Africa, and an extraordinary professor in Optentia Research Focus Area, North-West University, South Africa. Her research (which is locally and internationally funded) and publications focus on the resilience processes of South African CYP challenged by chronic adversity and account for how sociocultural contexts shape resilience.

Resilience in CYP is a multi-system phenomenon

The interest in human resilience – that is, the capacity to function and/or develop normatively despite exposure to risks associated with poor functioning or arrested development – is unceasing. This interest makes sense in a world where the risks to human health and wellbeing are rampant. CYP are not immune to these risks; in fact, they are often especially vulnerable to risk exposure. What enables their resilience and how to translate this knowledge is, therefore, a particularly pressing agenda.

The study of child and youth resilience is unequivocal that resilience is about more than personal strengths, such as self-regulation skill, willingness to seek help, or assertiveness. More accurately, CYP's capacity to adjust well to risk draws on multiple, enabling systems that are found in these young people (e.g. a functional stress response system) and around them (e.g. supportive relationships, quality health care, enabling laws or protective built/virtual environments). What this implies for those of us who wish to champion the health and wellbeing of risk-exposed CYP is that we need to better appreciate the intersectionality of resilience-enabling systems. We need to work as hard to facilitate resilience-enabling families, schools, digital environments and other relevant ecological systems as we do to advance CYP's personal strengths and skills.

Furthermore, the study of CYP resilience across diverse contexts offers unambiguous evidence that certain systems matter more for the resilience of some. These studies also show that which systems matter more is likely to be influenced by sociocultural dynamics and/or contextual realities. The same applies to the form that these systems take. In our current resilience work with African young people from stressed communities in South Africa, for example, we are learning that resilience-enabling families are central to CYP resilience. In many instances, those who report families as central to their resilience are in their mid-twenties. From a developmental perspective, one would expect older youth to be less reliant on family but the dearth of educational and employment opportunities available to CYP from stressed South African communities likely explains continued youth reliance on a resilience-enabling family system. These resilience-enabling families are seldom nuclear or headed by men. They typically include multiple parent-figures (e.g. sisters, aunts and/or grandmothers who co-parent younger members of the family). Amongst other reasons, this form relates to historic Apartheid laws that resulted in working African men being separated from their families and to traditional African families' valuing of intergenerational households and interdependence.

Another context-specific pattern in our work with young people from communities characterised by high levels of youth violence is that civically engaged youth seldom report their peers as resilience-enabling. As in other South African studies with youth from violent contexts (Humm, Kaminer, and Hardy, 2018), it is probable that the capacity to detach from anti-social peers is resilience-enabling (even if peer detachment is developmentally anomalous) (Sanders, Munford et al., 2017). Lastly, we are learning that specific clusters of contextual risks (e.g. residence in a violent or resource constrained community and membership of a non-supportive family versus residence in violent or resource constrained community) prompt CYP to prioritise resilience-enabling resources differently. Those whose community and family contexts are risk-laden rely more heavily on personal strengths, for instance.

Such contextual and cultural nuances discourage assumptions – including ones based on developmental theory – about which systems should be prioritised in resilience interventions with young people. Rather, interventions to support child and youth resilience should be tailored to fit specific individuals in each context at a specific point in time. To this end, practitioners are encouraged to use the following question to direct their resilience-enabling interventions: 'Which promotive and protective factors or processes are best for which people in which contexts at what level of risk exposure and for which outcomes?' (Ungar, 2019). In addition, awareness of contextual and cultural nuances encourages respectful responsiveness when practitioners and others work to facilitate resilience-enabling families, schools, digital environments and other relevant ecological systems. Given the South African example mentioned above, respectful responsiveness could mean raising parent-figure (rather than just parental) awareness of risks (such as the emotional and social risks of the digital world to child and youth mental health) and sustaining how these parent-figures contribute to child and youth resilience. Sustaining the contribution of these figures, who are invariably risk-exposed themselves, will demand practitioner attention to these figures' personal resilience too.

Unfortunately, our understanding of how best to sustain the resilience of parent-figures and other systems that contribute to CYP resilience (such as

(Continued)

supportive families, schools or built/virtual communities) is not particularly well developed. This was alluded to when Luthar and Ciciolla (2015) asked 'Who mothers Mommy?'. Their question advocated the importance of advancing insight into the resilience of those systems that are implicated in the health and wellbeing of risk-exposed CYP, especially when these systems are also risk-exposed. As with CYP, it is possible that exposure to moderate, or manageable, levels of risk can strengthen system capacity for resilience (what Michael Rutter referred to as the 'steeling effect') (see Rutter, 2007). As with CYP, it is also possible that a system's capacity for resilience is rooted in a combination of system-specific and ecological supports. There is an urgent need for these possibilities to be robustly investigated across diverse contexts and translated into best practice guidelines that will advance the resilience of those systems that matter for CYP resilience. In the meantime, practitioners are encouraged to respect the multi-system nature of child and youth resilience by actively supporting the resilience of the CYP that they serve, along with the resilience of all the other systems implicated in the resilience of these CYP.

PART II
THE IMPACT OF DIGITAL MEDIA

5

EXPLORING THE POSITIVE IMPACT ON MENTAL HEALTH

THE RHETORIC OF 'THE GOOD'

Learning points

After reading this chapter, you will be able to:

- Appreciate potential positive impacts of digital media on children and young people
- Critically assess the concept of digital citizenship
- Understand the role of digital media in building social skills.

Introduction

Scholars have acknowledged that in lay discourse and media portrayals of the relationship between digital media and mental health, this is typically rhetorically positioned as either 'good', 'bad' or 'ugly' (O'Reilly, 2020). O'Reilly noted that although digital media, and social media more specifically, are not inherently good, bad or ugly, and there is considerable overlap in these domains, it is a framework that is often deployed discursively to demarcate issues raised in relation to the levels of potential and actual risk and harm. For the sake of simplicity, we divide this part of the book into these three domains. However, in so doing, we remind you to remain critically reflective, and we point out some of the challenges with such a parsimonious demarcation as we develop each chapter, especially as many issues could easily fit into two or three of those domains.

In this chapter we focus on how CYP use digital media, to impact positively on their wellbeing and mental health. We note there are ways in which organisations can and do use digital media in supportive ways, but we turn our attention to those later in the book. The aim of this chapter is to illustrate how digital media can be used by CYP in positive ways and help them cope with stress to improve or maintain positive mental health. We start by looking at the ways in which different forms of digital media are used to build social relationships and improve communication and then how they are used for relaxation and entertainment, or to cope with adversity. Aligned also, are the ways in which identity is developed, especially during adolescence. In the modern world embedded with digital technologies, this can have a strong influence on young people's identity development (Ito et al., 2010). Digital media have great potential for mental health promotion, improving awareness and offering support.

Context

In this book, we have steered away from the idea that technologies can 'do' things to us, sometimes called *techno-romanticism* or *technological determinism*. Technological determinism is the proposal that technology has important effects on people's lives, but critics have argued that technology itself is socially determined (Adler, 2006). Adler noted that technology and social structures 'co-evolve' in ways that are non-deterministic and emergent, and the impact of technology depends on how these are implemented. We therefore encourage you to think about the interactions between technology, the CYP user, and perhaps even the intention behind the design of the technology (Levine, 2019). It is helpful then, for you to think about technologies as emerging from the society in which they are used, rather than external to that society. Whilst doing so, remain aware of how technology companies interact with society, who influences their development, and what their drivers may be. We question whether different perspectives are considered and represented in technological advances. Notably, much of the polemic of digital media and mental health casts the relationship in a negative way. However, digital media, and even social media, are not all bad.

In everyday discussions, there has tended to be a line of reasoning that digital media, and social media especially, are damaging a generation's mental health. However, it is very important that there is some balance to this view and recognition that there are ways these media are being used that can *protect* mental health and *promote* wellbeing in CYP. Indeed, there is a growing evidence base of the link between positive mental health and social media use (Dienlin, Masur and Trepte, 2017). It is crucial that we do not 'throw the baby out with the bathwater' and simply disregard digital media from young people's lives when many are using it in positive ways and have a good understanding of how to protect themselves online. Think about the following question and attempt the reflective activity in Box 5.1.

> Do CYP use technology in ways that are good for their mental health?

Box 5.1: Reflecting on the positives

List the ways digital media can be positive for CYP's mental health.

In your reflective diary it is worth challenging yourself to think of all the different ways in which digital media, including social media, has had a positive impact on CYP.

Evidence suggests that although 'the majority of young people are relatively resilient online, a minority report an online life in which they are at risk of multiple harms' (Asam and Katz, 2018: 281). Research shows, then, that many CYP are developing skills to stay safe online and many (but of course not *all*) have support in place when something upsets them, with most of them able to take steps to protect themselves (Mascheroni and Cuman, 2014). In other words, CYP can do well using social media if they are empowered to use these in positive ways and are well supported by adults in their lives. This was eloquently stated by the OECD (2018: 10):

> Children and young people should be empowered and supported to use digital technology well, so they can further reap benefits that social media provides. By talking with children about their use of social media, parents and carers should adopt an approach that works best for their child's age, interests and needs.

Consultations with young people

As part of our own research endeavour, consultation groups were run with 16–18-year-olds from Ashby-de-la-Zouch in Leicestershire (UK) and these were led by a young person rather than academics for authenticity. All were White British.

The purpose of these groups was to help us design our research project on the relationship between social media and mental health. In doing these consultation exercises it was agreed by the young people that social media use fitted into three domains: the good, the bad and the ugly. Thus, as part of the participatory and person-centred activity, three boards were created with those headings. The young people were asked to write statements on sticky notes and place them on the appropriate board. These boards and their ideas of the role of social media in their lives are introduced in this chapter and the others in this section of the book as a reflective and practical way of displaying what young people think and believe about the good, the bad and the ugly. Here we illustrate their reflection on the positive side of social media, which led to a discussion about the positive influences on mental health more specifically. We illustrate the participatory activity of sticky notes in Figure 5.1.

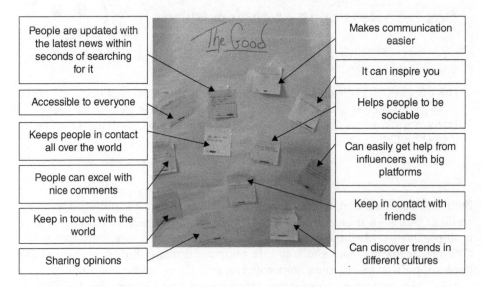

Figure 5.1 Young people's constructions of the good

During these consultation groups, the participants emphasised the importance of communication and staying in touch with people from all geographical locations. They recognised that this allowed them to *keep in touch with the world* (George, aged 17 years) and *keep in contact all over the world* (Lily, aged 16 years). They argued this makes *communication easier* (Dylan, aged 16 years) and enables them to *share opinions* with others (Rhiannon, aged 16 years). They felt social media can *inspire* (Madalyn, aged 16 years) and allowed others to provide *nice comments* (Tristan, aged 16 years). They also noted that social media can be a source of information as *people are updated with the latest news within seconds of searching for it* (Blaine, 16 years), and as Rose (aged 16 years) noted it also allows young people to *discover trends in different cultures*.

Some comments were discussed as general positive aspects of social media, such as Rose's idea about different cultures; others commented on how these positive ways of using social media, like sharing opinions and being inspired, can have a positive impact on their wellbeing more specifically. We followed up on these ideas by asking some young people to contribute their opinions in the form of expert voices for the purpose of this book. They were simply asked to write about 'their opinion of social media' and were not given any other assistance in producing their views. We note those contributions, as the views of Madalyn, Ryan and Isabella, were mostly positive, and are presented in Boxes 5.2, 5.3 and 5.4 respectively.

Box 5.2: Expert voice: Madalyn Heaton-Ward

Opinion on social media

The social media sites that I use are mainly Instagram and snapchat. Occasionally I will use Facebook as it is used by older generations more too, allowing me to connect with family, such as my grandparents even when I cannot physically see them. Additionally, I will rarely use Twitter for its 'witty' humour or to buy or sell tickets to gigs/concerts. However, as I said, taking most of my attention is firstly, Snapchat. This app allows me to interact with my friends quickly and easily. It allows me to share more than a conversation; it allows me to convey my moods and my successes with photos and videos. Secondly, Instagram allows me to be inspired by others' art and fashion, which is why I enjoy using this app. It enables me to keep up with ever changing trends and explore cultures without getting on a plane.

Sometimes I may feel the pressure to look good or post good content as it can be daunting having so many eyes on your content without seeing a physical reaction, but luckily I can say that I don't experience any negative comments online.

I use Instagram mainly to connect with other people's creations, which is a positive about social media. On the contrary, a negative aspect of social media is that it unfortunately gives a platform and some power to the minority of people that want to harm others, such as trolls and extremists.

I would say that the amount of time on social media is a total of probably around a few hours a day. I tend to use/look at social media when I wake up first thing in the morning, in my breaks at school and in the evening too. Another reason why I find social media a positive thing is due to the increasing use of social media by businesses and schools. For example, my school textiles department has one. This makes it possible for different resources to be easily accessible and shared to many.

News and movements can be formed by collective voices of many joining together. With a healthy mindset, there is much to be loved about social media.

Madalyn Heaton-Ward

School student aged 17 years (UK)

Box 5.3: Expert voice: Ryan Zappelline

Opinion on social media

I think social media can be very useful in the lives of young people. They are often a real-life escape valve. If used positively and without excess, they can do young people a lot of good. I see that it gives a great freedom for those who cannot interact personally. There they can talk without having to be 'stared' and without having to decipher what other people's facial expressions say. For many it is 'easier' to make friends virtually than physically.

It has occurred to me to be sad with people close to me, like my parents for example, and to resort to social media to see something that makes me happy, or to let off steam with friends, or even find ways to solve my problems with them. But since not everything is perfect, I also let myself become addicted to these media for a while.

I feel that our mental health depends on several factors working together so that it can function properly. So, to use the Internet itself, we have to regulate ourselves so that everything is in balance within our brain. No time abuse on it, mostly.

A testimony from real life: I studied at a school since I was 5 years old. I studied there until I was 13 years old. There was a boy in my class who didn't speak to anyone, except a boy. This other boy was very fond of talking. One day I came to him and asked him what he and the quiet boy were talking about so much. It was then that I discovered that the 'quiet' boy had a channel with more than 1,000 subscribers on YouTube. Today he has more than 3,000. Look at the social media there ...

Here's the tip, use it correctly and it will be very beneficial for you.

Ryan Zappelline

School student aged 16 years (Brazil)

Box 5.4: Expert voice: Isabella Maria Valério

Opinion on social media

Currently, social media are present in the daily lives of all age groups and social classes. This constant exposure makes us realise the influence they have on the public, indirectly or directly. It is not news to anyone how much social media can be used for evil, but here comes a subject that we must discuss more: if used for good, could social media be much more useful than they have been?

In an era of rising digital influencers, the demand for talking about real people's problems grows, which is to be expected, knowing that many of these influencers are inspiration for the audience that follows him. We should, whenever possible, normalise the feelings and anxieties that we humans always have and will still have. The trend is that the more a topic is commented on and publicised, the more people take the topic as normal; hence the constant struggle for representation of social minorities, which is a very important issue in this century. At the same time that we must give way to these people, with their experiences and speeches, we must also take advantage of this time of ascension, to spread the thought that yes, feelings are normal, in the same way that 'bad' days are also.

When one is in physical pain, the published texts or articles are numerous, at the same time as a shortage of resources is seen at a time when one is in a state of emotional suffering; this makes the subject more controversial, since there is so little comment: it almost becomes a burden, something to blame.

With technology, we have an infinite number of possibilities at hand, so why not make it a tool to help yourself, or help others? The influence that people have today within these media should no longer be used as a way to plant bad thoughts, anguish and comparison, in others; it should be used as a means to spread the importance of care and maintenance to mental health, which can, in many cases, cause more suffering than the physical pathology itself.

Isabella Maria Valério

School student aged 16 years old (Brazil)

The three young people provide a valuable insight into the role that social media play in their lives, as they provide a balanced perspective on the benefits and challenges, and ultimately, as Ryan notes, recognise that it is how they utilise digital platforms that is a crucial factor. They are clear that they use digital media, especially social media, and that this is important to them and to their identity, a topic to which we now turn our attention.

Identity

It is well known that a positive sense of personal identity is a crucial factor in positive psychological wellbeing. Identity and sense of self is important to CYP but is especially pertinent during adolescence. During this period, adolescents become more self-aware of their abilities and limitations, and they begin to address critical questions about their role and location in the social world (George and Odgers, 2015). Digital environments provide new ways for CYP to develop and explore their identity and promote a positive psychological profile. As Clarke (2009: 74) claimed:

Emerging identity is an important aspect of early adolescent development, and in our existing digital culture children have an immense opportunity to explore their world, be creative, play with identity and experiment with different social mores. Using SNSs is not only entertaining for children, but also highly creative and allows them to assert their identity in a totally unique way, checking out what their friends think of their creative endeavours

We invite you then to think about the following question:

> Do you think that CYP have separate digital and non-digital lives, selves and identities?

Evidence suggests that CYP themselves do not see their identity as digital or non-digital – in fact, they are not often given the opportunity to think about their identity at all. Talking about CYP's use of digital media with them can help them to think about how they see themselves and others around them. It can be helpful to reflect on how your views of this might influence your practice. Try the reflective activity in Box 5.5.

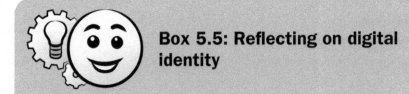

Box 5.5: Reflecting on digital identity

Consider in what way your view of a separate or blended digital and non-digital identity might influence your practice.

In your reflective diary challenge yourself to think about what your beliefs are around digital and non-digital identities and how they overlap. Why and how might this perspective influence the way you work with CYP?

Use of digital media offers adolescents, particularly, with a mechanism to discover different aspects of themselves, to foster their sense of personal identity, and opportunities to discuss their thoughts with others (boyd, 2014). Disclosing a sense of self online can generate trust and boost self-esteem (Valkenburg & Peter, 2009), and in this way social media particularly promote a positive self-image (Allen et al., 2014). Exploring identity via digital media can be especially helpful for those CYP who are more isolated and so have fewer opportunities for identity development as it enables them to join networks and be part of a digital community whereby they can explore their interests and find others with similar values (Glazzard & Mitchell, 2018). Glazzard and Mitchell note that through the digital world adolescents can develop their autonomy and interact with others without the close gaze of significant adults. This community building, sharing ideas and identity development online can be especially helpful to adolescents who are developing identities through which they express difference. For example, lesbian, gay or bisexual young people who have a potentially safe space to learn about others who share their sexuality can gain support from those who have had personal experiences and explore their sense of sexual orientation (George & Odgers, 2015). You may wish to reflect on the implications of these opportunities for young people in your care who come from cultures in which sexuality is contested.

There have, of course, been some concerns expressed by adults about the above developments and associated risks. It is, however, important that we remember that taking risks is part of the self-actualisation process which is a natural part of the young person's psychological development as they transition from adolescence into adulthood (Erikson, 1968). Adolescents may take risks online but can still have the tools to explore the Internet in a safe manner. Some degree of risk-taking can be positive for CYP to develop their resilience and learn strategies for staying safe and developing their coping skills when things are upsetting online (Livingstone et al., 2014), and peer-to-peer support and peer learning could be helpful in developing that. The solution therefore is not necessarily to ban CYP from digital media and their devices, as that can be problematic in other ways (which we discuss later), but instead to educate them to protect themselves, use digital media appropriately and provide support.

Social skills and building relationships

A central feature of identity for CYP is their relationships with others. Communication is a cornerstone of society and helps foster a sense of belonging and promotes social relationships (Fuchs, 2017). One of the most obvious benefits of digital media is that using them can provide a mechanism for CYP to promote and develop social skills, build relationships, maintain existing peer relations and reduce isolation (Ito et al., 2010). Thus, digital media provide a platform for sharing experiences or challenges (Fuchs, 2017). Although we refer to digital media broadly, social media play a role in social skills and building relationships. The role played by social media is likely to be different across the age spectrum. CYP will be at different points in their social and communication (language) development according to their chronological and developmental age (see Chapter 1).

Developmental ability is especially important to the formation and maintenance of peer relations as, according to Rubin (1994), peer acceptance depends on the following three competencies:

1. The ability to regulate emotions.
2. The ability to process social information.
3. The ability to display competent and desirable social behaviour.

Rubin argued that the opposite is true in terms of indicators of peer rejection that tends to be a consequence of:

- Emotional dysregulation.
- Impoverished social cognition.
- Displaying antisocial behaviour.

We consider what this means in practice in Box 5.6.

 **Box 5.6: What this means**

CYP who struggle to regulate their emotions and are prone to outbursts of anxiety or aggressive behaviour tend to be ostracised by their peers. Furthermore, this kind of behaviour can also be negatively treated by adults. The reason for the emotional outbursts or behaviour are, however, important as they may be indicative of a special educational need, an unresolved trauma, a mental health condition or developmental delay. The behaviour can be connected to mental health conditions, like conduct disorders or behavioural conditions, or may reflect ACEs like child abuse or domestic violence. CYP who find it challenging to regulate their emotions, display antisocial behaviour and/or struggle to comprehend social rules find it more difficult to make friends and interact in typical social situations. In turn, this may lead to limited peer support and challenges of communicating and building relationships online as well as offline.

Evidence suggests, then, that digital media can be helpful in promoting the development of these skills and in the initiation, building and maintenance of relationships in ways that are valued by CYP. Furthermore, this seems to have some universal appeal. For example, there is evidence that this is also the case for low-resource contexts. Research indicated that social relationships are intertwined with technology use, and in a study of 9–18 year olds' use of mobile phones in South Africa, Malawi and Ghana it was suggested that

> many young people across Africa obtain work and live off resources provided by social contacts: kin and friendship networks are crucial in this respect ... This requires careful nurturing of social relationships over time, and mobile phone contact is extremely valuable. (Porter, Hampshire et al., 2012: 149)

In contemporary society, children's friendships are a blend of on- and offline social interaction, with large numbers communicating via social media, interactive gaming and other digital media. For example, research that included 2,000 young people aged 8–17 year olds in the UK showed that:

- 52% used YouTube to chat to their friends daily.
- 75% used YouTube to communicate generally.
- 43% used WhatsApp.
- 43% used Snapchat.
- 38% used Instagram.
- 37% used Facebook. (UK Safer Internet Centre, 2018)

This study showed that boys were more likely to use interactive gaming to communicate with their friends and girls were more likely to use a range of social media, such as SNS and apps that enable communication with peers. Similarly, an American review of 36 studies showed that young people use digital technologies to share intimacy, display affection and arrange social gatherings (Yau and Reich, 2017). In Table 5.1 we illustrate some of the key factors about social interaction online that the British children thought were especially important.

Table 5.1 Factors of importance for online interaction (UK Safer Internet Centre, 2018)

Factor	Description
Focus on respect and support	CYP felt that an online environment should be kind, respectful and supportive, and felt that relevant adults could help make this a reality.
Instant replying	The survey showed that 73% of participants felt that it was essential that their friends responded to a digital message as soon as it had been seen.
Inclusion	The survey showed that 60% of participants believed it to be important to be included in group chats when initiated by their friends. It was shown that 40% felt left out if peers posted things but did not include them.
Online 'likes'	The survey showed that 51% felt it important that their friends actively 'liked' their status updates or posts, and equally 43% felt that their friends should actively ignore other people that they did not like.
Social interaction	Most CYP had positive experiences of social interaction online, with 83% having an experience of a peer being kind, 68% chatting to friends as it cheered them up and 89% being happy because of an online experience.

Interacting via digital media can be beneficial for CYP across the age spectrum. As we noted, children develop in many different domains and this has relevance for how they use media and how they interact with others via those media. Chronological and developmental ages will impact on how and to what extent they use digital media in that way.

In younger children, engagement with virtual worlds can offer them opportunities to play (Marsh, 2010) as technology can increase their understanding via videos and pictures (McPake, Plowman & Stephen, 2013). Through digital media children can discover and explore, and, in the early years, it can enable those children to belong to a community (McPake et al., 2013).

Children under the age of nine years now engage in a range of online activities, such as watching videos, playing games, finding information, doing their homework and socialising (Holloway et al., 2013). Communication and creative expression are important for young children as these are precursors to literacy. Thus, digital media – including technological toys and games – can facilitate children's operational skills, knowledge and understanding of their social worlds (Devine, 2012). Frequently, young children will connect with their peers through online gaming, and these spaces mean that they learn how to use devices quickly and at a young age, as well as connecting with others (which can be used in positive or negative ways). Indeed, Craft (2011) identified four important competencies described as four Ps (different from the four Ps covered in Chapter 2) that can be developed by young children in online environments and we outline these in Table 5.2.

Table 5.2   The four Ps (Craft, 2011)

The P	Description
Being Plural	Online spaces allow young children to connect with people and digital playmates in a multitude of play or social places, providing space to experiment with their own online presence.
Being Playful	Online spaces are co-exploratory in the sense that children are required to improvise with imagination. Young children then, can continue to play long after they have left the physical spaces in their offline environment.
Participation	Children access peers to play in both on- and offline environments and, in so doing, participate in many domains of life. They become an author, performer and audience. Digital play environments allow the sharing of ideas as they upload images, messages, recordings and animations.
Possibilities	The online environment allows children to explore possibilities as they translate what might be in quick and easy ways. For example, an avatar can swim, or cook or fly at a simple click of the mouse.

We note these competencies are important for children to develop, but it is important that as a practitioner you are aware that the development of such competencies depends greatly on the type of platform used, and the possibilities open to children. While some gaming has educational objectives built in, others do not, and not all digital environments are adequate for all children of different ages. Of course, we need to be mindful that younger children may be engaging in digital activities that are not entirely age appropriate. For example, even though SNS tend to have a minimum age, research has shown that children younger than that are still using them, for example 18% of 9–10 year olds and 25% of 11–12 year olds had a profile in 2013 (Livingstone et al., 2014). It is not fully understood yet whether children under the age of nine years have the necessary developmental skills to engage with this online world in an unsupervised, safe way, especially in terms of socialising in virtual worlds or on social networks primarily intended for adolescents (Holloway et al. 2013) and this may also be the case for older children.

Highlighted point!

It is important that younger children are provided with support and education to use digital media in safe ways, and that adults provide supervision of their online activities. Technology companies also have the responsibility of designing age-appropriate services which support children's development and respect children's rights.

As children develop and their social skills improve, and their friendships become more meaningful, many spend more time on screens interacting with others, as well as working together with screens to socialise or focus on a task (see e.g. Figure 5.2). This can have beneficial effects as CYP who spend time interacting with their offline friends via screens tend to feel closer to those friends (Valkenburg and Peter, 2007). Using social media can help CYP to improve their communication and technical skills and foster a social connection with others (Ito et al., 2010), and self-disclosure online can generate trust and positive feedback can boost self-esteem (Valkenburg and Peter, 2009). The older children get, the more complex and sophisticated their social networks and friendships become.

Figure 5.2 Friendships

Adolescents are an especially important group to consider in relation to social skills, communication and social interaction online. As noted, adolescents are a group that developmentally take more risks on- and offline (Keenan et al., 2016) and are forming their sense of identity. Adolescents use digital media for several reasons, including extending social ties, creating networks and communication (Davies and Eynon, 2013), and young people frequently join social networks because so many of their peers do so (Chou and Edge, 2012).

During adolescence, friendships become increasingly more important and this is of central importance to the psycho-social – and neurological – development of young people. As this age group tend to be heavy internet and social media users, it stands to reason that this is a platform through which many aspects of their social relationships are explored and built. It is also argued that some groups of adolescents may particularly benefit from engagement with digital communication. Adolescents who are socially introverted are perhaps less directly socially active (Glazzard & Mitchell, 2018) and therefore social media has potential to reduce isolation and loneliness (Royal Society for Public Health, 2019).

Adolescents may use a myriad of devices and platforms to keep contact with their peers. Indeed, it is frequently observed that this age group can be in the same physical space but still communicate with each other via digital media (how often do you see teenagers and even adults texting or WhatsApp messaging each other from across the same room?!). For some adolescents experiencing challenging emotions, difficult life circumstances or environmental risk, or for those with existing mental health needs, being connected via digital media can provide a supportive environment. Peer support can help them to feel acknowledged, connected and feel less different, which can promote positive mental health. Such peer support can facilitate coping strategies.

Highlighted point!

It is important to attend to social relationships and their digital mediation as it is well known that strong peer networks and social skills are connected to positive mental health; isolation and challenges in peer relationships, conversely, are associated with poor mental health (Bradford & Larson, 2009).

Given how important digital media, and more specifically social media, are in connectivity between adolescents it is unsurprising that young people report these as central to their lives. In our project, we received many descriptions of the positive connectivity that these serve. For example, many young people reported the social aspect of social media, and we cite quotations taken from the project in Figure 5.3.

It [social media] *makes you more social.*

It's a way of communicating with people, maybe like really good friends you wouldn't see very often.

It could be a way to connect with your old friends, people you lost touch with.

Figure 5.3   The social aspect of social media as reported by young people

At this point, it might be helpful to think about your own beliefs. We encourage you to reflect on this section and think about the ways in which digital media might be good for adolescent relationships and try the reflective activity in Box 5.7.

How might adolescents use digital media to promote positive peer relationships?

Box 5.7: Reflecting on adolescent peer relationships

Create a list of ways you think digital media can be positive for adolescent peer relationships.

In your reflective diary it is worth thinking specifically about adolescent relationships, connectivity and social interactions in a digital environment, and the potentially positive impact that this may have.

Relaxation and stress management

In the modern world CYP are coping with many stressors. For most, these are anticipated pressures associated with childhood and development, such as academic attainment and managing sibling relationships. For others, they face multiple adversities such as poverty, poor parental mental health, parental separation, bereavement, domestic violence, child abuse to name just a few. In some countries even greater adversity is faced, with community violence, conflict or war, displacement, malnutrition and so on. CYP sometimes argue that using digital media and engaging with their peers through social media helps them to relax and manage their stresses and stressors. Relaxation and stress management are different things, with relaxation generally being a pro-active measure and stress management being a reactive measure, but they are closely related, and we deal with them together here. There are many ways that CYP can manage their stress, and the Royal College of Psychiatrists (2020) provided a list of practical offline techniques that can be adopted by CYP to help them do so. We outline these in Box 5.8.

 **Box 5.8: Practical tips for managing stress**

The Royal College of Psychiatrists (2020) advises CYP to consider the following strategies for managing their stress:

- It is important that CYP have someone to talk to as dealing with stress alone makes it harder to manage.
- CYP need people in their life they can trust to help them work out how to tackle the causes of stress.
- Writing things down can be helpful and writing a list of the stressors on a piece of paper helps to cognitively process the problem. Taking each stressor in turn and making a list of ways to tackle it can sort things out.
- It is helpful to take a break from the sources of stress and do things that are enjoyable.
- Deliberately engage in relaxing activities.
- It can be helpful to do some physical exercise as this is good for the body and mind.

Interestingly, the list of practical ideas presented by the Royal College of Psychiatrists does not mention digital media, but the young people from our research study made a case for the value of this in relation to stress and relaxation.

We report on the descriptions provided by some young people about the protective role that digital media plays for their wellbeing as a mechanism for stress
management and relaxation. We present their views in Figure 5.4 (see O'Reilly
et al., 2018 for more detail).

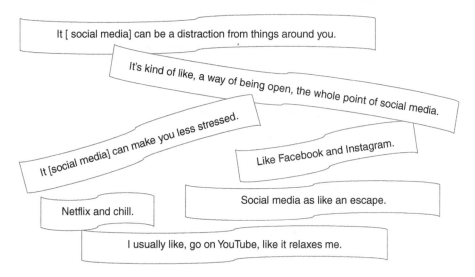

Figure 5.4 Using social media to relax and destress

Regardless of the type of society that a CYP might be living in, it is normal
to experience some stress. Stress is the body's reaction to feeling threatened or
under pressure. It is very common and can be quite positive in that stress can
be motivating to help us achieve things in our daily life, and can help us meet
the demands of home, work/school and family life. However, too much stress
can affect our mood, our body and our relationships – especially when it feels
out of our control. It can make us feel anxious and irritable and affect our
self-esteem. Therefore, when the stress becomes overwhelming for the CYP or
is consistent and long-lasting, this frequent feeling can lead to a negative
impact on mental health. Thus, we argue that it is possible that some CYP
engage in relaxation techniques as a proactive measure to support their wellbeing and to prevent stress from occurring. Relaxation then is one of the various ways in which CYP try to manage their stress.

There are psychological benefits for some CYP to being online, and it is
known that some use digital media to improve their mood and to relax. For
some, the use of social media can develop their self-esteem and their sense of
self-concept and give them a more positive view of themselves (Glazzard &
Mitchell, 2018). For example, when children share positive comments amongst
their peers it can have a positive effect (Children's Commissioner (UK), 2018),
and positive relationships online can be confidence boosting, especially for
those who find face-to-face interaction more challenging (Glazzard & Mitchell,
2018). We explain further in Box 5.9.

Box 5.9: What this means

Of course, using social media can be stress-inducing too, so it is crucial that we teach CYP to be kind to themselves and others online. They can be kind to themselves by:

- Monitoring their own physical and mental responses to their use of technology.
- Maintaining good digital privacy.
- Knowing when to step back from interactions that might be upsetting.
- Being mindful of risk and safety.

They can be kind to others by:

- Treating others in the way they would wish to be treated.
- Avoiding posting or sending messages in haste or anger.
- Remembering that there are usually real people behind the avatars and profiles, and that we do not know what those people might be thinking or feeling.
- Avoiding the use of hate speech.
- Being tolerant toward others.
- Being empathic.

Digital citizenship

We introduced you to digital citizenship in Chapter 3. In traditional studies of 'citizenship' in a broader sense, work has focused on public participation in political processes (Westheimer & Kahne, 2004), but contemporary conceptualisations of citizenship are now more inclusive of a broader range of civic behaviours like participation in community activity and collectively working toward solving community problems and addressing social injustice (Thorson, 2012). The idea of the digital citizen has garnered some support and you may find that there are some digital citizenship educational programmes as well as guidance in the literature that are designed to help promote respectful behaviour online (Jones and Mitchell, 2016). There are of course different elements of digital citizenship and these were described by Ribble (2017) as outlined in Chapter 4. To be a digital citizen, CYP need to understand how to navigate the Internet and participate in all aspects of technology (Young, 2014) safely and appropriately. Young argued that they must acquire an understanding of the rules associated with the digital world and appreciate the consequences if those norms are violated, thus needing to understand things such as the laws of privacy and copyright.

The concept and practice of digital citizenship has been criticised in the literature and so we argue that it is useful for you to engage in these ideas as you consider how much you agree with the notion. Critics have, however, suggested that by constructing technology as neutral or outside the societal struggles in which it is located, digital citizenship has become a way in which technologies are used to compel people to adopt skills, practices and ways of being that are not necessarily conducive to building empowered or happy lives (Emejulu & McGregor, 2016). As a result, there have recently been calls to think about digital citizenship more holistically and radically, particularly as we move beyond minority-world-dominated understanding of childhood. We encourage you to critically reflect for yourself on these issues by considering the expert voice from Professor Athina Karatzogianni about her work in this area. We provide her response in Box 5.10.

Box 5.10: Expert voice: Professor Athina Karatzogianni

The problem with digital citizenship

Digital transformations have undoubtedly had a strong impact on civic participation and on the ways in which active digital citizenship is conceived, perceived and experienced. Scholarly debates around the use of ICTs by non-state actors such as NGOs, protest groups, insurgents, militant and terrorist organisations are extensive, addressing issues such as surveillance and censorship (Zuboff, 2015; Bauman & Lyon, 2013) and the impact of ICTs on the ideology, organisation, mobilisation and structures of social movements (Morozov, 2011; Coleman & Blumler, 2009; Dahlberg & Siapera, 2007). Other scholarly debates address the role of digital networks in supporting social movements and protest groups around the globe (Gerbaudo, 2016; Castells, 2013); the influence of non-state actors on debating ethics and rights at all levels of governance – migration, the environment, the rights of cultural and other minorities – in the digital public sphere (Zuckerman, 2013; Karatzogianni, Nguyen & Serafinelli, 2016); and the use of ICTs by terrorist groups and online radicalisation (Conway, 2012).

Within this context, digital citizenship scholarship has revolved around access, commerce, communication, literacy, etiquette, rights and responsibilities, health and wellbeing, security/safety, digital inequalities, data justice, censorship and surveillance, and ICT use in the majority world (Mann et al., 2003; Benjali, Livingstone et al., 2017; Theron, Levine & Ungar, 2020). In terms of CYP, Global Kids Online has produced cross-national evidence based around children's use of the Internet, with particularly significant empirical evidence in regard to the majority world and digital inequalities, for example in relation to ICT use by young girls. However, this project does not particularly focus on ICT and civic participation. The DigiGen project could partially fill this gap potentially

(Continued)

as it investigates digital citizenship in adolescents with a cross-national comparison (DigiGen, n.d.). There are valuable insights regarding the role of political culture and forms of organisation development in relation to digital citizenship, as well as how digital activism and ideologisation processes emerge from a given socio-economic and political context – all issues which are not discussed in general ICT use by children and young adults' literature.

For example, Frau-Meigs (2014: 441) argues that

> citizenship has also led to an increased fight against censorship, to promote transparency and access. The general wellbeing of society has been predicated on media freedoms and rights, especially for voting adults (around 18 years old). This can sometimes run counter to children's expected wellbeing because their early exposure to all sorts of content and mediated conduct can be perceived as inhibiting their own civic agency.

Last, scholars do not yet understand how CYP develop political consciousness and crystallise their ideology, prior to developing theory on how the digital transformations and historical crises interact with this problematic. This is why it would be preferable to discuss ICT and civic participation, rather than use the term digital 'citizenship', as 'citizenship' is by definition based on exclusionary discourses, whilst it presupposes that the 'digital' with which one does 'citizenship' is unproblematic in its affordances, in any given country, and its concomitant historical and political context.

Professor Athina Karatzogianni

University of Leicester (UK)

Digital morality

We argue that an important dimension in the digital citizenship framework is that of digital morality. What we mean by this is digitally mediated morality, in the sense that morality in behaviour and expression is mediated via digital technologies. This is especially important when considering the anonymity that can be afforded online, in much the same way as older social psychology studies illustrated that the wearing of a mask that fully covers the face or some form of disguise can increase the likelihood of people engaging in antisocial behaviour because they cannot be easily identified (*not* the face coverings of mouth and nose required in COVID-19 times). In social psychology this was referred to as *deindividuation theory* (a term coined by Festinger, Pepitone & Newcomb, 1952), as the mask means that observers are unable to attribute the behaviour to the individual because they are hidden (Mann, Newton & Innes, 1982). In the modern world, the behaviour can be individual or in groups, but the core issue is that the screen can hide a person's identity and so means that those behind the screen might behave in ways that they might not if they could be seen (Flores & James, 2013). Thus, morality becomes applied to digital apps as CYP can do things digitally that they might not do in face-to-face environments as the behaviour is one-step removed.

Digital responsibility and morality are central for keeping CYP safe online. This responsibility is broad and involves a range of stakeholders, and these were outlined by Miles (2011) as:

- *Governments* should provide support and funding for research, to promote educational messages and craft reasonable laws, policy and legislation.
- *Law enforcement agencies* have a responsibility to find appropriate ways that tackle the highly sophisticated ways criminals are exploiting online weaknesses.
- *The Internet industry* must provide support for self-regulatory efforts in protecting CYP from the darker side of the Internet. Industry efforts require development of stringent privacy controls and educating their consumers to stay safe.
- *Teachers and educators* need to take responsibility for learning new and rapidly changing technology and find ways to integrate it in positive ways in the classroom.
- *Parents* need to become empowered to know what their children are doing online and how much.
- *CYP* have responsibility to behave in appropriate ways online, to develop resilience and coping strategies, and create a culture of supporting each other.

Amongst all the rhetoric of empowerment and protectionism we must not forget that the CYP are at the centre. Many interactions they are having in digital spaces are between CYP (although some are with adults). Younger populations spend a lot of time interacting with each other, and many of the negative consequences experienced are due to CYP posting or commenting in ways that could cause a reaction in others. One area that does need attention therefore is how adults promote a sense of responsibility and morality in these age groups so that they behave and communicate in ways that are positive.

CYP need to take some responsibility for their own behaviour online. They need to think about what they are posting, what others can see, what images they make public, how they protect their personal information and how they treat others, whether known or unknown. In our own work, this was something that adolescents recognised as they felt that they had a responsibility to use digital media carefully and responsibility; we show some of these perspectives in Figure 5.5.

Of course, protecting CYP online needs to be aligned with children's rights and the need to empower children to explore through the Internet (Huda, Jasmi et al., 2017). Notably, until recently little attention had been paid to children's rights in terms of the Internet and yet children should have opportunities to engage with technology to learn, express themselves and participate in their communities in meaningful ways (Livingstone & O'Neill, 2014). Livingstone (2019b) has led the field in questioning what children's rights might look like in a digital age around the world. She and her collaborators have raised fundamental issues that are relevant for practitioners working with children, including:

- The ways CYP's views can be expressed and accounted for when formulating digital policies.
- The importance of addressing online and offline discrimination to ensure all children have their rights realised in a digital world.
- The role of parents, other caregivers, school personnel.
- The ways in which countries around the world can understand their obligations to children's rights in digital environments.
- The relationship between children's rights in digital contexts in relation to non-digital contexts.

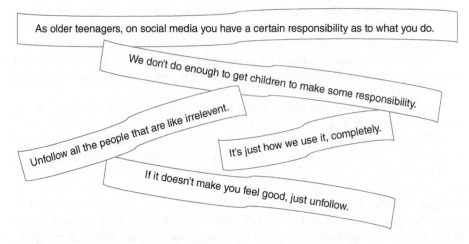

As older teenagers, on social media you have a certain responsibility as to what you do.

We don't do enough to get children to make some responsibility.

Unfollow all the people that are like irrelevent.

It's just how we use it, completely.

If it doesn't make you feel good, just unfollow.

Figure 5.5   CYP's views of responsibility

We encourage you to reflect on your position and try the reflective activity in Box 5.11.

In what ways are these points important when thinking about children's rights in a digital age?

 **Box 5.11: Reflecting on rights**

In terms of your own work with children or young people, take each point and think about its relevance to your organisation.
    Write in your reflective diary your views on each of these bullet points in terms of your own work with CYP.

More broadly in relation to digital technology, there have been efforts to consider what rights individuals might have in terms of acting in CYP's best interests and recognising their evolving capacities, and in Table 5.3 we outline briefly those provided by the Council of Europe (2018).

Table 5.3 Digital rights (Council of Europe, 2018)

Right	Description
Right to non-discrimination	This stipulates that all rights should be granted to the child without discrimination on any grounds.
Right to be heard	All CYP have the right to express themselves in the digital environment and their view should be given due weight.
Right to freedom of expression and information	CYP should be able to express themselves online and to seek and receive information through any media of their choice. High-quality online content should be available that is of social and cultural benefit to CYP. CYP should be encouraged to be active in communication and producing user-generated content.
Right to engage in play, and to assembly and association	The online environment provides opportunity for CYP to participate, engage in play and to peaceful assembly and association. CYP should be encouraged to foster inclusion, digital citizenship and resilience on- and offline. Children should access content appropriate to their age and maturity.
Right to privacy and data protection	CYP have the right to privacy and family life in the digital environment, including the protection of personal data.
Right to education	Opportunities should be offered to realise CYP's rights to education, including a right to digital literacy, educational programmes and resources.
Right to protection and safety	CYP have the right to be protected from violence, exploitation and abuse online.

It is also important that CYP can understand the risks they might face and have strategies to protect themselves by managing any negative things that might happen to them online (Edwards, 2018b). The very idea of responsibility and morality in on- and offline spaces is important for society, and responsibility can be thought of from different perspectives. Empathy is especially important for children in digital spaces, because online communication has limited social cues for children or young people to know how their communication is being interpreted or received (Ohler, 2011).

Highlighted point!

Empathy is the ability of the individual to share and understand the feelings of others.

In integrating empathy, children's rights, moral development and digital technology, we coined the concept of a 'digital ethics of care' (see O'Reilly, Levine & Law, 2020).

Digital ethics of care

The conceptualisation of a *digital ethics of care* is founded on the moral philosophy of an 'ethics of care', which is an alternative way of viewing morality from traditional ideas about rules or principles to guide behaviour (O'Reilly et al., 2020). The traditional ethics of care emphasises ethical relationships and sees morality as a central feature of social interaction, as something that occurs within and between persons. Ethical philosophers argue that empathy is central and responsible behaviour is possible because of the human capacity for empathy, and therefore any contemporary ethics approach must deal with the obligations that individuals have toward others, especially those or are suffering or endangered (Slote, 2007). Furthermore, ethics are closely connected with respect, which involves an openness to difference, tolerance of others and civility, and respect and disrespect are directly observable in CYP (James, 2009). Thus, the ethics of care position sees the individual as a moral agent who analytically addresses their relationships and considers the harms that they may inflict on others (Petterson, 2011). There were four elements to an ethics of care philosophy proposed by Tronto (2005), and we outline these in Table 5.4.

Table 5.4   Elements of the ethics of care philosophy (Tronto, 2005)

Element	Description
Attentiveness	This is where the individual attends to the needs of others and recognises what those needs are, so they can respond appropriately.
Responsibility	To be able to care for others, the individual needs to take responsibility, which links to obligation. Obligation is tied to pre-established societal and cultural norms. There is a relationship between obligation and responsibility.
Competence	To care for others means the individual must be competent to do so.
Responsiveness	Responsiveness means that the individual recognises the moral problem and is concerned to respond to conditions of vulnerability and inequality. Responsiveness is a method whereby inequality and the vulnerability in others is understood.

The ethics of care was developed primarily as a criticism of the idea that children develop their morality in stages as proposed by Kohlberg (1969) (see Chapter 1). It was argued in a seminal book by Gilligan (1982) that the staged view of morality was gender biased, and although men and women treat moral problems in different ways, neither is superior. This way of thinking is therefore gender neutral, as the moral approach is not based on principles or rules, but moral judgements are aligned with specific situations (Klaver, van Elst & Baart, 2014).

In Box 5.12 we provide some practical advice for promoting the positive aspects of digital and social media, which accounts for digital citizenship, digital morality and a digital ethics of care.

Box 5.12: Practical tips for promoting the positive aspects of digital and social media

- Spend time with the child or young person online together, encouraging them to explore.
- Discuss age restrictions with them and explain why it is important that they do not set up social media profiles when they are too young.
- Talk to them about the importance of being kind to themselves and others online.
- Teach them about the persistence of data online – it is close to impossible to remove online content once it has been uploaded. Encourage thinking about the long-term implications of having different types of content associated with them. Think about using phrases such as 'digital footprint' and 'digital identity'. What kind of digital footprint would the young person like to be associated with them in the long term?
- Guide them to think about how they can stay safe online. Provide them with good quality online safety information, avoiding moral panics.
- Progressively build trust as they grow older and more digitally competent, proving to you their capability and sense of safety.
- Encourage them to talk to you (or another trusted adult) if something upsets them on- or offline, so they have a trusted adult to go to if needed.
- Encourage them to explore and learn online and incorporate technology into their lives.
- Teach them how to spot the physical and mental signs that they are using digital technologies too much and to recognise any distress or discomfort they might feel.

Conclusions

We have shown in this chapter that there is great potential for CYP to use digital technology and social media in positive ways. In completing this chapter, we provide a reflective piece about the positive aspects of digital media for CYP from an expert in this field. In Box 5.13 we present the perspective of Professor Patti Valkenburg, who has been undertaking research in this area for many years.

Box 5.13: Expert contribution: Professor Patti Valkenburg

Role: Distinguished Professor

Organisation: University of Amsterdam

Brief bio: Professor Patti Valkenburg's's research interests include the cognitive, emotional and social effects of media and technologies on children, adolescents and adults. She is a fellow of the International Communication Association, the American Psychological Society, and the Royal Dutch Academy of Sciences. She is the author of 150+ academic articles and eight books. Her latest book 'Plugged In' was published in 2017 by Yale University Press.

The good, bad and ugly effects of digital media differ from adolescent to adolescent

The discussion in this book about the impact of digital media use on mental health is divided across three chapters that together discuss the 'good', the 'bad' and the 'ugly' effects of digital media on adolescents' mental health. As these chapters show, a growing number of studies have investigated these three effects of digital media, often with mixed results. Some of these studies have reported small beneficial effects of digital media on mental health, others have yielded small harmful effects, and yet others no effects whatsoever. Do these small and inconsistent effects found in these studies mean that we do not have to worry about the mental health effects of digital media, and that we can advise parents, policy makers and journalists accordingly?

In my view, such a stance would be premature; there are still too many gaps in the research literature to allow for decisive conclusions about the effects of digital media on youth. One crucial gap is that we still do not know how different online behaviours and experiences influence adolescents' mental health. Most studies have focused solely on the effects of the time adolescents spend with digital media (Odgers & Jensen, 2020). However, a growing number of researchers agree that measuring 'screen time' is too crude to yield valid results about the true effects of digital media (Prinstein, Nesi & Telzer, 2020). A sole focus on screen time may overlook online behaviours and experiences that may lead to opposite mental health effects. For example, adolescents' exchange of supportive information with their best friends should lead to quite different effects on their wellbeing than their exchange of harmful communication, as typically occurs in cyberbullying. Likewise, exchanging sexual messages between romantic partners may benefit adolescents' identity development, but when such sexual messages are distributed to the wider circle of peers without consent, they will have seriously harmful effects.

Another gap in the literature on digital media and mental health is that only a few studies have focused on differences in susceptibility to the effects of digital media use (Valkenburg & Peter, 2013). Just consider the two quotes below that were made in a qualitative study by Rideout and Fox (2018) on teens' online experiences:

> 'I like to look at what my friends are doing. It makes me happy to see them being happy.' (16 year old male)

> 'I scroll through feeds of everyone having fun with each other while I'm stuck at home doing nothing about it.' (15 year old male)

These quotes from two boys in middle adolescence reveal that the first boy gets happy to see his peers being happy online, whereas the second boy gets gloomy after the same experience. So, the 'good' holds for the first boy, while the 'bad' holds for the second. In one of our studies we indeed found that some adolescents get inspired when they compare themselves to others online, whereas others get envious when doing so (van Driel, Pouwels et al., 2019). Despite such telling individual differences shown in the study of Rideout and Fox (2018) and other qualitative studies, too few effect studies of digital media, including the ones discussed in this book, have investigated how CYP differ in their susceptibility to the effects of digital media. In one of our recent studies we have tried to quantify these individual differences. We found that about 17% of adolescents felt better after using social media, 9% felt worse, while the remaining majority of 74% experienced no effects at all (Beyens, Pouwels et al., 2020).

Our study supports the assumption that the effects that have been reported in earlier digital media research are small just because they are diluted across an immensely heterogeneous population of adolescents. This also aligns with anecdotal observations of parents that some of their children are highly vulnerable to certain media experiences, while others are not (or less) so. The findings of our study underscore the importance for future studies to explore individual susceptibility to digital media effects. After all, if we really want to understand the good, bad and ugly effects of digital media use on CYP, we first need to acknowledge that each individual child and adolescent is unique in their sensitivity to media effects.

6

EXPLORING THE POTENTIAL RISKS TO MENTAL HEALTH

THE RHETORIC OF 'THE BAD'

Learning points

After reading this chapter, you will be able to:

- Explain some of the challenges to mental health
- Critically assess the factors associated with fear of missing out (FOMO), impact on sleep and possible disconnection from society
- Recognise the risks associated with harmful content

Introduction

The research available examining the relationship between digital media and mental health in CYP has illustrated that there are some negative impacts and issues that warrant consideration. These negative, or as they are more typically framed 'bad' aspects of digital media can potentially lead to effects on self-esteem, upset the young person to some extent, or compromise their relationships, communication skills and/or safety (see O'Reilly, 2020). These issues are more day-to-day, commonly experienced issues and the impact tends to be less extreme than some other effects. We consider those more significant aspects in the next two chapters, where we consider the 'ugly' (as they are rhetorically constructed) elements. For the sake of division within the book, however, separating the bad and the ugly serves as a pragmatic way of breaking down the issues into chapters, but it is important to remember that they overlap and there is not a clear-cut differentiation between what is positioned as 'bad' and what is positioned as 'ugly', as some of the 'bad' when more extreme can become 'ugly'.

Highlighted point!

As we noted in the previous chapter, we are not endorsing the view that social media have inherent or deterministic qualities in either direction. Rather, we are acknowledging that there are aspects of digital and social media that are rhetorically positioned discursively as 'bad'.

The focus of this chapter is to unpack some of these general potentially negative effects of digital media use on mental health and explore how they might affect CYP in different ways. We consider the variable possible impacts on CYP's self-esteem, self-identity, communication skills, emotions, along with possible other harms. We outline some of the arguments that have connected such negative issues to digital content. These areas of CYP's lives are important as we seek to promote their wellbeing and rights, while still protecting them (and helping them to protect themselves) from harm. Indeed, one of the concerns we have raised is the general argument that some groups are more susceptible to the possible mental health harms associated with digital media use and some are more susceptible to taking greater risks than others online which *could* (but not necessarily) lead to a greater potential for harm. Before we consider the susceptibility of some CYP over others, we invite you to think about those you work with and consider who is more 'at risk' from the possible 'bad' side of digital media by undertaking the reflective activity in Box 6.1.

Which CYP are more susceptible to harm?

In the previous chapter we illustrated that our consultation groups reflected on how digital and social media influenced their mental health and wellbeing in positive ways. The same young people (aged 16–18 years) also reflected on the negative impacts that social media could (or in some cases did) have on

Box 6.1: Reflecting on susceptibility to harm

Thinking of the CYP you work with, who are those that you feel are most likely to take risks online and why? What impact might these risks have on those CYP?

In your reflective diary think about the CYP you work with. Consider what characteristics some of them have that may make them more susceptible to any negative effects of digital media in terms of their mental wellbeing. Think about where your perspectives of those characteristics are coming from. Check for unconscious bias.

their mental health. They created a board with a heading The Bad and put sticky notes on there with statements about what they considered 'bad'. We illustrate the participatory activity of sticky notes in Figure 6.1.

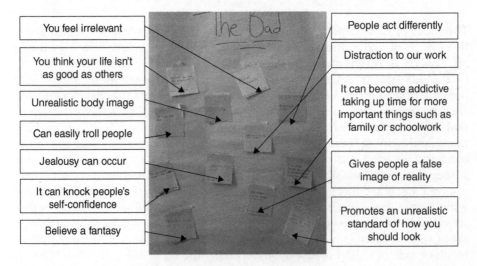

Figure 6.1 The bad side of social media

Rose (aged 16 years) noted that a challenge of social media is that *you think your life isn't as good as others.* Tristan (aged 16 years) argued that *jealousy can occur.* Thus, both young people recognise that the lives that others are portraying on social media can lead to negative feelings. Rhiannon (aged 16 years) argued that engaging with social media on a regular basis can make young people feel *irrelevant,* while Blaine (aged 16 years) noted that social media sometimes present a *false image of reality.* To summarise then, the young people in our consultation groups recognised and reported that there were aspects of engaging in social media that could influence them negatively and might lead to negative impacts on mental health. They noted that there were occasions when this had happened to them, as they had experienced lowering of self-esteem from negative online comments and had directly experienced jealousy when using Instagram and seeing others' positive lives.

Vulnerability and susceptibility to the 'bad'

In Chapter 4 we introduced you to the evidence and tensions about conceptualising CYP as vulnerable and indicated some circumstances when certain types of vulnerability might be important online. When CYP use digital media there are possibilities that they will be exposed to or take different types of risk. In Chapter 4 we showed the four Cs (see Table 4.3) used to characterise those different types of risk as content, contact, conduct (Livingstone et al., 2015). The nature of these risks, the extent of them, and the impact or potential for harm related to them is variable according to the child, their context, their vulnerability, their resilience and their support systems amongst other things. Indeed, research indicates that most CYP are not especially or frequently bothered by online risky experiences and most are able to respond to possible impact in positive and/or proactive ways to mitigate or manage those risks and attend to potential psychological impact (Livingstone, Haddon et al., 2011). However, there are some who are impacted more deeply or may have greater difficulties when adopting effective coping strategies and, as a result, their mental wellbeing is more severely affected by the risk and/or harm resulting from it (d'Haenens et al., 2013).

Some of the literature approaches risk predominantly from a developmental perspective. One argument put forward is that younger children are less well-equipped to handle digitally mediated risks than their older peers when exposed to or taking risks in the digital environment, particularly those children aged 12 years or younger. In other words, because of their age and cognitive maturity they may become more upset when things go wrong or when their friends or peers misuse their online profiles (Holloway, 2013) and the younger they are, the more likely they are to be upset. Younger children can consider it challenging to find age-appropriate content and lack the skills to cope with adversities online (Livingstone et al., 2014), and thus, as they grow older, their level of digital literacy improves, although consequently, they are more likely to become exposed to a greater volume of risk (Livingstone, Haddon et al., 2011) and they are more likely to do so with less or no adult supervision. See Chapter 1 where we outlined the developmental differences across ages. We also encourage you to recognise that many developmental studies are focused on CYP in the minority world. As a result, we need to ask ourselves some difficult questions about the contexts in which CYP are operating, and what makes one person more vulnerable than another at any point in time. It is therefore important to consider how factors such as risk interplay with mitigating factors such as support. The overall picture for each child will differ as risk and protective factors will interact within the context for that child.

There are groups that may be especially vulnerable to the possible negative effects of digital media. We remind you that the notion of vulnerability is contentious, and that it is fluid rather than fixed. In considering these groups frequently constructed as vulnerable, we refer you to Chapter 4 where we first critically assessed this concept. However, in the literature, some groups of children are certainly positioned as being more vulnerable than others. These are populations who have faced adversity or multiple adversities, or because of certain personal characteristics may not have the cognitive, social or emotional maturity to handle digital risks as competently. For example (this is not an exhaustive list):

- Looked-after children (those in care; fostered, adopted or in residential care).
- Children with mental health conditions.
- Children with disabilities or other forms of special educational needs or intellectual disabilities.
- Children who have experienced trauma.
- Children who have experienced domestic violence or abuse.
- Refugee children.

In other words, CYP who are struggling in some way in their day-to-day lives are more likely to have online experiences that are negative (George & Odgers, 2015). The harm experienced online by those who are already vulnerable tends to be of greater severity than harm experienced by their peers (Hinduja & Patchin, 2008). This can be explained, at least in part, by the resilience pathways and processes available to those in vulnerable groups. We need to reflect on whether they have access to adequate support structures, and/or the coping strategies and/or the resources needed to manage the challenges they experience because of vulnerability characteristics. Alternatively, it may be that these CYP have faced or are facing multiple adversities which means they are managing many other things, leaving them unable to cope with additional issues from the digitally mediated world. Because they are already vulnerable in their offline environments, they are more likely to receive negative feedback through digital media and are more likely to experience challenges in regulating their internet use (Koutamis, Vossen & Valkenburg, 2015; Underwood & Ehrenreich, 2017).

Highlighted point!

Some children who are vulnerable (offline) do not have the advantage of parental or carer advice for staying safe online and may lack the closeness of personal relationships which may lead them to seek compensatory support from the Internet (Livingstone et al., 2005).

It may be obvious that the greater the vulnerability and the more extensive the adversities experienced, the greater likelihood of CYP being impacted by negative experiences online and the greater the consequences to their mental health. However, while this may be the case for some, adversity and vulnerability do not *necessarily* mean that these CYP will be harmed, will have their mental health negatively impacted or that they will take greater risks, as for some the use of digital media can be beneficial (as we showed in the previous chapter). An example of this is children who have experienced trauma, and we asked an expert in this field, Dr Nikki Kiyimba, for her perspective for this vulnerable group, outlined in Box 6.22.

Box 6.2: Expert voice: Dr Nikki Kiyimba

Children experiencing trauma and digital media

One impact of digital media images, websites and social media on how traumatic events might affect CYP is the greater accessibility of trauma images and stories than was previously possible. Before the widespread availability of digital media, only those in close physical proximity to traumatic events would be affected. Now images are relayed within seconds, and the impact of global catastrophes and atrocities is more immediate, more widespread and less controlled. Potentially this globalisation of trauma may lead to a concerning 'desensitisation' of CYP to shocking events, or to a perpetual 'overload' of stress responses. Furthermore, social media are known to be used by some CYP to engage in cyberbullying. As a readily accessible platform for capturing and sharing images and posts, the possibility for CYP to use this medium to harm others is well known.

However, despite the well-founded concerns around CYP's engagement with digital media, there are benefits that can be utilised to support those therapeutically who have experienced trauma to aid their recovery and healing. For example, social media may be used to foster or maintain healthy age-appropriate social connections, which can be a great source of support and resilience for a child in the aftermath of trauma.

Additionally, trauma-focused software programmes can now be accessed online, meaning that CYP in rural or inaccessible locations can receive treatment such as web-based trauma-focused cognitive behavioural therapy. Similarly encrypted tele-health platforms also provide further possibilities for CYP to access therapy with a trained professional from their own homes.

Evidently, digital media present opportunities for those who have experienced trauma, and while the potential for negative impact remains a concern for practitioners, it is important to embrace the value that some digital media provide.

(Continued)

The world is now a different place and we can find ways to move forward to support those CYP who need it.

Dr Nikki Kiyimba

Clinical Psychologist and Senior Educator

Bethlehem Tertiary Institute (New Zealand)

Exposure to risk is a normal part of life, and managing risk and dealing with harm are important for learning coping skills (Smith & Carlson, 1997). One study framed this through the metaphor of orchids and dandelions, whereby orchid and dandelion children evolve in ways that reflect the continuum of susceptibility (Boyce & Ellis, 2005). Boyce and Ellis explained that like delicate flowers (e.g. orchids), most CYP will develop positively or thrive when they are placed in conditions of support but decline when in conditions of neglect. Others (e.g. dandelions) can thrive across a range of environments and thus the negative consequences do not *necessarily* or *absolutely* follow as they have other factors at play. We argue that in adopting this metaphor we must remember that it is not the responsibility of the CYP to survive and thrive, but it is the systems around them that create the conditions to enable them to do so. Therefore it is the ecosystem, not the individual, that enables thriving or encourages decline.

In accounting for different aspects of the ecosystem it is important to bear in mind that there are different elements that need to be considered. In terms of susceptibility to psychological harm when online there are different types of susceptibility, which were outlined by Valkenburg and Peter (2013) as:

- *Dispositional susceptibility*, which relates to the dimensions of the child that may predispose them to selecting or responding to media, such as gender, personality, beliefs, values, temperament, genetics, attitudes, moods and motivations. Some of these become stable across time (e.g. temperament), whereas others are more transient (e.g. mood).
- *Developmental susceptibility*, which relates to the use of media and the individual's responsiveness to it as related to their cognitive, social and emotional development.
- *Social susceptibility*, which relates to the social-context factors that may influence the CYP's use of media and their responses to media, including the micro-level contexts of peers/friends, institutional contexts including work or school, and societal aspects such as cultural norms and values. Thus, the systems around the CYP will be influential on their online use and their responses to it.

In discussing these various forms of susceptibility in terms of CYP's use of digital media, Valkenburg and Peter (2013) created a model to explain this and we outline this in Box 6.3.

Box 6.3: Key research evidence

Susceptibility model (Valkenburg and Peter, 2013)

Valkenburg and Peter (2013) created the differential susceptibility to media-effects model (DSMM). This model was a theoretical one created to explain why some CYP are more susceptible to the effects of digital media than others. This model had several propositions, but three key ones are:

1. The effects of media are conditional and depend on the three susceptibility types referred to earlier (dispositional, developmental and social). In other words, the impact, and any possible negative effects on the CYP, depend on the individual and their personality, intellect, temperament and so forth, the level of developmental maturity, and the social environmental systems around them.
2. The effects of media are indirect, in the sense that they are moderated by the three response states (cognitive, emotional and excitative). In other words, it is not the case that engaging in digital media directly causes a negative impact on the CYP.
3. Differential susceptibility variables have two different roles in the media effect process: they act as a predictor of media use; and they act as a moderator of the effects of it. In other words, it is argued that the effects of the environment on the outcomes of CYP are moderated by temperament in ways that can either be advantageous or maladaptive. Thus, some CYP are more susceptible to negative influences in the environment, but equally may receive greater benefit from positive influence.

In terms of proposition 1, media effects are conditions in the sense that they are dependent on the dispositional, developmental and social susceptibility variables, and these exert a moderating influence but also assert an interactive moderating function.

In terms of proposition 2, media effects are indirect. In other words, the effects of media are mediated by the emotional, cognitive and excitative response states of the individual engaging with it and thus are the route to media effects. The examples given by Valkenburg and Peter were that cognitive response relates to attention to, retention of and absorption of content as well as how they process that information. Additionally, emotional states are those reactions to media messages and characters such as sadness, anxiety and happiness. Excitative response state refers to the physiological arousal experienced by that person in response to the content.

In terms of proposition 3, different susceptibility variables have multiple roles, and the three types of differential susceptibility (dispositional, developmental and social) have two conceptual roles. First, they predict the selection of media and exposure to it. Second, they stimulate or reduce the influence that media might have by influencing how they respond to it.

Fear of missing out

The fear of missing out (FOMO) can drive some CYP (and adults) to attempts to be constantly connected via digital devices, even at times that are not entirely appropriate. FOMO is quite a new concept where the individual is reluctant to miss out on important information or social events from others in their social network (Przybylski, Murayama et al., 2013). FOMO is when an individual believes or perceives that others are having more fun than they are, or living better lives, and is the general feeling that they are missing out on something especially important that is being experienced by others. Interestingly, the FOMO has become an entry into the dictionary and is defined by the Oxford English Dictionary as a feeling of anxiety experienced by an individual when they believe that an exciting or interesting event may be happening somewhere else, often a feeling aroused by seeing posts on social media (Oxford English Dictionary, n.d.). Thus, FOMO is an apprehension that others might have rewarding experiences without involving the individual and therefore the individual tries to stay constantly connected to what others are doing (Przybylski et al., 2013) and individuals need instant gratification (Turkle, 2011).

This FOMO can lead CYP to feel under pressure to check their social media constantly. In other words, the constant checking of social media is a compulsivity to stay updated with online platforms (Stephen & Edmonds, 2018), and this compulsivity leads to much higher levels of social media engagement, which can consequently increase FOMO (Glazzard & Mitchell, 2018). One study by Damjanovic and Dayman (2015) showed that this FOMO is a pervasive phenomenon amongst adolescents, and we describe this in Box 6.4.

 **Box 6.4: Key research evidence**

Research study on FOMO

Damjanovic and Dayman (2015) reporting on the fifth annual National Stress and Wellbeing Australia survey found that Australians had higher levels of stress, depression and anxiety by the end of the study and this was related to FOMO. Their key statistics were that:

- 66% of adolescents wanted to share their details online when they were having a good time.
- 60% were worried when they found out that their friends were having fun without them.
- 51% experienced anxiety if they did not know what their friends were doing.
- 78% thought it was important for them to understand their friends' 'in-jokes' (a joke only understood by those in that group).

Overall, the study showed that adolescents were worried they were having fewer rewarding experiences than their friends and felt anxious when they thought they might be missing out on something.

FOMO can be problematic as it involves negative expectancies and cognitions that can play a role in problematic internet use (Wegmann & Brand, 2016). The fundamentally social aspect of FOMO means that CYP may be susceptible to negative impacts on their wellbeing. Thus, adolescents who score high on FOMO report more negative mood states and this can also make social anxiety worse, including negative mental health outcomes (Milyavskaya, Saffran et al., 2018). For example, Turkle (2011) argued that FOMO is associated with lower mood and life satisfaction, higher levels of social media engagement, and in adults can lead to behaviours like distracted driving or social media use when they should be focusing on something else, like a university lecture or work task. Furthermore, FOMO can increase stress and lead to reduced sleep (Milyavskaya et al., 2018). This link to sleep is especially problematic, as biologically and psychologically sleep is very important for CYP and is a well-known correlate to poor mental health. In a study by Scott and Woods (2018) of adolescents aged 12–18 years, they showed that going onto social media at night was associated with later bedtimes, increased pre-sleep cognitive arousal and shorter sleep duration, and this was associated with FOMO for some CYP and therefore it is necessary to tackle this.

Impact on sleep

FOMO is not the only aspect of digital media that relates to sleep and, more broadly, the impact on CYP's mental health as connected to sleep, and it is important to explore this further. On average, adolescents need between 8.5 and 10 hours of sleep each night, but the majority get less than 7 hours per night (Emsellem, Knutson et al., 2014). As noted, poor sleep quality contributes to poor mental health, and can increase anxiety, depression and low self-esteem (Alfano, Zakem et al., 2009), and this is one area that does have compelling evidence of a negative effect on CYP (see Hale & Guan, 2015 for a review). This is especially problematic, as older research indicates that as many as 80% of adolescents who own a mobile phone sleep with it (Lenhart, Ling et al., 2010), with 90% using social media day and night (Duggan & Smith, 2013). Furthermore, one-quarter of children reporting missing meals or sleep because of the time they spent on the Internet (Livingstone et al., 2014) (e.g. see Figure 6.2).

The young people in our own study also recognised that sleep was an issue. Importantly, however, they kept their phones close by at night and, despite recognising that it was problematic, still allowed their phone to disturb or impact their sleep, as shown in Figure 6.3.

Figure 6.2 Digital media and sleep

> *You know when you get a message, you just want to open it and I think a lot of people like, I mean, late at night I think it's kind of it keeps me awake at night.*

> *So then I'm tired the next day. It kind of affects your concentration, I think.*

> *I had an experience of that with WhatsApp where lots of people were messaging at the time, I'd go to sleep at about 10 o'clock at night and then I felt the need, even when there was no one messaging me just to keep checking and it did affect my sleep.*

Figure 6.3 The effect of digital media on sleep

Because of the way social media function, there is a likelihood that sleep will be disturbed unless the individual takes active steps to prevent it. Some phones have various functions to prevent the noise and light from notifications from occurring, but these must be activated by the individual. Of course, very simply, one option is to turn off the phone during night-time hours. If such an action is not taken, then the individual may receive incoming alerts during the night, and this may disturb sleep. Consequently, this leads to poor sleep quality. Indeed, there is much evidence that demonstrates that an increased use of digital media (and social media especially) is associated with poor sleep quality for adolescents (e.g. Scott, Gardani et al., 2016).

Poor sleep quality is an important area to consider, especially when caused by checking social media and/or the phone through the night because, as we have reiterated in this section, poor sleep is associated with higher levels of anxiety and depression, as well as lowered self-esteem (Woods and Scott, 2016). George and Odgers (2015) identified three pathways through which this occurs, described in Table 6.1.

Table 6.1   Pathways for impaired sleep (George & Odgers, 2015)

Pathway	Description
Displacement	Digital media, social media and screen time can displace sleep time for CYP.
Emotion	Digital media and/or online interactions can lead to emotional arousal and this can make it more challenging for the child or young person to fall asleep and to stay asleep.
Melatonin stimulation	The bright lights from the screen, or the electromagnetic radiation from mobile phones, can disturb melatonin activity and sleep rhythms.

Although we can be confident that poor sleep quality is linked to poor mental health, and that use of digital media during the night can lead to poor sleep quality, we still need to understand this relationship better. As noted,

> [a]s adolescents' lives become increasingly wired, it will also be important to understand how the use of multiple devices and modes of communication interfere with sleep and what can be done to offset these effects (George & Odgers, 2015: 845)

With respect to both FOMO and sleep, adults may need to think about the role models they provide. If parents are always on social media and take their phones to bed, it is difficult to expect CYP to do otherwise. It may be useful for the whole family to leave their phones away from sleeping spaces. This may, however, be practically difficult as families increasingly rely on mobile phones rather than landlines and use functionality on the phone for things they need, like an alarm clock for waking.

Self-esteem

Self-esteem can be fragile, especially in CYP. Adolescents especially are developing their confidence and a sense of who they are. Self-esteem is particularly important to keep them psychologically healthy and therefore behaviour that risks damaging self-esteem can be highly problematic. There are ways in which using social media and other forms of digital devices can impact positively on self-esteem, although some types of use can decrease self-esteem (Griffiths, 2014).

Studies have found that more frequent digital media use is also related to lower self-esteem (Vogel, Rose, Roberts, & Eckles, 2014). This could be explained by the fact that receiving negative feedback and engaging in upward social comparisons through digital media would help decrease self-esteem in adolescents (Vogel et al., 2014). In this sense, it could be argued that the association between overall digital media and lower self-esteem might simply reflect an increased exposure to the carefully constructed profiles of others that are deliberately designed to emphasise their positive characteristics (Gonzales & Hancock, 2011), and the consequences of this can be a diminishing of the young person's feelings of their own self-worth (Woods & Scott, 2016). Therefore, if greater emotional investment in digital media, especially social media engagement, is associated with lower self-esteem, this would suggest that adolescents who feel a strong emotional connection to social media sites would be most at risk because these highly invested individuals may be more vulnerable to upward social comparisons and negative feedback through social media as suggested by previous studies (Vogel et al., 2014).

Recent work has shown that in 18–24 year olds there has been an increase in the number of girls who are dissatisfied with their body, with 70% who would consider cosmetic surgery (Royal Society for Public Health, 2017). In a UK survey of young women aged 11–21 years, there were concerns about the effect of social media specifically on self-esteem: 55% felt that it should not be permitted to advertise plastic surgery or diet pills via online or social media platforms; 52% believed that if an image had been airbrushed or altered there should be a label to identify it as such; and 46% felt they had to remind themselves that social media are not a reflection of reality (Girlguiding, 2019a). Furthermore, with the rise of celebrity culture, there has been a rise in the volume of selfies being taken and an increased use of photoshop (Frith, 2017b).

Highlighted point!

The rise of smartphone cameras, online filters and image-manipulation techniques, and the abundance of idealised images of beauty portrayed over social networks has increased the pressure to conform to beauty standards (Frith, 2017b).

This increased pressure to conform to beauty standards is perpetuated online, and this can encourage harmful behaviours and negatively impact on self-esteem (Royal Society for Public Health, 2019). It is important, therefore, to make CYP aware that what they see online is not always a true reflection of reality. It is also important to support them so that they can feel comfortable and satisfied with themselves and their bodies.

Risks of isolation, disconnection from society and breakdown of relationships

One frequent argument is that digital media – and social media especially – are leading to the breakdown of social, personal and familial relationships. The rhetoric claims that CYP are increasingly becoming disconnected from their physical spaces and face-to-face relating as they turn instead to communicating via digital technologies. Particularly strong advocates of this polemic claim that we are hurtling toward an isolated society whereby they become disconnected from people and their families. For example, Turkle (2011) argued via analysing a set of case studies that new technologies were interfering with people's ability to communicate effectively as they chose to interact via the phone rather than face to face. Turkle characterised these young people as being *alone together*, claiming they are missing out on important socialisation experiences. This rhetoric is something that is readily repeated by parents and practitioners working with CYP. For example, parents often worry that the constant use of mobile phones by their teenage offspring is preventing them from effectively communicating with each other (George & Odgers, 2015).

Highlighted point!

Despite the concerns, there is little evidence that shows that the time adolescents spend online displaces face-to-face interaction with their parents, and moderate technology use does not predict a declining parent–child relationship quality (Williams and Merten, 2011).

Although the concerns raised by parents, professionals and certain scholars are frequently expressed through different outlets, it is important to examine the evidence. In the previous chapter we highlighted that we are writing this book at the time of the COVID-19 crisis, and we have seen the positive side of technology for connectivity in a time of social isolation and social distancing, as mediums like WhatsApp, Skype, Zoom, Teams, Facetime and other digital media have provided ways for CYP to stay connected to extended family members and friends. You need to decide about the validity of the negative rhetoric by exploring research and thinking reflectively about the opinions, experiences and concerns of those who place the best interests of CYP at the centre of their work. To help you critically consider this perspective we encourage you to try the reflective activity in Box 6.5.

What are your views on the idea that CYP are increasingly disconnected in their personal relationships?

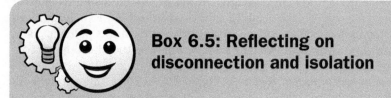

Box 6.5: Reflecting on disconnection and isolation

To what extent do you agree or disagree that digital media are leading to a disconnection of CYP from society?

In your reflective diary reflect on your personal view of this issue, but really think about why, and, where possible, write down examples.

It is argued that there is little rationale for the assumption that serious irrevocable disconnections are happening between young people and society, or young people and their families (Selwyn, 2009). Nonetheless, as responsible adults, we must remember that face-to-face connections are crucial for positive mental health and there are some CYP who struggle to form friendships and may turn to digital relations instead (Glazzard & Mitchell, 2018). They could become more vulnerable online and it is important that adults recognise who those children are and promote positive use of digital media and online safety.

Harmful content and online negative experiences

The Internet is full of content: videos, images, films, text, news and so on. It is perhaps unsurprising that sometimes CYP click on a link that leads them to witness something that they find upsetting. Of course, just because this content upsets one child does not mean that it will upset another, and just because the content upsets them does not necessarily mean that it will be harmful or long-lasting. However, this exposure to potentially harmful content can have some impact. This may range from mild discomfort or embarrassment, or may be more persistent and long-lasting or may feel traumatic. The nature of the content, their age, their personal experiences and resilience (individual and social – see Chapter 4) will play a role in this. This is especially important as we must remember that some of the upsetting content that CYP are exposed to is created by CYP themselves.

Smahel et al. (2020) described six different types of harmful content, with some user-generated and some professional or presented by various media that were considered to be the most problematic for CYP:

1. Hate messages.
2. Gory or violent images.
3. Content suggesting ways to be very thin.
4. Content describing experiences related to taking substances.
5. Content showing ways to physically harm the self.
6. Content illustrating ways of dying by suicide.

In this study, they asked CYP about their negative online experiences in broad terms related to the past year as to whether anything bothered them or upset them in some way, and respondents described many different experiences like being exposed to online sexual or aggressive content, harassment and bullying, hacking, shared personal information, reputational damage, viruses, spam and advertisements. Smahel et al. (2020) described therefore that some CYP reported serious problems with significant negative impact (like cyberbullying) and others, problems that had little negative impact, like technical problems.

Being exposed to harmful content via digital media is something that CYP regularly face when online. Statistics suggest that 15% of UK 9–16 year olds reported being bothered, feeling uncomfortable or upset by something seen online (Livingstone et al., 2014). In Europe, the latest EU Kids Online research (Smahel et al., 2020) shows similar trends among 12–16 year olds.

Digital stress

Harmful or upsetting content, and certain kinds of digital experiences, can lead to digital stress. In other words, the experience of being upset by something online can leave the CYP feeling stressed. In a study of 648 personal accounts of adolescents, for example, Weinstein and Selman (2014) identified six dominant digital stressors and we describe these in Table 6.2.

Table 6.2 Six digital stressors (Weinstein & Selman, 2014)

Digital stressor	Description
Impersonation	Impersonation involves an individual masking their identity in the digital world. The purpose of impersonation tends to be to slander, mock or embarrass the individual being impersonated. This tended to function through hacking or through fake accounts.
Receiving mean and harassing personal attacks	This is when individuals or groups use social media platforms to send unwanted messages and personal attacks to another.
Public shaming and humiliation	While personal attacks are typically directly messaged to another and done so privately, public shaming operates in the public domain and usually involves humiliating messages.

(Continued)

Table 6.2 (Continued)

Digital stressor	Description
Breaking and entering accounts and devices	Breaking and entering is when a young person logs into the online account of another or looks through their digital devices without consent. This tends to take one of two forms. First is curating contact lists, which is the practice of searching through another person's digital address book or contacts and editing or deleting them. Second is reading and sending messages. This reading is intended to do harm rather than simply gaining access.
Pressure to comply with requests for access	A pressure to comply means that there is a stress related to managing requests for access to accounts or digital images when the request is from someone close to the individual. This often occurs in romantic relationships.
Feeling smothered	Some CYP feel a pressure to have constant access to others, and even close others can lead to feeling smothered.

Weinstein and Selman (2014) noted that these digital stressors were viewed as stressful and problematic by CYP. They argued that the first three stressors are fundamentally a product of cruelty and meanness moving online. This includes the reciprocal relational conflict as proposed by Marwick and boyd (2011), as well as more explicit incidents of violence such as cyberbullying (discussed in the next chapter) as characterised by power and asymmetry. Weinstein and Selman argued that these three components constitute Type 1 digital stress, which is fundamentally an expression of relational hostility. The remaining three digital stressors are not stressful because of the content per se, but more because of peer relationships. This Type 2 digital stress therefore flows from the reality of adolescents' use of technology as driven principally by a desire to communicate with others (see e.g. boyd, 2014). Type 2 stress thus stems from the challenges that adolescents face in navigating connections, closeness and intimacy online.

The challenge then for CYP is that they are living in a world with new outlets that lead to or contribute to their stress and distress, but also one where they have platforms to express their emotional states and share with others who have similar concerns. While we discuss this emotional expression in the next chapters, not all emotional expression is significant or severe. It is important to note, though, that not all support-seeking and emotional expression is viewed as positive, and often these kinds of posts are viewed as attention seeking. Indeed, as our language evolves in relation to digital media, we are seeing new terms all the time.

An example of a relatively new concept that has entered popular discourse is that of *sadfishing*. Sadfishing, put simply, is when an individual puts up a post about an emotional state or problem in a bid to attract attention, sympathy or to gain an audience in the number of likes or viewers. It was a concept proposed by Reid (2019), where in an internet post she argued that after viewing a teaser campaign of Kendall Jenner she saw the Internet go 'bonkers'.

Yet, the ultimate posts of Jenner were eventually disappointing and did not reflect the hype or media hysteria. Reid argued that sadfishers maximise the drama to try to create engagement on social media, and noted that it is not a judgemental term for those who are genuinely being open about their mental health challenges in public forums. However, she notes that it is important that CYP recognise that their mental health need is not going to be alleviated by likes or messages of support and that social media fail to address any of the causes of that mental health need. Reid cited a Digital Awareness UK survey of 50,000 young people aged 11–16 years and reported that when they went online to talk about their problems in genuine need of support, they were highly likely to be disappointed and rarely received the response they needed.

Conclusions

In this chapter we have considered some of the potential negative aspects of digital media, and social media, on CYP's mental health. We have shown that there are a range of issues that have potential to harm the wellbeing of CYP and expose them to psychological impacts, which can be damaging. In completing this chapter, we provide a reflective piece about some of the challenges that relate to digital media for CYP and mental health from an expert in this field. In Box 6.6, we present the perspective of Dr Megan Moreno, who has been undertaking research in this area for many years.

Box 6.6: Expert contribution: Dr Megan Moreno, MD, MSED, MPH

Role: Academic Division Chief of General Pediatrics and Adolescent Medicine and Vice Chair of Digital Health

Organisation: University of Wisconsin-Madison

Brief bio: Dr Megan Moreno is the principal investigator on the project Social Media and Adolescent Health Research Team (SMAHRT). SMAHRT focuses on ways that technology can be harnessed to improve adolescent health.

Learning lessons from our work on SMAHRT

The patient was referred to me for 'abdominal pain', a lovely 18 year old in her senior year of high school. After our introductions, I asked her the common

(Continued)

question, 'When did your abdominal pain start?' Many adolescents will answer this question with vague or nondescript answers like 'maybe a month ago' or 'in spring?' or 'I have no idea'. Not many of us remember the exact onset of these types of issues. To my surprise, this patient answered: 'Around 8am on April 21st, I think it was a Thursday.' In further discussion I learned that this was the time that she had logged onto MySpace (these days we refer to this as a 'vintage' social media platform). Her friends had posted embarrassing pictures of her that they had taken without her consent. She realised the pictures had been distributed throughout her school and was horrified to see that her brother may have seen them as well. Fast forward a few weeks, she hadn't been to school since, and was now sitting in our children's hospital, referred for abdominal pain.

While this case happened over 10 years ago, it is memorable to me as I remember thinking, what is this technology that has enough power to land this patient in clinic with severe abdominal pain? The impact of technology, and social media especially, has been a source of interest for my research ever since. I've been interested in examining the ways that social media can augment issues with self-esteem, heighten emotions and damage relationships. I've continued to see adolescents and young adults in clinic who share stories of negative consequences and outcomes from their experiences with social media.

My research team is the Social Media and Adolescent Health Research Team (SMAHRT). SMAHRT's three core areas of work include: 1) providing education to adolescents and families towards safe digital media use; 2) developing tools to assess digital media use and understand beneficial and problematic internet use; and 3) to both test and interpret messages within social media to promote healthy behaviours. Our values include a collaborative, interdisciplinary approach, as well as seeking and supporting the excellence that comes from diversity in science. Our team includes staff, trainees and interns who all contribute to group projects and conduct their own individual research projects.

In our research, we've examined the relationship between time spent on social media and depression symptoms. This type of study examines the impact of social media at the population level by seeing what relationships there are within large groups. In these studies, we have not identified a positive relationship between quantity of social media use and depression symptoms. This research supports that at the population level, across all teens in a given study, there just isn't a causal relationship between social media and depression symptoms. However, we can also consider if there are groups of adolescents who are at risk for depression symptoms related to their social media use. These types of studies require different approaches that go beyond the population to understand groups within that population. We've examined this relationship using a method called Latent Class Analysis. This approach allows the researcher to identify groups within larger study populations. These groups may be linked by demographic characteristics such as age group or gender, or by reported behaviours on social media, or by similar levels of depression symptoms, or all three. In these studies, we've identified that there are defined groups of adolescents for whom increased time or investment in social media is linked to increased depression symptoms. Other groups do not experience this relationship. Thus, we've learned over and over through the evidence we've created, as well as that of others, that the impact of social media on adolescents is not uniform. It is unlikely that social media itself is negative for the entire population of teens (thank goodness). However, there are at-risk individuals and groups, and a future direction for our work is to understand which groups are at risk.

Another lesson we've learned through our work is that all social media is not the same. It is important to consider what aspects of social media may be associated with negative consequences. Early research studies tended to look at specific platforms and compare them, considering which platform was 'worse' in promoting bullying or poor self-esteem. While some platforms, such as Yik Yak, which seemed designed to promote anonymous bullying (and has since been discontinued), were obvious culprits, most others are more complex. More recently studies have considered that each platform has certain affordances, or functionalities. These functionalities or affordances may include tagging photos, linking other's profiles to yours, or developing a 'story'. Research is starting to explore how certain affordances are more likely to generate negative consequences than others. Conversely, some affordances may lead to more positive outcomes. Understanding these technologies at the functional or affordance level is a future direction we continue to work towards in our research.

In conclusion, not all adolescents are the same and not all have the same risks or consequences of social media use. Further, not all social media are the same, and within each platform there are different functionalities and affordances that may convey different types of risk or benefit. It is complicated, which also makes it endlessly interesting.

7

EXPLORING THE NEGATIVE SIDE OF DIGITAL MEDIA

THE RHETORIC OF 'THE UGLY'

Learning points

After reading this chapter, you will be able to:

- Identify the challenges associated with cyberbullying
- Evaluate the literature related to sexting, pornographic content and grooming
- Understand the implications of exploitation and online abuse

Introduction

Much concern around digital media and mental health relates to severe and challenging issues, which cannot be ignored. Indeed, these challenges have drawn much media attention and contributed to the pervasive negative view of social media and the rise of the Internet. We refer to this as the *ugly* side of digital media. Some groups of CYP are more at risk than others, as we have demonstrated earlier. We bring these different groups back into focus in this chapter as we outline some of the more potentially severe impacts on mental health, and again think about the main four Cs of online risks (Content,

Contact, Conduct, Contract). Over the course of the next two chapters, we focus on several of these issues. Although there is some overlap between these two chapters (and even some overlap with the previous chapter), here we explore the problematic side of digital media that may impact on mental health, and in the next chapter we focus more specifically on mental health itself and its relationship with digital media.

Specifically, in this chapter we consider challenging problems that occur online, some more common than others, that have the potential to negatively impact on the mental health and wellbeing of CYP in various ways. We attend to some of the key concerns emphasised by practitioners from different fields in terms of the possible risks for children's mental health. We open the chapter with one of the most common concerns for parents, teachers and others as we focus on cyberbullying and trolling, whereby digital media can be used to target victims, which can affect their self-esteem, wellbeing and mental health. In so doing, however, we will distinguish between potential online risks and potential detrimental effects. Some are a consequence of being exposed to potentially harmful content, contact or conduct. In other words, when we consider these issues, we will explore how a risky type of conduct (bullying another), a risky contact (being bullied) and harmful content (bullying material being shared) can collectively or separately lead to harm (three of the four Cs discussed previously). We also look at how online spaces can be used by adults to inflict harm on CYP, and consider problems of grooming, while also thinking about how they might be exposed to sexual behaviour from viewing pornography to sexting.

While, in a chapter like this, it is important to cover these 'ugly' areas of digital media, we again remind you that we are not taking a technologically deterministic position, as noted in the previous chapter. We recognise though, that we are inevitably constrained by space and therefore each section is intended simply as an overview to help you reflect on these issues for the CYP you work with. The chapter is not designed to give an in-depth review of the evidence in each area, but if there is a topic that you find particularly pertinent to your work, we would encourage you to follow up some of the references we cite.

Young people's rhetoric of the ugly

Before we go into the individual aspects of what have been positioned as especially concerning, we summarise these from the perspectives of young people. We follow up some of these issues in the next chapter where we continue our discussion of the more challenging side of digital media but are more specifically focused on specific mental health conditions as we turn our attention to issues such as self-harm, anxiety, depression and eating disorders. We also consider problematic internet use, which has sometimes been referred to as 'internet addiction', despite not actually being officially classified as a clinical condition. As a result, here we only include the contributions relevant to this specific chapter and provide the rest in the next chapter.

In our consultation groups with 16–18 year olds, they considered the more problematic side of digital media, social media and the Internet. We point out here for clarity that these young people conflated the terms 'digital media', 'social media' and 'the Internet', and in putting up their sticky notes on a board labelled 'The good', 'The bad' and 'The ugly' sometimes the same issue appeared on two boards (e.g. impact on self-esteem). We nonetheless illustrate their perspectives of what constitutes 'ugly' in Figure 7.1.

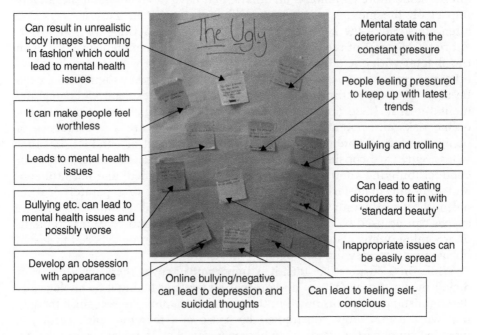

Figure 7.1   Young people's constructions of the ugly

The young people avoided specifically making personal reference to themselves as individuals; they repeated the general rhetoric of the ugly aspect and thus this became the title of this discussion board. This covered more general impact on mental health, with mental health deteriorating *with constant pressure* as reported by Tristan (aged 16 years), to more specific issues. Some young people discussed the problems of bullying and the inappropriate sharing of images online. Bullying was discussed in depth with all young people, seeing this as a problem in their school life. Madi (aged 16 years) noted that bullying and trolling were important challenges in modern schooling. Dylan (aged 16 years) specifically made the link between bullying and mental health, with Rhiannon (aged 16 years) connecting bullying to *depression* and *suicidal thoughts.*

Cyberbullying

Cyberbullying must be regarded as a serious health problem. (Dehue, Bolman & Völlink, 2008: 218)

Cyberbullying is a serious and growing social problem. It refers to intentional and repeated harm that others inflict via a digital device (Hinduja and Patchin, 2009). Using digital technology, bullies send threatening messages, spread vicious rumours, post embarrassing pictures or launch personal attacks on another individual to humiliate the receiver (Brown & Marin, 2009). Notably CYP may engage in bullying behaviour and may also be a victim of such behaviour from another or others (Lampert & Donoso, 2012). Figure 7.2 represents the problem of cyberbullying, illustrating some of the cruelty that CYP can display through text and images to others.

Figure 7.2   Cyberbullying

There is now a significant literature on cyberbullying and efforts are made to synthesise our knowledge on the topic. In one such meta-analysis of the literature, three key issues were identified, outlined in Box 7.1.

Box 7.1: Key research evidence

Meta-analysis of cyberbullying evidence

Kowalski, Giumetti et al. (2014) examined 131 research studies of cyberbullying. In this meta-analysis they identified three important findings:

(Continued)

1. Estimates of cyberbullying varied considerably and tended to range from prevalence figures of 10–40%. These statistics varied according to how cyberbullying was defined and related to the age of the victims.
2. There was a significant overlap between those CYP who bully others via technology and those who bully in person. They found bullies tended to target their victim both on- and offline.
3. The impact and effects of cyberbullying were profound on the victims. There were a range of mental health and physical health problems because of that behaviour.

We address these issues in the main text.

A core challenge in generating scientific evidence in the field of cyberbullying is defining it, and we have already given broad definitions. Different attempts have been made to categorise cyberbullying, as well as other forms of online aggression. For example, some authors claim that some of the behaviours (like harassment, cyberstalking) are forms of cyber-aggression, whereas others amalgamate them as forms of cyberbullying. For instance, Willard (2007) included eight different types of cyberbullying in a typology, as outlined in Table 7.1. We encourage you to think about whether you agree or not that each of these eight types constitutes cyberbullying, or whether you find creating 'types' of online bullying useful at all.

Table 7.1 Eight types of cyberbullying (Willard, 2007)

Type of cyberbullying	Description
Flaming	This includes angry or vulgar online exchanges.
Harassment	Repeated sending of insulting or nasty messages.
Denigration	The spreading of rumours and gossiping about a person with the intention to damage their reputation or friendships.
Impersonation	There is intent to cause someone else to get into trouble or damaging someone's reputation by pretending to be that person and/or sending material on their behalf.
Outing	The sharing of secrets or humiliating information of another via the Internet.
Trickery	When individuals engage in behaviour to convince someone to share humiliating information and then make that information available online.
Exclusion	This type of cyberbullying is the intentional exclusion of another from online groups with the intention of hurting the other.
Cyberstalking	This refers to the repeated harassment of someone so that the other individual feels afraid or threatened.

Often cyberbullying is an extension of in-person bullying, and the behaviour is frequently expressed by those same CYP online as offline, and thus it is not *always* anonymous. A central issue is that the cyberbullying behaviour can become sustained as the victim struggles to hide from it as there is potentially 24/7 exposure and the victim may feel they have no escape.

Cyberbullying is a concerning problem, but it is challenging to determine how common it really is. The statistics for CYP are variable and are different both within and across countries depending on the study. For example, statistics from the USA suggested that victimisation rates ranged from 20.8–40.6% (Hinduja and Patchin, 2010a), with a more recent study suggesting it is as high as 59% of adolescents (Anderson, 2018a). Recent UK figures suggest that 21.2% of 11–19 year olds had experienced cyberbullying that year (NHS Digital, 2018), with some arguing it is 7 in 10 CYP reporting it (Royal Society for Public Health, 2017). Extrapolating from various statistics, Douglas (2012) suggested that in the UK there were over 340,000 CYP aged 11–16 years who are experiencing persistent bullying via technology. In Europe, a survey in 2014 compared data from a 2010 version of the study and found that cyberbullying had increased from 8 to 12% overall, with girls seeming to be more affected as their rates had risen to 15% (Livingstone et al., 2014). These studies suggested that younger children (aged 9–10 years) had seen an increase in cyberbullying. Evidently then, cyberbullying figures are difficult to determine, and some studies report statistics much lower than others, and so we encourage you to think about the definitions and methods these different authors used and how realistic these figures might be.

Cyberbullying is a concern for parents, and a global phenomenon. As this behaviour occurs online it is frequently hidden from parents, with CYP experiencing it in silence. In one study of 1,000 parents of those aged 10–14 years, more than 90% of the parents were concerned about online bullying (boyd and Hargittai, 2013). In a recent UK study, 40% of parents of children aged 5–15 years had increasing worries about their child becoming a victim of cyberbullying (Ofcom, 2017). One of the reasons why parents are so concerned about cyberbullying is because it is so much more difficult to monitor than in-person bullying, because perpetrators have options to remain anonymous from their victims, and because the bullying behaviour can impact on the victim at any time of day or night (George & Odgers, 2015).

For CYP, cyberbullying is seen as a pervasive and entrenched part of modern life. For many young people it is simply accepted that this is an area of conduct that they are likely to encounter at some point, and most young people know someone who has been a victim of negative online comments and, for some, cyberbullying behaviour. Consider the comments from the adolescents in our research study in Figure 7.3. In response to a general open question about what they believed were the negative aspects of social media, lengthy discussions were had across all our focus groups on cyberbullying.

Cyberbullying is well known to have a negative impact on the victims, and consequences for their mental health and wellbeing. It is this we now address but, first, we would encourage you to reflect on the issues we have presented so far about cyberbullying and try the reflective activity in Box 7.2.

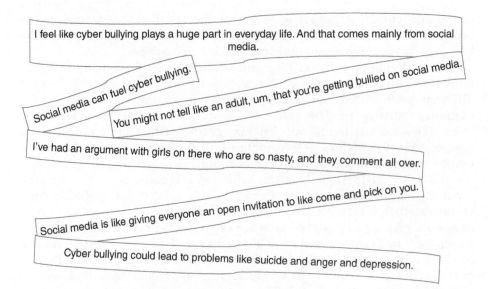

I feel like cyber bullying plays a huge part in everyday life. And that comes mainly from social media.

Social media can fuel cyber bullying.

You might not tell like an adult, um, that you're getting bullied on social media.

I've had an argument with girls on there who are so nasty, and they comment all over.

Social media is like giving everyone an open invitation to like come and pick on you.

Cyber bullying could lead to problems like suicide and anger and depression.

Figure 7.3 Young people's comments on cyberbullying

What are the main problems of cyberbullying?

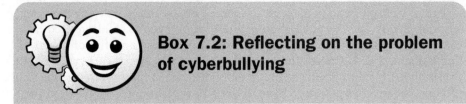

Box 7.2: Reflecting on the problem of cyberbullying

What do you think are the key problems of cyberbullying?

Write in your reflective diary a list of the things you think make cyberbullying especially problematic in your context. You might find it helpful to compare cyberbullying to in-person bullying. What do you think distinguishes cyberbullying from in-person bullying, and what specific implications do you believe this has for CYP's mental health?

Notably, cyberbullying takes place on different platforms including texts or apps, photo messaging, videos and online games, as well as a wider range of social media platforms (Ofcom, 2017). What is especially problematic about cyberbullying is that the bully is not present to see and witness the reactions of the victim first-hand (Anti-Bullying Alliance, 2019). Because of this lack of physical and social cues, the bully or bullies lack the feedback to induce empathy. Of course, another issue relates to the intent of the behaviour, which can be ambiguous. Frequently the behaviour is clearly cyberbullying, and it is sustained and repetitious. However, it is important to remember that when receiving information via technology in text format, there are no cues like tone of voice or body language, and thus the offence or hurt may not have been intended (Glazzard & Mitchell, 2018). You may want to revisit our earlier discussion about a digital ethics of care (O'Reilly et al., 2020) in Chapter 5, where we considered some of the issues about CYP responsibility, morals and empathy when interacting with others online and some of the challenges they can face in their online conduct.

Consequences and tackling cyberbullying

Although there is a clear relationship between in-person bullying and cyberbullying, the potential effects of cyberbullying may lead to high levels of internalising and externalising symptoms of mental health conditions (Waasdorp & Bradshaw, 2014). We encourage you to reflect on the reasons for this before you read further into the chapter by engaging with the reflective reflective activity in Box 7.3.

What experiences do you have of CYP and cyberbullying?

Box 7.3: Reflecting on the impact of cyberbullying

What are your views on cyberbullying and its effects on mental health?
    Write in your reflective diary your views and experiences of cyberbullying for CYP and the effects you feel that this form of bullying has on the victims.

There is consensus that there are considerable consequences for the victims of cyberbullying. CYP who encounter this form of conduct online, like in-person bullying, are usually subject to social isolation, social withdrawal, low self-esteem, anxiety and depression. Furthermore, the bullying conduct can impact the victims' academic performance, and lead to emotional trauma (Ma, Phelps et al., 2009). A major concern for practitioners, parents and society is the connection between cyberbullying to self-harm and suicide. Evidence has shown that there is a relationship between being a victim of cyberbullying and these consequences (Daine, Hawton et al., 2013). It is important to stress that situations of online risk do not always result in harm, but when harm arises the impact on a child can be devastating. Research demonstrates that cyberbullying has the 'potential to inflict serious psychological, emotional, or social harm' (Patchin and Hinduja, 2006: 149) leading to problematic outcomes including:

- Depression, (social) anxiety, having negative social views of oneself (Dempsey, Sulkowski et al., 2009).
- Embarrassment, fear and upset, as well as avoidance of the Internet (Wolak, Mitchell & Finkelhor, 2006).
- School absence and lower grades (Willard, 2006).

In extreme situations, this has led to suicide, or attempted suicide on the part of the victim. A recent meta-analysis that brings a body of evidence together has identified that cyberbullying is much more strongly related to suicidal ideation and behaviour than in-person bullying is (Van Geel, Vedder & Tanlion, 2014). Self-harm and behaviour that influence suicidal ideation and social media are an area that we return to in the next chapter (Chapter 8).

It is probably obvious to you that when CYP move away from physical spaces into virtual places, the pervasiveness and intensity of those peer relations increases. When engaging with in-person bullying there is the likelihood of eventual physical separation between the bully and the victim, but for cyberbullying this physical separation does not happen as the bullying conduct follows the victim around through their own digital devices (Mesch, 2009). Importantly, the mask of the Internet, hiding behind a screen (whether anonymous or not) can mean that the bully is more likely to go further in their aggression than they might in person. Also cyberbullying may not be a visible activity so that others may be less able to intervene and curtail it, and therefore the aggressor may manage to escape accountability for their actions.

Often, cyberbullies have some knowledge of their victim and the nature and style of personal communication is considered a risk factor, in the sense that victims tend to be more open in sharing their personal information online (Mesch, 2009). This is especially important in terms of any vulnerabilities that are known to perpetrators. Evidence suggests that some groups of CYP are more likely to become victims of cyberbullying: for example, those with disabilities (MacArthur & Gaffney, 2001); those with mental health conditions; and those from lower socio-economic indices (d'Haenens et al., 2013). In Chapter 4, we identified that some groups are more vulnerable to risk and harm than others, and these CYP might need more attention from practitioners and families to keep them protected from risks like cyberbullying. Indeed, research has shown that young people with behavioural and emotional mental health conditions do experience high levels of bullying and cyberbullying (Hart and O'Reilly, in press). Furthermore, it is important to be mindful of the bystander effect. Research has illustrated that CYP are less likely to defend a victim or report online aggression as they grow older, and therefore adults need to facilitate them to think more critically about their role in the cyberbullying and ways in which they might be able to help victims (Leduc, Conway et al., 2018).

We argue that cyberbullying is a social issue that needs an integrated interprofessional and multidisciplinary effort to tackle. CYP must learn to take responsibility for their online conduct (O'Reilly et al., 2020), and victims can be encouraged to report incidents of cyberbullying, as well as developing proactive coping strategies that are facilitated by effective socio-ecological environments (Papatraianou, Levine & West, 2014). Notably though, deleting the bullying messages does not 'delete' the problem and therefore it is crucial to have a positive, caring school ethos to help tackle this issue. Often social media sites have anti-bullying policies, but it is arguable that technology companies have generally been slow to intervene in cases of abuse (Glazzard & Mitchell, 2018) and often appear only to act in the wake of social pressure and when it may be too late.

A key issue in tackling cyberbullying, however, is disclosure by the victim. Indeed, CYP often resist reporting their bullies because they fear that parents will remove their devices (Englander, 2013), or they may be frightened that the problem will escalate if parents intervene. Often CYP are reluctant to report to their parents or their teachers (Blumenfeld & Cooper, 2010), this may be exacerbated if they feel that their parent or teacher will not understand, or if the quality of that adult–child relationship is not strong. Nonetheless, parents are the most likely adults CYP will turn to if they are being cyberbullied, and many of them feel that parents will address this problem (Anderson, 2018a). We return to the role of parents later in the book. Clearly, we need new strategies to create environments that are not only safe for, but which stimulate victims to disclose (George & Odgers, 2015). There are also signs that parents and practitioners can look out for, identified by Glazzard and Mitchell (2018), and we outline these in Box 7.4.

Box 7.4: Practical tips to identify signs of victimisation from cyberbullying

Glazzard and Mitchell (2018) argued that there are many signs that a child or young person might be a victim of cyberbullying. Practitioners and parents need to keep an eye out for these:

- Withdrawal from family.
- Resistance to allowing adults near their devices.

(Continued)

- Making excuses to stay off school.
- Exclusion from social events.
- Weight loss.
- Changes in appearance.
- Mood changes.
- Lowered self-esteem.
- Sleep difficulties.
- Increase in risk-taking behaviours.
- Anxiety.
- Experience nightmares.
- Self-harm.
- Taking substances.

There is considerable overlap between the signs identified above and other problems such as depression discussed in the next chapter, but being aware may help lead to earlier identification. Often cyberbullying occurs between known peers and the link to schools cannot be ignored. Because of this it is important that teachers and administrators are knowledgeable about cyberbullying and schools must include cyberbullying in their anti-bullying policies (Devine & Lloyd, 2012) so that potential incidents can be prevented, detected and/or dealt with effectively and promptly. However, schools alone cannot deal with cyberbullying. Schools can work with parents and other practitioners, but social media companies also have a responsibility to act (Glazzard & Mitchell, 2018).

Highlighted point!

We must remember that the bullies themselves need attention as they are also at risk (Cowie, 2013). Also, remember that bullies may be victims of bullying too.

Trolling

While trolling has been considered another form of cyberbullying, it is distinctive (Griffiths, 2014). Trolling, like cyberbullying is an online activity with negative intent and actions that seek to harm others. Trolling via social networking or social media platforms usually involves the posting of inflammatory, abusive and malicious messages (Hardaker, 2013) and the severity of trolling can be quite minor, such as 'accidental trolling' (i.e. just speaking one's mind), to more extreme and deliberate acts, such as posting messages to cause grief to bereaved families (Hardaker, 2013). Trolls frequently assume an anonymous identity online and hide behind the screen. Trolls may also work to persuade others into pointless online discussion to provoke or antagonise them (Herring, Job-Sluder et al., 2002). Herring et al. (2002) noted that there are three types of message usually sent by trolls:

1. Messages from a sender that seem to be sincere.
2. Messages from a sender that are designed to attract predictable responses.
3. Messages from a sender designed to waste the time of others by provoking arguments that are futile in nature.

Research into trolling has found that the main reasons individuals engage in this negative behaviour are to gain attention, revenge on a known or unknown other, and boredom (Schachaf & Hara, 2010). Evidence suggests that trolling can be felt to operate as a status-enhancing activity as the troll draws approval from likeminded others and may receive greater recognition than they achieve offline (Chamorro-Premuzic, 2014). Trolling not only occurs via social media, but also via interactive gaming. In a study focused specifically on gaming, with 125 gamers included, it was found that trolls in this context tended to be young males and their trolling behaviour tended to be sexist and/or racist or designed to intentionally mislead others (Thacker & Griffiths, 2012). Thacker and Griffiths showed that when young people witnessed trolling it was positively associated with self-esteem, whereas being a victim of trolling was negatively associated with self-esteem. Other work has demonstrated that in gaming, trolls often engaged in this behaviour because they found it funny, although one in six did not believe that their abusive messages would harm another, and half of the adolescents in the study believed it was acceptable to say things online that they would not in person (Rice, 2013).

Some victims are more resilient to the online trolls and their actions, typically perceiving those perpetrators to be of a lower intellectual level to themselves, and in some cases confronting them (Maltby, Day et al., 2016). We would encourage you to think about vulnerability again here in this context and refer to Chapter 4. The more vulnerable a CYP is, the less resilient to trolling they are likely to be. Indeed, Maltby et al. suggested that the implicit personal theories individuals hold about trolls may ameliorate the effects and act as a protective factor. In other words, as we have shown throughout this book, some individuals are more vulnerable to the impact of certain types of online risks than others, as is the case of trolling.

Sexting

Sexualisation and sexual activity as mediated via the Internet or social media have become more problematic over time, and there has been a rise of sexting, particularly amongst adolescents. 'Sexting is the term that describes sending nude or partially nude images via digital media' (Betton & Woollard, 2019: 146). There are a range of reasons why young people may choose to send messages with sexually explicit content or images, as outlined by Cooper, Quayle et al. (2016):

- To flirt with another individual.
- Consensual activity within their personal intimate relationships.
- For experimentation as associated with adolescence.
- Pressure from a romantic partner or a friend.
- To explore their sexual identity.
- To express intimacy.

The European average of 11–16 year olds reporting receiving sexual messages via their mobile (cell) phone was 11%, although lower in the UK at 4% (Livingstone et al., 2014). In a survey of 1,034 adolescents aged 15–16 years in the USA, 20% had sent a nude or semi-nude image and 30% reported receiving one (Fleschler-Perkin, Markham et al., 2013), and a similar US study showed 15% sending sexually explicit messages or videos (Rice, Rhoades et al., 2012). A more recent meta-analysis carried out by the University of Calgary suggests that these figures are rising (Madigan, Ly et al., 2018). These CYP are putting themselves at risk, with a potential for emotional distress and mental health difficulties for those who are victims, especially if those images are shared without their knowledge or consent (O'Keeffe and Clarke-Pearson, 2011), or made available in the future. Recent work by Martellozzo, Monaghan et al. (2016) has identified that sexting is quite common, and we outline that work in Box 7.5.

Box 7.5: Key research evidence

Statistics about sexting

In a study by Martellozzo et al. (2016), with the National Society for the Prevention of Cruelty to Children (NSPCC) and the Children's Commissioner (UK), some concerning figures have emerged about CYP's engagement with sexting.

The study involved 1,001 children aged 11–16 years, and there were several key findings:

- None of the CYP described sexting in terms of taking or sharing self-generated photographs of naked bodies or body parts. Instead, they saw sexting as writing and sharing sexually explicit or intimate words to a known other, usually a romantic partner.
- Most CYP had not taken a naked selfie, although 12% had taken a topless picture of themselves, 4% had taken a picture that showed their bottom half

naked, 3% had taken a full naked picture of themselves, and so in total 14% had taken naked or semi-naked photographs of themselves. Just over half of these had shared that image with another, and most of them sent it to someone they knew. However, some had sent the image to strangers.

The challenge for practitioners (and for parents) is managing any consequences or harms that may result from this sexting. CYP (like many adults) do not always think through the possible consequences of their actions, and once photographs are posted online they are almost impossible to remove (Ahern & Mechling, 2013). Unfortunately then, sexting can lead to humiliation and reputational damage both in- and outside of the school context (House of Commons Science and Technology Committee, 2019). There is always a risk that the image may be shared or passed on without the consent of the individual, or it may be accidently forwarded to others and this can lead to shame and humiliation for the victim (Betton & Woollard, 2019).

More research is needed to consider the content-creators' perspectives in more detail, questioning why CYP produce and share this kind of content, and for organisations to think through what might be done to prevent this from happening. It is thought that often girls sext as a way of getting some attention, or because of peer pressure or pressure from their romantic partner. Indeed, evidence shows that a primary reason why girls engage in sexting is because of pressure and of a fear of losing the boyfriend (Van Ouytsel, Van Gool et al., 2017). Furthermore, work in this area has identified that sexting tends not to occur in isolation but seems to be part of a cluster of risky sexual behaviour amongst young people (Rice et al., 2012).

The impact and potential for harm in relation to sexting is therefore an important concern, and some CYP are identified as more vulnerable to these risks. For example, in a study of 422 CYP, it was found that younger children, those from less affluent families and those with low self-efficacy, felt more intensely harmed by sexting (d'Haenens et al., 2013). Furthermore, in another study, 50% of CYP aged 10–15 years had used live streaming apps, but over half regretted posting content and experienced negative comments and were at greater risk from grooming (Cherry, 2019). Rice et al. (2012) therefore argued that practitioners ought to discuss sexting in an adolescent-friendly way with the CYP they work with in broader conversations about sexual activity, prevention of sexually transmitted diseases and pregnancy, and that sexting ought to be included in school-based sexual health curricula.

Pornography and viewing inappropriate sexual content

Before we start to consider the issues related to viewing inappropriate sexual content online for CYP, it is important to keep this in context. This was demonstrated by Nash, Adler et al. (2015: 3):

It is important to note at the outset that the vast majority of children's online experiences and interactions are not about sex or pornography, and that for most, their Internet and technology use deliver significant benefits in terms of social, educational and creative engagement ... it is vitally important that harms and benefits are weighed up appropriately, and that the potential for positive experiences is not undermined by a heavy-handed and restrictive approach.

In this section, our primary focus is on considering the challenge that many CYP (deliberately or accidently) may be exposed to pornography or violent sexual content that *may* (although not necessarily or definitely) impact negatively on their mental health, their self-esteem or their emotional wellbeing, or may give them a misguided sense of sexual relationships or views of the opposite sex. It is important to recognise that some CYP actively seek out online pornography, and the NSPCC (2020) offers several reasons why they do this, including:

• For sexual arousal.
• For humour.
• Out of curiosity.
• To learn about sex and sexual identity.
• To push boundaries.
• To be disgusted.
• Because of peer pressure or relationship pressure.

Pornography is more accessible than ever before and is an industry that has significant economic impact. Clearly, pornography, especially that with violent sexual content, is readily available through the Internet. Indeed, it is a fact that large numbers of CYP have seen online pornography, with many coming across it by accident rather than actively seeking it out. Recent evidence has shown high figures, and we outline this in Box 7.6.

 **Box 7.6: Key research evidence**

Martellozzo et al's 2016 study, with the NSPCC and the Children's Commissioner (UK), gave some insight into CYP's engagement with online pornography. While not all of this will necessarily be problematic or negative, and not all related to mental health, we outline their general findings here to give you a full overview.

The study involved 1,001 children aged 11–16 years and there were several key findings:

• 28% of 11–12 year olds had seen pornography online.
• 65% of 15–16 year olds had seen pornography online.

- 28% had found material accidently, whereas 19% had sought it out.
- 87% of boys and 77% of girls thought that pornography failed to help them understand the importance of consent.
- 53% of boys and 39% of girls thought the pornography was a realistic depiction of sex.
- More boys than girls continued to watch pornography intentionally.
- Older children were more likely to view pornography than younger children, regardless of intention.
- Girls were more negative about pornography than boys were.

What we can see from this, and from discussions on this issue more generally, is that moral issues aside, not all engagement with pornography is problematic or unhealthy. The age of the young person, the nature of the pornographic content, the intention or not to seek it out, and the perceived individual impact are all relevant factors to consider. Adults often find CYP's exposure to pornographic content as problematic, as this may impact young people's expectations of sexual relationships, it can affect the way women and men are perceived, and there is the potential to induce sexual violence. Pornography can raise unrealistic sexual expectations and can portray women as sexual objects whose function is to satisfy men's sexual pleasure. CYP may be shocked, confused or upset by watching this material. Of course, the range of sexual material available varies from what is described as 'soft porn' right through to more seriously violent and damaging content. These findings prompt us to think about not only the types of pornography CYP may encounter but, importantly, the impact of that consumption on their wellbeing and mental health.

This evidence also suggests that there are some gender differences in attitudes and motivations about online pornography. In another recent study, the Girlguiding Group (UK) (2019b) focused specifically on girls. In their survey with over 1,600 girls and young women aged 7–21 years, they found that 70% of the 13–21 year olds believed that the rise in access to online pornography was contributing to women being treated less fairly. In 17–21 year olds, there was a range of concerning findings:

- 80% believing that it encourages society to see women as sex objects.
- 78% feeling that it encouraged sexual stereotyping.
- 71% believing it normalised violent behaviour toward women.
- 66% feeling it puts pressure on girls to have sex before they are ready.
- 53% thinking it coerced girls into sexual acts because boys are copying what they see.

Such easy access to pornographic content is concerning for practitioners and parents, especially as evidence suggests that there is a relationship between viewing this and poorer mental health, although it is not necessarily a *cause* (Betton & Woollard, 2019). However, there is limited evidence to suggest any direct linkage between exposure and children's psychosocial development

(Ybarra & Mitchell, 2005). However, Ybarra and Mitchell did note in their study of 10–17 year olds, that those who *sought out* pornography online were twice as likely to show characteristics of depressive disorder, and they had a less-positive relationship with their caregivers when compared to those who used offline pornography or did not seek it at all, but this exposure is not likely to be the direct cause of these problems. As we know that CYP who experience depression tend to be more isolated (Matthews, Danese et al., 2016), we must therefore be mindful of the potential impact that online pornography has, and we outline some of the different perspectives in the literature in Table 7.2.

Table 7.2 Potential impact of online pornography on CYP

Impact	Description
Viewing increases the odds of teenage pregnancy	Young people who are exposed to sexual content via technology (including television) are more likely to become pregnant or impregnate a female, probably due to increased likelihood of initiating sexual contact (Chandra, Martino et al., 2008). However, we would caution that it is important not to oversimply this issue as there are also many other factors that influence adolescent pregnancy. Adolescent pregnancies are a global issue, with many neither planned nor wanted (WHO, 2018a).
Viewing can increase the risk of depression	As we have noted, there is a relationship between depressive disorder in those who view online pornography, although the direction of this relationship remains unclear. Whichever direction this relationship is, it is an important one, whether viewing lowers mood or if low mood leads to more viewing.
Viewing pornography may hinder socially appropriate sexual development	The regular viewing of pornography can distort and disorient adolescents during a phase when they are learning to manage their sexuality and sexual identity (Peter & Valkenburg, 2008)
Viewing pornography may create distorted expectations of sexual relationships	Young people who regularly view and engage with pornography might have lower levels of sexual self-esteem (Morrison, Ellis et al., 2006).

We recognise that this is a challenging area to research for several reasons, and these were outlined by Nash et al. (2015):

- Direct experimental studies testing the effect of pornography are not possible for ethical reasons; you cannot deliberately expose CYP to it.
- Studies exploring the effects tend to consider correlational relationships and not establish causation.
- Longitudinal studies could provide more useful information, but these are expensive and relatively uncommon.

Given the potential for such negative impact on CYP, it is important that practitioners (and parents) consider what they can do to reduce accidental viewing and manage intentional viewing. As practitioners, it is important that you are careful not to blame, punish or invoke shame in the CYP you are working with, and instead openly discuss this and keep channels of communication open (Betton & Woollard, 2019). Furthermore, governments also have responsibility in this area. The UK government claims it is the first country in the world to bring in age-verification for online pornography with measures that started in July 2019 and sanctions imposed on those who fail to comply (Department for Digital, Culture, Media and Sport, 2019). This measure means that commercial providers of online pornography are required by law to conduct robust age-verification checks on its users. The Department for Digital, Culture, Media and Sport (2019) argued that this move was in response to 88% of parents of children aged 7–17 years calling for controls to stop them seeing pornography online. There are, however, steps that you as a practitioner can take to help address this problem that are child-centred, and the organisation Internet Matters (2019) outlined these, which we describe in Box 7.7.

Box 7.7: Practical tips for dealing with internet pornography

There are some things that you can do as a practitioner (or indeed as a parent) to manage this:

- Have age-appropriate conversations with CYP and explain carefully that there are some sites that are intended only for adults.
- Encourage CYP people to talk to you if they see something that upsets them online.
- Encourage critical thinking skills in CYP so that they can appraise the images they see online appropriately.
- Facilitate coping strategies to help them deal with online content that they find uncomfortable. This can include strategies like closing the laptop, turning off the screen, overriding the webpage with something else, seeking adult help.
- Make sure that you are prepared to answer questions they have about sex and relationships.
- For young children you might want to limit the likelihood of exposure to inappropriate content by setting up filters or parental controls on devices.
- Get some support yourself from other practitioners (or parents) so that you have a source of help.
- If a CYP is actively and intentionally seeking out pornography online, then try to have calm conversations about why and point them to sources of support if they have strong emotional reactions.

Although some adults might think about actively blocking content on the CYP's computer, and there may be some arguments for the appropriateness of this, there are important issues and challenges to think about in doing so. In a recent report, Zaman and Nouwen (2016) highlighted some of the advantages and disadvantages of blocking and filtering content including:

- Many blocking filters and other such steps are not always as efficient as adults believe them to be.
- These kinds of filters may give parents a false sense of security.
- Those companies that offer blocking or filtering software tend to be commercial companies and therefore it is important to be aware of any possible privacy risks.
- As children grow older, adults need to be more mindful of violating the child's right to privacy and therefore open dialogue and communication is encouraged.

(We discuss the role of parents in more detail later).

Grooming, online abuse and child exploitation

Perhaps one of the arguably most concerning aspects of digital media has been the growth of online abuse. This is abuse that is facilitated using internet-enabled technology and social media (NSPCC, 2018). The NSPCC notes that online abuse can take many forms, such as stalking, harassment (remember that earlier in the chapter some authors constructed these as forms of cyberbullying, and we questioned the different types of definitions there), threats, sharing sexual materials, sexual exploitation, sexual communication and grooming. The NSPCC also recognises that this side to digital media is one area that has a significant and long-lasting impact on CYP's mental health and wellbeing.

Grooming

Grooming has been defined as when an adult 'builds an emotional connection with a child to gain their trust for the purposes of abuse or exploitation' (Glazzard & Mitchell, 2018: 52). Unfortunately, and unacceptably, child sex offenders are using the Internet to view and share abusive material, as well as to groom them online.

Not all adult strangers that communicate with CYP online have the intention to groom or any sexual intent toward them. Despite this, and although research shows that only a few CYP use online communication to meet adults as most communicate with peers and family, grooming remains one of the biggest concerns among parents and other adults today. Indeed, although grooming is relatively rare and the numbers of groomed children are low, the consequences can be significant for those CYP:

> Possibly the greatest public and policy concern for children's safety on the internet has focused on the risk that a child will meet someone new online who then abuses them in a subsequent face-to-face meeting (…) However, previous research suggests that the risk of harm from a face-to-face meeting with someone whom one first met on the internet is low, not least because children increasingly use the internet to widen their circle of friends, with very few using online communication to meet adults (whether deliberately or inadvertently). (Livingstone at al., 2011: 85)

It is deeply concerning that strangers are pressurising CYP to do things they do not want to do, including participation in sexual conversations or asking them to send sexual images (Glazzard & Mitchell, 2018). It is therefore crucial that there are mechanisms in place to teach CYP safe practices, warn them of the risks of talking to strangers online, and encourage them to disclose any such activity. Adults who groom CYP will invest considerable time establishing their relationship with their victim. They do this in different ways, as described by Glazzard and Mitchell (2018):

- Pretending to be someone they are not (typically pretending to be a child too).
- Offering advice or support.
- Buying them gifts.
- Giving the child attention.
- Utilising their profession or reputation.
- Giving the child compliments.

Findings from a European study suggest that offenders often target vulnerable CYP and that victims of grooming are mostly female, and aged 13–14 years (Davidson, 2011), which suggests that we need to find better ways to protect those from vulnerable groups from these negative aspects of digital media. This includes CYP with existing mental health conditions, especially because those with conditions are more likely to take risks online (Livingstone & Palmer, 2012)

Any CYP who becomes a victim of grooming is one too many. The figures regarding prevalence are mixed, but parents are certainly concerned about this issue. For example, in a recent study by Ofcom (2017), 39% of parents were concerned their child might give out personal details to inappropriate people, and 25% of their sample of 12–15 year olds had been contacted by a stranger. In a European study, 17% of the 9–16 year olds had been in contact with someone they had not met, but it is important to note that only 3% had followed through from online to in-person contact (Livingstone et al., 2014). We present a real case example from Pakistan as our expert Dr Sajida Hassan, who works with vulnerable young people, reports from her experience in Box 7.8.

Box 7.8: Expert: Dr Sajida Hassan

Grooming in Pakistan: Case example

The Internet has made child sexual exploitation and abuse available on demand; the ever-increasing use of live-streaming has made the digital sphere a difficult place to be a child. Child abuse is unfortunately a common occurrence in Pakistan, which tries to cover itself under the guise of religion, but it is shocking and sad that paedophilia or child abuse is rampant in Pakistani society. Today, stalking and luring children seems to have become common on the Internet. The predators are on the hunt for children who may easily fall in their trap. The predators usually play on the emotions of children and teenagers, especially those with unresolved personal issues and in need of emotional support. Once the children open up, the predators begin introducing sexual content in their chats.

I have worked with a 14 year old (who I call Saima here), who was active on social media and regularly shared pictures of herself and friends online. She was lured into friendship by an older man online who initially approached her on Facebook using a female ID. He encouraged her to share information and gradually encouraged her to share personal pictures. He then started to blackmail her and for months she struggled with guilt and depression and a lack of courage to share her plight with her family and friends. When things got completely out of hand, she finally had the courage to share with her mother, who reported the case to the police helpline. The perpetrator was arrested and Saima was encouraged to take counselling and healing art sessions. She now shares her story to help other teenagers to become more aware of the danger of online exploitation.

Dr Sajida Hassan

Child and Adolescent Development Programme (CADP), Hussaini Foundation, Karachi

As a practitioner you are likely to have safeguarding practices and policies to help protect CYP from grooming and other sexual exploitation or abusive behaviour, and these extend to online spaces. In the online world think about how organisations collect, process and save children's personal data, and how these help you to think about how to listen to them, respect their rights and how you might play a role in keeping children safe. In terms of thinking about these issues, we asked a safeguarding expert to outline some of the issues faced, and this can be found in Box 7.9.

In this box Simon has presented a common perspective on the issue and outlined some concerns often expressed by teachers and parents. We argue that the context is nuanced and complex, so we encourage you to think about

Box 7.9: Expert voice – Simon Genders

Safeguarding children on the Internet

The essential messages for parents and teachers about keeping children safe have completely changed for the digital age. Worries about 'stranger danger' for children 'out and about', have been replaced by fears for children ensconced in their bedrooms on tablets and mobiles. The Internet is often seen as a playground for paedophiles. They use a scatter-gun approach, messaging hundreds of children to find the one, who in that vulnerable moment, decides to respond. Their methods of grooming are devious and highly skilled – honed over time. They use false identities and scan children's digital footprints to find out about their interests or vulnerabilities. They exploit these to become trusted online 'friends' and make an invitation to meet up. The unsuspecting child becomes trapped. Abuse also happens in livestreaming apps where children as young as seven have become victims of serious abuse on camera.

So, the challenge for parents and teachers is to adapt to the dangers of this changed world – to equip children with the knowledge and skills they need to manage their own online safety and to feel confident to report their concerns. Recent surveys in Leicestershire schools suggest that online-safety education is improving. Older children are less likely to meet up with online contacts and less likely to send a self-taken sexual image. The challenge is now to engage more effectively with parents – to spread the message about risk, to encourage regular conversations with children and to keep up to date with the changing digital world, its opportunities and its risks.

Simon Genders

Safeguarding Development Officer

Leicestershire County Council

this perspective and consider if and how it resonates with your own, and if and how opportunity can be promoted while safeguarding CYP, by undertaking the reflective activity in Box 7.10.

To what extent do your professional policies work to protect CYP from grooming and other forms of exploitation online?

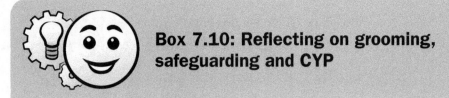

Box 7.10: Reflecting on grooming, safeguarding and CYP

Do you feel your professional policies and practices go far enough to protect CYP?

We encourage you to reflect on your professional policies and practices and ask yourself:

- Are you aware of what your local professional safeguarding policies state?
- To what extent do you feel they are good enough to protect CYP online?
- What experiences do you have of taking steps to safeguard CYP online?
- Why is it so important to have good safeguarding policies and practices in your organisation?

Child exploitation and online abuse

Child sexual abuse or exploitation material – usually referred to as 'child pornography' – child sexual exploitation or child trafficking are global problems that some argue have been exacerbated by the Internet and digital media, and are phenomena that relate to grooming because of the intention to sexually exploit the CYP. We recognise that 'child pornography' is a term that is widely used in many areas of the world, including within legislation. However, child advocates all over the world condemn the use of the term because the CYP depicted in these images or videos are not willingly producing pornography and instead are victims in these instances. As Broadhurst (2019: 3) rightly explains,

> the victims of these crimes are children who are subject to sexual exploitation or abuse. The term Child Exploitation Material (CEM) or Child Sexual Abuse Material (CSAM) are preferred to 'child pornography' commonly used in the laws of many jurisdictions because it does not convey the gravity of the sexual assault often associated with the production of CEM.

Child exploitation and online abuse are closely-related phenomena, also linked to grooming as discussed in the previous section. We therefore address these two issues through the expertise and voices of two internationally known scholars who work in these areas. Rather than ending our chapter with one expert contributor, for this chapter we are privileged to have two, with Sharon Cooper talking about exploitation in Box 7.11, and Tink Palmer talking about tackling online abuse in Box 7.12.

Box 7.11: Expert contribution: Dr Sharon Cooper, MD, FAAP

Role: CEO of Developmental and Forensic Pediatrics

Organisation: University of North Carolina at Chapel Hill School of Medicine

Brief bio: Dr Sharon Cooper is the CEO of Developmental & Forensic Pediatrics, P.A., a consulting firm which provides medical care to children with developmental disabilities, and provides medical care, research and training, and expert witness testimony in cases of child maltreatment. She serves on the boards of several national and international organisations focused on protecting children from violence.

The complexity of victimisation in child sexual exploitation

Though access to Internet and communication technology of a digital nature only became publicly available in the mid-1990s, the use of these technologies to commit crimes against children has abounded at an alarming rate. Organisations such as ECPAT International began to track the numbers of children reported to be exploited by nation, and continues to monitor the changes in types of victimisation. Historically, the types of victimisation were easier to monitor: sexually abusive images (previously referred to as child pornography), child sex trafficking, cyber-enticement and child sex tourism. However, the 21st century has brought markedly increased methods of victimisation, with a learning curve for intervention and treatment lagging far behind. Even the term 'trafficking' is expanding as the recognition that some forms of sexual exploitation are for the expressed purpose of the dissemination (or trafficking) of abusive images, videos or live-streaming content.

Presently, the types of child sexual exploitation have dramatically increased, and research focused on specific methods of victimisation remains primarily grounded in the criminal justice field, though the complexity of mental health outcomes clearly indicates a need for multidisciplinary responses. Part of this difficulty rests upon the clear digital evidence without consistently knowing the identity of the victims. In addition, even when children are located and rescued, therapists are at a loss for treatment strategies because of a lack of robust research regarding best practices. Examples of this deficit in the field are seen in the fact that though there are improving medical guidelines for children and youth who have been victims of commercial sexual exploitation through sex trafficking, the mental health interventions remain diverse and, in the USA, unavailable to victims who are seen as having co-operated in a criminal enterprise.

(Continued)

It is imperative that those who work in this area of crimes against children avoid thinking in a silo manner; for example, focused only on the most apparent evidence such as abusive images, or images that appear to be self-generated and might constitute self-exploitation. Internet and communication technology (ICT) grooming is frequently present in digital victimisation and its occurrence must be acknowledged and addressed when victims succumb and produce images which should be considered as the kinds of behaviours seen in compliant victims.

The nature of these types of crimes against children has often revealed that children may be caught in a web which may include being duped, groomed, coerced, drugged, intimidated, blackmailed, kidnapped, transported nationally or internationally, imprisoned, beaten, tortured and in some cases killed. There is no other form of child maltreatment with such a diverse list of potential outcomes, and those who seek to rescue and rehabilitate children with such life experiences are understandably very challenged.

Avoiding the 'silo thought process' requires that those who treat these children consider that discovery of an image may be the beginning of a therapeutic relationship, but abuse and neglect often precede the discovery of sexual exploitation for a significant amount of time. The probability of polyvictimisation (PV) is high in this population of child survivors. Polyvictimisation is defined as exposure to multiple kinds of victimisations and focuses on the prevalence of multiple kinds of exposures (Finkelhor, Omrod & Turner, 2007). The term often includes common victim profiles such as children who have been involved in the child welfare, juvenile justice and mental health systems (Ford, Wasser & Connor, 2011).

In addition, the polyvictimisation associated with child sexual exploitation significantly worsens outcomes for children in that they are often subjected to organised abuse (Salter, 2013; C3P, 2017). The connection between PV and the development of complex trauma (CT) is now recognised as an important sequela. CT is defined as exposure to multiple interpersonal traumatic events and their wide-ranging, long-term impact (Spinazzola, Habib et al., 2013). In light of these dynamics, the risks for self-harm are magnified with the complex nature of abusive images, online sex trafficking and organised abuse resulting in suicidal ideations and/or attempts in 83% and 60% of survivors, respectively (C3P, 2017).

Most professionals in the field of child maltreatment are accustomed to one victim and one offender. Additional training is warranted when a case becomes an apparent multi-victim case as is seen with offenders who are teachers, coaches, clergy, doctors and other types of offenders who are single perpetrators with easy access to many children. However, from the perspective of the complexity of victimisation, multi-offender cases are exceedingly traumatic and do untold harm to anyone, but especially children.

This realisation has challenged mental health care providers for such children who have been victims of abusive images, child sex trafficking, child sex tourism and the more recent digital pay-for-view victimisation now referred to as 'online sexual exploitation of children' (Sinclair, 2020). Online blackmail (referred to as 'sextortion') may represent organised abuse either from the production level or more likely the distribution outcomes as the demand continues to grow. As agencies worldwide seek to address the mental health needs seen in sexual exploitation, three highly-victimised populations should be a priority: urban communities of colour where PV and poverty intersect; human trafficking and commercial sexual exploitation of child victims; and the lesbian, gay, bisexual, transgender and questioning (LGBTQ) youth (Musicaro, Spinazzola et al., 2017).

Intervention for victims of child sexual exploitation should include attention to the sequelae of ACEs with medical engagement, as these survivors more often than not develop health consequences as a result of long-term cortisol mediated toxic stress. They should also have ongoing mental health intervention as cited above. It is important to be mindful of the increased risk for dissociation in children and adolescents who have experienced sexual exploitation, particularly if the abuses included sadism and child torture. 91% of survivors of abusive images reported that their psychiatric diagnosis/diagnoses were directly linked to the presence of abusive imagery (C3P, 2017).

Finally, many of these victims have experienced spiritual wounding, and attention to the mind, body and spirit may provide the most holistic treatment options for children and youth whose lives have been upended in a manner never before imagined (Messina-Dysert, 2016). One size typically does not fit all, and those who provide intervention and treatment should consider being flexible in the treatment options.

Box 7.12: Expert contribution: Tink Palmer, MBE

Role: CEO

Organisation: Marie Collins Foundation

Brief bio: Tink Palmer has worked with children and their families for the past 47 years and has specialised in child sexual abuse over 40 years. She is an experienced clinical and forensic practitioner, manager, trainer, policy maker and strategist. Tink first began working with children abused via the new technology in 1998 and has since developed a professional interest and expertise in this area. Tink has written widely on the issue of harm to children online. In 2017 she was awarded an MBE for her services to sexually abused children and founding the Marie Collins Foundation.

Tackling online abuse and grooming of children

It was in 1998 when I was managing a therapeutic unit for children who had been sexually abused that I received my first referral regarding online sexual

(Continued)

abuse – a group of children had been made the subjects of abusive imagery. At the time I was the manager of a therapeutic unit offering services to children and their families for whom sexual abuse was an issue. This initial referral was the start of my growing recognition that the needs of children harmed online require a differential professional response to that of children when the Internet is not a conduit. Since that time I have worked both in the UK and internationally to better understand the impacts of internet-related abuse on the child victims and their families, to develop recovery strategies for the victims and to update training modules for safeguarding professionals working with sexually abused children when the Internet is one of the conduits for their abuse.

In 2011 I founded the Marie Collins Foundation, which is a children's charity. Our vision is that 'all children who suffer sexual abuse facilitated by the Internet or otherwise, are able to recover and live safe and fulfilling lives, free from fear and positive about their future.'

The MCF works in partnership with police, health, children's services, NGOs, education personnel, industry members, government departments and those working in the legal profession and judiciary. We

- offer direct services to children and their families affected by abuse online.
- provide training for professionals.
- work alongside those assisting children in their recovery.
- influence national policies and strategies regarding appropriate responses to children harmed online.
- participate in research initiatives to better inform evidence-based practice.
- engage the media in responsible and informed debate.

Over the past nine years we have learnt a great deal about the sexual abuse of children online and the following outlines the differential nature of online abuse and its implications for the child victims. Although the scale of the problem is unknown, online sexual offences against children have risen exponentially in the last five years. Three years ago, the National Crime Agency (NCA) reported that, at any one time, over 80,000 people within the UK were committing sexual offences against children. Currently in 2020, that number has risen to over 300,000 with approximately 700 people being arrested per month for online sexual offences against children and 900 children being safeguarded per month – and the number is expected to rise in the coming months and years. We truly have a public health issue that needs addressing if we are going to better protect children in the generations to come.

What are the features of the Internet that facilitate the online abuse of children and have enabled those intent on causing harm to the most vulnerable members of society to reach children in a way they would never have been able in the past? Children are easily accessible – unlike in the offline world, there are very few obstacles for perpetrators to overcome to enable them to make contact with a child. There are no 'external inhibitors' such as protective adults and safe locations that might block a perpetrator's attempts to reach a child.

Online activity is 'hidden' and able to take place in relative secrecy. It is quick – no longer is there the need to go through a lengthy grooming process as is usually the case offline – and most online perpetrators go on sites which they know children occupy and take a scatter-gun approach in the knowledge that they will inevitably be able to groom an unsuspecting child. A further feature of the Internet is that it acts as a disinhibitor. Most children with whom we have worked at the Marie Collins Foundation report that they would never behave as they do online in the real world. Finally, the Internet supports and eases the dissemination of self-generated content and it is a global form of communication and interaction.

There are four key elements that differentiate the online sexual abuse of children from that which occurs offline: the way CYP communicate online; discovery as opposed to disclosure of the abuse; the grooming process; and the impacts on the victims. When communicating online young people are quick to connect with people they don't know and to share personal information with them in a way that they don't do offline. It is 'normal' for them to share personal images and to use sexualised language – to quote one young person, 'I would never use the language that I use online when speaking to friends in the real world'.

We know that prior to the Internet, child sexual abuse was a hidden issue, but some children did disclose what was happening to them and sometimes a concerned adult might realise that a child was being abused and would report it. It is very rare for a young person to disclose what is happening to them online and, in most cases, their abuse is discovered. Thus we know that children are not going to tell us what is happening to them, and this can be due to a number of reasons – some don't realise they are being groomed and believe the perpetrator to be their friend so there is nothing to report, according to the young person. Many feel complicit in the abusive scenario and are conscious of the sexually explicit language they have been using and the imagery they will have shared, and some are fearful of the repercussions on the part of the perpetrator should they tell anyone about what is happening to them.

For offline grooming of children for sexual abuse to occur, the perpetrator needs to have the motivation to want to do it, to overcome their internal inhibitors (their conscience), to overcome their external inhibitors (creating opportunities to be alone with a child) and to overcome the child's resistance (i.e. doing it and getting away with it). In the online world the grooming process is quicker and easier – perpetrators rarely struggle with their internal inhibitors and have barely any external inhibitors (obstacles) to overcome to enable them to make contact with a child. As in the offline world, the groomer may take a number of approaches from the 'I'm the only one who understands you' stance to that of love and romance and/or to that of fear inducing.

The fourth key element that differentiates online sexual abuse from that of offline is the impacts that the abuse has on the victims. Many feel

- impotent regarding the fact the abuse was discovered when they were not wanting to disclose.
- high degrees of shame – particularly when the inappropriate/illegal images they have sent of themselves are discovered.
- responsibility for the activities that have occurred.
- dismay when they endeavour to cope with the feeling of non-resolution regarding their abusive experiences because the images of their abuse may be available for others to see for years to come.

(Continued)

At the MCF, we offer face-to-face sessions with children and their parents/ carers as well as virtual meetings. All children attend our service for as long as they require our support – one young person received our support over seven years. Our over-arching principle is if you place the needs of the child victim and their family at the centre of any investigation or professional intervention you are likely to better safeguard the child and to achieve a proportionate and appropriate response within the criminal justice system. For more information about the work or training offered see www.mariecollinsfoundation.org.uk.

Conclusions

It has been suggested that there is a marked increase in requests for support by CYP about issues they have experienced online, such as sexting, grooming and viewing sexual material (Childline, 2016). It is adversities such as these that CYP have been facing online that have been the focus of this chapter. There are therefore several challenges that may be faced by CYP and adults need to take some responsibility to protect children from these potential issues and technology companies need to do some work to prevent these challenges occurring. Furthermore, there is a need to equip CYP with the skills to manage any risks they are exposed to in these areas, and to provide support for CYP impacted. Some CYP are already in vulnerable situations and these individuals are more likely to be targeted for abuse or violence and these CYP might find it more difficult to deal with and are less likely to report those difficulties.

8

EXPLORING WHEN DIGITAL MEDIA IMPACTS ON MENTAL HEALTH

THE RHETORIC OF 'THE UGLY' CONTINUED

Learning points

After reading this chapter, you will be able to:

- Identify some mental health challenges related to digital media
- Critically assess the concept of excessive Internet use
- Identify evidence in relation to self-harm, suicidal ideation, and suicide

---

Introduction

In this chapter we develop further our discussion on some of 'the ugly' sides of digital and social media, more specifically in terms of mental health. We address several mental health issues that have been highlighted through the negative rhetoric in this area and return again to conduct, contact and content related to digital media. We begin our discussion with two common areas of mental health – those of anxiety and depression – and consider how these mental health conditions (as well as emotional states) are relevant to the discussion of digital media and mental health. Digital media can play a supportive role for CYP who are experiencing mental health need, but there are also concerns about the role of websites or apps that encourage maladaptive behaviour, like those that encourage eating disorders or self-harm. We therefore consider some of the issues that CYP face such as self-harm and suicidal ideation as connected to digital media. Self-harm as a challenge of emotional regulation has been a long-standing behaviour in CYP with evidence to suggest it is rising. Digital media have become a source of sharing, information-seeking and possible behaviour encouragement and this is discussed. Suicidal ideation, intent and completion as influenced by digital media is one of the areas that has been most controversial and discussed, along with cyberbullying (as discussed previously). We guide you through some of the evidence on this. We also look at new ideas around excessive internet use, gaming disorders and the lay use of the notion 'addiction'. As with the previous chapter, the chapter is not designed to give an in-depth review of the evidence in each area, but if there is a topic that you find particularly pertinent to your work, we would encourage you to follow up some of the references we cite.

We also want to acknowledge that our perspectives on mental health in this chapter come from a very particular paradigm – or set of ideas – that is, located in research in the minority world. New research movements emerging from the majority world (e.g. Ratele, 2019) are beginning to question some of these ideas. There are some cultures globally in which experiencing depression is not something to be embarrassed about, or to be medicated, but could be a link to an ancestral past or a spiritual journey. Bakow and Low (2018), for example, investigated *ukuthwasa* (a calling to being a traditional healer) in KwaZulu-Natal, in relation to mental health conditions such as depression. Their study highlighted that it is crucial to consider cultural factors when making decisions about how to treat such conditions. For this reason, parents and teachers may want to be fully aware of cultural perspectives relating to the mental health of the children in their care, and the messages about mental health that might emerge from local communities, relatives and friends.

Anxiety and depression

In the media, panic discourses around the relationship between digital media and mental health exist, with commonly-cited issues being anxiety and depression. Importantly, both can be experienced at mild, moderate or severe levels, and they can have considerable impact on the quality of life of CYP. However, non-pervasive feelings of anxiety and low mood are part of the normal range of human emotion and do not in themselves constitute a condition in clinically diagnosable terms. The concepts of anxiety and depression have become embedded in lay discourses and are often used by CYP (and indeed adults) in general ways which differ from how clinical practitioners may use them. Some CYP make claims to feeling anxious when they are a bit stressed or worried about something, and say they are depressed when they are experiencing low mood. However, the possible impact of digital media on emotions and emotional regulation resulting in low mood or anxiety of any level is something that can be concerning. Before we consider the relationship between anxiety, depression and digital media, we first provide a brief description of anxiety, and then, for context, depression.

Anxiety

It is important to remember that feelings of anxiety are normal, and everyone gets anxious sometimes. Human beings experience stressful situations as part of normal daily life and the brain reacts. When faced with an anxiety-provoking situation the brain engages a 'fight or flight' mode to stay and deal with the source or run from it (Day, 2017). In normal circumstances, however, when the situation calms down or the individual removes themselves, they usually relax, but if individuals feel stressed, worried or anxious when there is an absence of stressors or provoking situations, then anxiety may become a problem (Young Minds, 2019). If the CYP consistently feels anxious and stressed, has physical symptoms (like palpitations) regularly, and it is affecting their daily activities (by preventing them from doing usual things), then the CYP may be experiencing an anxiety condition – referred to as an *anxiety disorder* (see APA, 2013). There are several major types of anxiety disorder and we do not describe them all, but the more common ones include:

- *Generalised anxiety disorder*, which is a constant and intense feeling of anxiety.
- *Social anxiety*, which is when there is a fear that others will judge them in social situations.
- *Phobia*, which is anxiety specific to places, objects or situations even if there is no real danger.
- *Obsessive compulsive disorder* (OCD), whereby the CYP has uncontrollable or recurrent thoughts and behaviours that feel necessary to repeat. The anxiety is related to fears something bad will happen if they fail to do so.

As a practitioner there are signs and symptoms of anxiety conditions, or even lower levels of anxiety, that you can look out for. The earlier these are identified and managed the sooner the CYP will be given support and the issues can be tackled before they escalate. We provide some tips for spotting anxiety and anxiety conditions in CYP, as provided by the National Health Service (NHS, 2017) in Box 8.1, so that if necessary, you can signpost the CYP to appropriate services or, for milder cases, useful sources of support.

Box 8.1: Practical rips for spotting anxiety (NHS, 2017)

There are some signs that you can look for in CYP that will indicate if they are anxious or experiencing an anxiety condition and these include:

- Trouble concentrating on their schoolwork or other activities.
- Difficulty sleeping and may experience nightmares.
- Avoiding some situations that they find uncomfortable.
- Changes in appetite.
- Mood swings, expressing anger or irritability.
- The individual may seem to be worrying a lot or have negative thoughts.
- The individual may seem tense or fidgety.
- Crying a lot.
- The individual may come across as clingy.
- Might complain of physical symptoms such as stomach ache or feeling generally unwell.

Depression

Like anxiety, it is within the range of normal experience for CYP to experience low mood and to feel sad. Often these feelings of sadness are in response to external events, like a bad day at school, falling out with a friend or missing a significant family member while they are away. Depression as a clinical condition, however, is more persistent and concerning but may be mild, moderate or severe with the need to categorise to ensure appropriate management and care.

Depressive disorders in the classification systems fall under the broader classification of *mood disorders*, and a core characteristic of depression is low mood. Whilst depression commonly occurs without mania, mania without depression is less common, and bipolar disorder is characterised by episodes of mood disturbance at the two 'poles' of depression and mania. The principal features of mania are of elevated mood and increased energy, disinhibition and little requirement for sleep or food. In CYP mania is uncommon and may be related to substance misuse.

For a CYP to be diagnosed with a depressive disorder (i.e. depression), they must be experiencing at least five of the major symptoms consistently for two weeks or more, and they should have depressed mood or less feeling of interest or pleasure (ICD-11). Indeed, ICD-11 identified a range of different symptoms, and as a practitioner you can look for signs of these in the CYP you work with. We outline these in Box 8.2.

Box 8.2: Practical tips for signs and symptoms of depression and depressive disorder (ICD-11)

There are some signs that you can look for in CYP that will indicate if they are depressed or experiencing a depressive disorder and these include:

- Low or depressed mood.
- Lowered interest or pleasure in activities.
- Reduction in ability to concentrate.
- Low self-worth or excessive guilt.
- Sense of hopelessness.
- Recurrent thoughts about death or suicidal ideation/attempts.
- Impact on sleep.
- Change in appetite or weight.
- Reduced energy or feelings of fatigue.
- Psychomotor agitation or retardation.

Note: In mania, the symptoms and signs will often be the opposite of those in depression.

For a diagnosis of mood disorder or more specifically of depression, there are characteristics that the child or young person displays that are persistent and affect quality of life. Our author, Nisha Dogra, describes a case study from a time when she was working as a psychiatrist in Box 8.3.

Box 8.3: Expert voice: Professor Nisha Dogra

Case study

Sally was a 15-year-old girl and presented with a four-month history of struggling with her schoolwork which declined significantly during this time. Her concentration was very poor, and she struggled to complete work in class or at home. This was exacerbated by the fact that she was due to sit her GCSEs. Up until about six months before she was doing well in school with a good group of friends. She used to be actively involved in school activities, but this had fallen away as have social activities with friends at the weekend. She was overwhelmed

(Continued)

by feelings of guilt that she felt a burden to her family and her friends. She had not shared how bad she felt as she did not want to worry anyone. She also felt guilty that someone who had all that she had should think of ending her life, but she could not really see a future in which she would feel better.

She had regular thoughts of self-harm but was torn by her mixed feelings – part of her felt that if she did harm herself her family would be upset, so that prevented her from carrying out her thoughts. At other times she felt it would be in her family's interests if she did end her life so she could stop being a burden. She had thoughts of taking an overdose when no one else was at home, but, to date, guilt has prevented her from acting on her thoughts. However, the urges were getting harder to resist.

She did not sleep well. She lay in bed worrying about everything that had happened and worrying about what she had done wrong. She dreaded waking up in the morning and facing the day ahead. At other times she slept for long periods but felt no more rested, waking feeling 'zombie like'. Her appetite was poor, and she lost some weight.

Emeritus Professor Nisha Dogra

University of Leicester

Indeed, CYP may present with low mood as the primary complaint (this must be mostly pervasive over time for depression to be diagnosed) or they may present with irritability instead, as well as a range of biological, affective and cognitive symptoms of depression. These were described by Dogra et al. (2017) as including:

- Changes in behaviour.
- Self-harm or thoughts about self-harm.
- Feelings of hopelessness.
- Negative self-image and low self-esteem.
- Losing interest and enjoyment in usual hobbies.
- Reduced motivation or enthusiasm.
- Reduced energy and readily fatigued.
- Poor concentration.
- Sleep problems (e.g. waking early, usually unrefreshed).
- Reduced appetite.
- Weight loss or failure to achieve expected weight gain.
- Inability to keep up at school or a drop in academic performance.
- Frequent vague, non-specific physical symptoms, such as headache or tiredness.
- An increase in moody, irritable, snappy, aggressive and hostile behaviour (often noted by parents).
- Reduced emotional reactivity.
- Substance use (which may have been a precipitating factor or may be used to some extent as self-medication).

They may also present with features of disorders that are commonly comorbid with depression, such as anxiety, compulsive behaviour and oppositionality.

Anxiety, depression and digital media

In understanding the relationship between anxiety, depression and digital media, it is important to recognise that the rates of anxiety and depression have risen over 70% in the past 25 years, with many factors being connected to this rise, and some concerns about the role of digital media (Royal Society for Public Health, 2017). Anxiety and depression, while normal emotions can become severe and when they meet the threshold for clinical criteria, are collectively classified as *emotional disorders*. In a recent UK survey, it was shown that 8.1% of 5–19 year olds had an emotional disorder, with rates being 10% in girls and 6.2% in boys (NHS Digital, 2018).

Although the evidence is clear that there are rising rates of emotional conditions in CYP, a recent review has found mixed findings in terms of the connection between these and the use of digital media, especially social media (Seabrook, Kern & Rickard, 2016). The world has changed in many ways, with digital media being one factor. While social media specifically are associated with higher levels of both anxiety and depression (Woods & Scott, 2016), this does not necessarily mean that social media are the cause of these higher incidence rates. For instance, it may be the case that young people who are anxious use social media more to mediate the effects of the anxiety (Hamburger & Ben-Artzi, 2000) or low mood. Another example may be that the poor sleep created by an overreliance on digital media may lead to anxiety and depression, and therefore the relationship is mediated by sleep (Woods & Scott, 2016). Furthermore, overreliance on digital media may reduce quality of relationships and decrease physical activity, which are protectors of mental health and again, these factors may mediate the relationship between anxiety, depression and digital media (Viner, Aswathikutty-Gireesh et al., 2019). Arguably, the direction of the association between digital media and social media use with anxiety and depression remains unclear. On the one hand, it may be that those who are more emotionally invested in their media platforms are at greater risk of increased anxiety and depression because of the feelings of isolation or distress they experience when they are disconnected, but it is also possible that depressed adolescents may use digital media more to regulate their low mood, in similar ways as CYP and adults use TV viewing for emotional regulation (Chen & Kennedy, 2005).

Of course, we must not forget that digital media may be a positive force in the lives of those with anxiety or depressive conditions. CYP diagnosed with an anxiety and/or depressive disorder may turn to the Internet for health information for their conditions, to chatrooms or discussion boards for sources of support, and social media to seek validation of their feelings and experiences. For example, in one study of 23 adolescents diagnosed with depression, they reported that while there were some negative challenges, like cyberbullying and negative comparisons with others, the use of social media for sharing positive content, sharing humour, creating content and connecting socially was important to them (Radovic, Gmelin et al., 2017). In a systematic, narrative review, Best, Manktelow and Taylor (2014) found that 13 of the 43 studies analysed, reported beneficial outcomes regarding social media and communication such as increased self-esteem and 'belongingness' resulting from social networking opportunities, which may, in turn, indirectly impact upon feelings of wellbeing. They claimed, however, that these benefits were potentially indirect and could be encouraged by a broader perception that they were feeling supported.

One area where digital media have been considered potentially helpful to those experiencing anxiety and depression is the rise of celebrities and 'influencers' who disclose their own personal mental health struggles and coping strategies (Young Minds, 2019). As the celebrity culture is highly influential on CYP, the disclosure of such emotional challenges has for some been useful in validating their own feelings and encouraging them to reach out for help. A recent example of this (and there are several) is that of celebrity vlogger Zoe Sugg (Zoella), who turned to YouTube to disclose her anxiety challenges and to reveal her need for professional help, and actively encouraged others to manage a calmer life (Young Minds, 2019). Such celebrity culture can be influential in reducing stigma, raising awareness and supporting young people in coping with their conditions. While we note that much of the celebrity culture is typically self-promoting, can potentially be misleading or inaccurate, and only represents one version or understanding of a mental health condition, they are nonetheless influential in today's society and active high-profile challenges to the stigma of mental health are important. There are also excellent websites available offering young people tips for how to manage some of their emotions and prevent escalation, such as the NHS website and the Young Minds website (UK). Thus, the broader use of the Internet for information seeking is important (and we talk more about health promotion and information later in the book).

Excessive Internet use

When two of the most influential technology figures in history, Bill Gates and Steve Jobs,reported that they rarely allow their own children to use the very products that they have created, it is very telling indeed. In conversations with the *New York Times*, Steve Jobs revealed that he did not allow his children to use the new iPad and imposed limits on screen time. Bill Gates reported that he implemented screen time restrictions on his daughter and did not allow his children to have a smartphone until they were 14 years old (Weller, 2017). This was in part due to an unhealthy attachment to certain games (Akhtar and Ward, 2020). One of the key concerns about digital media, social media and the Internet is that more broadly of *addiction*. It is important to note that there is limited sound evidence about this phenomenon of addiction in a clinical sense, and differentiating excessive use from clinical addiction is not always a straightforward endeavour (Livingstone et al., 2014).

Highlighted point!

The concept of 'internet addiction' is controversial and one that has been subject to considerable debate. In part this is due to challenges in defining addiction, especially in relation to the changes in the brain, and because of divided opinions amongst professionals in terms of whether this is a symptom of an existing mental health condition or exists as a condition in its own right.

The new DSM-5 does not have a diagnostic category of internet addiction or social media addiction, but it does have internet gaming disorder (Betton & Woollard, 2019), and the new ICD-11 has a condition of digital and video gaming as a disorder (WHO, 2018b). We return to the issue of gaming and excessive use shortly. We introduced you to ICD-11 and DSM-5 back in Chapter 2 and remind you here what these are in Box 8.4.

Box 8.4: What this means

Describing ICD and DSM

ICD-11 is the 11th edition of the *International Classification of Diseases*, and this system conceptualises physical and mental health. It is described by the World Health Organization as the gold standard for diagnostic health information.

DSM-5 is the 5th edition of the *Diagnostic and Statistical Manual of Mental Disorders* from the American Psychiatric Association (2013) and classifies mental health conditions only.

It is recognised that the idea of being addicted to digital media is contentious and that more research is needed (Royal Society for Public Health, 2019). In clinical terms diagnosing addiction is a complex task because the symptoms vary (Lemon, 2002). In talking about addiction to technology, it is described broadly as excessive interactions between people and machines and develops when the person becomes dependent on a device to give them psychological benefit (Griffiths, 1999). According to Mascheroni and Òlafsson (2014), there are five key characteristics of excessive internet use that can have an adverse effect on CYP:

1. Sacrificed eating or sleeping because of using the Internet.
2. Feeling unhappy or bothered when their access to the Internet is restricted.
3. Surfing the Internet even when they are not especially interested.
4. Spending time online instead of doing schoolwork or spending time with family.
5. Attempts to reduce time spent online but not being able to do so.

Addiction to technology is different from addictions to other things, like substances or gambling, as the individual may continue to act normally or in a socially acceptable way (Griffiths, 1999). There are some warning signs of digital media overload, and some CYP may start to show signs of social isolation as they become 'addicted' to technology and start to experience withdrawal effects and they begin to see the online aspects of their life as more important than their physical spaces (Glazzard & Mitchell, 2018).

This is an area where there are a range of different terms used and many specifically refer to the smartphone, including:

*   Smartphone overuse (Kim, Min et al., 2017).
*   Smartphone addiction (Pavia, Cavani et al., 2016).
*   Smartphone use disorder (Lachman, Sindermann et al., 2018).
*   Problematic smartphone use (PSU) (Baggio, Starcevic et al., 2018).

Of course, these raise some issues and controversy. First, this is partly because there is a problem in ascertaining how much smartphone use is too much use, and it is difficult to determine what leads to detrimental effects (Loid, Täht & Rozgonjuk, 2020); consider our earlier discussion about screen time. Second, this is partly because of confusion over terminology and the challenge that not all internet, digital media or social media use occurs through the smartphone, but can also occur on other devices like laptops, tablets and gaming consoles. Nonetheless, research is indicating that 10–25% of smartphone users do display behaviour that is consistent with excessive use (Smetaniuik, 2014), as it involves dysfunctional behaviour and detrimental outcomes (Billieux, Maurage et al., 2015), and is correlated with generalised anxiety disorder symptoms (Coyne, Stockdale & Summers, 2019).

Although the evidence about addiction to technology is complex, in different studies young people themselves have self-reported various levels of 'addiction' to devices and online technologies. It is a core concern for young people that they will become addicted to their media, which will take away from other areas of their lives. This has been a concern for CYP for a long time as, in an older study, young people believed that it was possible to become addicted to the mobile phone and argued that this device often dominated young people's thoughts, checking it on a regular basis, and some become 'addicted' to it (Walsh, White & Young, 2008). Indeed, the adolescents we talked to as part of our research study commented as such (see Figure 8.1).

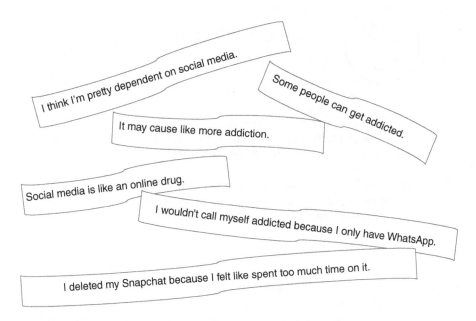

Figure 8.1 Comments on excessive use

However, what we must be mindful of is that young people often make passing reference to their online activities as being addiction, and this feeds the rhetoric (boyd, 2014). Extreme Internet use is, however, not especially common, although it is difficult to define in terms of the number of hours. One study defined extreme and excessive use as more than six hours per day and did show that only a small number of CYP use the Internet this much, but those that do tend to have less life satisfaction, are lonelier at school and are at greater risk of being bullied (OECD, 2017). It is certainly the case that there are CYP who develop an unhealthy relationship with digital media, and some develop obsessions with gaming or social media which negatively impacts their emotional development and academic performance (boyd, 2014). However, boyd argues that we must be sensible in our approach and balanced in our perspective, as it is easy for adults to blame digital media for young people's behaviour and ignore cultural, social and personal factors. We have encouraged you throughout to form your own opinions on these matters and to interpret the evidence accordingly, and we point you to the reflective activity in Box 8.5.

Do you believe CYP can become addicted to the Internet, social media and/or gaming?

Box 8.5: Reflecting on addiction

Do you think CYP are becoming addicted?

We encourage you to reflect on your professional policies and practices and write some responses to these three questions:

1. Do you think CYP are becoming addicted to the Internet?
2. Do you think they are becoming addicted to social media?
3. Do you think they are becoming addicted to gaming?

We also asked an expert in this area for an overview of the notion of 'internet addiction' while recognising that this term is contentious, presented in Box 8.6, and we asked another expert to consider excessive internet use in vulnerable children, presented in Box 8.7.

Box 8.6: Expert: Dr Daria Kuss

Excessive internet use

With the ubiquity and mobility of the Internet, health practitioners and researchers are raising concerns about addictive internet use. Research in this area indicates that individuals do not become addicted to the medium of the Internet per se, but to the activities they engage in. Gaming is one of the activities that has received research interest over the past 30 years. This research shows that gaming addiction symptoms are akin to symptoms of substance-related addictions, including salience, mood modification, tolerance, withdrawal, relapse and conflict. A behavioural addiction, such as gaming addiction, may develop without the requirement of ingesting a psychoactive substance. Instead, it may be the consequence of repeated engagement in a behaviour which over time sensitises the brain's reward system, requiring increased exposure to gaming to result in a similar pleasurable/numbing effect in comparison to earlier exposure, contributing to the development of addiction symptoms.

In 2019, the WHO included 'gaming disorder' in ICD–11 as a fully recognised mental disorder. This historical diagnostic move not only supports socio-political considerations of conducting research and providing treatment, but also destigmatises individuals who are experiencing associated symptoms, as the disorder is understood to have a neurobiological basis. In addition to addiction-related problems associated with gaming, the research community has started looking into other uses of the Internet which have been linked with addiction symptoms. These include, but are not restricted to, using social media, online pornography, online dating and online shopping.

Dr Daria J. Kuss

Chartered Psychologist, Chartered Scientist

Nottingham Trent University

Box 8.7: Expert voice: Dr Seyda Eruyar

Attachment relationships and excessive internet use in children

Considering the risks that the Internet poses, such as compulsive attendance to online gaming, pornography and social networking, parents are cautious about excessive use of the Internet by their children. Indeed, excessive internet use might have a disruptive impact on children's social, cognitive and emotional development as well as their mental health. However, we know that some children might not show such a pattern of addiction or compulsive behaviour towards internet use. What protects these children from the adverse impact of the Internet can be understood within the scope of ecological systems theory (Bronfenbrenner, 1979), which suggests that the development of children largely depends on their relationships with the environment that they are nested in (i.e. family and society).

Accordingly, secure attachment relationships with parents and peers could prevent maladaptive internet use in children. Epidemiological evidence germane to the issue suggests that children who securely attached to their parents are less likely to use the Internet excessively, whilst children with pre-occupied or fearful attachment styles are more likely to become addicted to the Internet. Insecure peer attachment, which is characterised by having difficulty in trusting others and a high level of alienation, moreover, might cause children to spend more time in the virtual world in which they feel relatively comfortable

(Continued)

without the feeling of loneliness and inadequateness in their relationships. Since insecure attachment patterns carry a high risk for future peer relationships and various types of mental health problems related to excessive internet use, attachment-focused interventions could be implemented with families as a preventive measure for excessive internet use.

Dr Seyda Eruyar

Assistant Professor of Psychology and Head of Department

Necmettin Erbakan University, Turkey

Risks and gaming

In the previous section we mentioned gaming in the context of excessive internet use, and this is because gaming has become a concern for some practitioners and parents. Interactive digital media like video games are a relatively new media, and there are positive and negative impacts of these for CYP's physical and mental health, and these ever-more sophisticated types of media mean that the effects of child-initiated virtual violence are potentially more profound than more passive media like television (Council on Communications and Media, 2009). While some argue that computer gaming has harmful effects on the young brain, emotional regulation and behaviour (e.g. Greenfield, 2014), others have claimed that there is limited robust scientific evidence, and therefore question the validity of those negative arguments and suggest that they risk misleading parents (Bell, Bishop and Przybylski, 2015). We must recognise, however, that some of the other 'ugly' aspects of digital media use occur via gaming platforms, whereby they can be used for cyberbullying, trolling and spreading fake information that can impact self-esteem and identity.

In some ways the arguments and fears around CYP's gaming, as possibly linked to increasing aggression or violence, are interconnected to older arguments of media, and television more specifically. This is especially the case as older evidence showed that by the age of 18 years, the average young person had viewed approximately 200,000 acts of violence on television (Huston, Donnerstein et al., 1992). The impact of television on CYP's behaviour has received considerable attention over the years. These arguments are now being replicated to gaming. Recently, there has been more of a focus on computer/video games, many of which are now interactive, social and internet-based (Sarriera, Abs et al., 2012). One area related to excessive internet use (and related to the idea of addiction) is specifically gaming with a social/interactive dimension.

Nonetheless, while evidence for the possibility of specific gaming disorders may be increasing, the boundaries between excessive and addictive use of interactive gaming still need more research. In one study by an Internet Gaming Disorder Working Group in the UK and based on the DSM criteria, found a prevalence rate of between 1 and 9% (Gentile, Bailey et al., 2017).

This group reported that the aetiology of this condition is not very well understood, although they identified impulsiveness as a risk factor. Thus, the parameters of this gaming disorder are not especially well defined, and there are some concerns about defining it as such. The classification is concerning because of the limited evidence base upon which it is based (Aarseth, Bean et al., 2017). Aarseth et al. argued that the operationalisation leans too much on existing classification of substance use and gambling criteria, and there is a lack of consensus regarding symptomology or assessing problematic gaming. They further highlighted the problem of moral panics about video-gaming, which they argued could result in the premature application of diagnosis from mental health practitioners using a confirmatory approach rather than critically examining the boundaries of normality. Indeed, they go so far as to argue that the formal diagnostic category should be removed from the classification systems so that public health resources are not wasted and to avoid the harm from labelling to healthy video gamers. We encourage you to critically reflect on these three concerns outlined by Aarseth et al., and outline what these mean in Box 8.8.

Box 8.8: What this means

There are three concerns raised by Aarseth et al. (2017):

1. They pointed out that the quality of the research base is low. There is only limited evidence on the new classification of 'internet gaming disorder'. Problematically, scholars doing work in this area have not yet reached consensus on the issue, and in an article authored by many different scholars, these disagreements are highlighted (Griffiths, Van Rooij et al., 2016). Furthermore, many of the clinical studies are speculative and have small sample sizes, and often patient numbers in research do not always correspond with clinical reality (Van Rooij, Ferguson et al., 2017). Aarseth et al. argue that because of this disagreement and the lack of evidence, it is premature to have this as a classification that can be used by mental health practitioners to classify and categorise CYP.
2. The classification of 'internet gaming disorder' is based heavily on the criteria used to categorise substance use and gambling addictions. Aarseth et al. note that although some comparison with other forms of addictive disorders can provide useful information, it should not be the fundamental basis when applied in the exploratory phase of understanding a new issue. It is noted that there are significant differences in the behavioural profiles of the different conditions and in understanding the withdrawal effects or

(Continued)

tolerance of use (Griffiths et al., 2016). Thus, Aarseth et al. point out that applying symptoms associated with substance use disorders to gaming behaviours can pathologise thoughts, feelings and behaviours that are normal. It is possible then, that these CYP will be labelled and classified as problematic when they have little or no functional impairment and experience little or no harm because of their gaming.

3. It is highly problematic that there is no consensus regarding the symptomology and assessment of gaming. Aarseth et al. point out that the symptoms of problematic gaming have tended to be based on flawed interpretations of survey data, flawed applications of statistical analysis and a reliance on psychometric evaluations where patient interviews were used to differentiate clinically relevant symptoms from normal behaviour. They note then, that misclassification of these issues might lead to worse treatment outcomes.

While quite often the arguments around gaming, violence and impact on mental health have revolved around adolescents, as well as addiction or excessive use, it is important to remember that younger children often play them too. Some are interacting through gaming media on age-appropriate games and others on games intended for older age groups.

Inappropriate websites promoting maladaptive behaviour

One of the major Cs that we identified earlier in the book was that of content, and how CYP might interact with inappropriate or potentially harmful content online that may negatively influence their mental wellbeing. Although there is a broad range of online content that may be considered part of the 'ugly' side of digital media (we discussed pornography previously), we focus on websites that encourage maladaptive behaviour in young people that is to their detriment such as pro-ana and pro-self-harm or suicide sites. Also, some common physical illnesses such as diabetes mellitus and asthma have potentially fatal outcomes if young people are advised to misuse their treatments.

Pro-ana and pro-mia websites

The two most common eating disorders as classified by the diagnostics systems we talked about earlier (DSM and ICD) are *anorexia nervosa* and *bulimia nervosa* (although there are others). To give you a basic understanding of these two eating disorders, the typical features of both conditions are summarised below. In practice, there may be considerable overlap between these two disorders and co-morbidity with other psychiatric conditions, and so this is just a simple overview to aid your understanding. Here we provide a summary of ICD-11 criteria for anorexia nervosa:

- Body weight is at least 15% below that expected (or failure to gain expected weight in pre-pubertal patients).
- Weight loss is self-induced by avoidance of fattening foods, which may be accompanied by self-induced vomiting, purging, excessive exercise, use of appetite suppressants.
- Body image distortion with a dread of fatness.
- A widespread endocrine disorder manifested as amenorrhoea in females or loss of libido in males.
- Delayed or arrested puberty occurs with prepubertal onset

A summary of ICD-11 criteria for bulimia nervosa includes:

- A preoccupation with eating and a craving for food gives rise to episodes of binge eating.
- There is a morbid dread of fatness and a strong desire to be unhealthily thin.
- The fattening effects of food, and especially binging, are counteracted by self-induced vomiting and/or laxative abuse and/or alternating periods of starvation and/or medication (e.g. appetite suppressants, thyroid preparations, diuretics).

From a practitioner perspective, suspicion about the possibility of the above disorders may be raised by the above symptoms/signs but also those as highlighted in the practical tips Box 8.9.

Box 8.9: Practical tips for spotting the signs of eating disorders

Practitioners (or indeed parents) can be alert to signs of eating disorders such as:

- Being secretive around food, often not wanting to eat with others.
- An increased or new interest in nutrition which is somewhat different from what might be considered usual in that age group.
- An increased interest in preparing food for others.
- Obsession with calories counting and restricting foods consumed.
- Increased physical activity (which may appear rigid or obsessive rather than healthy).
- Regular weighing.
- Distorted perceptions about body image.

The challenge is that CYP, especially girls but increasingly boys too, are often given conflicting societal messages about their bodies, some of which are conveyed through social media as we discuss below. While obesity is common, and often has psychological consequences such as low self-esteem and depression, it is not regarded as a primary psychiatric disorder. However, even CYP who are not obese may consider they are, given that so many images on the web are airbrushed and project often unattainable and unrealistic body shapes. Indeed, during our consultation group, the challenge of dieting, idealistic notions of beauty and the risk of developing eating disorders were raised by the young people. In minority world societies there has been a shift in thinking about physical beauty and body shape, with many girls and young women, and indeed young men, desiring thinness as the ideal. In contemporary thinking being thin is now considered the weight goal, and this is referred to as 'thinspiration', leading to CYP developing negative perceptions about their own body image (Ricciardelli and McCabe, 2001).

The UK eating disorder charity BEAT (n.d) described pro-ana (i.e. pro-anorexia) and pro-mia (i.e. pro-bulimia) websites as those with content online that promote the harmful behaviour and mindset which contributes to some eating disorders. They note that websites and social media where this content is found imply that such eating behaviour is a lifestyle choice as opposed to symptoms of an illness. BEAT noted that sometimes it is assumed that those posting content on these sites are deliberately malicious and aware that they are misrepresenting symptoms. However, this is typically not the case, and they are often experiencing an eating disorder themselves. Eating disorders are very complex conditions and often the individual has complicated feelings about their illness and the possibility of recovery. BEAT report then, that one reason why pro-ana and pro-mia content appeals to so many of those who aspire to thinness is that it is a space where they feel understood and share common goals. On the pro-ana websites there is encouragement of disordered eating and dieting, promoting thinness as the source of beauty (Syed-Abdul, Fernandez-Luque et al., 2013). Syed-Abdul et al. noted that consultation of these websites is often by those who already have an eating disorder, as they see the information as trustworthy and informative, but it is also a source of support for those who are dieting and trying to achieve thinness.

A core issue and concern about these pro-ana websites is that they propose unrealistic and often unachievable ideas about thinness and therefore this is a public health concern, especially as some young people are more susceptible to being influenced by the content (Syed-Abdul et al., 2013). It is, however, important to remember that much of the pro-anorexia content that is on the website has been developed and created by those online communities, by those young people with disordered eating or an eating disorder (Wilson, Peebles et al., 2006). In other words, with the perpetuated ideology of beauty, there is increased pressure on young men and women to conform to a certain unrealistic and often impossible idea of what they should look like. This expectation around beauty and body standards drives some CYP to websites that encourage dieting, provide beauty tips and encourage exercise. However, for some, these behaviours and the desires that drive them are maladaptive and can become clinically and physically problematic.

In one recent study that examined pro-ana content on YouTube there were some concerning findings, and we present this study by Syed-Abdul et al. (2013) in Box 8.10.

Box 8.10: Key research evidence

Pro-ana content on YouTube

Syed-Abdul et al. (2013) studied YouTube content. In this research they accessed YouTube to search for videos with questions that related to anorexia nervosa. For the study, the authors selected the 30 most viewed videos for each of their key concepts, which were:

- Anorexia
- Anorexia nervosa
- Pro-ana
- Thinspo

This meant that there were 120 videos in the sample, plus a subset of 30 random videos that had more than 5,000 views, giving 150 videos in total. However, when some were removed for copyright reasons, there were 140 videos included in the study, which was 11 hours of viewing. Their key findings were:

- 29.3% were rated as pro-ana.
- 55.7% were informative.
- 15% were neither.

They identified that the 40 most viewed videos (20 of the pro-ana and 20 informative) between them had been viewed 61.13 million times. The important finding here was that the pro-ana videos were favoured three times more than the factual sites designed to give information, and these videos featured very thin models and were framed in ways to inspire others to become thin beyond the point of healthy. Indeed, one-third of the videos promoted anorexia as a lifestyle.

Typically, the pro-ana and pro-mia websites are viewed negatively, and many adults argue that they should be shut down. We encourage you to critically reflect here though, as some have argued that these pro-ana websites can help CYP to feel understood and respected (Tierney, 2007). Tierney argued that when CYP experience an eating disorder, they are more likely to be open and honest about their eating behaviours online and to online communities than they are to practitioners or other adults in their lives. Because of this transparency, they can therefore find the posts on these sites supportive. Evidently, the use of these websites and social media platforms can be positive or problematic to those CYP who are vulnerable (Betton & Woollard, 2019) and practitioners need to recognise that these websites may serve a purpose for some (Teufel, Hofer et al., 2013). The difficulty therefore is how practitioners and parents might help these CYP to make decisions that are good for their mental health and to understand how they are gaining benefits from sites and social media that ostensibly appear destructive (Betton & Woollard, 2019).

Self-harm and suicide websites

Arguably one of the most concerning aspects of the Internet and social media are those platforms and websites that promote and encourage self-harm behaviour and suicidal behaviours. Pro-self-harm/suicide websites are those webpages or social media content that encourage the behaviour, and display methods of self-harm and suicide (Minkkinen, Oksanen et al., 2017). Minkkinnen et al. argued that part of the challenge is that victimisation is a significant factor for self-harm and suicidal behaviour in young people, and much of the victimisation also occurs online (e.g. cyberbullying) and can push them toward these websites.

This issue has created a lot of controversy, as on one hand some CYP find that these function as sources of support, a community where they are understood, can be themselves and completely open and honest about their thoughts, feelings and behaviours. On the other hand, they pose risks, there is the problem that they encourage highly-risky behaviour, and in more extreme cases there have been cases where an individual has died by suicide (either deliberately or by misadventure) after engaging with digital media.

One example of this is Instagram's #selfharm, which was utilised to build a self-harm community and was dedicated to that behaviour (Simmons, 2014). This was concerning for adults, regulators and parents as CYP and adults share images of their self-harm and risk glamorising the behaviour. Instagram responded to the concerns and blocked users from searching for content on the platform related to this hashtag (Moreno, Ton et al. 2016). However, the persistence, and perhaps need, for such an outlet by that community should not be underestimated. As Moreno et al. showed, what happened consequently was a revised hashtag #seflharmm, and then, when blocked, #self-harmmm, and this could continue. Moreno et al. argued then, that the challenge is that parents, educators and clinical practitioners can struggle to understand how to interpret hashtags and other social media displays. While we are going to go into much more detail on this particularly challenging side of digital media and mental health, we offer some practical ideas to encourage CYP who engage in self-harm to find alternative sources of support in Box 8.11.

Box 8.11: Practical tips for encouraging CYP who self-harm to find alternative sources of support

There are some things that you can do as a practitioner (or indeed as a parent) to encourage CYP away from damaging websites that encourage self-harm:

- Be prepared to openly discuss self-harm with CYP.
- Accept that whatever our perspectives, the self-harm serves a function for the CYP and alternative managing strategies may be required before stopping self-harm is viable.
- Discuss with the CYP strategies of minimising risk and reducing problems like infection to the wound or accidental death, if they feel they cannot stop self-harming.
- It may be useful to visit the websites together and discuss their potential benefits and disadvantages and find legitimate and useful information.
- Encourage them to seek professional support and help.

Self-harm

A noticeable thread that is emerging in our discussion of both cyberbullying and trolling, and of maladaptive websites, is that of self-harm and suicide. The relationship between self-harm, suicidal ideation/intent and digital media has been discussed in terms of cyberbullying and trolling, but it is also important in terms of issues like depression, social isolation, peer pressure, seeking the perfect life and so on. In this section of the chapter we consider the challenge of self-harm and social media, the new phenomenon of 'digital self-harm', and the risks of suicidal ideation, intent and completion as mediated by digital technology. We deal with each of these in turn. Before we do so, we encourage you to reflect on your practice in helping CYP who self-harm or experience suicidal ideation by considering our two questions, and to think about your beliefs about any connection to social/digital media by undertaking the reflective activity in Box 8.12.

What do you think about the relationship between social media and suicidal ideation, suicide attempts and completed suicide?

Box 8.12: Reflecting on social media, self-harm, and suicide

In your opinion, what is the relationship between social media and self-harm?

What do you think of the relationship between social media and suicidal ideation, suicide attempts and suicide completions?

We encourage you to reflect on the CYP you work with. Think about how much self-harm and/or suicidal ideation you find in your work and consider the extent to which you think that is connected to their digital and social media usage. If none of the CYP you work with self-harm, then treat this as a more hypothetical exercise and consider what your personal beliefs are.

Self-harm, sometimes referred to as non-suicidal self-injury (NSSI), is an area frequently discussed in relation to digital media. Self-harm behaviours are increasing in CYP and therefore governments, services, practitioners and researchers need to pay much more attention to this issue (Townsend, 2019). Townsend argued that there is a clear connection between self-harm and suicidal ideation, intention and completion, and argued therefore that front-line practitioners are important in prevention and intervention, with research needed to develop early intervention. This is especially important as the American Psychiatric Association contemplates whether self-harm ought to be classified independently as a mental health condition (rather than a behaviour associated with emotional conditions), and called for evidence to inform the decision. Currently NSSI criteria are outlined in DSM-5 with empirical studies operationalising samples of children, young people and young adults to determine the prevalence rates, characteristics, clinical correlates and possible independence of such a disorder, yet empirical data are needed with direct and structured assessment of the DSM-5 criteria so that they may be reliably assessed and validated for a possible diagnosis of NSSI disorder (Zetterqvist, 2015).

Self-harm is a very complex issue, especially in CYP. Self-harm behaviours typically include cutting or scratching the skin, burning, poisoning, banging limbs, hair pulling, punching oneself or surfaces and tying ligatures round the neck (Brophy & Holmstrom, 2006). It is argued that self-harm behaviour is a coping mechanism for those CYP with poor emotional regulation (Zimmerman & Iwanaski, 2014), or it can be a form of self-punishment (Klonsky, Glenn et al., 2015).

Self-harm and suicidal ideation are most commonly seen in adolescents (Hawton, Saunders & O'Connor, 2012). However, there is evidence showing that self-harm is beginning earlier in childhood, and its prevalence is rising in younger children (Simm, Roen & Daiches, 2008). It can be challenging to accept that very young children are self-harming and/or have suicidal ideation, but the evidence to show this is emerging. For example, one longitudinal study over 25 years looked at children under 15 years and found that children as young as 8 years presented to hospital for self-harm (Hawton & Harriss, 2007), and in the UK nearly 800 children of primary school age (5–11 years) presented to hospital for self-harm, representing an increase of 10% compared to the previous year (Marshall, 2015). There is limited research with these younger children, but that which has been conducted has shown that 8% of a sample of 665 children aged 7–11 years were engaging in self-harm in the USA (Barrocas, Hankin et al., 2012). In a recent unpublished qualitative study with 7–11 year olds led by Sarah Adams (University of Leicester), teachers, parents and children provided examples of a range of behaviours that constituted self-harm and believed that if left unsupported would grow worse in adolescence. This small body of work has important meaning, and we outline this in Box 8.13.

Box 8.13: What this means

There are three key points being made by this evidence:

1. Children of pre-school age, and those in primary (elementary) school, can and do engage with self-harm and therefore it is important that you are mindful of this when engaging in your practice. Just because they are young is not a reason to believe they are not capable of harming themselves.
2. The reasons why younger children engage in self-harm are probably like those of adolescents, predominantly emotional release and coping or self-punishment. We need more research with younger age groups.
3. Although the number of younger children presenting to hospital is rising, we must remember that most children who self-harm often do not present to services and yet early intervention as well as prevention are very important. You may play a role in spotting the signs and promoting early intervention.

While suicide attempts are more prevalent in adolescents than younger children, there have been cases of younger children attempting to hang themselves (Scott, Crossin et al., 2018), and possible suicidal thoughts or intent are certainly a concern for teachers and parents (Simm, Roen & Daiches, 2010).

However, it is also important to bear in mind that there are questions around their cognitive ability to understand death and its permanence, and questions about whether their true intent is to die.

Although a growing concern in younger children, self-harm rates in adolescents are a long-standing issue for practitioners and parents. The rates of self-harm in adolescents are growing, especially for those with existing mental health conditions (NHS Digital, 2018). Given that adolescents are prolific users of digital technologies such as social media it is necessary to consider if there is a relationship between them and what that might be. Many adolescents are using social media for positive reasons related to their self-harm as they engage with these platforms to learn about self-harm and its consequences, find safe ways to treat their wounds, and support others or seek support for their behaviour. It is therefore important to reflect and take a critical position on digital media and self-harm, and we must not forget the possible positive side. Research by Seko, Kidd et al. (2014) has suggested there are two main issues in the motivation for posting self-harm pictures online that can be positive for the individual:

- The first relates to the individual benefits, like self-expression, reflecting on the self-harm experience, and soothing the urge to engage in further behaviour.
- The second is more socially connected and includes motivations such as offering emotional help to others, seeking support from others who experience self-harm, and raising social awareness. Some young people see the Internet as a safe space to express their feelings.

Figure 8.2   Social media and self-harm

Clearly, there are benefits to those who self-harm as they engage with the Internet (Dyson, Hartling et al., 2016) and some are fostering supportive communities (Devon, 2018b). However, on the uglier side, some individuals use these sites to encourage others to self-harm, push them further in their behaviour and offend, insult or troll them, leaving them further distressed, as Figure 8.2 portrays.

Highlighted point!

We encourage you to remember that social media are not necessarily the reason for or cause self-harm behaviour incidents and neither are they necessarily the reason why this behaviour began, and so it is possible that society may be placing too much emphasis on this relationship (Devon, 2018a).

There is evidence of some connection between self-harm and digital media. For example, in a recent study of CYP who presented to hospital following an incident of self-harm, 26% of them had viewed self-harm and suicide content online, which compares to only 8.4% of adults (Padmanathan, Biddle et al., 2018). Google tends to be the primary search engine CYP obtain information from about self-harm (Lewis, Mahdy et al., 2014). Problematically, however, Lewis et al. noted that individuals are frequently exposed to unreliable and inaccurate information about self-harm, and such poor-quality information might impact on their self-harm decisions, especially as there was minimal information about effective treatments or sources of support. This is especially important as in terms of social media (and some websites like Wikipedia) the content is peer-generated, and CYP post content about their self-harm to build communities around this shared interest (Moreno, Kota et al., 2013).

These self-harm communities can be important for the CYP who use them, but the concerns lie with the possible negative impact that they may have. Evidently, CYP are rather savvy at finding ways to circumnavigate imposed restrictions. It is important to recognise that although many companies' terms of use do discourage displays of self-harm on their platforms and place warnings about dangerous content, more robust actions are needed to address self-harm content and respond quickly to any type of content that could potentially damage the users of their platforms, especially CYP.

One of the main issues raised about CYP's self-harm and digital media is that of *normalisation*. Self-harm is maladaptive as a coping strategy, or form of emotional regulation or self-punishment technique, and therefore is a behaviour that requires intervention. CYP can find it challenging to disclose their self-harm (Bostik & Everall, 2006), meaning they often do not get the support they need. It is problematic then, if they normalise their self-harm and harbour beliefs that they do not need help. In a systematic review, it was shown that when individuals (adults or children) search for information about self-harm, they are likely to encounter violent and explicit imagery, and such content may normalise the behaviour (Daine, Hawton et al., 2013) or lead to social contagion (Whitlock, Powers & Eckenrode, 2006).

It is important that those working with CYP seek to understand how they are using digital media in terms of their self-harm and to learn about how these platforms are influencing or helping them in their choices (Betton & Woollard, 2019). There may also be a need to consider those CYP for whom self-harm is a maladaptive coping mechanism whilst they learn more appropriate coping strategies, and those whose self-harm is more pervasive and is not replaced by more appropriate strategies. Clinically, over the last 25 years, there is anecdotal evidence to suggest that for some CYP in some contexts, self-harm is almost perceived as a normal coping mechanism at a certain point in life.

Digital self-harm

While digital media can have positive and negative impact in terms of self-harm, an area that is considered especially problematic is that of digital self-harm; that is, harming oneself via digital means. Digital self-harm is when an individuals create online accounts and deliberately use these accounts to send hurtful or threatening messages to themselves (Patchin & Hinduja, 2017). It was in a blog post by danah boyd (2010) where this concept of digital self-harm was coined, also referred to as 'self-trolling' or 'online self-harm', as she noted the increase in behaviour by young people of posting nasty comments to themselves anonymously and then responding. The concept of digital self-harm therefore refers to the posting or sharing of harmful content about oneself in an anonymous way, via SMS, email, gaming consoles, web forums or virtual environment (Patchin & Hinduja, 2017). This phenomenon drew public attention with a high-profile case in the UK, and this is outlined in Box 8.14.

Box 8.14: Key research evidence

High-profile case of digital self-harm

In 2013 the phenomenon of digital self-harm became publicly highlighted when a 14-year-old girl called Hannah Smith from Leicestershire in England anonymously sent hurtful messages to herself on the social media platform Ask.fm. Hannah subsequently died by suicide and left her family devastated.

Initially, investigators believed that her death by suicide was influenced by cyber-bullying, because of the hurtful comments on Ask.fm. However, on closer inspection it was found that the comments came from her own IP address and indeed, Hannah had been digitally self-harming. (Davies, 2014)

Problematically, there is a very limited evidence-base on digital self-harm, and it is a challenging phenomenon to research as it remains relatively hidden. We therefore have very little information about why CYP engage in digital self-harm and can only speculate that the reasons are like those for other types of self-harming. It has been argued that this type of self-harm is a cry for help, or an effort to trigger compliments from peers as they defend the individual against the believed harassment (boyd, 2010). There have been two large studies in this area, and we report their findings in Box 8.15.

Box 8.15: Key research evidence

Evidence on digital self-harm

In 2012 Englander published a study with 617 college students, finding that 9% of them had engaged in digital self-harm during their time in secondary (high) school. Englander found that both males and females engaged in digital self-harm and the reasons were:

- To attract attention from their peers.
- To prove that they were able to handle the negative comments.
- To encourage others to be worried about them.
- To get attention from adults.
- Because they felt angry about someone and wanted to start a fight.

In 2017 Patchin and Hinduja administered a survey to a nationally representative sample of 5,593 12–17 year-olds, and this focused mostly on cyberbullying, bullying and related behaviour, but they found some interesting findings related to digital self-harm. From this study they found:

- Of the respondents, 6.2% disclosed that they had anonymously posted something online about themselves that was 'mean'.
- Of that 6.2%, 51.3% reported doing this once, 35.5% reported a few occasions, 13.2% reported many times.

(Continued)

- Of the full sample, 5.3% reported that they had anonymously cyberbullied themselves.
- Of that 5.3%, 44% said they had done this once, 37.2% reported a few times, and 18.4% reported many times.
- The findings showed that boys were more likely than girls to engage in digital self-harm.

Suicidal ideation, suicidal intent and suicide completion

Research suggests that suicide rates have increased (Curtin, Warner & Hedegaard, 2016).

In the USA, there were more than 30,000 suicides across all age groups, and nearly 1 million across the globe every year (WHO, n.d.). Globally, self-inflicted injuries are the leading cause of death for young people aged 15–19 years, and the 10th leading cause of death in 10–14 year olds (Patton, Coffey et al., 2009). Examining the relationship and the fears about digital media and its relationship with suicidal behaviour is an important issue. This is because there are growing concerns that the Internet, and social media more specifically, might play a role in suicide-related behaviour (Fiedorowicz & Chigurupati, 2009). This is especially important for CYP as they engage heavily with digital media.

In the UK, a national inquiry into suicide and mental health in CYP was conducted with 595 children under the age of 20 who had died by suicide across two years, and 23% of them had a record of suicide-related Internet use (Appleby, Kapur et al., 2018). This is not to say that the use of the Internet caused the suicide or even contributed to it, but it does show that many who died by suicide also engaged with those kinds of sites. However, this does raise questions of whether adolescents who have lower mood and are more prone to suicidal ideation spend more time on digital media, or if the digital media lowers their mood and contributes to their suicidal ideation. Indeed, evidence suggests that young people who spent the highest volume of time on screens were more likely to have high depressive symptoms or at least one suicide-related outcome than those who spent less time on devices (Twenge, Joiner et al., 2018).

As we recognised earlier in the previous chapter, one of the related factors that connects social media specifically with suicidal behaviour is in the context of cyberbullying and thus we return to that issue here. There have been many high-profile cases of the connection between cyberbullying and suicide in recent years (Lester, McSwain and Gunn, 2009). A survey of 2,000 children (in middle school) showed that victims of cyberbullying were almost twice as likely to attempt suicide than those who were not (Hinduja and Patchin, 2010b). Of course, it is important that you consider these kinds of statistics critically and reflectively, as we have encouraged you to do throughout the book. These figures are not saying that cyberbullying is a sole predictor of suicide in CYP, but that being a victim can increase the risk of suicide by amplifying feelings of instability, isolation and hopelessness, and this is especially risky for those who have existing psychological difficulties (Hinduja & Patchin, 2011) or other vulnerabilities.

Highlighted point!

The relationship between cyberbullying and suicidal behaviour has been coined *cyberbullicide*, which refers to when suicide is either influenced directly or indirectly by a young person's experiences with aggression or bullying online (Hinduja & Patchin, 2009).

A second major concern for society is the possible media contagion effect (Williams, 2011) as message boards, social media and various other online platforms have been used to spread information about methods of suicide, and as a means to obtain 'how to' descriptions of suicide (Luxton, June & Fairall, 2012). We must also remember that some people use social media and related platforms to livestream their own suicide attempts (or deaths by suicide), where they may be encouraged to complete the act and die by others via online comments. One cross-sectional study of 990 members of online suicidal ideation communities found that the likelihood of suicidal ideation and intent augmented with the increased numbers of communities that the individual belonged to, the proportion of suicidal peers in their network, and the extent of social isolation (Masuda, Kurhashi & Onari, 2013).

On the positive side, we would also encourage you to think about the ways in which digital media and the Internet might be used for suicide prevention and support for those with suicidal ideation or intent. In one study of 240 websites examining 12 suicide-associated terms, researchers found that while half were pro-suicide sites, with chat rooms, the other half provided factual information (Biddle, Donovan et al., 2008), including sites that have a wide range of videos to promote suicide prevention (Luxton et al., 2012). Social media and social networking can help young people form social connections between peers and raise awareness of suicide prevention programmes, crisis helplines and other sources of support (Luxton, June & Kinn, 2011).

Suicide prevention is essential and is the goal of the WHO (2014b). All practitioners working with CYP have some responsibility for this and can work together to support them. Understanding the risk factors for suicide and investigating suicide completions can tell us important information, and we need more evidence on the mediating or linking issue of digital media.

Conclusions

In this chapter we have considered the ugly side of digital technologies by considering the more direct relationship between digital media and mental health. In completing this chapter, we provide a reflective piece about self-harm in younger children and consider the role that social media might play. Sarah Adams reports her research project on self-harm and emotional regulation in children aged 7–11 years in Box 8.16.

Box 8.16: Expert contribution: Sarah Adams

Role: Lecturer in Education

Organisation: University of Leicester

Brief bio: Sarah Adams works as a Lecturer in Education, at the University of Leicester. She specialises in child mental health in schools and serves on the National Institute for Clinical Excellence Committee on self-harm. Her research uses qualitative approaches to take a person-centred view of these issues.

Self-harm in younger children

Self-harm in the primary school age range may feel a difficult topic to discuss and research. However, primary school leaders are reporting an increase in the number of children self-harming (The Key, 2017), a concerning statistic which cannot be ignored and one that needs addressing to reverse the increasing trend.

There is a small growing literature that is examining self-harm in younger children. For example, one study in Australia found there were 1,558 ambulance callouts between 2012–2017 for self-harm in children 7–11 years old (Scott et al., 2018), and an American study found that 7.6% of 8–9 year olds had engaged in self-harm (Barrocas, Hankin et al., 2012).

I would argue then, that self-harm is an important issue to attend to. Indeed, self-harm is everyone's business, and researchers, clinicians, carers and those with lived experiences should share the messages (Townsend, 2019).

Understanding what may lead up to a child engaging in harmful thoughts and behaviours is a complex area and one which needs rigorous investigation. Drawing upon the adolescent research, self-harm has been identified as a coping strategy to aid emotional regulation when having uncomfortable feelings and experiencing intense emotions. This suggests that when a young person experiences intense emotions and thoughts they may opt for a coping strategy that is harmful to themselves as a release.

One of the issues in understanding self-harming behaviours in children is comprehending what the term means. From a medical perspective, self-harm is defined as 'any act of self-poisoning or self-injury carried out by an individual irrespective of motivation' (National Institute for Health and Care Excellence (NICE), 2013: 6), although this excludes self-induced psychological harms (McAllister, 2003) and the more contemporary notion of digital self-harm. Digital self-harm has been defined as the deliberate act of posting anonymous hurtful content about oneself through social media, which can also be known as 'self-bashing'.

Children's usage of digital media is increasing, which has led to a plethora of research exploring the benefits and harms. However, it is unknown if children in the primary school age range who self-harm are accessing supporting material or material which triggers and maintains harmful thoughts and behaviours.

In my own project focusing on emotional regulation and self-harm in 7–11 year-olds, social media and social gaming were raised as important to children's lives. We ran 16 focus groups to discuss the wider issues of mental health, emotional regulation and self-harm. We ran groups with parents, educational professionals and with children aged 7–11 years old. Educational professionals were mostly teachers, but included special educational needs coordinators, teaching assistants and head teachers. The focus of these discussions was on coping with big emotions and self-harm. Because self-harm is a difficult issue to talk about with children, the aim of our focus groups with this population was to talk about emotions and emotional regulation in a way that mirrored traditional classroom discussion-based activities.

Many different issues came up in the focus groups with the children, parents and educational professionals. There was experience of self-harm in the age group, and they had different ideas about what constituted self-harm, defining it in various ways. They did recognise the traditional formats, like cutting and self-poisoning, but also more subtle ways such as self-punishment, digital self-harm and eating disorders. Notably, they also discussed the challenge of overusing digital games and saw this as a form of addiction. Some parents particularly were worried that their child might become addicted to the digital games.

While the adult participants recognised that self-harm challenges were likely to increase or be more problematic in adolescence than during the younger ages, they were concerned that the self-harming behaviours seen in younger children would increase and get worse as the child got older. They also worried that as the children would also increase their engagement with social media use this could be problematic.

In discussions about why younger children might engage in self-harm there were various different reasons proposed, and often these reasons were consistent with those posed for adolescents who self-harm. Mostly it was agreed that young children used the self-harm as a way to cope with their stress and to manage their emotions. Such a release of emotion was connected to their social, linguistic and cognitive development as the adults felt that they did not

(Continued)

have the maturity to cope with big emotions, or deal with the range of pressures they faced, and this included some of the digital media those children used.

Overall, it is clear that there is a lot more to be done with this age group, in terms of researching self-harm, but also in terms of their digital and social media use. It is also important to remember that parents report spending more time and effort monitoring and supervising their child's use of digital devices, and the Internet. Some of the children were using digital media in positive ways and for leisure and schoolwork. For others, some parents and teachers had concerns about their engagement with digital media, and were worried about issues like bullying and digital self-harm.

PART III

PRACTICAL IDEAS FOR FAMILIES AND PROFESSIONALS

9

THE ROLE OF PARENTS AND CAREGIVERS

Learning points

After reading this chapter, you will be able to:

- Examine the construction of the family unit
- Critically assess the role of parents in digital media and mental health
- Identify ways of mitigating risk

Introduction

In writing this chapter we recognise that CYP are raised in many different circumstances by single or multiple adults, including biological parents, legal guardians or other primary caregivers. For the sake of space, we do not list all these different variations each time we reference these different carers and instead use the broad notion of 'parents' throughout. This is not to diminish the relevance of other types of carers and/or families, but simply reflects the space available. If you are a practitioner working with CYP, then it is probable you will also work with their families, even if it is in a marginal way. It is impossible to discuss any issues related to CYP without some reference to the home environment. There is generally a tendency to see families as largely beneficial for CYP, and protective of their mental health. Whilst this is usually the case, it is important to be mindful that families can be a very negative experience for some, and furthermore, a significant number of CYP grow up without a consistent and/or supportive family. Therefore it is important in the context of mental health and digital media to think about the role that parents play.

Parents play a crucial role in raising children and facilitating their transition toward independent adulthood. Parents usually act in their children's best interests to promote their wellbeing and safeguard them from harm. In today's world, mitigating risk, monitoring behaviour and protecting CYP from harm means parents need to consider digital media. While this is a complicated and challenging task for parents, there are many areas of importance and lessons to be learned.

This chapter deals with a range of issues in the context of parenting children in a digital world. Before we focus specifically on the digital context, we open more widely with a general discussion about the nature and formation of families, and the challenge of parenting and parenting styles. In so doing we consider the role that parents play in modelling behaviour and teaching responsibility to their children which, as we have shown, has an impact on their online conduct and their digital ethics of care. The chapter also includes discussion of *sharenting*, whereby parents share aspects of their children's lives on their own social platforms, to consider the role parents have in their child's digital footprint. We then examine parental concerns about their children's digital lives and the strategies available for parental mediation of this usage. We close the chapter with practical ideas for supporting CYP in their digital media usage and integrate this with a practical discussion of mental health support, alongside some thoughts about how parents themselves might engage with digital media. It is important that parents can recognise the impact that their own relationship with digital media has on their child's behaviour and to take active steps to encourage CYP to engage with non-screen activities like sport or dance which are known to improve mental health (Children's Commissioner, 2018).

Examining the definition of family

Defining the family is a more complex and challenging endeavour than it may first seem, but ways of thinking about what constitutes the family, biologically, socially and culturally, are important for thinking about the place of digital media within the home. Definitions of the family vary from country to country but may also vary within countries, and defining family structure types can be difficult. Before we discuss this, we encourage you to create your own definition using the reflective activity in Box 9.1.

What is a family?

Box 9.1: Reflecting on a definition of a family

What constitutes a modern family and why is that important for the digital world?

Write in your reflective diary your own personal definition of a family. Think about what factors you are using to define the family in that way and why it might be important. We also encourage you to think about why your definition of the family might be relevant in terms of digital media and mental health. As you read through the chapter we deal with these different issues.

Although families are typically considered in terms of biological and genetic connections, it is now recognised that social and psychological connections are also important factors that may play a part in how someone decides who is part of their family. There are many different definitions of the family and over time these definitions have changed and evolved. Legal, economic and social definitions frame the ways in which families are supported and viewed by society (Beauregard, Özbilgin & Bell, 2009). Historically, families were constructed as having at their heart a biological connection, but being part of a family extends far beyond biology in the modern world. Indeed, it is impossible to define the extent of the family, as this is personally, legally and culturally determined. For example, some cultures may regard members of the extended family, such as grandparents, as an important influence in their day-to-day life, while other cultures would regard this as unhelpful and intrusive. There are many routes into a family such as birth, adoption, fostering, sexual relationships and marriage. Dogra et al. (2017) suggest that for the purpose of working with CYP in a mental health context, a pragmatic functional rather than structural definition of family would encompass all those involved in meeting the child's immediate emotional and developmental needs as defined by its members. Levin and Trost (1992) proposed a definition of family as two or more people who define themselves as family. In practice, families usually have little difficulty in defining themselves, but difficulties arise when the professional working with them does not share the family's views on membership because of their own cultural and personal expectations. It is also important to be mindful of the legal implications regarding who has the authority to make decisions for the family.

Families are diverse and constitute different ways in which people come to live together; modern families do not automatically conform to social norms, rather they evolve and translate their own family culture (Dallos & Draper, 2010). The structure of the family and the members within that family unit will play an important role in the way the child develops. The family structure impacts on family dynamics in terms of how members behave and interact (Garfield, 2009) and, as already mentioned, will vary considerably across different contexts. Garfield noted that families can positively impact CYP as they provide economic resources, love, values and companionship, as well as teaching them how to cope with adversity as they embrace common belief systems and deal with crises together. This is important for the integration of digital media in family life. Although there have been concerns about digital media eroding family ties and connection, there is evidence to suggest that digital media have extended family connections as families engage in on- and offline activities together (Livingstone, Blum-Ross et al., 2018). In other words, embracing digital media can bring families closer together, can improve their communication, and can provide new ways to entertain.

The family in need

When considering the family and its role for mediating any positive or negative impacts of digital media on child mental health, it is necessary to recognise that all families are different. Ideologically, in the minority world there are normative standards of a family, regarding how the family interacts together and influences the child. This notion of the 'normal' family is often unspoken or taken for granted (Dodd, Saggers & Wildy, 2009), and the inadequacy of existing definitions of the family can lead to unfortunate consequences for those whose conceptions of the family do not align with the narrow, normative legal, economic or social definition (Beauregard et al., 2009). However, there are very few 'normal' families in that families tend to be unique entities and often have their own way of doing things. Indeed, discourses of children's mental health and illness are influenced by personal, interpersonal, institutional and national ideas regarding what is seen as best for children (Strong & Sesma-Vazquez, 2015). Furthermore, there are difficulties in the societal view that parents take responsibility for child-rearing practices and act in the best interest of the child. This idea positions responsibility for the child's behaviours, moral reasoning and outcomes in adulthood with the parents. However, few families manage to achieve the ideological standards, and some families encounter challenges or difficulties that impact or affect the upbringing of the child in different ways.

Society has commonly blamed parents for any mental health or behavioural challenges in children, and parents must navigate this social gaze on their rearing practices (O'Reilly & Lester, 2016; Patrika & Tseliou, 2016; Singh, 2004). Clearly, then, when CYP do have their mental health negatively impacted by digital or social media, the lens of judgement frequently turns to parents. However, this rhetoric of blame is not always appropriate, and certainly is not helpful, and often families need support to manage the adversities they face, rather than societal criticism. It has been recognised that the family system has a profound impact on the child and much psychological distress is a consequence of those relationship processes (Stratton, 2010), and therefore the family system is one that requires attention.

Highlighted point!

Families can face all types of adversities that may affect their ability to function and cope. It is important to foster a supportive narrative to help parents manage any impact of these on their child's mental health, although many are often out of their control.

In cases where the child does have specific mental health needs, the challenges of family functioning can be addressed by family therapists to help families work more effectively together to meet each other's needs. In family therapy it is argued that the difficulties faced by an individual child are likely related to the broader family system and all family members can play an important role to promote positive mental health and address any need. We therefore asked family therapist and academic Professor Tom Strong to comment on the issues of digital media in family functioning, and outline his response in Box 9.2.

Box 9.2: Expert voice: Professor Tom Strong

Families and family therapy

In responding to the rise of television, Marshall McLuhan (1967) famously wrote: 'the medium is the message.' He related such media developments to changes Harold Innis studied in transportation for how each change transformed Canada's social economy: in transitioning from canoe to railroad travel, different settlements and economic possibilities resulted (Innis, 2017).

(Continued)

McLuhan's message still pertains to how society is currently being transformed by social media, despite an enduring feature of family life.

While neurocognitive or even media design reasons partly account for excessive social media use in families, Bateson (1972) recommended we look for patterns that connect. Family life acquires its familiarities through becoming highly patterned. However, such family patterns can be disrupted by unforeseen developments (e.g. illness) introduced by one member, thereby begging new patterns in how members respond to each other. Excessive social media use can overtake how family members relate in often unintended ways, bringing unwanted patterns of conflict, stuckness or disengagement.

Unwanted family patterns persist through how members react to each other. Reflecting upon and addressing how unwanted predictable patterns of reacting (Couture & Strong, 2004; Tomm, Wulff et al., 2014) recur is a therapist's challenge when helping families caught up in such patterns. Patterned reactivity has an almost gravitational pull, and responding differently requires identifying the micro-interactions where it occurs and responding in preferred ways. Problematic social media use is a relational challenge, requiring members' attentive responsiveness and creativity to break from its patterned pull – not unlike dance partners finding new steps together.

Professor Tom Strong

Weklund Studies in Counselling Psychology

University of Calgary

The family and culture

We note that families, in many ways, are unique entities. We have already shown that it can be challenging to define what constitutes a family and any definition provided is culturally relevant. CYP's mental health is often influenced by the family life cycle provided by Carter and McGoldrick (1989). In this model they identified eight stages:

1. *Family of origin experiences*: maintaining relationships with family members and peers.
2. *Leaving home*: developing adult-to-adult relationships with parents and starting a career.
3. *Pre-marriage stage*: selecting a partner and deciding to marry.
4. *Childless couple stage*: Developing a way to live together.
5. *Family with young children*: Adjusting to family life and adopting parenting roles.
6. *Family with adolescents*: Allowing adolescents more autonomy and adjusting to midlife marital issues.
7. *Launching children*: adjusting to living as a couple again and to in-laws and grandchildren.

8. *Later life*: Coping with physiological decline, making room for experiences of the elderly and dealing with loss.

It was this model that Dogra, Frake et al. (2005) utilised with Indian mental health professionals. In doing so they recognised that the Carter-McGoldrick model was not immediately transferable or translatable to the Indian context, and even in minority world contexts it has received some criticism. Yet, as the model noted, in life and development there is inherently change in the social context and practice. Thus, the way in which families as a unit, or the individual members within it manage that change will have implications for the whole family (Dogra, 2010b). In other words, the stages of the family life cycle might vary between and within cultures, but the concept of different stages of development is likely to hold true. Practitioners then can compare their own experiences and those of the families they have worked with using the model as a benchmark for other experiences (Dogra, 2010b). We point out here that for the purpose of our discussion it is not necessary to debate the benefits and criticisms of the model, but rather we acknowledge that the issues that may arise around families in any cultural or local context will be important as families are influenced by not just their culture, but also by other demographic factors like their socio-economic status or their environment as rural or urban.

Parenting styles

Intrinsically linked to the construct of the family is the role of the parents. Ultimately, the ways in which parents bring up their children, the rules they set, the reward and punishment systems they impose and the values they reflect will have a significant impact on CYP's engagement with digital media, and the support they have from parents if and when things do not go as expected in the online environment. It is important to consider then, the type of parenting you might be facing in your work with CYP.

In this section we focus on parenting styles in general to give you some context, and later in the chapter we more specifically connect with digital media. It should be noted that the idea of parenting 'styles' has come under criticism recently, as neglecting the complex *processes* and pathways that comprise parenting journeys. We suggest that the fluidity and change inherent in technology use can help us to see parenting in the broadest possible sense. Nonetheless, the idea of styles does have some relevance and is still used today. The typology of parenting was developed by Baumrind (1966), who identified authoritative, authoritarian, permissive and uninvolved parenting styles. Maccoby and Martin (1983) divided permissive parenting into two subtypes: neglectful and indulgent, or laissez-faire. From a minority world perspective, authoritative parenting is sometimes described as the 'preferred norm' in that parents demonstrate high control but are also responsive to the child's needs. Parenting styles will have implications for children's digital media use, and therefore we go through each in turn.

Authoritative

Baumrind (1991) argued that child outcomes from authoritative parenting tend to be more positive because this kind of parent tends to display high levels of warmth and high levels of control. He noted that parents are usually reasonable and nurturing and although they set high expectations, they tend to explain disciplinary rules clearly and engage in dialogue with the child. Consequently, children of these parents tend to have greater competence, exceptional maturity, assertiveness and self-control (Baumrind, 1991). Furthermore, these CYP tend to do well academically and have positive social orientation (O'Connor & Scott, 2007), and tend to be happier, more socially competent and have higher self-esteem (Yardi and Bruckman, 2011). Research evidence that has explored authoritative parenting has reported that these parents tend to employ child-centred disciplinary practices, using verbal reasoning, and thus they tend to raise CYP who have higher levels of moral reasoning and prosocial behaviour (Krevans & Gibbs, 1996). Research evidence has shown that authoritative parenting is likely to be the most effective parenting style, but it must be remembered that it is also the most demanding in terms of parental energy and time (Greenberger & Goldberg, 1989). This is because there are clear standards set, limits to what is permissible, but the reasons for those are explained during dialogue with the child (Yardi & Bruckman, 2011). Problematically, there is a systemic inequity for those families who are facing adverse circumstances, and this may impact on their family functioning (as we indicated earlier) (Kohen, 1998).

Authoritarian

Parents who adopt an authoritarian style tend to combine low levels of warmth with high levels of control (Baumrind, 1991). Baumrind noted that these parents tend to use a strict style of discipline for their child, characterised by low levels of negotiation, lack of communication, limited flexibility, high use of punishment and high expectation. Thus, authoritarian parents tend to have unreasonable expectations that their rules are obeyed but do not give the child any reason or explanation for them (Yardi & Bruckman, 2011). Research evidence suggests that when CYP experience excessive parental control from early years it tends to correlate with negative outcomes, like increased anxiety (Chorpita & Barlow, 1998) and childhood depression (Rapee, 1997), and this may be a consequence of limited opportunities to develop autonomy for independent exploration of the environment (Bowlby, 1977). Research also suggests that the low warmth associated with authoritarian parenting is associated with child outcomes like hostility, anti-social aggression, delinquency and rebelliousness (Baumrind, 1991). Furthermore, CYP of authoritarian parents tend to have the poorest adjustment (O'Connor & Scott, 2007).

Permissive

Permissive parents are those that exhibit high levels of warmth, and display low levels of control (Baumrind, 1991). Baumrind argued that these parents tend to act more like a friend to their child than a parent, typically employing low-level discipline with few rules, have little or no expectations and provide virtually no guidance or direction. He noted that while parents with a permissive style do tend to be loving and nurturing, they usually allow their child to solve their own problems. These parents take some responsibility for their child and the child's behaviour, but they tend to avoid confrontation and are not demanding (Yardi & Bruckman, 2011). Research suggested that this permissive parenting style results in a lack of involvement, follow-through and confidence in parenting ability, and these were important factors predicting child problem behaviours as reported by teachers and parents (Calzada, 2000). This may be due to the over-indulgence of the parents leading to CYP having a decreased social competence and they may struggle to achieve academically (Chen, Liu & Li, 2000).

Uninvolved

Baumrind (1991) described the uninvolved parent as one who combines low levels of warmth with low levels of control and one who does not adopt a specific style of discipline. He argued that this kind of parent tends to have little interest in parenting, with limited communication and nurturing, and consequently the child is given a great deal of freedom. Thus, these uninvolved parents are neither demanding of their children, nor responsive to their child and their needs (Yardi & Bruckman, 2011). Although ostensibly freedom and autonomy may feel like positive aspects of childhood, when this is not controlled and overseen because the parent shows little interest in their child or their behaviour, the outcomes tend to be negative. Research has indicated that these CYP tend to feel rejected and therefore exhibit externalising behaviours like aggression, delinquency, attention problems and hostility (Barnow, Schuckit et al., 2002). It is thus clear that these factors strongly influence emotional and social development and a sense of self. How the child's sense of self, parental and wider expectations interplay with each other are of great relevance in child mental health.

It is inevitable that different parental styles will be found in all cultures, though the parenting style's interactions with other factors may lead to different outcomes. McLoyd et al. (2000) argued that different child-rearing practices between different ethnic groups may be demonstrating diversity within groups and/or the lack of rigorous research rather than real differences. The child's perception of discipline and the parent may also be relevant in the way these styles play out. Dwairy (2004) and Dwairy and Menshar (2006) demonstrate that culture is difficult to separate from social context and gender issues. In a Palestinian sample, different types of parenting styles were associated with different problems (Dwairy, 2004). A study with an Egyptian sample found that in rural communities, parents used authoritarian styles with boys and authoritative styles with girls, whereas in urban areas the authoritarian style was used for girls (Dwairy and Menshar, 2006).

Parental digital skills

Given how important parents are to CYP and their use of digital technology, it is helpful to think about how their parenting strategies might be enhanced or limited by their own digital abilities. Inevitably, some parents will have higher levels of digital competence than others, and some will require more guidance and assistance than others. Indeed, digital literacy is more than simply the functional skills to operate online; it also requires an ability to critically assess information and to develop social and communicative skills, as well as content-creation skills (van Deursen, Helsper & Eynon, 2015). Thus, the digital skills of parents and of their children are more relevant in mediating internet use than previous forms of media like television viewing (Livingstone, Òlafsson et al., 2017).

There is evidence to suggest that parents with greater levels of digital skill and digital literacy, and parents of younger children (who are potentially less digitally competent at a younger age) are more likely to oversee their child's internet use (see Nikken & Schols, 2015). These parents are better placed to solve technological problems, give advice, mitigate risks and facilitate positive engagement with a range of different platforms. Parents who play an active role in their child's use of digital media can do so for learning, helping their child build relationships and entertainment (Farrugia, Grehan & O'Neill, 2017). Conversely, Farrugia et al. noted that parents who lack digital competence and may be overly concerned about the risks associated with digital and social media will find it more challenging to support and advise their child about online matters or may not recognise the risks, and may find navigating the online environment a challenge.

For some families, there is a significant gap between parental and child knowledge (Mascheroni & Cuman, 2014), but we must be cautious as that is not necessarily always the case. Recent work shows that personal levels of digital skills are diverse and this impacts on whether individuals can take advantage of the opportunities that the Internet offers (Litt, 2013). For some parents, then, guidance is needed so that they can help their child in the modern world (Children's Commissioner, 2018), and it may be that in your role as a practitioner you can provide some of this guidance where appropriate. It is argued that this guidance should be aimed at different ages of children. In other words, recommendations have been made that parental educational packages are created that target different developmental groups, in ways that outline how parents can maximise benefit and minimise risk while promoting internet-safety education (Holloway et al., 2013). Furthermore, we would also recommend that guidance recognises different types of families, and some parents will need specific guidance because of their vulnerabilities. Also, different parents have different attitudes and beliefs about digital media which will have to be accounted for in any conversation. Livingstone and Blum-Ross (2020) conceptualised parents broadly into three genres (i.e. clusters of practices) in terms of approaches to digital parenting, and we describe these in Table 9.1.

Table 9.1   Approaches to digital parenting (Livingstone & Blum-Ross, 2020)

Cluster of practice	Description
Embrace	This is when parents seek out digital technologies for them and their families to gain skills.
Balance	This is when parents try to balance the risk and opportunity by encouraging some digital practices but not others.
Resist	This is when parents try to reduce or stop the time spent on digital technology.

Parental concerns

When considering the role of parents in children's digital lives and in protecting and safeguarding their mental health it is necessary to attend to the concerns raised. In the general rhetoric of moral panic around the possible negative impacts that digital media, and more specifically social media might have on CYP's mental health, parents are often at the centre and are at least key recipients of those kinds of arguments. Parents can find it challenging to understand the extent to which digital media plays a role in their child's life and, while they do see some benefits of this, they also have concerns (Symons, Ponnet et al., 2017). For instance, in the UK, most parents feel that the benefits of being online outweigh the risks and that they can trust their child to be responsible online (Ofcom, 2017).

Research has shown that online safety is a major concern for parents as they express fear about the potential impact that digital media use might have. In a survey of 1,000 parents in the USA of children aged 10–14 years key concerns expressed were that their child might meet a stranger online, with one in three of them being worried about cyberbullying because of the impact that this conduct has on wellbeing (boyd and Hargittai, 2013). A qualitative study in Kenya and Nigeria found similar concerns from parents about the impact of social media on puberty-related behaviour, alongside reflections on comparisons with television and radio consumption (Bello, Fatusi et al., 2017). Amongst all their various concerns, there are seven fears most commonly expressed by parents, as outlined by George and Odgers (2015):

1. Concerns about who their child is interacting with online.
2. Cyberbullying.
3. The possible interference of online relationships with in-person friendships.

4. The digital divide between adolescents and their parents.
5. Damage to the adolescents' sense of self and identity.
6. Possible effects of mobile technologies on adolescents' cognitive performance.
7. Negative effects on sleep.

We discussed most of these issues in earlier chapters and encourage you to reflect on those. Here we look at how and why these concerns manifest for parents and how that relates to parenting.

Parental mediation

Parenting styles, skills and strategies need to be adapted to suit the use of the Internet, digital media, gaming and social media in CYP's lives. The quickly evolving changes and enthusiastic embracing of these through mobile devices exerts a strong influence in the home, leaving parents with a significant responsibility (Terras, Yousaf & Ramsay, 2016). The way in which parents respond to this is by implementing mediation techniques to safeguard their child's interests online. This has commonly been referred to as 'parental mediation', which represents different ways in which parents become involved in their child's use of digital media, especially internet-enabled technology (Khosrow-Pour, 2018).

Highlighted point!

It is important to acknowledge that not all researchers and practitioners adopt the term 'parental mediation', and some resist this term (Khosrow-Pour, 2018), favouring the notion of 'proactive media monitoring' as not all strategies mediate media use but may still protect CYP (Padilla-Walker, Coyne et al., 2012).

This is particularly important because of the growing 'bedroom culture' in the minority world, where many CYP use the Internet on their own in the bedroom (Livingstone, 2007). This use of the Internet in private settings can make it challenging for parents to monitor and mediate their child's online behaviour (Symons, Ponnet et al., 2017). Despite these difficulties, parents frequently apply mediation strategies. One study, for example, showed that 86% of British parents mediated their child's internet use, with 67% restricting access and 45% using technical solutions like filters (Mascheroni & Cuman, 2014). Again, this is an area that has some cultural variation, as parenting practices are tied to cultural norms. One US study measuring ethnicity and parental monitoring of White, African American, Hispanic and Asian parents showed that they did indeed use parental mediation strategies in different ways (Connell, Lauricella & Wartella, 2015). Connell et al. demonstrated that Asian parents were most likely to limit the time allowed for their child to spend on screens, with Hispanic parents limiting their children's time the least.

Parental mediation and our understanding of these techniques is not new. Early work on mediation stemmed from concerns about the practice of CYP viewing television, and the related screen time (Nathanson, 1999). Nathanson argued that this included active mediation, restriction and co-viewing. These broad conceptualisations that were applied to the context of television were further categorised in different ways as applied to digital media use. These were described as strategies for 9–16 year olds by Livingstone, Haddon et al. (2011):

- Active mediation of internet use by active discussion or sharing the activity.
- Active mediation of internet safety.
- Restrictive mediation.
- Technical controls.
- Monitoring by checking the CYP's online activities after use.

Understanding the ways in which parents mediate and control their child's use of digital media is important for you as a practitioner. As a responsible adult you may also be using mediation techniques with the CYP you work with, or you may be advising parents on this matter, or you may be communicating with them about how they engage relevant adults in these matters. You may also be able to have some input on advising parents about ways in which they can mediate their child's use of these media, while respecting children's rights. We therefore explore the main types in turn. In so doing, however, we stress that parents are likely to try out several different mediation strategies in their effort to maximise opportunity and minimise risk, and their choices are likely to be shaped by their values and personal preferences (Livingstone and Blum-Ross, 2020; Livingstone, Òlafsson et al., 2017).

Active mediation

Active mediation is described as a strategy parents employ to engage their child in conversations about media content, both negative and positive, and apply strategies that CYP can use to be more aware of negative content and how to avoid it (Padilla-Walker, Coyne et al., 2012). The key to active mediation is communication: parents talking to their child about their online practices (Livingstone & Helsper, 2008). In other words, parents talk to their child about safety, give them advice and help them address problems as they arise

(Betton & Woollard, 2019). By using active mediation parents encourage their child to develop their critical thinking skills and reflect on the content they are consuming, and as such this type of mediation has a more protective effect against possible negative impact (Collier, Coyne et al., 2016).

Restrictive mediation

Restrictive mediation is an alternative strategy that can be used by parents. Some parents reported restrictive mediation techniques by blocking their child's access to devices or using filters or blocking certain features (Vaterlaus, Beckert et al., 2014). Some parents use restrictive techniques by imposing rules on peer-to-peer communication by banning instant messages, or emails or other social media communication channels (Livingstone & Helsper, 2008). In other words, restrictive mediation is where parents set rules for their child and restrict their access to the use of digital media and curb the amount of time the child is allowed to spend online (Betton & Woollard, 2019).

Co-using

In traditional work the idea of co-*viewing* was related to television and parents mediating the amount of time spent watching screens. Thus, the notion of co-*using* relates to the parent co-listening, co-reading or co-watching the media, meaning that the parent consumes the media with their child (Dorr, Kovaric & Doubleday, 1989). For co-viewing, or co-using, in relation to technology this mediation strategy is not as straightforward as it was for television, as parents were able to engage in other tasks while a television was on, but many uses of the computer or mobile device require the co-use to be active (Livingstone & Helsper, 2008). Co-using then is when parents are actively using the Internet, digital or social media with the child, helping them post pictures or comments and being present while the child is using these (Betton & Woollard, 2019). Co-using (or co-viewing) is conceptualised in two ways when related to digital media, as outlined by Chakroff and Nathanson (2008):

- *Intentional co-using/viewing* is when the parents are actively concerned about the potential impact that the media might have on their child and therefore choose to actively view or listen with the child.
- *Passive co-using/viewing* is when the parent is circumstantially in the same room as the child who is consuming media, but not necessarily actively engaging with those activities.

Monitoring

Monitoring is an important mediation strategy as it can occur on a range of levels and may engage the child or may not. Parents may engage in monitoring and checking their child's digital footprint, and may check on their internet history, messaging and posting of images, and may monitor the number of minutes used on the phone and data usage (Vaterlaus, Beckert et al., 2014). They may do this overtly or covertly (Livingstone & Helsper, 2008). Parents should be careful to adequately assess the potential impact of their chosen monitoring strategies, ensuring that their children's privacy and rights are respected.

Technical restrictions

An increasing number of digital surveillance and restrictive tools are becoming available for parents to use to impose technical restrictions on their children's use of technology (Betton & Woollard, 2019). The age of the child appears to have some impact on what kind of restrictions parents impose, with parents of very young children more likely to impose parental controls (Livingstone et al., 2018).

Of course, there are different influences on parents and cultural values and religious beliefs, and their own upbringing may have an impact on their choices. In Box 9.3, we describe some research from Saudi Arabia that considers parental mediation of social media use.

Box 9.3: Expert voice: Najwa Albeladi

The role of parental mediation in the relationship between adolescents' use of social media and family relationships in Saudi Arabia

My study explores the effect of parenting mediation strategies on family relationships and the use of social media among Saudi teenagers. A quantitative research design was used, including questionnaires with data collected from 393 Saudi students aged 13–18 years from intermediate schools and high schools (two boys' schools and two girls' schools). The key results of this study showed:

- Over one-third of students (35.62%) reported that they spent between 3–5 hours per day on social media.
- Another 30.79% spent more than 6 hours daily on social media. The most popular social media sites among Saudi teenagers were Snapchat and Instagram.
- Around 28.1% of participants used social media for entertainment purposes.
- 24.9 % used social media to communicate with their families and friends.
- 18.8% used social media to share and find out new information.

(Continued)

Saudi teenagers indicated that on their social media accounts, they were friends with either of their parents (47.07%) or with both (35.62%). Furthermore, they reported that either father or mother (39.95%) and both father and mother (35.11%) were mostly aware of their activities on social media.

The data showed a significant negative correlation between excessive use of social media and family relationships (cohesion and expressiveness), while a significant positive correlation was found between excessive social media usage and conflict, which means that the cohesion and expressiveness between family members decreased when the adolescents used social media excessively. This is probably because cohesion can result from CYP spending time with their parents and siblings.

Finally, regarding the impact of parental mediation on family relationships and social media use, the results presented that monitoring and technical parenting mediation strategies were found significantly associated with social media use and family relationships. The study showed that technical mediation has a negative influence on family relationships. From the viewpoint of the teenagers, the result found that some parental mediation strategies (such as active mediation of internet use, restrictive mediation and active internet mediation of internet safety) had no impact on Saudi adolescents' social media use. This is indicative of the varying degrees of effectiveness of these strategies in various countries and cultures, as well as the extent to which parents have correctly implement these strategies. See Albeladi and Palmer (2020) for more detail.

Najwa Albeladi

Researcher and PhD student from Saudi Arabia (studying at University of Leicester)

Research in parental mediation is growing, especially as parents attempt to balance children's right to privacy and their need to learn and engage with digital media. Parents need to ensure that their strategies are age appropriate and respectful of children's rights. In Europe, a survey of 6,400 parents of 6–14-year-olds identified that there are two prominent mediation strategies: enabling mediation, which is associated with increasing online opportunities and subsequently risks; and restrictive mediation, which minimises risks but also reduces opportunities (Livingstone et al., 2017). A similar European study of parents found that they tend to use at least two forms of active mediation of internet use (68%), most commonly including communication and being close by when the child is online (Mascheroni & Cuman, 2014). This study reported that active mediation in terms of CYP's internet safety was common (77%) but setting rules was less common. Consequently, it was argued that different types of mediation are applied related to the context of internet use, the age of the child and so forth. Furthermore, it has been recognised that restrictive mediation is negatively associated with child-initiated support-seeking from parents, and thus an enabling mediation strategy promotes CYP's agency and encourages child-initiated requests for parental support (Livingstone, Òlafsson et al., 2017). Notably, then, it may be helpful to combine restrictive and active approaches to stimulate the CYP's autonomy (Valkenburg, Piotrowski et al., 2013).

We asked several parents their views of digital media and how they keep their children safe, and in Box 9.4 we outline their responses to our question.

Box 9.4: Expert voice: Darren Doherty, Amber Dumbelton-Thomas, Caitlin McReynolds and Rowena Wilding

Parental opinions

We present four UK parents' views:

I have two daughters aged 7 and 10. I currently don't think they're old enough to have social media accounts. They do browse the internet and browse YouTube and watch TV shows and music, but I wouldn't want them to have their own accounts and post things, far too young with preying people and trolls and goodness knows what else.

They have lots of fun playing games and can chat securely to friends on WhatsApp. They can do so many other creative things on their tablets and educate themselves in constructive ways. Their school and we [their parents] educate the girls about the dangers of social media and they seem to be alert to it.

Darren Doherty

I think social media is part of life so as parents we should focus on kids developing a sensible attitude. My kids are 10 and 12. They have Xbox accounts and they both have phones. They won't have Facebook or Instagram accounts until they are 13. They know not to share real identities online. My eldest has WhatsApp but doesn't seem bothered by social pressures. If he did, I might monitor differently. Digital media are now a part of life, and the challenges that COVID-19 has more recently presented, mean that my children are relying more on technology for social connections and education.

I like them chatting and collaborating on Minecraft or Fortnite. It's the YouTubers that worry me most: they are so young and opinionated, with huge audiences. So, I have taught the boys about fake news and conspiracy theories: alongside safety that's probably the most important thing we can do.

Amber Dumbleton-Thomas

As a full time lecturer of business and teacher training (FE & HE) since lockdown I have been teaching my full timetable from home, finding new ways of working, and adapting my teaching resources, especially as when delivering

(Continued)

teacher training it's imperative that I 'model' best practice in my delivery, so I have been using Zoom, Teams and YouTube, often videoing practical activities to appeal to all learners. I have also been home-schooling my daughter (age 7) who, due to the high emphasis on technology at school, I'm very strict on not allowing her a computer, a tablet or access to online gaming, in order to promote more balance and practical skills. However, the sheer volume of work for me has been so high that despite my best efforts at creating engaging activities, I have relented and given her the morning to play on a cheap tablet I bought two years ago for a long flight; she now plays Roblox, Minecraft and various other games, which has meant I can actually spend the morning working, supervising home learning in the afternoon, then get back to my work in the evening.

It's been the only way that I can balance childcare and work. I've even got into one of the games myself which helps me wind down in the evening and appeals to my 'completer finisher' nature. We've also embraced some incredible online resources like the ones on BBC bitesize which are so engaging for young people. It's definitely changed my attitude to technology; my daughter even self regulates her time online herself some days, and while I will always encourage balance, the use of technology for me is a lot less detrimental than I had thought.

Caitlin McReynolds

As millennials, my husband and I grew up during the decade in which digital became commonplace, hitting our teens as mobile phones became a necessity rather than a luxury, and social media began to gather momentum.

In that context, it makes sense that digital technology plays a huge role in our lives, and in the choices we've made in raising our children. Digital communication makes the world a smaller place; my children can video call family members in another country at a moment's notice.

Video technology has opened opportunities for them that we may not otherwise have been able to offer; they take immersive French lessons on their Kindle and have piano lessons via video link. We believe that by supervising them in using and navigating the digital tools available to them now, we are setting them up to be able to use them safely and responsibly on their own as they grow older.

Rowena Wilding

Benefits and challenges of mediation

The fundamental challenge is balancing rights, freedom and autonomy against the need to protect CYP from any potential harm. In the online environment a degree of trust can be helpful, especially as children grow older and demonstrate a greater capability of looking after their own interests.

Adults, therefore, question whether CYP have the maturity and capacity to protect themselves from harm, and if it is decided that they do not, then it may be necessary to treat them paternalistically (Mathiesen, 2013) (we acknowledge the gendered nature of this framing). Mathiesen argued that the paternalistic argument is based on four basic premises:

1. That parents have an obligation to protect their children from harm.
2. When CYP are online, they are at risk of harm.
3. To protect CYP from harm, information about children and their activities is required.
4. A useful way to gain this information is via parental monitoring.

It is argued by Mathiesen then, that the logical conclusion of paternalism based on these premises is that parents have a duty to monitor their child's online activity.

This paternalistic position tends to result in two main responses from parents, as shown by Gabriel (2014):

• Banning their child from participating in the online culture by reducing or removing the risk, typically by banning them from the Internet.
• Blaming the CYP, putting them down or criticising them for their use of the Internet in ways that might not be socially acceptable.

However, Mathiesen cautions that accepting this parental position encourages a broader consideration of its relevance in the online context and the possible counter-view. Before we present this, we encourage you to reflect on this paternalism perspective and think about the extent to which you agree or disagree with it.

We therefore encourage you to try the reflective activity in Box 9.5.

To what extent do you favour a paternalistic position?

Box 9.5: Reflecting on paternalism in the context of digital and social media

To what extent do you feel that a paternalistic position is acceptable for protecting CYP online?

(Continued)

Write in your reflective diary your own view on this matter. Do you feel that parents need to take a paternalistic position in terms of monitoring and mediating their child's media usage? Why do you feel this? To what extent should CYP have autonomy and freedom online?

Paternalism has its merits and is well-intentioned as its primary goal is to protect CYP from harm. However, Mathiesen (2013) noted that there are some problems with implementing this position in the context of online behaviour. Mathiesen argued that this position makes several assumptions in this context that can be challenged:

- It assumes that CYP are facing genuine threats online.
- It assumes that monitoring online behaviour provides parents with useful information.
- It assumes that parents can use that information to make decisions that ultimately protect their child from any harm.

You may be able to see, however, that these assumptions are not entirely appropriate and therefore have been subjected to some critique. In Mathiesen's (2013: 267) own words:

[M]y view is that, while these objections to the necessity and effectiveness of monitoring generally weaken the case for monitoring, they do not defeat it. For that, it must be shown that children have a right to privacy that overrides the paternalistic justification for a policy of monitoring.

In other words, the challenge to parents taking a paternalistic position relates to the issues of respecting the child's privacy and autonomy. Thus, Mathiesen outlined three main objections to this position:

1. Risks are likely overstated. Although parents may have a role in monitoring their child's use of the Internet and their engagement in social media, the overstating of risk is arguably a symptom of the moral panic. However, it is important to note that CYP's internet and social media use is not completely risk free and the risks may be sufficiently significant to warrant some monitoring.
2. Arguments have been put forward that monitoring is ineffective and therefore serves no function.
3. Some scholars argue that the monitoring itself might lead to harm.

Arguably, it is more effective to educate CYP, encourage them to behave responsibly and teach them about the possible harmful aspects associated with social media use (Gabriel, 2014), and we argue that a 'digital ethics of care' framework is a useful way to do this (see O'Reilly et al., 2020). Furthermore, research has suggested that for those CYP whose use of the Internet has been restricted, they are less exposed to risk and therefore potentially less able to cope with other kinds of risk when they emerge, because the more CYP use the Internet the more skills they develop (Mascheroni & Cuman, 2014).

Simply banning or heavily restricting CYP's online activity is likely to have detrimental effects as they may not only resent this but will also have reduced opportunities to learn how to use the Internet responsibly (Glazzard & Mitchell, 2018) and may be disadvantaged in comparison to their peers. It is important that CYP are given a chance to develop their resilience as parents are leading childhood to become 'tame' with their *helicopter parenting*, that is, intensive parenting (Creasy and Corby, 2019). Creasy and Corby argued that because of this CYP's lives are being stifled, with parents and other adults seeking to remove all risks by taking over decision making and restricting what they do, which ultimately reduces their opportunities to engage, explore and learn.

Simply imposing rules or setting boundaries is unlikely to be helpful, especially if the parent–child relationship is not strong and/or positive, and this approach to mediation is likely to make that more fragile (Edwards, 2018a). Additionally, research suggests that having no or little exposure to the digital world is a disadvantage (Przybylski & Weinstein, 2017), as CYP who are restricted may feel that they are excluded by their peer groups if they are not allowed online and this may interfere with their social lives (Clarke, 2009). Interestingly, research indicates that mothers tend to be more restrictive than fathers and are more restrictive with girls than boys (Livingstone, Òlafsson et al., 2017).

Highlighted point!

Research indicates that simply restricting use of digital or social media encourages the CYP to resist this and can prompt some to hide their use, which means they may not turn to their parents in a time of need (Asam & Katz, 2018).

Parents tend to use a combination of parental mediation approaches to manage their child's digital media use, especially in terms of managing social media and helping keep their child safe (Ofcom, 2017). Research indicated that parents tend to favour active mediation techniques of talking to and engaging their child and encouraging their child to use the Internet for educational purpose (Livingstone et al., 2014). Furthermore, CYP do report that they want support from adults. For example, research has shown that 77% of them wanted their parent to support them if they encountered something concerning online, although 25% felt that their parents did not understand their online lives (UK Safer Internet Centre, 2018).

Notably, as children grow older there is typically a decrease in mediation practices, and adolescents tend to be less receptive to parental rules (Symons et al., 2017). This coincides with the problem that managing digital media use and setting boundaries about screen time becomes more difficult as the child grows older (Ofcom, 2017). This is important as it also relates to the child's development, as when the child reaches adolescence they strive toward independence, rely more on their peers and begin to develop their own sense of identity, and this blends on- and offline. This is something generally recognised by parents, and Edwards (2018a) provided an overview, described in Box 9.6.

Box 9.6: Key research evidence

The journey to digital independence (Edwards, 2018a)

Edwards (2018a) showed the journey toward digital independence on the developmental spectrum as consisting of the following.

- During infancy, it is important for parents to limit their children's access to digital media to set up good patterns for the future, and instead of using screens, create time with the child to play and go outdoors. Very short periods on digital media can provide sensory stimulation, with appropriate games and activities.
- As the child reaches three–five years, they become increasingly exposed to technology as part of their exploration, and there are many apps that facilitate learning and entertainment. However, screen time should be an addition to other activities, not a substitute for them. Supervision of this age group is necessary as they learn to navigate the Internet.
- As the child reaches middle childhood and their tweens, they can read and understand the content of websites. Some parents allow their children of this age to own their own phone. This means that it becomes more challenging to supervise and monitor their use of digital and social media as they are more private in their use of the Internet.
- During adolescence, digital and social media are significant to connect with others and grow their friendships. Furthermore, this age group begin to recognise the issue of credibility of information and they start to critically assess the information they find online.

Practical support and mitigating risk to mental health

Thus far, we have highlighted the important role that parents play in supporting their children, creating boundaries, safeguarding them from harm and mediating risk. We have also shown that parents have a range of different concerns about their children's welfare online. Many of those concerns relate to the potential impact that digital or social media may have on their child's mental health and wellbeing. There is therefore a range of evidence published with practical ideas to help parents (and practitioners) to support a healthy approach and guard against risks to their mental health. First, in Box 9.7 we present some guidance for promoting healthy and positive engagement with digital and social media as outlined by Edwards (2018a).

Box 9.7: Practical tips for promoting healthy engagement (Edwards, 2018a)

There are several strategies parents can be encouraged to use to help their child take a healthy approach to digital and social media used, including:

- Co-constructing family rules with the child and agreeing a social media plan at home.
- Making sure that there is a time when it is agreed that smartphones, tablets and computers are turned off. Ideally this should be at least two hours before bedtime.
- Agreeing that the phone should not be checked in the morning until other more important tasks are achieved such as brushing teeth and eating breakfast. In this way the phone can be incorporated into the morning routine but is not of paramount importance.
- Setting boundaries around important family activities like mealtimes or family communication points in the day. Parents ideally need to model appropriate behaviour, so need to ensure they also follow the rules and are clear about why they are broken if they are.
- Encouraging an open dialogue and trusting relationship with the child will help to open channels of communication. In cases where certain social media platforms or apps are upsetting the child, parents can encourage the child to uninstall these.
- Having open and honest conversations about the photos and videos the child views can be helpful. Reminding the child that photos and videos are frequently heavily edited and not realistic will help them realise that.
- Having conversations about what is realistic and reminding the child that it is simply not possible to go to every event or be part of every conversation.
- Parents need to consistently be there for their child, being open and supportive.

It is important when applying these strategies that parents are active in their parenting. An involved, nurturing parent will ultimately communicate effectively with their child, promoting healthy use of digital media while working to safeguard against risk. It is necessary that parents in carefully monitoring their use, while consulting and engaging their child, will need to also be mindful of the signs that their child might be using these media in negative ways, be negatively impacted, or using these media too heavily. Glazzard and Mitchell (2018) listed several ways in which parents can be mindful of any potential digital media overload and we describe these in Box 9.8.

Box 9.8: Practical tips for signs of overload (Glazzard & Mitchell, 2018)

There are several strategies parents can be encouraged to engage with to identify any possible overuse of digital and social media, including:

- If the CYP is experiencing anxiety or low mood, they might be using digital or social media to help them feel better. These children should be encouraged to find healthier ways to deal with their emotions.
- If the CYP shows signs of social isolation and is engaging with social media as a substitute for face-to-face interaction, it is important to have some supportive conversations to manage this situation.
- If the CYP is showing signs of feeling stressed, being angry or frustrated, or possible signs of depression, this may be an indication that they are using digital and social media too much.
- If the CYP expresses anger or frustration when they are prevented from using digital devices or asked to put them away, this could be a sign of withdrawal effects.
- If they are turning to digital or social media because they are experiencing adversities in other areas of their life such as school, this may result in problematic engagement.
- If monitoring the CYP's social media use shows that they are gradually increasing their usage, then it is important to raise attention to this issue and start to find alternative ways to spend time.
- If the parent starts to feel that the online world is becoming more important to the CYP than the offline one, it is important to open a conversation about this.

Parental influence

Social learning theory posited that children are perceptive regarding what their parents are doing, and they observe and model those behaviours and attitudes (Bandura, 1977). Although this theory is not perfect and has been subjected to some critiques from different disciplines, at its simplest it is fair to say that CYP learn from their parents. This is also the case with online behaviour. It can be difficult for parents to set boundaries and expectations for their children in terms of content and use of digital media (Livingstone, 2013), and yet parents must become aware of their own online behaviour and their own engagement with these platforms. In other words, parents need to model being a good digital citizen, including how they treat other people online, as their children will be observing and modelling this behaviour (Glazzard & Mitchell, 2018).

Highlighted point!

If parents are using digital media in irresponsible ways, or are offensive or aggressive online, then their children may replicate this behaviour (Glazzard & Mitchell, 2018).

Glazzard and Mitchell (2018) argued that this also extends to other digital decisions like screen time. Parents who spend considerable time attached to devices, staring at screens, failing to engage with face-to-face conversations because of distractions of the smartphone, are likely to be mirrored by their children. Research of 2,300 parents of children under eight years showed that parental time spent on screens, including television, smartphones, computers and tablets, was associated with the amount of time their children spend on screens (Lauricella, Wartella & Rideout, 2015; Terras, Yousaf & Ramsey, 2016). If parents are establishing rules and boundaries around device use, social media engagement and gaming, then they need to acknowledge such rules in their own use. In other words, parents 'have a responsibility to model the responsible use of social media' (Glazzard & Mitchell, 2018). A recent narrative review demonstrates how important this is by collecting a range of evidence and commenting on it, and we provide an overview of this in Box 9.9.

Box 9.9: Key research evidence

Narrative review by Terras and Ramsay (2016)

Tarras and Ramsay (2016) presented a narrative review of evidence that examined parental practices concerning digital communication technologies and apps, and more specifically they focused on smartphones in terms of how they relate to the use of technology by their children. They noted that there are two important factors to consider:

- Parental technology use is closely related to that of their child.
- Despite parents expressing concerns about the nature and extent of their child's mobile (cell) phone use, parents themselves frequently engaged in unsafe internet behaviours and excessive smartphone use at home.

CYP are inevitably influenced by their family's views of digital and social media. Although CYP may have a sound technical knowledge, it requires more than this to function online. As a practitioner you might be able to help parents to support their children by considering these issues in open communication with the parents you work with. This may further extend to supporting parental and child digital skills. Understanding the influence of parents is important in the context of digital media and mental health. Specifically, in terms of digital media and the Internet, two parenting dimensions are considered especially important: parental control and parental warmth (Valcke, Bonte et al., 2010). Valcke et al. argued that when it came to internet use, parents often resorted to authoritarian styles and this parenting had an important impact on their child's engagement with the Internet. It is helpful, then, to think more broadly about how influential parents are in terms of their child's online behaviour, their mental wellbeing and self-esteem, and in meeting their basic needs. Indeed, parenting styles are argued to act as a risk or protective factor for cyberbullying victimisation, with those parenting styles with warmth practices being a protective factor, but authoritarian parenting being a risk factor for cyberbullying (Martínez, Murgui et al., 2019). There is limited research however on parenting styles in terms of influence on parental mediation.

Sharenting

An important aspect of internet safety that parents do not always consider is that of sharenting and the role they play in exposing aspects of their children's lives online. Sharenting is a new concept but one that is now recognised by dictionaries. For example, in the Collins Online Dictionary, sharenting is defined as a habitual use of social media by parents to share photographs, events and news about their children. In other words, sharenting denotes when parents share information about themselves and their children via the Internet/social media (Blum-Ross & Livingstone, 2017) without necessarily having the consent of the child. Many parents are using social media platforms to share with others posts about their children, and this can start before their child is born as they share pictures of ultrasound scans and then map their child's lives through social media (Lazard, 2017). There is a social side to sharing ultrasound photographs (see Figure 9.1) as this is a form of communication that is about sharing the joy of pregnancy, and a media side, related to the ongoing storage, analysis and mining of images and data that corporations may use to track its users (Leaver, 2015).

Figure 9.1 Sharenting

It is arguably unsurprising that there is such a large volume of sharenting practices going on. We live in an era where smartphones have sophisticated cameras and enable parents to capture the nuances and details of their children's lives. Indeed, the most common practice of sharenting is the sharing of photographs, with scientific research showing that 98% of parents surveyed posted pictures of their children on Facebook (Bartholomew, Schoppe-Sullivan et al., 2012). Notably, mothers are typically sharing more photographs and more frequently than fathers (Lazard, 2017). Clearly, this sharenting satisfies a range of needs for parents, as it encourages their need for self-realization and social approval (Brosch, 2016). Brosch also noted that some parents may feel socially isolated and deprived of adult company, and the use of digital and social media enables them to connect with other parents.

Although there are some positive associations of sharenting, this side of social media has attracted a range of criticisms. Some go so far to say that this parenting activity is a means of showing off to others, and in the popular press is thought to be a form of digital narcissism (Lazard, 2017). More commonly, however, concerns are raised about the digital footprints of children all over the Internet that set out children's private lives without the children being fully aware of this. It is therefore the case that these children's digital footprints are being created at a time when they are too young to understand or to provide their consent, and their 'future ability to find, reclaim or delete material posted by others is uncertain' (Holloway et al., 2013: 5). This is especially the case for some parents who excessively share intimate details of their children (Brosch, 2016). Problematically, this raises a possible conflict between parental rights and privacy and children's rights and privacy (Steinberg, 2017). Steinberg noted that parents may be well-intentioned and share aspects of their children's lives without thinking about how their posting may impact their child's wellbeing through disclosing information and images of their children. This therefore raises several questions as presented by Blum-Ross and Livingstone (2017):

- Is sharing a child's image publicly a violation of that child's privacy?
- What if the parent's purpose is to reveal and reflect on their own parenting?
- Who should decide when to share a family photo?

These questions are important as parents must have responsibility for safeguarding their child's privacy, and yet they frequently share information in public spaces (Betton and Woollard, 2019). Importantly, there has been some research that has examined the perspectives of CYP about these issues. It has been shown that some do feel uncomfortable when their parents share photos of them online, but often parents were not aware of their views on this (Children's Commissioner, 2018).

A related area concerning children's privacy is that of the growing number of surveillance tools available to parents to observe their children. There are a growing number of tools available to parents, like baby monitors, nanny-cams, GPS tracking devices and surveillance tools (Marx & Steeves, 2010). Marx and Steeves reported that parents are actively encouraged to buy surveillance tools under the rhetoric of keeping their children safe as responsible parents would. Thus, there are a wide range of digital media available to parents. This includes wearable technologies which are becoming increasingly popular. One such example is the 'smart sock', which is a surveillance boottee which allows parents to monitor the baby (Leaver, 2015). In Chapter 1 we provided a discussion of children's agency and children's rights, and such surveillance has created some tension between parental monitoring and keeping children safe, and children's rights to privacy and agency. For example, some parents are using GPS trackers in a child's bag or pocket to keep a watchful eye on their child and noting where they are (BrickHouse, 2009). Furthermore, some parents are putting features on their child's smartphone to track and control children's physical location, with some parents feeling comforted knowing where the child is.

A final thought: Parents allowing access to their own social media

It is worth mentioning at this point in the chapter that one way in which parents influence their children is through their own social media accounts. Some parents appropriately or inappropriately allow their child to access and use their own social media accounts and related digital platforms. Some parents will allow their child to use their smartphone or tablet and they do not always supervise this usage. This tends to be the case with younger children as they are less likely to have their own accounts and may not have their own devices either (Children's Commissioner, 2018). However, the Children's Commissioner noted that when children are accessing their parents' social media accounts, the adult and child's social worlds become blurred and children can be exposed to adult content not suitable for their age, which some children do find concerning. Some parents go further by helping their child to set up a social media account despite the age restrictions and become complicit in helping their child lie about their age (Hargittai, Schultz & Palfrey, 2011). Hargittai et al. noted that this was because some parents believed it acceptable to violate restrictions if they felt the platform enhanced education, family communication and/or social interaction with their peers.

Conclusions

In this chapter we have considered the role that parents play. In completing this chapter, we provide a reflective piece about working with families in a digital world from an expert in this field. In Box 9.10, we present the perspective of Vicki Shotbolt, who is the CEO of a parent-focused organisation, Parent Zone.

Box 9.10: Expert contribution: Vicki Shotbolt

Role: CEO

Organisation: Parent Zone

Brief bio: Vicki Shotbolt is the founder and CEO of Parent Zone. Parent Zone is an organisation that aims to help parents and families to navigate the challenges of a connected world. Thus, the work that Vicki does focuses on digital family life.

(Continued)

Parent Zone – digital family life

A curious thing happened when technology first hit family life. We collectively overlooked the profound impact it was going to have on parenting. We anticipated the democratisation of knowledge, were surprised by many of the risks and felt hopeful about the flexibility it would bring to the workplace. We transformed businesses and empowered managers to use technology properly. We invested in schools to make sure they were connected and ready to educate CYP for a digital world. Almost no resources went towards the crucial business of parenting.

There was some inevitability to this forgetfulness. Despite widespread understanding of the impact parenting has on a child's outcomes (the single biggest impact alongside poverty), parenting remains something that we struggle to talk about. We quite rightly respect family life as a space that is private. Parenting is a task that is personal, based on individual choices that need to be left to individual parents. 'Every family is unique' and 'you know your child best' are oft repeated messages that are absolutely true. But there is another truth, and that is that researchers have been studying the impact of parenting styles since the early 1960s. We know a huge amount about what children need from their parents. We understand things like parental attributions – the explanations parents give for their child's behaviour – and we have well evidenced, robustly tested parenting programmes designed to support good enough parenting. All this work should have prepared us to have effective support ready to help families adapt to the new demands of parenting in a digital world. It should have helped us to anticipate some of the issues that technology would bring to the parent–child relationship and the challenges that parents would face in a connected digital world – but it didn't.

There are numerous reasons for that. The first is that we tend to take for granted the huge societal role parents play. They are the ultimate forgotten workforce: raising the next generation with love and enthusiasm because that role of 'Mum or Dad' is such a joyous one. But the fact that we don't think of them as a collective workforce means that we don't consider their personal development needs. Imagine a company that told all of its employees that from Monday, they would be required to adjust to new devices, new interactions with their customers, a different level of information about their own work and also the work of all their competitors – and furthermore there would be no training. They were going to be asked to just 'get on with it'. That's pretty much what we did to parents.

We also fell into the trap of thinking that if it was digital it was different. Only people specialising in it were thinking about the impacts – and those people tended to ignore anyone working in separate but very relevant fields. If you were outside the 'tech circle' you were happy to be excluded because it was difficult and unfamiliar – and you were probably busy enough dealing with 'real world problems'.

The third and perhaps the most pervasive reason we didn't talk about the impact technology was going to have on parenting is the one that persists. It is the simple fact that we don't like talking about parenting. We're very comfortable discussing what parents need to know or what we'd like them to do – we're pretty quick to point out parents who are 'getting it wrong'. But parenting support, parenting techniques, parenting styles – all of these things are simply not mainstream. We prefer to adopt the approach that lots of young people like to take when they're talking about studying for exams. The super-cool kids are the ones who claim to be able to get A-stars without putting in any work. We know the truth is that they are studying hard – but it's way cooler to be seen to be smashing it with ease. That's what we do with parenting. We put pressure on ourselves to do it with ease and make asking for help a sign of failure – instead of a sign that you're putting in the work that's needed to do a difficult job well.

Finally, it was the speed of change. When hard science is moving fast it's difficult for social science to keep up.

As a result, parents were ill prepared to raise digitally resilient children. We simply hadn't thought about them properly at the start. We gave them messages and advice that actively undermined good enough parenting. We gave them information that pushes the parenting styles that are least good for children.

So we have a lot of work to do – and that is the work that Parent Zone does. We start with what we know about parenting support and effective parenting styles. All of our messages are crafted with authoritative parenting in mind because that is the style that works best. We think about how we can help parents to do accurate behaviour attributions so that they can respond to the correct issue. Our inbox demonstrates what that looks like in practice. Take this case study.

A parent contacts us because they're worried about the amount of time their child is spending gaming. During the conversation it emerges that he has changed school – and countries – twice in the previous three years and was about to be moved again. In addition, his parents' marriage had broken down and whilst it had been very amicable, he had been 'a bit upset'. Our job was to help the parent start to attribute the behaviour – excessive gaming – to the right cause.

What we see here is that a parent's ability to parent well is negatively impacted by messages that do not promote confident, authoritative parenting and accurate attribution. Give a parent a digital cat to kick and that's what they tend to do. Tell them that they are digital immigrants and can't possibly guide their children through difficult digital spaces and they will back off and retreat to authoritarian parenting. Offer them tools that will 'save them a job' and we are offering them a shortcut to failure. A way out to uninvolved parenting.

The future could be very different. By asking 'What do children need from parenting?' we could get closer to a proper model of support for parents. That will include well designed, family friendly digital spaces. It will also include information that is accessible, evidence based and empowering. We can parent this generation to flourish in a world that might look different again to this one, but the key to doing that can only be found in the knowledge we already have about supporting good enough parenting.

10

THE ROLE OF SCHOOLS IN MENTAL HEALTH AND DIGITAL MEDIA

Learning points

After reading this chapter, you will be able to:

- Explain the role that schools might play in mental health
- Explain the role that schools might play in digital media and safety
- Understand the importance of educator wellbeing

Introduction

As CYP spend much of their time in education, schools play an important role in monitoring, educating and protecting children from the possible negative impact of digital media. They also foster an environment of collaboration and shared responsibility with the CYP in their care, including other stakeholders such as parents. In the age of increased mental health condition prevalence, those in education are finding that they are taking more responsibility for educating CYP about mental health, reducing stigma, raising awareness of mental health, and supporting those with diagnosed conditions in the classroom through an agenda of inclusion. In this chapter, we cover several areas that are important for schools: the responsibility that schools have in mental health; in raising awareness and supporting those with need; the value of using digital media in schools to achieve this; and how schools can educate children to use digital media responsibly in ways that help protect mental health. The wellbeing and mental health of teachers and other school personnel is also important, and we consider the challenges they face in the current climate. For simplicity in our chapter when we are referring to those involved in educating children broadly, like teachers, head teachers, teaching assistants and the like, we use the term *educators* to include all groups, and when we are just referring to teachers, we use that term.

School responsibility for mental health

Mental health is becoming increasingly an issue for schools and is now on the agenda. Not all educators will feel they have the necessary specialist skills or training background to engage in tasks that attend to positive mental health, and the challenge of working with CYP with significant mental health conditions can feel difficult for some. In our own research educators and young people talked about this issue, despite that we did not specifically ask about this. The participants in our own research had different views about how schools might support the promotion of positive mental health through education and how they might meet mental health needs in those that required support. Interestingly, there were four key issues that arose in this research (see O'Reilly, Adams et al., 2018):

1. Educators felt that mental health promotion, prevention and intervention was not the primary role of a teacher.
2. Educators reported that they felt they had limited skills to manage the more complex mental health conditions.
3. Young people reported that they relied heavily on their teachers for mental health education and, in some cases, support for their own wellbeing.
4. Educators and young people felt that parents also played an important role.

To help you understand these perspectives we provide the educators' views in Figure 10.1 and the young people's views in Figure 10.2.

Clearly, these views show that schools could have an important role in the promotion of mental health and for those educators supporting CYP with mental health need. Our research is congruent with other studies that have also shown that schools are at the forefront of promoting positive mental health, reducing stigma and educating them about mental health issues, as CYP report wanting to learn about mental health in the school environment (see also Bone et al., 2015). Schools cannot work in isolation though and partnerships with other agencies, such as mental health services, are important to succeed (Svirydzenka, Aitken & Dogra, 2016).

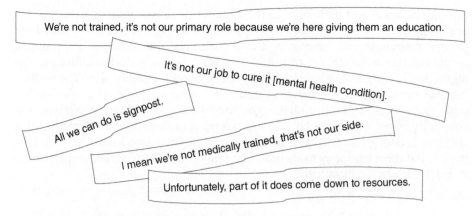

Figure 10.1   Educator perspectives

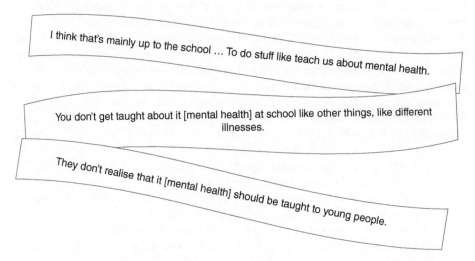

Figure 10.2   Young people's perspective

Schools have always taken their responsibilities toward CYP seriously, but our research, and the evidence base more broadly, indicates that educators have some concerns about dealing with mental health. The educators in our study reported that they lacked time, training and other resources, and this is hindered further by the limited opportunities they have for debriefing or formal supervision, which is consistent with other work in the field. What was particularly interesting from the perspectives of the educators and the young people was a general conflation of different levels of mental health and illness. Our participants moved from talking about positive mental health and wellbeing in basic ways, to talking about more significant levels of mental health conditions, as well as issues of emotional trauma, self-harm and suicidal ideation. For schools then, a multi-tiered approach of mental health promotion, illness prevention and intervention for those diagnosed is needed (Vaillancourt, Cowan & Skalsk 2016). We consider what this means for schools in Box 10.1.

Box 10.1: What this means

The research evidence suggests several things:

- That young people feel that teachers have a role to play in teaching them about mental health as an educational resource, as part of their education, in the same way as they teach about other issues, like sex education or digital safety.
- That young people feel that teachers play a role in supporting their mental health needs, at least in the sense that teachers may be the first adults they confide in if they are feeling anxious, depressed or are self-harming.
- That teachers do not always feel they have the confidence, skills or training to manage mental health in the classroom, particularly when this need is more complex.
- That teachers may need support in managing any additional responsibility that might be given to them.

We asked Zoe Chapman, a secondary school teacher, and Luke Whitney, a primary school head teacher, what role schools might play in children's mental health. We asked them about the role schools play in mental health and how that is enacted in practice; their views are expressed in Boxes 10.2 and 10.3.

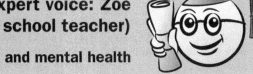

Box 10.2: Expert voice: Zoe Chapman (secondary school teacher)

Schools and mental health

Under the Children Act 1989, teachers have a duty of care towards all pupils to ensure the welfare and safety of all children. This clearly must include a responsibility for supporting their mental health and wellbeing. With issues such as

(Continued)

low self-esteem, anxiety and depression becoming increasingly common in children, I firmly believe that schools should be supported to implement effective support processes and to be able take the necessary steps to promote positive mental health.

This is, however, different from being entirely responsible for the mental health of every child. Teachers, typically, do not hold qualifications in mental health, nor are the majority trained to be able to identify or diagnose specific mental health issues; nor should they be. However, all schools should have access to local authority and NHS support and should be able to signpost families in the right direction for support. Unfortunately, the current situation where there are waiting lists of over a year for some children and families to access support from child mental health teams means that many schools are buying in counselling services as the waiting list for NHS referrals is so long; this inevitably has an impact on school budgets.

Ultimately the responsibility for child mental health must lie with the parent/carer of each child, but schools do have responsibility for promoting positive mental health and identifying key trigger areas such as social media, relationships and assessment and exam stress, for example, and so there needs to be wider support for school leaders and teachers with access to high-quality, fully funded training and resources.

Mrs Zoe Chapman

Secondary school teacher

Leicestershire

Box 10.3: Expert voice: Luke Whitney (primary school head teacher)

Schools and mental health

To assign 'responsibility' to any one agency is unhelpful. Children are known to a range of professional services, and all are secondary to parents. The real question coalesces around the support we give to families to nurture child mental health, giving our CYP the skills they need to cope.

At Mayflower, we believe that the education system can create intolerable pressure to achieve against national benchmarks. This serves only to promote anxiety in our parents, which will be passed on to their children. Anxiety is the enemy of what good schools set out to achieve, most notably engagement, wellbeing and, interestingly, high academic standards.

To combat this, our staff understand that engagement and wellbeing lead to academic success, not the other way around. We passionately believe that children who engage, and show high levels of wellbeing, will succeed socially, emotionally and academically. Our mission is to create engagement and wellbeing for all, giving children a broad, creative, skills-led curriculum, enveloped by compassion, pastoral care, parental outreach and a strong sense of purpose by linking provision to the UN Sustainable Development Goals.

Central to this is the structured teaching of mindfulness, allowing our children to live in the moment, and acquire skills to manage their often conflicting emotions. Joy, happiness and laughter characterise our school, and we know the children take this learning home every day. They are the vanguard of our parent partnerships, supporting their families to promote better mental health.

Luke Whitney

Head Teacher

Mayflower Primary School (Leicester)

As we have discussed, the extent to which schools can address mental health, in terms of information seeking and awareness and supporting those diagnosed, is an area that has garnered some controversy; we therefore encourage you to reflect on your position on this and try the reflective activity in Box 10.4.

To what extent do you think schools have a responsibility for mental health in their students?

Box 10.4: Reflecting on responsibility

How much responsibility do you think schools have to promote positive mental health?

How much responsibility do you think schools have to identify difficulties in students and support?

Write in your reflective diary your views on both questions; we move on to consider these in the next sections of the chapter.

A good example of this challenge has been highlighted in the UK. Recently, the British government has proposed that schools need to take more responsibility for child and adolescent mental health, and has committed funding to support training (Public Health England, 2017); yet educators themselves often feel they lack confidence and skills to implement this effectively, and report being pressured by other demands of their job, such as academic targets, meaning that they have insufficient time for intensive pastoral care (i.e. the facility of a school to protect the physical and emotional health of its pupils) (O'Reilly, Adams et al., 2018). The initiative has been criticised for failing to commit sufficient funds to ensure success, and for failing to recognise the broader context and issues at stake, making it a 'sticking plaster solution' (Sims-Schouten, 2017). Without additional support and funding for services, both inexperienced and specialist mental health services, teachers and other educational staff will have no place to which they can signpost more complex cases (Karim and O'Reilly, 2017).

Mental health promotion in school using digital media

We first introduced you to the differences between promoting positive mental health, preventing ill health, and providing interventions to those with need in Chapter 2. There have been calls for schools to play a more significant role in mental health promotion as we discussed there. Some approaches to mental health promotion in schools have shown some success, although the resources required to implement this fully can make this challenging. For example, mental health promotion needs to be integrated through a provision of a continuum of intervention programmes and services which need to focus on the social and emotional learning of all students in school, but also actively involving young people, school personnel and the wider community (Weist & Murray, 2008). Reflecting the 'whole school approach' (see Weare, 2000), which requires input from senior leaders, embeddedness in the school policy and curriculum design, needs care and support for CYP from school personnel and expects engagement with parents.

Despite the significant challenges, schools can do much to promote positive mental health, educate about mental health, reduce stigma and raise awareness of mental health. Digital media are one tool in the armoury to achieve this. One of the positive and encouraging endeavours arising in some contemporary societies is the role that digital media may play in such health promotion activities. In a recent scoping review, it was concluded that technology can be used effectively to help young people promote their positive mental health and create positive change (Zinck et al., 2013). The use of digital media in such activity within schools has, however, received only limited attention. Social media especially has an information dimension, a media-related dimension and a social dimension (Kaplan & Haenlein, 2010). Because of this, it has started to be embraced for physical health promotion (Fergie, Hunt & Hilton, 2016) but also has potential to be used for universal mental health promotion (O'Reilly, Svirydzenka et al., 2018).

For this to be utilised in schools effectively, however, we need a better understanding of how CYP engage with health information online (Fergie et al., 2016). Digital media *could* be used more actively as part of mental health promotion programmes. In our own work on this issue, educators and young people proposed that there are a range of benefits for promoting mental health in this way (O'Reilly, Dogra et al., 2018). Our participants argued that learning about mental health and illness through different platforms was important and social media, and more broadly the Internet, could be a helpful educational tool if supervised by teachers in the classroom. In other words, the young people in our study thought it was helpful that they could use digital media to seek out information about mental health and illness but wanted their teachers to work with them to assess the credibility and trustworthiness of the information to validate their learning.

Highlighted point!

CYP can only learn effectively about mental health and illness if the information they are engaging with is both credible and appropriately presented. Furthermore, the information needs to be accessible, based on solid evidence, and should be age appropriate.

CYP tend to prefer quick, accessible and sometimes anonymous ways to find out information about mental health and illness; digital media can be a useful way to make this happen. The involvement of educators in the engagement of young people with digital media for health education could, however, be important. Evidence shows that universal mental health promotion activities should be sequenced and coordinated using an active form of learning (Durlak, Weissberg et al., 2011). We therefore asked Mark Bowler, an educational psychologist, about possible ways in which this could be achieved, and this is presented in Box 10.5.

Box 10.5: Expert voice: Dr Mark Bowler

Digital media, mental health promotion and schools

Using digital media for mental health promotion could arguably provide educators with a fast, cost-effective and efficient way to support CYP in learning about mental health and as a tool for raising awareness and reducing stigma.

(Continued)

Young people access digital media for a variety of reasons and often for a large proportion of their time. This can lead to an assumption that screen time for CYP leads to negative effects. Of course, there are occasions where this discourse has some truth, but social media is one of the most common activities undertaken by CYP.

In moderation, use of social and digital media can be very powerful and informative. We all routinely turn to digital media of some form or another when we want to research something, find an answer, explore perspectives, seek validation, and CYP are no different. Accessing social or digital media can still be considered a form of social interaction, which can have both educational and psychological benefits.

I think there can be a (mis)perception by adults that CYP sitting in front of a screen is unhealthy and socially isolating. However, a common reason they turn to online media is to communicate with others. Therefore, if patterns of online communication reflect how CYP communicate in person, then it makes sense to have information that they might be seeking available to them.

Providing information about mental health online could be valuable and, because information is accessed in a behind-the-scenes manner, it could reduce stigma. Whilst online mental health promotion could be fast, informative and cost-effective, there is always a caveat. The private nature of accessing information could be detrimental in that it could be overwhelming, lead to comparisons and not be what the person was looking for.

Dr Mark Bowler

Educational Psychologist, Staffordshire

There are also steps educators can encourage CYP themselves to do to take care of their own mental health in relation to their use of digital media. As we have shown throughout the book, thinking about mental health is closely linked with thinking about other aspects of development such as self-awareness, real versus 'fake' social media profiles, understanding interactions with online groups and our own digital 'footprint', and our digital ethics of care. We encourage you to work with CYP to remember these key facts about mental health and social media as outlined by Page, Held and Levine (2020):

1. We depend on each other as human beings. We need to communicate with others. We argue, and we make friends.
2. Companies need us to use social media to make money.
3. Not everyone feels strong all the time.
4. What we say, type, share and do on social media should aim to promote better lives for everyone.

Further advice has been proposed by Edwards (2018b), and we outline this in Box 10.6.

Box 10.6: Practical tips for CYP to care for their mental health (Edwards, 2018b)

Educators can encourage CYP to look after their own mental health by:

- Encouraging them to take breaks from their digital media and screens and engage in other activities they enjoy.
- Reminding them to ask for support if it is needed and to suggest sources of support that they can access.
- Show them that it is not healthy to compare themselves to others, in the classroom environment or online. Remind them that not everything online is real or trustworthy.
- Encourage them to care for their diet, get enough sleep and engage in exercise.
- Seek out trusted adults and talk to them when they have concerns or are struggling.

Supporting students using digital media

Schools around the world are becoming more creative about how they can help provide support for their students. For example, a group of researchers in the USA carried out a review of the literature on the ways digital technologies can be used to treat mental health issues in majority world countries (Naslund, Aschbrenner et al., 2017). They found 49 studies that showed that there was potential for online, text messaging and telephone support interventions for CYP to be supported with their mental health need. The researchers placed the interventions into four groups, many of which involved schools, health centres or families at the heart of the intervention:

1. Technology for supporting front-line care and educating health and education workers.
2. Mobile tools for detection and diagnosis.
3. Online self-help programmes.
4. Substance misuse prevention and treatment programmes.

Despite limitations relating to access, the researchers found that digital technologies, if used effectively, had potential to extend health workforce capacity within the school environment to support mental health, which was particularly valuable in cases where there was a need to support clinical cases in remote or hard-to-reach regions, or put patients in touch with each other.

There was also the suggestion that technologies could have a role to play in mobilising efforts for intervention earlier than might be otherwise realised when CYP reach crisis point and require professional intervention.

There are a range of text message services across the globe that work in different ways, and we give you just one example here from the UK that operates within schools, via a text messaging service called ChatHealth. This service covers both physical and mental health, but much of the message traffic is for the more sensitive areas like sexual health and mental health. We provide the evidence available on this service in Box 10.7.

Box 10.7: Key research evidence

Evidence from ChatHealth (UK)

ChatHealth is a two-way communication platform that provides a mechanism for young people aged 11–18 years to communicate directly with school nurses in an anonymous way through SMS text messages (Palmer, 2019). Palmer reported that ChatHealth is held on a secure web-based message management app and it is managed and run through school nurses. ChatHealth has potential to have a positive impact on the health of young people, although there is currently limited empirical evidence. However, this is a service that is reaching about one million adolescents in England, and audit data suggests that young people really value this anonymous means to access school nurses (NICE, 2017). The messaging service is mostly used for questions about mental health and sexual health, although all areas of health are covered. NICE reported that there are important key features built into the SMS service including:

- An out-of-hours automated response, directing young people to alternative services while the school nurses are not on duty.
- An automated fail-safe, including flagging unread messages and system notifications.
- An availability management, which includes shared access to caseloads and the ability to respond to conversations on behalf of other nurses if they become unexpectedly unavailable.

This SMS service was developed by Leicestershire Partnership NHS Trust, and was develop in consultation with the Royal College of Nursing, the police, health professionals and service users to ensure that it was fit for purpose (Endicott and Clarke, 2014). Endicott and Clarke noted that the school nurses were instrumental in the development of the service as they wanted to ensure that young people had alternative sources of support when the service was closed, wanted to ensure patient information was kept safe, and wanted a record-keeping system that was quick and easy.

One of the founders of ChatHealth, Caroline Palmer, has with others developed the service. She has also provided support and monitoring for school nurses across England and we therefore asked for her view on the value of text messaging generally, and ChatHealth specifically, for mental health support in adolescents. We report her view in Box 10.8.

Box 10.8: Expert voice:
Caroline Palmer

The value of text messaging

Health care delivery for our smartphone generation of service users needs to be innovative, age appropriate and easily accessible.

ChatHealth is a safe and secure messaging service that enables service users across the country (including young people) to message a health professional for NHS and evidence-based health advice. In today's world there is information all around us, including online and this can sometimes be incorrect or provided by inappropriate sources; however, service users may not be aware of this. To help combat this and to ensure access to evidence-based health information, ChatHealth is managed by health care professionals and enables service users to access bespoke health care advice and support.

Young people particularly report that they like the anonymity of ChatHealth. They feed back that they like to ask questions that they may feel embarrassed about, and they report ChatHealth enables them to access health care in a way that they don't feel judged. Young people ask questions about a vast range of issues, from concerns around their physical development through to raising concerns they have around their emotional health and wellbeing.

Enabling service users to access health care in ways that are easy and age appropriate encourages service users to take ownership of their health, seek support from services in a timely way and engage through their own choice, increasing the likelihood of much more positive and long-lasting improvements for their health.

Using digital technology within health care can sometimes feel scary for professionals; however, when implemented in a safe way like ChatHealth it is proven that health care professionals engage really well and can see the benefits for their service users.

Caroline Palmer

Digital Development Clinical Lead

Queen's Nurse

Leicestershire Partnership NHS Trust

Before you continue with the chapter, we would encourage you to think about what these challenges of delivering support via text messages by undertaking the reflective activity in Box 10.9.

> What are the challenges of using text messages to support students in school?

Box 10.9: Reflecting on the challenges of using text messages or other non-face-to-face channels in schools

What do you believe might be the challenges of supporting school students with mental health need via text messages?
  In your reflective diary, try to answer these questions:

• Do you think the service would have different impact if different digital technologies were used instead of text messaging?
• Would you find a resource like this useful? Why, or why not?

Using digital media to support those with mental health conditions

Educators are key adults in the lives of CYP and are well placed to see the early indicators of emerging difficulties (Department for Education, 2016). For this to work effectively, they need to have the competencies and skills to recognise the indicators, to support and help CYP in the classroom, and signpost to appropriate agencies or organisations, as well as work with parents. Indeed, signposting can become a central and important activity for schools in supporting CYP when they display signs of more serious mental health challenges.

  However, evidence suggests that teachers typically feel least confident in dealing with CYP with mental health conditions (Rothi, Leavey & Best, 2008; O'Reilly, Adams et al., 2018). They report that they have limited skills and a lack of training (Reinke, Stormont et al., 2011), and argue that they are not always able to differentiate between typical and atypical mental health (Loades and Mastroyannopoulou, 2010; Mbwayo, Muthoni et al., 2019). Although governments are seeking to provide further training to schools to find a cost-effective way of addressing the challenge of meeting mental health needs, this is not a straightforward endeavour. As we noted earlier in the chapter, the UK government, for example, is pledging that all secondary (high) schools are to receive mental health training (Public Health England, 2017). While this is a positive investment in education, it is also potentially misguided as it does not fully account for the factors which might impede its success and holds a misguided assumption that *high-quality* training can be easily found and implemented (O'Reilly, Adams et al. 2018).

Highlighted point!

Training school personnel in mental health requires financial resources, time for them to leave the classroom, their motivation, and opportunities for consolidation of learning.

We want to emphasise that schools are only one agency that is important for meeting the needs of CYP with mental health conditions. It is remembering that not all those with mental health need will want it addressed in the school environment. Some may find it challenging to trust school personnel and may not want their peers to become aware of their difficulties (Hart and O'Reilly, 2017), or in some cases the school environment may be contributing to their difficulties. Furthermore, it is important that society and governments do not overestimate what can be achieved in schools, especially for those with more complex mental health needs. These more complex young people require multidisciplinary input and specialist services (Williams and Salmon, 2002).

Being mindful of educators' own mental wellbeing

In the modern educational environment, there is arguably a greater pressure on schools than ever before. We live in a period punctuated by limited time, lack of training opportunities, insufficient resources, virtually no opportunity for educators to debrief or obtain supervision and increased pressure in terms of their primary role. As we have noted, schools are being charged with increased additional responsibilities related to CYP's mental health, relationship and sex education, safeguarding, and digital literacy, among others. Engagement with digital media has provided new ways for parents and others to communicate with teachers, which for some may lead to abuse, trolling or criticism. It is therefore inevitable that educators themselves are going to feel this pressure, find the educational environment challenging, and may experience threats to their own mental health and wellbeing. This is concerning as teachers' own mental health is very important. An example of this challenge came from data in the UK from a recent survey that was carried out by the National Union of Teachers, which found that almost 50% of the 3,000 teachers they surveyed were seriously considering leaving the profession, with one prominent reason being their own mental health (Adams, 2017). We present an important review of the evidence about educators' mental health in Box 10.10.

Box 10.10: Key research evidence

Review of teacher mental health (Gray, Wilcox & Nordstokke, 2017)

Gray et al. (2017) in their review of the evidence reported that many teachers experience high levels of stress in their daily job, and this can contribute to burnout causing many to leave the profession. Education personnel are crucial members of the public service workforce and therefore their mental health is critical. It is necessary to support teachers and find ways to contribute to their resilience. Collectively education personnel and the CYP are influenced by a range of factors, and importantly this includes those factors associated with the school climate as a positive school ethos can contribute to both CYP and teacher mental health, and this provides an optimal environment to support student learning and growth. In this review of the literature, they found that there are many significant demands on teachers, including expectations of them to manage the classroom and promote gains in students' learning. The review also found that this has become increasingly difficult as class sizes have grown and there is now a greater complexity and diversity of needs across the student body, which is juxtaposed with reduced resources and funding. Additionally, the increased prevalence of mental health need in the student body means that teachers are addressing new challenges that historically were dealt with by families and communities more extensively. It is crucial that these issues are dealt with effectively as a positive school environment and teacher mental health are foundational for student learning and academic attainment. We need to empower teachers, strengthen the school climate, and find ways to empower CYP in managing their mental health needs and promoting their learning.

Educators might be hindered in their ability to support their students who are diagnosed with mental health conditions because the stressors associated with their profession can impact on their abilities (Kidger, Gunnel et al. 2009). For example, educators might experience excessive workloads, challenges with their students' behaviour, meeting school targets, examinations and inspections (Naghieh, Montgomery et al. 2015), to name just a few.

If educators are to respond to these challenges effectively, they need to be able to offload the emotional impact that working in this way may have. Our own research highlighted how important this can be. Our educator participants felt that their general lack of opportunity to debrief and offload any emotional impact when dealing with troubled CYP did have a negative impact on their own mental health. They identified a range of issues that impacted on their wellbeing, and we outline a small selection of their quotes in Figure 10.3.

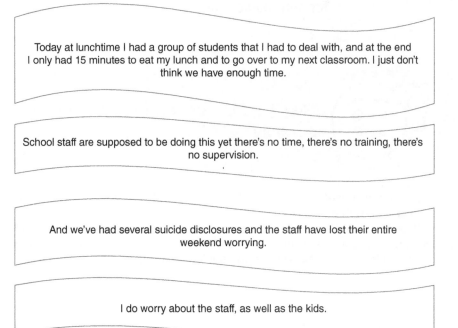

Figure 10.3 Issues impacting educator wellbeing

Schools working with parents

We acknowledge that schools do not operate in isolation. Indeed, schools spend considerable time engaging and communicating with parents. It is in CYP's best interest for schools and parents to work together as parents play a crucial role in maintaining positive mental health in CYP and supporting those with mental health need, as we discussed in the previous chapter.

We encourage you to reflect on your own views of the role that digital media might have as a communication tool between schools and others and direct you to the reflective activity in Box 10.11. As you reflect on this, think about some of the dramatic changes that COVID-19 has brought about in education. During the time of writing, the COVID-19 pandemic has dramatically increased – and some might say changed – the volume and nature of use of technology to deliver teaching and learning. We suggest that this presents new, realistic opportunities for families, communities and services to place what we understand about CYP more centrally in our activities as practitioners (Levine, Morton & O'Reilly, 2020).

> What are your views about the role of digital and social media for communication at school?

Box 10.11: Reflecting on the role of schools

What might the benefits and challenges be for schools in using social media to communicate with parents?

Write in your reflective diary your views on what you believe might be the benefits of school personnel using social media to communicate with parents and the wider community. What do you think the challenges of this might be?

Glazzard and Mitchell (2018) emphasised the importance of empathy toward parents and the building of trust by being collaborative. They noted that this is especially important if educators find a need to report concerns about a child's use of digital media. Likewise, if a parent discloses concerns, it is helpful for educators to actively listen and work with parents.

Notably, some schools have moved to using social media to facilitate home–school communication and to market their organisation. Schools no longer need to print out letters to parents as they can text, email, WhatsApp, post messages on Twitter or Facebook, and blog about events, information, important messages and so on to reach them. Thus, the communication aspect of social media can allow schools to create a broader community of practice and promote inclusivity if everyone has access to mobile technology. Of course, this also provides a mechanism for parents to communicate with the school, by sending texts, instant messages, emails or blogs. Parents can share their thoughts online and review the education their child is receiving. This can be of benefit and can also present challenges for schools.

Conclusions

In this chapter we have considered the roles of schools in using digital media to promote mental health, educate about mental health and support those with need. We have illustrated the potential for using digital media for communicating with CYP and for communicating with parents. In completing this chapter, we provide a reflective piece from an expert in this field about the role schools might play in promoting positive mental health and protecting vulnerable CYP in relation to digital media. In Box 10.12, we present the perspective of Dr Jessica Lester, who has been undertaking research in digital media, education and mental health for many years.

Box 10.12: Expert contribution: Dr Jessica Lester

Role: Associate Professor of Inquiry Methodology

Organisation: Indiana University, USA

Brief bio: Dr Jessica Lester is an Associate Professor of Inquiry Methodology in the Department of Counseling & Educational Psychology in the School of Education at Indiana University, Bloomington. Jessica has published over 80 peer-reviewed journal articles, as well as numerous books and book chapters focused on discourse and conversation analysis, disability studies, and more general concerns related to qualitative research.

Digital technology and schools

Increasingly, the world is going virtual, with primary and secondary schools being no exception to this reality. With the rise of new technologies, there is now more than ever before a range of ways that people can interact, engage in networked communities, and even generate data. We are now all living not just with technology but through technology. For many people, including youth, smartphones and other personal devices offer quick and easy access to information and networked communities. From monitoring early warning signs or symptoms to delivering interventions, emerging technologies offer new and innovative ways to work at the intersection of CYP and mental health. Indeed, there remains a critical need to continue examining the place of the digital world in promoting mental health with CYP in schools and other contexts. A plethora of national and international reports, as well as more localised

(Continued)

surveys, have highlighted the growing need for mental health supports for CYP. As such, the very notion of a 'mental health crisis' is widely accepted, with many countries calling for more swift action and resources. It has long been documented that mental health services are chronically under-resourced. However, technological innovations are being positioned as one possible (and promising) avenue by which to expand access to mental health supports (Bucci, Schwannauer & Berry, 2019).

Interestingly, some CYP have reported that social media, and other digitised spaces, serve to connect them to others and various supports and communities in meaningful ways. In fact, some research has even highlighted that CYP frequently turn to digitised spaces to receive mental health supports (Rideout and Fox, 2018). Significantly, some of the scholarship in this area has pointed to the potentiality of augmenting and delivering mental health supports in digitised ways. Uhlhass and Torous (2019), for example, argued that 'current models of care and diagnosis create significant obstacles' and thus forwarded the idea of digital spaces as 'first entry points for clinical services and education' for CYP. Specifically, in their own work, they used a web-based screening platform, which participating youth found to be useful. What Uhlhaas and Torous, as well as a growing number of other scholars, offer is a window into how digitised forms of mental health support can and should expand how CYP might gain access to mental health supports. The idea of digital or telemedicine is not particularly new; however, what it means for mental health care is still unfolding. From using digital tools such as text messaging to smartphone apps to virtual reality environments, there are now a wide range of ways in which youth mental health might become 'more digitised'. Of course, the mere existence of such digital tools does not equate to their utility in addressing mental health concerns. For instance, some scholars have suggested that not all digital tools are evidence-based and therefore may not adequately address mental health (Bry, Chou et al., 2018). Further, the sheer abundance of web-based information is often unregulated and can be overwhelming for the consumer. Certainly, there are a range of benefits and concerns associated with digitised mental health tools (see Bucci et al., 2019, for instance). Nonetheless, the potentiality of tapping digital resources more fully, particularly as a means of responding to CYP's mental health in schools and elsewhere, is what the future of mental health care involves (at least in part). How to pursue both the development and effective use of digital tools to support CYP's mental health will most definitely entail engaging with potential ethical concerns and embarking on transitioning (at least in part) traditional care practices to more digitised practices. While there is no simple pathway forward, the evidence abounds that digital tools hold great potential for supporting mental health; yet, what remains essential, particularly in schools, is access to the necessary resources and training to make this a reality.

11

THE ROLE OF MENTAL HEALTH AND OTHER RELATED SERVICES

Learning points

After reading this chapter, you will be able to:

- Recognise the challenge of help-seeking for mental health conditions
- Identify the challenges of assessing online information
- Critically evaluate the role of online health services

Introduction

Organisations with practitioners who identify, diagnose, treat, support, promote, prevent, CYP's mental health needs have a crucial role in understanding and managing the relationship between digital media and mental health. Formal mental health services, as part of the health service in most countries, are tasked with a range of activities that are central to identifying, assessing, diagnosing and treating mental health conditions in CYP. Other organisations and agencies, such as social care agencies, youth organisations and charities (amongst others), will also play an important role, especially in terms of promotion, prevention and early intervention, as well as referring on to or recommending more specialist support for those in need. All practitioners across the spectrum of mental health services working with CYP, ranging from the very specialised such as child psychiatric services to those in more community context such as youth leaders, sports coaches and the like, will need to have some understanding of the role that digital and social media play in the lives of this population and the way that supports or negatively impacts on their mental health and emotional wellbeing.

In this chapter, we examine the ways in which mental health practitioners and organisations may successfully engage with digital media to carry out their roles more effectively. We move through the broad spectrum of internet-enabled aspects of mental health service, organisation, agency and support, and contextualise this in relation to the challenge of traditional help-seeking in terms of differing mental health need. We start with the more general issues of CYP using internet-enabled technology, digital media to access and assess mental health information and the challenges of appraising the quality of this. This is aligned with the possible value of using digital services to promote mental health, and we build on discussions of this from earlier in the book. Mental health practitioners have an important role to play in this field. We consider what they can do to promote mental health and provide support for those with mental health conditions. We also review how their own beliefs may influence this process. Many services, including mental health services, now use technology to deliver services and some of these are discussed, alongside young people's perspectives and the usefulness of specific mental health apps. The chapter concludes with a brief consideration of how digital media might be used to address inequalities in mental health. Although the focus of this chapter is on mental health, we access research and evidence generated from physical health where relevant to our discussion.

Technological advances

The rise in smartphone use and mobile apps has provided opportunities for learning, peer-to-peer support, and intervention 24-hours per day (Kamel Boulos, Wheeler et al., 2011). Problematically, however, we have large gaps in our knowledge about *how* CYP are using digital media to support their health needs, despite the increased access to health information and intervention through smartphone technology (Wartella et al., 2016). We only have limited evidence about the effectiveness of this information and intervention in terms of mental health (Seko et al., 2014). Nonetheless, it has been argued that the digital revolution has transformed society and altered the work of mental health practitioners working with CYP (Rafla, Carson & DeJong, 2014). Rafla et al. (2014: 472) argued that this transformation in mental health practice has posed

> both challenges and opportunities for mental health clinicians working with teens. Practitioners may discuss online activities with patients to better understand them and to promote their healthy development, augment face-to-face treatments with

online therapies, or organize their practices more efficiently using technology. On the other hand, adolescent patients may be at risk due to their online activities. Clinicians need to be knowledgeable about and mindful of professional, ethical and clinical risks in using Internet technologies in practice.

Of course, digitally mediated activities are not an unmitigated good. Some inspection processes, and more recently during the COVID-19 pandemic, we have seen all too clearly how rapid and comprehensive acceleration of technology use can act as a tool for poor managerial practice, leaving practitioners overwhelmed and client expectations unmanaged.

Similarly, the term 'digital colonialism' has been used since the late 2000s to refer to the ways large technology companies use the tools at their disposal (e.g. proprietary software, the cloud, internet services) to process data about users, and target advertising (or more sinister activity) at them (Kwet, 2019). For digital colonialists, technology infrastructure acts as the railways and sea-going routes of the colonial periods did, enabling companies to expand their reach across the globe, extracting profit (albeit data instead of spices) while power and resources are concentrated in the minority world. Practitioners – and the managers and leaders structuring their services – need to be mindful of these tendencies in the ways they design and deliver mental health support with and for CYP (see Young, 2019).

The challenge of help-seeking for mental health conditions

As we noted earlier in the book, the Internet broadly, and digital and social media more specifically, have become a common and popular way for CYP to learn about mental and emotional health, as well as for seeking out support, intervention and identifying with others. This needs to be considered in the wider context of help seeking. It is widely recognised that much mental health need is unmet. It is the case in wealthier countries, but there can be nearly 100% unmet need in the majority world (Verhulst, Achenbach et al., 2003). Despite the high prevalence of common emotional conditions like anxiety and depression in CYP, many do not receive any help or treatment even when the condition becomes more significant and clinically diagnosable (Mariu, Merry et al., 2012). It is well known that education about mental health and illness is crucial, as well as providing prevention strategies, and detecting and supporting mental health conditions are essential to lessen the global burden of mental health challenges in adulthood (Patton et al., 2016).

There are many reasons why CYP are so frequently unsupported regarding their mental health needs, from basic interventions to complex treatments. One reason may be that accessing mental health information and treatment is not always straightforward. There may be many potential barriers as well as a lack of services available. Additionally, family perspectives about mental health and illness will strongly influence if formal or informal help is sought. Prejudice and misinformation may also influence how family or peers understand mental health conditions and how they should be managed. Before you go further, we would encourage you to think about what these barriers might be by undertaking the reflective activity in Box 11.1.

> What are the barriers to help-seeking?

 **Box 11.1: Reflecting on barriers to help-seeking**

Thinking in the context of mental health need, what do you think the main barriers might be to help-seeking?

In your reflective diary, create a list of the barriers that parents might face in seeking help for their child when they suspect there is a mental health need. Create a second list of the barriers you feel the CYP might face in help-seeking for their own mental health.

Although there are various barriers to help-seeking, such as resources, availability of appropriate services, transport, time, awareness and recognition of the problem, we focus here on one of the highlighted central barriers, that of stigma. We do not repeat the definitions and detail covered earlier in Chapter 2. Here we focus specifically on the role of stigma in help-seeking behaviour. The fundamental barrier of stigma as associated with mental health and illness is a huge challenge for meeting need as this relates to broader issues of trust, fear and confidentiality (Gulliver, Griffiths & Christensen, 2010). Indeed, in their meta-analysis, Guilliver et al. reported that concerns about others finding out were a central issue, alongside discomfort in disclosing mental health symptoms, as well as the challenge that many were not able to recognise that they needed help.

Stigma is everywhere in relation to mental health conditions and this is a significant factor in people's decision making regarding whether to request help from mental health services (Rüsch, Corrigan et al., 2009). This stigma shrouding mental health conditions tends to be pervasive and global. For example, in India many CYP refuse to seek out help for their mental health because of stigma, as well as a lack of knowledge about mental health and negative responses from their peers (Chandra, Sowmya et al., 2014), and this is also the case in minority world countries too (Jorm, Korten et al., 1997; Pinfold et al., 2003).

For CYP, the fear of stigma, being judged by their peers, being subjected to bullying, and the possibility of being treated differently may encourage avoidance from seeking information, support and/or intervention. Indeed, research has noted that young people especially can find communication with adults in authority challenging (Drury, 2003). Thus, the combination of these issues can result in CYP not utilising services that might support their mental health, even if services are available.

A useful starting point for mental health information and intervention may then be the wide range of internet-enabled modalities. This is because online support and information can be accessed anonymously, which reduces concerns about stigma and can remove barriers (Boydell et al., 2014). Research has shown that CYP enjoy the user-friendliness of online platforms for their health, the immediacy of the platform and the privacy that such technology affords them (Matthews, Doherty et al., 2008). Furthermore, in a time when there are economic and resource constraints on services, it is likely that digital technologies will play a greater role in the provision of mental health support and reflect a responsiveness to young people's preferences and finding ways to best meet their needs (Betton & Woollard, 2019). We now consider how digital media can be helpful in the context of mental health, starting with information seeking, and move later toward intervention for clinical conditions.

Accessing and assessing mental health information online

Information is available in abundance through the phone, tablet, computer or television. If CYP want to learn about emotions, positive mental health or any of the mental health conditions that are known, they can seek this information out privately and quickly. Indeed, CYP are accessing large volumes of information through internet-enabled devices (Betton & Woollard, 2019). This therefore provides opportunities for changes in attitudes toward those with mental health conditions and to improve mental health literacy (Korda and Itani, 2013).

Highlighted point!

The notion of mental health literacy was coined by Jorm et al., 1997) and is intrinsically linked to the notion of health literacy which refers to the capacity of young people to make sensible health decisions in their daily lives (Kickbusch, 2008).

Mental health literacy is an evolving concept and one that is a determinant of mental health with possible benefits to individual and public mental health (Kutcher, Wei et al., 2016). Thus, mental health literacy refers to the knowledge and abilities that are necessary to benefit positive mental health (Jorm, 2012). In contemporary understandings, it is argued by Kutcher et al. (2016) that mental health literacy has four main aspects in that CYP require:

1. An understanding of the mechanisms necessary to obtain and maintain positive mental health.
2. An understanding of mental health conditions.
3. An ability and effort to decrease stigma associated with mental health conditions.
4. A drive to facilitate help-seeking efficacy.

Framing mental health literacy through these four domains advances our earlier conceptions of the term as being simply knowledge about mental health conditions (Bjørnsen, Eiletsen et al. 2017).

Arguably, then, mental health literacy can be developed with the help of the Internet, digital and social media. Indeed, for more sensitive health topics, like mental or sexual health, CYP sometimes prefer the Internet as a source of information and support than face-to-face sources (Wartella et al., 2016), although they may want that information validating by an adult (O'Reilly, Adams et al., 2018). Young people report feeling empowered online and are more comfortable seeking out health information this way, especially mental health information (Nicholas, Oliver et al., 2004). For example, one study showed that 85% of young people used the Internet to seek out health information, compared to 10% who used books and 3% who used newspapers (Wartella et al., 2016). Wartella et al. noted that the key areas of health that these young people were seeking information on were stress and anxiety, but also depression and other mental health issues, drug and alcohol use, as well as physical health issues like sleep, colds and flu and general hygiene. Specifically, CYP want this health information to be delivered via social media and video sources (Fergie et al., 2013). Notably, research has indicated that there are three different types of internet users who sought health information as outlined by Fergie et al. (2016) which we outline in Table 11.1.

Table 11.1 Typology of online health information seekers (Fergie et al., 2016)

User	Description	What they do
Non-engagers	These are those who tended to rely more on offline support and therefore engaged less with user-generated content on the Internet. They tended to have strong offline support and engaged less with user-generated health content and avoided accounts of others' experiences.	These CYP tend to rely more heavily on family and friends for health support and information. (Of course, not all CYP have this available to them.)

User	Description	What they do
Prosumers	This group described the least support in their offline lives and tended to engage both in the production and consumption of health-related user-generated content.	These prosumers tended to have reliable emotional support from friends and family or services, but also produced and consumed user-generated content.
Tacit consumers	These individuals consumed health-related content and information but did not produce it.	These individuals tended to consume much user-generated content about their own health, but also had offline support from friends, family or services. They regularly explored user-generated content to supplement these offline resources.

Misinformation and assessing credibility

While CYP frequently turn to the Internet and social media for information about mental health and mental health conditions, it is important that they can assess the quality of the information accessed. This is even more crucial given the range of content providers contributing to and user-generated content available through the Internet. Research has shown that although people should critically evaluate the information they are engaging with, they often feel that they do not have the time, energy or motivation to do so (Metzger, 2007), or they may simply not have the necessary digital literacy skills to do so confidently. Furthermore, there is a risk of confirmation bias with online health information-seeking, as individuals find information online, and then seek further information that confirms it, which makes it difficult to separate the genuine from the fake (Swire-Thompson & Lazer, 2020). The ability of CYP and even adults to differentiate credible, trustworthy information from fake or untrustworthy information is an important one, especially in the context of health information.

CYP do have some awareness that not everything they engage with online is factual or truthful and many know that there is a lot of 'fake' news available. Indeed, many CYP seek out mental health information using the Internet and social media, but frequently want that information validated for accuracy by adults, or specifically seek out trusted sources (Fergie et al., 2013; O'Reilly, Adams et al., 2018). Indeed, as Swire-Thompson and Lazer (2020: 439) articulated:

> No longer is a patient a passive recipient of health advice but they can have an active role in consuming and evaluating health information. However, laypeople are not health experts, and there may be a cost to people having the freedom to research their own ailments. Is the ability to access one's own health information helping or hindering? Answering this question feasibly depends on three factors: (a) the general quality of health information online, (b) whether people are able to come to the correct health conclusions themselves, and (c) if people do not come to the correct conclusions, how much harm is it causing them.

The role and views of mental health practitioners

Mental health practitioners who work with CYP and their families have a fundamental role in providing appropriate support. Those working within mental health services assess, diagnose and treat CYP with mental health conditions and they can play a role in mediating and considering the extent to which their clients are engaging with digital and social media. Betton and Woollard (2019) argued that mental health practitioners could benefit from a three-step approach:

> **Step one**: Those working with CYP can ask for information about the individual's online practices and behaviour, while being cautious of making assumptions that buy into popular rhetorical tropes.
>
> **Step two**: They can make inquiries that seek to understand the behaviours, but more importantly, the meanings of those for CYP, and any impact of them.
>
> **Step three**: The process of becoming an ally. This is where the mental health practitioner can help the child or young person to make good choices about online behaviour that can promote positive mental health and resilience.

In so doing, mental health practitioners need to maintain awareness that CYP will take some risks online and that this is a normal part of development, so they need to be careful not to be judgemental. Their role is to help them develop knowledge and resources to minimise any possible adverse effects (Betton & Woollard, 2019). Indeed, mental health practitioners need to be mindful about and reflect upon their own views of digital and social media. In our own research we found that mental health practitioners tended to have quite negative views of social media specifically (rather than digital media generally) and we outline some of these in Figure 11.1.

However, they did see some potential value in using digital and social media to raise awareness of mental health, decrease stigma and to provide necessary support and interventions. These perspectives are outlined in Figure 11.2. However, we still have a lot to learn about how to do this most appropriately.

Various organisations worldwide who work with CYP and their families are grappling with different ways in which they can engage these populations to protect, promote and treat health. A good example of this is a recent new initiative in Brazil that came about in response to the COVID-19 crisis: ASEC Brazil and Pampili 'Light, Mind, Heart' led by Juliana Fleury. This was a nine-week programme of activities delivered in a virtual environment by trained and volunteer psychologists with groups of three children per session. In Figure 11.3 we cite some of the professionals' views of transforming their mental health support to online technology.

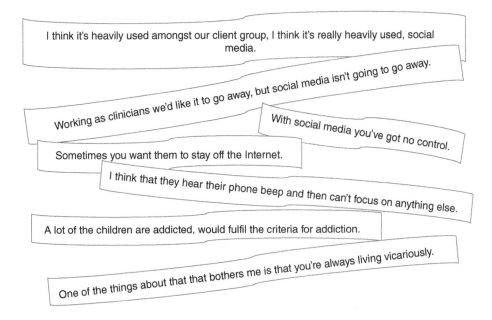

Figure 11.1 Mental health practitioners' negative views

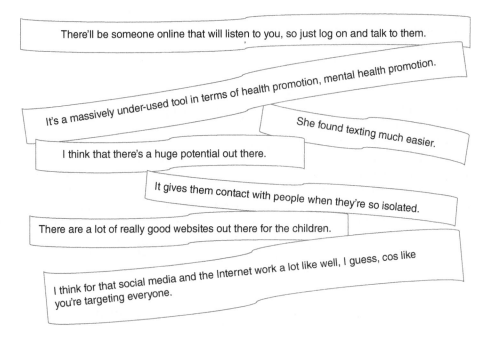

Figure 11.2 Mental health practitioners' views of the value of digital and social media

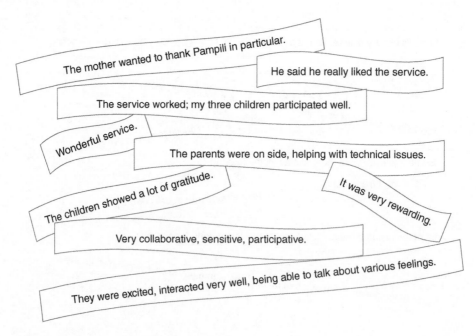

Figure 11.3 Professional perspectives

Mental health practitioners need to remain informed about the developing trends in which different media and technologies might be used, including social media, websites and smartphone apps (Rafla et al., 2014). Rafla et al. noted, however, that it is important that the practitioners learn how and why CYP are using these and to identify any individuals who might be more vulnerable.

For mental health practitioners to engage with digital and social media, websites and apps in the delivery of information, support and/or interventions, they need to be skilled to do so and reflect on their own perspectives. Betton and Woollard (2019) argued that steps need to be taken by health care services across countries so that mental health practitioners have the appropriate digital skills and knowledge. They argued that it would be helpful if practitioners undertook a training needs assessment to reflect on how to incorporate digital skills and confidence by assessing their own training requirements. Betton and Woollard (2019) also argued that mental health teams could think further about how to include digital media to facilitate service improvement, redesign and innovate projects, incorporating digital (or social media) cafés and promoting ways for CYP to share information and experiences.

Delivering services: eHealth and mHealth

Thus far in the chapter, we have considered how digital and social media might be adopted to provide information about mental health, reduce stigma and raise awareness, and as a mental health promotion tool, as well as considering the role that mental health practitioners play in considering the extent to which CYP might be engaging with digital or social media. Such positive aspects of these media are relevant to CYP in the general population. In addition to these important roles that digital and social media might play, they are also being harnessed by health services and other organisations as a mechanism for service delivery, new interventions for mental health, and supplementary aspects of health care provision. There are several ways in which digital and social media can be used to improve health care pathways and to reach wider populations of CYP, through the Internet (eHealth) and the mobile phone (mHealth).

Smartphone ownership, especially in CYP, has distinctly altered the way in which they interact with the world, and the way in which they engage with health care providers (Endicott & Clarke, 2014). A new body of health care has emerged using mHealth, which refers to the use of mobile and wireless technology to help health care providers support individuals to achieve their health objectives. This is part of the broader eHealth, which is the use of ICT in health care (WHO, 2011). The WHO noted that there is tension in definitions of mHealth, but generally involves the capitalisation of the mobile phone's utility of voice and SMS as well as its other functionalities like Bluetooth technology, and third-, fourth- and fifth-generation mobile telecommunication (3G, 4G and 5G).

Technology in a simple form of telephone support has been around for quite a while now and many support organisations provided a way for CYP to call in and ask for help. Many of these have evolved with the development of technology and now provide a suite of options to allow CYP to contact them. We provide an example of an international helpline below in Box 11.2.

Box 11.2: Expert voices: Patrick Krens and Angharad Wells

Child helplines to support mental health

A young person was experiencing feelings of low self-esteem, and talked about feeling isolated and depressed, often crying. His mother had suffered from depression and felt he had received little praise, guidance or support. He felt he was not good enough and compared himself unfavourably to those around him. He felt lost and unsure in life and was struggling to feel complete. He didn't know who else to turn to, so rang a child helpline.

The counsellor at the child helpline talked with him about how childhood experiences can often affect the way we see ourselves in the world. Together,

(Continued)

the young person and the counsellor explored the barriers to trying out new things, and how to start making new friendships and strengthen old ones. The young person had been given the opportunity to join a camp, so together with the counsellor he talked about the ways in which he could explore this possibility (Child Helpline International, 2019).

This is just one example of how child helplines provide vital support to CYP who are experiencing mental health issues. In 2019, child helplines around the world fielded over 2 million counselling calls (Child Helpline International, 2020) from CYP. Of these 554,000 were concerning mental health – the main reason for contact globally – with many CYP calling about fear and anxiety, suicidal thoughts, depression and self-harm. To keep up with the changing needs and preferred communication methods of CYP, child helplines use a variety of communication methods aside from telephone, SMS and online chats, including WhatsApp, Facebook, Messenger, automated 'chat-bot' services and online peer-to-peer forum boards. As well as providing free counselling support and emergency assistance, child helplines also work to introduce CYP to follow-up services.

Recognising the link between digital media and mental health, many child helplines also run outreach programmes to promote digital wellbeing, developing apps to warn CYP of inappropriate online content, providing workshops to teach school children about respectful relationships online, and using vloggers, bloggers, radio and television to raise awareness about impacts of internet overuse on our health.

Child Helpline International is a network organisation of 168 members in 139 countries and territories. We coordinate information, viewpoints, knowledge and data from child helplines, support the creation and strengthening of child helplines, and ensure their recognition as an essential part of child protection systems.

Patrick Krens, Executive Director,

Angharad Wells, Programmes, Operations and Communications Officer

Child Helpline International

There now exists a wide range of technology-enabled approaches, including simple texting, social media, e-counselling/therapy, machine learning, health apps and so on. It is not possible to provide a detailed account of all existing mHealth approaches, but we introduce some of them below.

There are many reasons why mHealth has been growing and increasing in popularity. The use of mHealth means that services can promote treatment accessibility, symptom and activity monitoring, tracking treatment progress, providing personalised feedback and motivational support; it has portability and flexibility in use and can potentially improve treatment or medication adherence (Carter, Burley et al., 2013; Harrison, Proudfoot et al. 2012). Furthermore, mHealth has global capability, and although minority world countries show greater levels and diversity in activity than majority world countries, they are nonetheless widely used (WHO, 2011). The WHO noted though that those in the African region were the least active in terms of mHealth. Given the relatively high levels of mobile phone ownership in the region, this appears to be a missed opportunity.

Highlighted point!

Because of the growth in mobile phone ownership, there is greater potential than ever before to reach larger sectors of the population worldwide with mental health information, promotion and support.

The simplicity of text messaging and instant messaging

Perhaps one of the simplest uses of digital media for health care services in mental health is that of text messaging (SMS) and instant messaging. Text messages utilise mobile technology for communication, while instant messages are internet-based communication tools. Any messaging function, be it SMS, instant messaging or anything else, can be and are being used by health care providers to engage CYP about mental health. This may be because of the popularity of these forms of communication. It is also worth noting that for those with no internet access, text messaging remains the most prevalent form of phone communication (Forgays, Hyman & Schreiber, 2014; Lenhart et al., 2010). Furthermore, text messaging is convenient, low cost and quick, and is therefore a useful tool to engage CYP, and is also appealing to those who are socially anxious and more challenging to engage in face-to-face services (Reid and Reid, 2007).

Evidence now suggests that CYP prefer to contact health practitioners in this way, especially for sensitive issues. For example, research by a UK child service called Childline showed that 78% of the young people who contacted them for help preferred to use email or online chat rather than picking up the telephone and speaking to someone (Frith, 2017a). Indeed, the young people who engaged in our focus groups referenced how important this messaging service on Childline was as a source of trusted support for CYP (see Figure 11.4).

I prefer the way Childline is done because it's a well-known, it's a well-known sort of website where, it's got adverts and stuff and everyone knows what it is.

Yeah if you want an online chat with a counsellor you have to sign up. I think that's kind of good because then like… It makes you feel like you can trust it.

Figure 11.4 Young people's views on Childline's messaging service

There are many ways in which health care providers might use text messages (including web-based text messages) for mental health and a recent systematic review conceptualised these into four main categories (Berrouiguet, Baca-Garcia et al., 2016). They argued that these four categories are:

1. For appointment reminders to promote attendance.
2. For information provision to impart one-way information to patients.
3. For support as a way of encouraging patients to engage or take care of their mental health.
4. To promote self-monitoring procedures.

One area that has expanded quite significantly, at least in health care in the minority world, is the use of text messaging to reduce non-attendance rates and reduce related costs. For example, in the UK a research study illustrated that the use of text message appointment reminders resulted in a 25–28% reduction in psychiatric treatment appointments and was a cost-effective method for enhancing engagement of patients in treatments, regardless of age, gender, ethnicity or diagnosis (Sims, Sanghara et al., 2012). Similarly, in the USA, a study examining 13–17 year old patients in mental health services in low-income areas found that text message reminders significantly improved rates of appointment attendance and improved patient satisfaction (Branson, Clemmy & Mukherjee, 2013).

The use of text messages (and instant messages) may be one-directional, whereby services send information to a patient, but there is no facility for the patient to message back. Alternatively, they can be bi-directional, where a communicative exchange is possible, and patients might ask questions or send information back to the practitioner. Thus, text or instant message interventions connect clinical practitioners with CYP between visits to the clinic, which can increase treatment or medication adherence and may enhance the clinical relationship (Makela, Paavola & Stenman, 2010). Those messaging services that allow social interaction between CYP and their health care practitioner potentially have greater scope for information, adherence and support. This is because the CYP can clarify information if needed.

Highlighted point!

While some governments may see texting as a cost-effective solution to demand, it should not be seen as a stand-alone intervention method and is not a supplement to traditional face-to-face intervention (Mason, Ola et al., 2015).

Text or instant messaging in health care with CYP can provide a comfortable and familiar method of communication. It may improve initiation of help-seeking and promote engagement (Summerhurst, Wammes et al., 2018). Furthermore, they provide a low-cost convenient form of connection while giving CYP a sense of control, and privacy (Gibson & Cartwright, 2014). This can be especially helpful for CYP who have mental health conditions that are characterised by social isolation and withdrawal or communication impairment (Summerhurst et al., 2018). Indeed, Summerhurst et al. noted that providing CYP with mood or anxiety conditions the option to message offers them a less anxiety-provoking means to interact with the supporting practitioner.

Other message-based systems have also indicated some levels of success. In research where WhatsApp had been used there were some positive effects reported, as this platform allowed sharing text, documents and images and therefore led to an improvement in clinical decision making (Kamel Boulos, Giustini & Wheeler, 2016). Kamel Boulos et al. argued that the value is broader than clinical value, as individuals can subscribe to WhatsApp alerts that are relevant to their health care needs, which can lead to motivational messages that encourage healthier lifestyles or provide information. However, in a recent review, research suggests that there are some concerns with using WhatsApp for health (Mars and Scott, 2016). For example, the review showed that many individuals had little understanding of how their information was being transmitted and stored, and there were concerns about confidentiality and data security.

Machine learning

Most computers at the time of writing follow a set of instructions – called 'algorithms' – that are coded into software that runs on a computer. The algorithms tell the computer exactly what steps to take to solve a problem or carry out a task. Machine learning is different. Here, computers are given many real-world examples of data; they learn from the data, and then apply it to new situations (The Alan Turing Institute, 2019). The advancement of machine learning is vast and an area of exponential growth and investment. The value of machine learning for addressing emotional wellbeing and mental health is developing. There is insufficient space in this chapter for us to give you a full picture of the potential, limitations or potential risks of this field, but it warrants a brief introduction. We provide some evidence but would encourage wider reading if it is of interest or relevance.

A synthesis of data through a meta-analysis of machine learning identified four domains of mental health apps that are useful for you to think about (Shatte, Hutchinson & Teague, 2019):

Detection and diagnosis: A body of evidence that examines the identification and diagnosis of mental health conditions in individuals through machine learning. This includes the development of pre-diagnosis screening tools and the development of risk models to identify a person's predisposition for or risk of developing a mental health condition.

Prognosis treatment and support: A body of evidence that aims to predict the progression of mental health conditions or to explore treatment or support opportunities for these conditions.

Public health apps: A body of evidence that uses large epidemiological or public data sets (including social media data) to monitor mental health conditions and estimate prevalence.

Research and clinical administration: A body of evidence that aims to improve administrative processes in clinical work, mental health research and health care organisations.

We are also seeing new forms of AI emerging. For example, there has been a growth of the use of *chatbots* that interact with CYP via automation (Hollis, Falconer et al., 2017). 'Chatbots are automated conversational agents that act as personal assistants, helping the user navigate to the information they require' (Betton & Woollard, 2019: 79). Betton and Woollard noted that there are a range of different chatbots available and some of these are designed to act like therapists and are available on app stores. These chatbots use evidence-based therapies, like cognitive behavioural therapy, and are engaging with the end user by mimicking a text-based conversation. It was further recognised though, that chatbots are in the early stages and there is a risk that they might interact in ways that are inappropriate or cause distress to the CYP.

The Alan Turing Institute in the UK is leading work on the use of machine learning and AI for mental health activity, mainly focused on early diagnosis, prediction and intervention. Its goal is to provide the basis for more efficient and effective clinical assessment, and to develop personalised health tools for screening and intervention. There are, of course, enormous ethical and privacy implications for their research. It may be useful to consider what the implications of these new tools and resources are for your practice with CYP. Would you use them? If so, how? What are the risks?

To help our understanding of the potential of machine learning for the field of child and adolescent mental health, we asked Professor Effie Law to elaborate, and we outline her response in Box 11.3.

Box 11.3: Expert: Professor Effie Law

Automatic multimodal emotion recognition and mental health

Automatic multimodal emotion recognition (AMER) has been the pivotal research challenge in the field of affective computing for about two decades. The recent advances in Machine Learning (ML) have accelerated the application of AMER in a variety of contexts, including mental health. ML, as a subfield of AI, is to predict a phenomenon of interest (e.g. a person's emotional response to a specific stimulus) based on patterns inferred from existing data. Instead of using explicit instructions, ML relies on algorithms and statistical models to enable computing systems to infer and predict.

As the term 'multimodal' implies, AMER aims to detect human emotions from speech, facial expressions, body postures, gaits and a range of physiological signals (e.g. brainwave, heart rate, skin conductance). The increasingly versatile social media, IoT and wearable sensors allow people's psychophysiological data to be measured implicitly and analysed with ML methods to recognise emotional states, which can be fed back to individuals in visual, audio and/or textual form in their personal device (e.g. mobile phone). In addition, an AI-based recommendation can be offered to individuals by selecting from their personal repertoire the most relevant emotion regulation strategy to deal with a specific situation. While research studies show that AMER can detect emotional health conditions such as depression and anxiety, the accuracy still needs to be improved for its wider use in everyday lives (Ringeval, Schuller et al., 2019; Schuller, 2018).

Overall, for AMER to realise its full potential for enhancing mental health, there are several formidable challenges to overcome at the technical (e.g. context awareness) and societal (e.g. ethics) levels. ML/AI holds great promises as well as risks. Technology should be harnesseed as an ethical and trustworthy tool to serve human needs and values, contributing to people's wellbeing in meaningful ways.

Professor Effie Law

Professor of Human–Computer Interaction

University of Leicester

The role of mental health apps

There has been a growing number of mobile apps for health. For example. In 2011 there were 1,056 health and fitness apps to download from the Apple App Store (Liu, Zhu et al., 2011), and in 2015 an estimated 165,000 apps related to health across the mobile phone range (Riaz, 2015). There is now an increase in the number designed to help with emotional regulation, wellbeing, stress management, mental health promotion and managing aspects, symptoms or characteristics of certain mental health conditions. Notably, of these apps, there are many designed especially for CYP.

Highlighted point!

It has been argued that health care providers should aspire to empower CYP to self-care for their mental health and have control, and one way to facilitate this is with an increased availability of digital tools and mental health apps (NHS England, 2015).

These smartphone apps are now a growing aspect of mental health practice and provide opportunities for improvements to practice (Betton & Wollard, 2019). Betton and Woollard noted that the use of apps means that practitioners can screen patients and patients are able to track aspects of their condition, like their mood or anxiety. Furthermore, patients can document any side effects of medication for the mental health condition or identify what triggers their anxiety or low mood and worsening symptoms. Thus, health apps provide almost immediate and cost-effective support and are now a 'new form of infrastructure' to communicate health information and advice, as well as reconfiguring health-seeking behaviour (Trnka, 2016).

Research examining the quality and effectiveness of health apps is also growing, particularly around those that assist users in gaining control over their screen time and the research about effectiveness of digital wellbeing interventions is mixed, and thus 'these contradictory findings suggest that what digital wellbeing is, and how it can be attained, remains ill-understood' (Vanden Abeele, 2020: 4). A cautious attitude is necessary if one considers that there are a multitude of mental health apps and most have not been evaluated. Moreover, the results of those that have been evaluated are inconsistent. For example, Donker, Petrie et al. (2013) reported on four trials that described three apps for depression, and three studies describing one app for stress, and one substance use study. In their appraisal of the research, they reported that the quality of research was relatively low and that there was limited examination through that research of the sustainability over the longer term. They argue that it is problematic that there are more than 3,000 mental health apps for Android, Microsoft and Apple devices that people can download freely, and this compares to only eight apps with an evidence base as shown through their review. It is challenging then, that there is little regulation of apps. In the USA, for example, the apps are not regulated by the Food and Drug Administration (FDA) so cannot be quality assured (Rafla et al., 2014).

In the UK, however, the NHS has established a specific NHS Apps Library of digital tools that they have assured to be safe, secure and effective for widespread public use (Betton & Woollard, 2019). Betton and Woollard noted that the number of apps that are available in the NHS library is comparatively small against those commercially and widely available. It is therefore essential that CYP can critically assess the source and quality of the apps they are downloading to help with their mental health or mental health condition. We consider what this means in practice in Box 11.4.

Box 11.4: What this means

There are several things then, that you as practitioners, and CYP themselves, could be thinking about before an app is downloaded and used. Betton and Woollard (2019) give the following guidance:

- It is important that anyone downloading a health app should think about the privacy and security of the app. The app should have a clear and understandable privacy statement and terms of use.
- This means that when downloading an app, it is important that beforehand the individual is confident that any data that is entered through the app will not be sold on by the company or used to target them with commercial products.
- In other words, it is worth thinking about whether there is a charge to download the app, and the value of that charge.
- This means that evidence is important. It is helpful if the app is informed by evidence, and there are ways to check that. It is useful to check if the app has been reviewed by practitioners or peers with relevant knowledge and experience.

As most of the apps have no evidence or very limited evidence to support the effectiveness, quality or the privacy assurance of them, much of this quality appraisal needs to be undertaken by the person downloading it.

E-counselling and e-therapy

One significant change in mental health care that has been facilitated by digital tools is that of e-counselling and e-therapy. These are modalities of mental health practice interventions that are delivered by qualified counsellors or therapists via the Internet (although we note that not all counsellors are regulated or belong to a governing body; in the UK those who are accredited counsellors belong to the British Association of Counselling and Psychotherapy [BACP]). These are usually real-time synchronous conversations between the practitioner and client over a web-based portal and may be supplemented with other digital communication such as email or messaging, or sometimes solely rely on a messaging platform and are only text-based conversations. Online counselling or therapy can vary widely and refers to anything from online support groups and bulletin boards, to more formal counselling and therapeutic interventions through synchronous video conversation, to email and to instant messages (Mallen & Vogel, 2005). See Figure 11.5 for an example.

Figure 11.5 E-counselling and e-therapy

These can be felt to be more convenient as it means service users are not reliant on geographical location and travel. For some families, the use of video-conference therapy reduces the barriers of treatment-seeking and this can be helpful for those with anxiety, depression and suicidal thoughts. (Fairchild, R., Ferng-Kuo et al., 2020). For some services it is a cost-effective way of delivering mental health interventions like cognitive behavioural therapy (CBT) or basic counselling. For those patients who are self-funding it can be more cost effective. Evidence from research with adults suggests that this modality of therapy and counselling is as effective as face-to-face interventions (Reynolds, Stiles et al., 2013). Furthermore, the recent COVID-19 pandemic has presented new challenges for global health services. While the mental health consequences of this pandemic are not known at the point of our writing this book, emerging evidence suggests that video-conferencing and telehealth could be upscaled to serve isolated regions and meet increased demand (Wind et al., 2020). Furthermore, 'better use of online treatment delivery could have a lasting positive effect on reaching vulnerable families and on delivering more effective services' (Hoekstra, 2020: 738). However, delivering counselling, therapy or support to CYP raises additional issues, not least because of their added vulnerability due to age and cognitive maturity. Safeguarding concerns need to be accounted for by mental health practitioners. Despite the challenges, we are seeing a growth in online therapeutic services and, along with it, a growing evidence base.

Given the significant connection of CYP to digital devices, especially the mobile phone, it is not surprising that there are benefits for them to seek mental health support and intervention via these devices. Early studies have illustrated that key attractions to receiving counselling or therapy via messaging or video-conversations for young people include factors such as a feeling of privacy, a sense of an emotionally safe environment, feeling less emotionally exposed or vulnerable than for face-to-face, not feeling too personally invested or exposed and feeling better protected (King, Bambling et al., 2006; Young, 2005). Thus, the independence and the possibility of anonymity are key reasons why young people might seek mental health support online, alongside the level of control they have in the counselling environment (King et al., 2006; Young, 2005). Furthermore, therapists report that this type of online support can improve initial engagement and provides a less confrontational way to support clients, which can be used in addition to face-to-face interventions (Furber, Crago et al., 2011).

In an Australian study of school counselling services, Glasheen and Campbell (2009) found that boys especially were reluctant to self-refer to see a practitioner in person. They found that the privacy and relative anonymity of online counselling was important but argued that any chat-based counselling platform needed to be visually attractive. In the UK, an established form of online counselling for young people aged 11–25 years, called Kooth, offers support for emotional and mental health problems with trained counsellors. It also has themed moderated message boards and a secure web-based email option (Betton & Woollard, 2019). We asked Tom van Daele in Belgium to comment on how these kinds of services are being used in the current COVID-19 crisis to support mental health and how that might be helpful. We outline his commentary in Box 11.5.

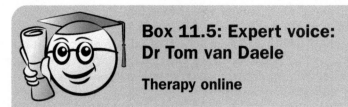

**Box 11.5: Expert voice:
Dr Tom van Daele**

Therapy online

Digital technology can be helpful when offering therapy to children and adoles-cents. Over the past two decades we have managed to offer increasingly better digital tools and interventions to people struggling with their mental health. As we initially had to rely on the limited means that technology like the World Wide Web offered, services were primarily textual and tailored to adults, though.

Because of technological advances, it is now also possible to create rich and challenging virtual environments that can also engage a younger crowd. Much work nevertheless remains to be done, as good practices are increasing, but seem still fairly scare. The 2020 coronavirus pandemic illustrated the urgent need for this. When therapists started looking for alternatives for their conven-tional face-to-face therapy, it quickly became clear that they could rely to some extent on online consultation to support their adult patients. For those who were younger (and especially for the very young), however, few alternatives were available. An important next step will therefore be to invest in the development and research for online interventions, serious games and other innovative approaches for children and adolescents. We might still use these as add-ons for conventional therapy, or we could potentially also rely on them as means to enhance our care from a distance, when circumstances require us to do so.

Dr Tom Van Daele

Head of the Expertise Unit Psychology, Technology & Society

Thomas More University of Applied Sciences, Belgium

Clearly, digital media brings opportunities for counselling and therapy and evidence to be used to underpin best practices and learn from different styles and forms of practice (Hill, Martin et al. 2017). Hill et al. noted that in the UK, and in many other countries ranging across the economic spectrum, the demand for mental health services exceeds supply. Therefore it is crucial that service providers find innovative ways to meet need on a limited health budget. For example, research in South Africa illustrated that there is an impe-tus for evidence regarding use of public health services by CYP, and that despite the comprehensive legal and policy framework which is committed to improving adolescent health, there are still systemic and structural factors that hinder effective provision and child-centred services (Mokomane, Mokhele et al., 2017). Mokomane et al. argued that amending health facilities to provide ways that are convenient for young people is essential. We would argue that these would need to be supplemented by careful legislation to protect the inappropriate use of CYP's data relating to mental health.

There are challenges associated with these therapeutic interventions for CYP that warrant consideration. Throughout the book we have encouraged you to critically reflect on evidence, and to reflect on your own thoughts and opinions. Before you go further, we would encourage you to think about what these challenges of delivering counselling or therapy via video, email or text/instant messages (which we discussed earlier in this chapter) might be by undertaking the reflective activity in Box 11.6.

What are the challenges of e-counselling or e-therapy for CYP?

Box 11.6: Reflecting on the challenges of e-counselling or e-therapy

What do you believe might be the main challenges of e-counselling or e-therapy for CYP?

In your reflective diary, try to create a list of the challenges that you think are important for CYP who might use digital tools to access therapy or counselling.

One of the core barriers to the wider-scale adoption of e-counselling and e-therapy is the lack of acceptance by health professionals (Topocco, Riper et al., 2017). A significant challenge for the quality and credibility of e-counselling and e-therapy is the attitude, acceptance, role and skill of the therapist or counsellor. A challenge for these practitioners is access and time for high-quality training with new technologies and the challenge of communicating with clients in a different way (Glasheen & Campbell, 2009). In a study with 19 mental health practitioners who work online through a youth mental health service, these practitioners reported that it was often the case that their clients presented with highly-complex problems and high levels of psychological distress that could be challenging to manage online (Dowling and Rickwood, 2014). They felt that in the online environment they had multiple roles to assess, provide emotional support and deliver evidence-based therapeutic interventions, and to do this they used online chat as well as video-enabled face-to-face counselling, but retention of clients could be difficult.

It is often the case that clinicians are concerned that the lack of non-verbal cues might hinder the therapeutic process and therapeutic relationship and may ultimately undermine the achievement of effective therapeutic change (Glasheen & Campbell, 2009). Furthermore, there may be safeguarding issues, as risk assessments are an important part of mental health assessments, and ongoing questions about self-harm or suicidal ideation can be challenging to manage (Kiyimba & O'Reilly, in press). Whilst a young person may prefer online counselling, it may not be the appropriate treatment for them if their needs are complex and require more specialist interventions. The role of counselling here may be to steer the young person towards more appropriate services. We have also yet to learn how CYP may access or benefit from such supports.

Highlighted point!

We must remember that while these digital forms of counselling or therapy might appeal to young people, they do not appeal to all CYP, and there are CYP who do not want counselling or therapy in this way (Betton & Woollard, 2019).

Hill et al. (2017) argued therefore that where interventions are evidence-based, they can help improve clinical efficiency in cost-effective ways that increase access to treatment. However, the evidence base is central to this. As one of our mental health practitioners in discussions about e-counselling and e-therapy pointed out (see Figure 11.6), there is a lot of this kind of intervention available to CYP that has no quality assurance or evidence underpinning it.

I think there is, I know that there's counselling online but my experience of it was that actually, it's often just quite poor quality, that people use online stuff to develop, what they really mean is cheaper stuff, which isn't necessarily quality assured.

Figure 11.6   Mental health practitioner's view of e-counselling and e-therapy

Hill et al. (2017: 65) argued:

Through our experience of digital mental health innovation, we have all been struck by the lack of guidance and formalised approaches to development within e-health.

CYP may find e-counselling or e-therapy appealing and therefore it is important to have a clear evidence base (Gibson & Cartwright, 2014). A core concern relates to the effectiveness of these kinds of therapies or counselling strategies when compared to the effectiveness of face-to-face interventions (Mallen and Vogel, 2005). Although the evidence for these modalities is growing, we still have a long way to go before we fully understand the benefits and risks of treating CYP's mental health conditions using digital technology.

CYP's views about using digital media in health

CYP are certainly embracing digital and social media and the Internet for their mental health. As we have discussed in this chapter, this engagement with digital media ranges from learning about mental health and mental health conditions, raising awareness and reducing stigma, to seeking out help through text or instant messaging, e-counselling or e-therapy, and the use of mental health apps. As we cautioned in the previous section of this chapter, there are concerns about the evidence base, the quality of the information/apps/intervention as well as the quality of the evidence itself, and you need to be active in appraising it. We also cautioned that not *all* CYP have a preference to learn about mental health in this way as they are able to recognise that not everything they see online is credible and not *all* CYP want support through digital platforms.

In our own focus groups in the context of mental health, the young people (aged 11–18 years) had different opinions about the value of digital and social media, and the Internet generally, for learning about mental health, supporting their mental health, and treating any mental health conditions. While young people, educators and mental health practitioners felt that digital media could be harnessed for mental health promotion and support, they were also cautious about overstating the benefits (O'Reilly, Dogra, Hughes et al., 2018). Young people's positive views are presented in Figure 11.7, and their concerns in Figure 11.8.

As the evidence base is limited, we argue that it is important to listen to the views of CYP, but also caution against treating them as a homogenous group. All CYP are unique, and while conceptualising them into certain categories can be helpful for understanding the broader issues at stake in relation to mHealth, their needs will be unique. We have shown from our discussions with young people that mHealth can be helpful for a range of aspects of mental health, but that there are challenges too. This is consistent with other work. For example, in work with young people aged 16–24 years, Trnka (2016) found that the use of health apps was seen as convenient and a mechanism to allow them to take charge of their own health, and they engaged with a broad range of health-related technologies to support their emotional and mental health.

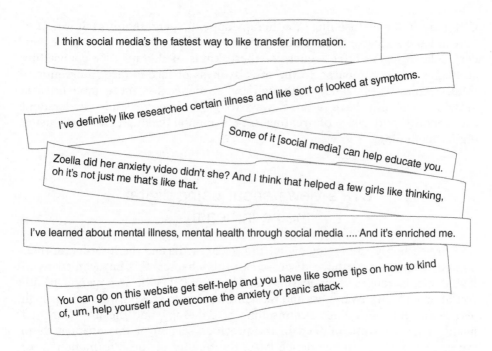

I think social media's the fastest way to like transfer information.

I've definitely like researched certain illness and like sort of looked at symptoms.

Some of it [social media] can help educate you.

Zoella did her anxiety video didn't she? And I think that helped a few girls like thinking, oh it's not just me that's like that.

I've learned about mental illness, mental health through social media .... And it's enriched me.

You can go on this website get self-help and you have like some tips on how to kind of, um, help yourself and overcome the anxiety or panic attack.

Figure 11.7   Young people's positive views of digital mental health

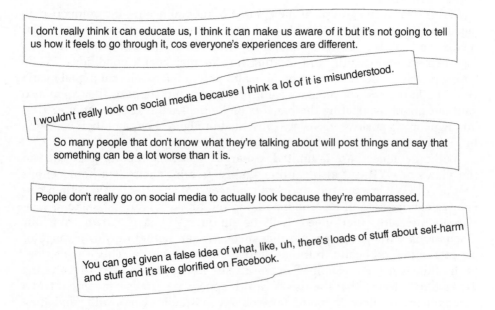

I don't really think it can educate us, I think it can make us aware of it but it's not going to tell us how it feels to go through it, cos everyone's experiences are different.

I wouldn't really look on social media because I think a lot of it is misunderstood.

So many people that don't know what they're talking about will post things and say that something can be a lot worse than it is.

People don't really go on social media to actually look because they're embarrassed.

You can get given a false idea of what, like, uh, there's loads of stuff about self-harm and stuff and it's like glorified on Facebook.

Figure 11.8   Young people's negative views of digital mental health

Conclusions

The potential for e-health is tremendous, though it must be remembered that not all content is readily transferable, for cultural and other reasons. Also, as with face-to-face health care provision, 'one size fits all' is unlikely to be useful or successful. In completing this chapter, we provide a reflective piece about the benefits and challenges of supporting CYP using digital media from an expert in this field. In Box 11.7 we present the perspective of Kirsty Donnelly, who works for a leading child charity in the UK (NSPCC and Childline) and who has been working in this field for many years.

Box 11.7: Expert contribution: Kirsty Donnelly

Role: Childline Community Manager

Organisation: Childline (NSPCC)

Brief bio: Kirsty Donnelly is the Childline Community Manager and sits within the Childline Online Services Team, the team responsible for Childline's digital offerings. She manages Childline's communities of young people on the Childline website and social media channels and creates the safeguarding policies and procedures for user-generated content on these platforms. Starting with Childline in 2010, she moved from the counselling service to the online service in 2016. She uses young people's usage of digital and social media platforms to continue to develop Childline's online presence and peer support whilst also providing expert advice to external organisations on setting up online communities and platforms with robust safeguarding procedures in place.

Childline: Using digital technology to support and empower young people

Initially created in response to a television programme about abuse, Childline was first set up in 1986 as a dedicated telephone helpline to provide CYP with a safe place to talk when they didn't have anywhere or anyone else, using what has since become one of the most recognisable UK telephone numbers: 0800 1111. At that time, some CYP would have to leave where they lived to make phone calls from public phone boxes, it being the only way they felt able to speak to someone about what they were experiencing in their lives, and for many their only access to a telephone. From the initial launch and focus on abuse, the types of issues that CYP wanted to talk about changed with their

(Continued)

having a place, some for the very first time, where they felt able to talk openly about all different feelings and situations they were facing.

As conversations changed, so too did Childline, expanding into what is currently now 12 bases across the UK covering Scotland, England, Northern Ireland and Wales, as well as one additional virtual base that was created at the end of 2020 in response to COVID-19. Technology also changed with the increasing use of mobile phones and access to the Internet and in 2009, Childline launched its online service, introducing a chat service allowing CYP to contact via a Childline account on a dedicated Childline website. Website development also allowed different features and resources to be added, offering peer support in the form of message boards, a problem page called Ask Sam where young people could anonymously submit letters online, and the creation of content providing information and advice on a wide range of issues. This increased the offering to allow freedom of access, variety and choice, all still within safeguarding frameworks. The expansion into an email service, referred to internally as 'personal inbox' (PIB), allowed CYP to have another means of contacting a counsellor, thus further increasing the help and support options available to them. However, technology changes rapidly and it's essential to be responsive to these changes not only to keep up to date but also to provide the best service possible.

In 2016, Childline turned 30 and amongst the celebration of all the help and support provided to CYP over the years also came a period of reflection; reflecting upon how the world had changed in general and for CYP, and thinking about how Childline could and must change to keep up with technical developments and solutions to ensure its continuing ability to be there for CYP, but also to ensure its continuing appeal and accessibility. There was the realisation too that site content must be dynamic to encourage and to have continued appeal to return visitors. It was clear that technology could be used in new and different ways to reach and support more and more CYP, but also that continual evolution and adaptability would be key to building upon the access and choice when using Childline.

That year saw the redevelopment of the Childline website, really bringing Childline to life in the digital environment, but more importantly, with a focus on CYP having access to a wider and improved range of resources to be able to find information and support for themselves in a way that worked best for them across different devices. Attention was paid to how such content and support would be displayed on these devices: thinking around the variations between desktop and mobile displays; with increased access to invaluable peer support on the message boards and its changed layouts and additional features; the integration of images created by a young person via the art box tool and the ability for these to be shared during an online counselling interaction; site colours chosen by young people taking into consideration the emotional impact a colour can have with background customisation options in a young person's online private locker, a place where all their notifications and counselling emails are stored, to allow their private space to be a place to reflect them. A changed font and very specific usage of colour and capitalisation on the site allowed easier use and accessibility, meeting the needs of CYP with different ranges of abilities and the introduction of a mood journal and a mood tracker gave them a private, online diary feature where they could write entries whilst also looking at their changing moods over time to both recognise when they might need extra support and to celebrate all the good, allowing self-reflection. Later, there was the launch of the Childline app For Me, offering the same site resources and access to counsellors but providing CYP, those using iOS due to the higher proportion of mobile contacts at the time via these devices, with another choice as to how they want to access Childline.

Today, a CYP can contact the Childline counsellors directly on the same Freephone number as in 1986, and they can still make contact via 1-2-1 chat and via Childline email but with improved functionality that continues to be developed. The Childline website allows any CYP in the UK, the Channel Islands and the Isle of Man to create an account to access the counselling service online. The technology behind the 1-2-1 chat service allows a young person to be on a desktop or a mobile device to type back and forth to a counsellor, talking about anything at all. This allows a choice as to how a CYP perhaps feels more able to express themselves if they do not feel comfortable or able to call, as well as the ease of access in a confidential way.

Over the years, the proportion of those contacting online versus phone has risen to over 75% and with increasing demand can come longer wait times. An extra benefit of technology is what is now possible to provide CYP with whilst they are waiting in the queue for a chat. Upon entering the chat waiting room, a young person can view top tips for getting the most from their chat to feel prepared and confident to even feel able to begin the process of engaging, and it also provides an opportunity for them to be shown helpful links as well as their being able to freely navigate around the website without losing their place in the chat queue. This allows them, should they wish, to seek out information and advice, to try relaxing and calming activities, to pass the time being creative using the art box or playing a game with therapeutic elements. They can also just get a real sense of all that Childline can be to and for them. Sending an email can allow them time to reflect on what they wish to say and to send at a time that works for them. As email is not a live service, they can also choose when they want to come back and read the reply while also being able to re-read the support and advice any time they wish, sometimes months or even years later to look back on the steps they've taken and to remind them of how far they have come.

The wide range of public and private user-generated content now available in the form of Ask Sam letters, mood journals, images a CYP has created and message board posts alongside a nickname they can choose for their Childline account continues to have a hugely wide appeal with user-generated content submissions only continuing to increase, some young people only using these channels and the support they provide. Such content requires moderation to assess risk, both to an individual and to the wider Childline community when content is public, and our content management system allows queuing systems to make the experience as efficient as possible whilst allowing Childline to effectively safeguard at all points, and to respond appropriately to the different types of help and support that may be needed. Recording systems also ensure that appropriate information is stored and available to best support a young person, capturing their use of Childline to

(Continued)

have a holistic picture to better assess risk, both current and over time, but to also better support. The birth of social media allowed Childline to be on YouTube and Facebook very early on with the expansion into a now thriving Instagram page and community, with campaign advertising also taking place on Snapchat and, very recently, on Tik Tok. Using such available technology allows the reach of a much wider and diverse range of young people on the platforms they themselves are actively using, raising awareness of Childline and all the resources and support it can offer.

The introduction of self-help tools such as new and improved games and the Calm Zone, an area of the site displaying different tools, videos and activities a CYP can use to feel calmer and less stressed, increases all they have available, whenever they choose to access at any time, day or night. The recent introduction of the Childline Helper assists CYP to seek out relevant information and advice, using a quiz mechanic to determine what each individual may benefit the most from and to provide them with activity options to help improve mood. The Boost Your Mood tool brings together a game and self-help where a young person can play pinball and choose the types of activities they may wish to try to help their mental wellbeing. It is also about providing a visually attractive and appealing experience for young people, to allow them to engage with resources and content in the way that they choose, whether using one specific resource or channel or a combination of all that is available.

Technology also allows us to introduce personalisation on the site, tailoring highlighted content to suit the time of day, for example a focus on getting to sleep and muted colours to offer a calming, relaxing environment featured going into the late part of the evening. Personalisation also allows those young people under 12 years of age to have direct access to the under-12s section of the website. Launched in 2018, the Childline Kids site allows younger visitors access to a variety of topics with language tailored to them and the overall aim focusing on speaking to a trusted adult or to Childline. Upon entering their age at the time of signing up for an account, personalisation allows this age group to be automatically directed to the 'Kids' section.

As we seek to further grow peer support and self-help tools, we must look to technology to allow us to develop and innovate. Upcoming projects will introduce a chatbot, not to divert from all that is currently available nor to take away a CYP's access to the counsellors but to enhance their experience of visiting the Childline site, to further guide them to relevant content and support in the format that could work best for them whilst also helping to manage the counselling service demand and wait times for those times a young person may not need to speak to a counsellor as what they are looking for already exists in content or through the words of other young people. Developing a Coping Kit will also allow young people to increase their resilience and their own ranges of self-help toolkits.

As Childline looks to the future, our digital offering will only grow and develop, feedback from young people themselves shaping and informing what will be available and improved upon across all aspects of Childline, it being clear that technology at various levels is both central to the lives of CYP and to the support and empowerment Childline will continue to give to them.

12

CONCLUSIONS

Learning points

After reading this chapter, you will be able to:

- Appreciate the involvement of government and policy
- Assess the role of technology companies
- Identify future directions for research and practice

Introduction

Through our writing across this book, we have explored a range of issues relating to the relationship between CYP and mental health with respect to digital media. We have attempted to appraise critically the growing evidence-base that has pointed to the positive relationship between mental health and digital media, as well as contextualise in a balanced way some of the broader concerns about the possible negative impacts, and the more severe issues that society faces in relation to this. Indeed, it is crucial that researchers and practitioners do not get led into the moral panic and negative rhetoric that currently shrouds digital media, especially social media. So, throughout the book we have encouraged you to critically reflect on the evidence to form your own opinions so that your perspectives and your practice are evidence-based.

In this summary chapter, we synthesise the core issues that we have raised and discussed throughout the book to draw some conclusions about the field. We draw your attention to the importance of some of those issues in relation to the wider policy landscape by considering the role of governments and technology companies, while making some suggestions about future directions. We finalise some key messages for practitioners to consider the role that they play in dealing with this complex relationship.

The broader picture – government and policy

There is little disagreement that CYP's mental health has a significant impact on their educational attainment and subsequent employment opportunities, as well as on their physical health and mortality. As we discussed, there is a complex nexus of relationships between society, family, peers and school that can impact positively or negatively on CYP's mental health and wellbeing (Weare, 2000). The increased demand and the high levels of unmet need mean that many governments are trying to find ways to support CYP through different services, such as education, youth services, charities, in the home and so forth. Recent rhetoric now proposes that CYP's mental health is everyone's responsibility (The Health Foundation, 2014; Tamburrino et al., 2020) and that there is 'no health without mental health' (Prince, Patel et al., 2007; Department of Health, 2011; WHO, 2005a). However, the extent to which different practitioners and services can meet those needs is dependent on the intensity and complexity of the difficulties experienced, the numbers of CYP coming forward within any one organisation, and the range of other demands on professional time. Additionally, it raises the issues of parity. Staff not trained in physical health would not be expected to manage physical health problems and yet CYP experiencing mental health conditions may find themselves being supported by a practitioner with little to no training in mental health.

Globally, the WHO (2005b) has been calling on national policy to account for the need for mental health training for frontline workers across multiple sectors and this was returned to as an important issue in 2013. For example, the WHO's comprehensive mental health action plan 2013–2020, adopted by the 66th World Health Assembly, calls for a multisectoral approach emphasising

> a comprehensive and coordinated response for mental health requires partnership with multiple public sectors such as health, education, employment, judicial, housing, social and other relevant sectors as well as the private sector, as appropriate to the country situation. (WHO, 2013: 10)

This plan was described by the WHO Director-General at the time, Dr Margaret Chan, as a landmark achievement because it focuses international attention on a long-neglected problem, namely child mental health, and is firmly rooted in the principles of human rights.

This plan also calls for a change in the attitudes that perpetuate stigma and discrimination that have isolated people since ancient times, and it calls for an expansion of services to promote greater efficiency in the use of resources. The four major objectives of the plan are to:

1. Strengthen effective leadership and governance for mental health.
2. Provide comprehensive, integrated and responsive mental health and social care services in community-based settings.
3. Implement strategies for promotion and prevention in mental health.
4. Strengthen information systems, evidence and research for mental health.

In the plan, the four objectives are accompanied by specific targets and these are to provide the basis for measurable collection action and achievement.

We would also point out that there is an issue of equality in relation to these issues. While there are some clear benefits of digital media, there is not enough evidence to guide policy and practice across the globe, and majority world countries especially lack formal research evidence (Livingstone, Lemish et al., 2017). Indeed, Livingstone et al. point out that there are signi-ficant inequalities and therefore there must be a greater culture of sharing best prac-tices internationally so that the risks and opportunities can be balanced. The challenge then, is that although there is much to be gained in the digital age, there is currently only limited robust evidence to guide policy and this is nec-essary to ensure sustained benefits for CYP (Livingstone et al., 2017). Livingstone et al. highlight the problem of the significant inequalities in soci-ety, and these have reinforced the effects of social and digital exclusion.

Policy is also pertinent in the context of education, and we considered the role of schools earlier. There are many guidelines for education in terms of supporting CYP in the classroom. For example, in the UK, the Department for Education (DfE), and the House of Commons Education and Health Committees (HCEHC) have argued that both the education and health sector have a respon-sibility to support CYP who have mental health conditions. In South Africa, a national crime prevention strategy has created a space in which health staff and teachers have been trained in mental health skills. The strategy is linked to the National Mental Health Policy Framework and Strategic Plan. This approach has been particularly important for low resource contexts – in South Africa for example, where funding for specialist mental health staff is extremely limited (Docrat, Lund, and Chrisholm, 2019). Governments therefore have a central role in developing policies that attend to CYP's mental health need, but also in managing some of the possible ill effects that digital media may have, and they do this through digital regulation.

It remains a fact that traditional legislation is not always effective in a digital media environment; arguably more tailored ideas are needed. Policymakers have increasingly become aware of the risks concerning social media (European Commission, 2008), especially for CYP, and a few regulatory initiatives have already been taken to address some of these risks. For instance, in February 2009, several SNS providers subscribed to a self-regulatory charter titled 'Safer Social Networking Principles for the EU' (SSNPs) (O'Connell et al., 2009), following a public consultation on online social networking by the European Commission (Staksrud & Lobe, 2010). However, the results of the two independent evaluations of the implementation of the SSNPs (Donoso, 2011; Staksrud & Lobe, 2010) showed that there was significant room for improvement. These findings question the effectiveness of this type of regulatory initiative: although the commitment of the SNS providers to take steps to make their services safer is to be applauded, the concrete implementation of such safety measures is of course crucial to achieve actual protection. Notably, this is not providing a clear base for enforcement and neither does it provide a compelling incentive for compliance and so we must question if self-regulatory instruments are helpful enough to prevent risk and protect rights and values (Lievens, 2011). Clearly, therefore, there is a role for technology companies to play.

The role of technology companies

Technology companies are frequently charged with not doing enough to address issues raised that have consequences for CYP's mental health. There has been some discontent recently about the role that large corporations play in promoting positive mental health and wellbeing in CYP through digital technology. Large tech giants like Google, Apple, Microsoft, Facebook (to name just a few) arguably have some responsibility in terms of protecting CYP in online spaces and doing more to help them stay safe, promote their mental health and guard their self-esteem. It is a challenging endeavour to monitor and regulate digital media, especially social media, but there are strong calls for technology providers to do more to help. Not surprisingly, new movements focused on 'wellbeing-driven technologies' are on the rise, but these movements must be based on up-to-date and effectively translated evidence if they are to be successful (Vanden Abeele, 2020).

Many in society see these large companies as bearing some responsibility – as do some of the companies themselves. For example, the CEO of Twitter disclosed that they were not effective enough at dealing with trolling incidents. In 2014 a group of powerful media companies in the UK (BT, Sky, the BBC amongst others) initiated a new not-for-profit organisation called Internet Matters intended to support safer and more effective use of digital and social media with CYP and their families; similarly, the ICT Coalition for Children Online was formed to help younger internet users to make the most of their online experiences and deal with any risks. However, despite this admission and moves for change, little appears to have been done (Hern, 2015), particularly globally. At this point, we would encourage you to reflect on your own views by trying the reflective activity in Box 12.1.

As the 5Rights Foundation (n.d.) states on their website

The digital services that children and young people use are not designed to meet their needs or uphold their rights. Many services simply ignore the presence of child users (under 18s) altogether. Design decisions are driven more by the commercial requirement for data than by advanced consideration of a child's best interests. Where design decisions are taken to promote their welfare online, they often come after the fact - provoked more by tragedy and public outrage than by any prior assessment of the impact on children and young people. The failure to anticipate the presence, rights and needs of children and young people, by design and default, severely limits the potential of digital technology as a positive force in their lives.

To what extent do you think that technology companies have a role in protecting children's mental health?

Box 12.1: Reflecting on responsibility and corporations

Write down a reflective piece about the extent to which you believe the technology companies have a responsibility to attend to the challenges of protecting CYP's mental health.

In your reflective diary think about your own views on this matter. How much responsibility should technology companies take to protect CYP, to keep them safe and monitor what is posted? What challenges might they face in doing so?

Donoso, Verdoodt et al. (2016) argued that there is a growing body of knowledge about CYP's engagement with digital media, and this evidence is helping to inform policy-makers, governments, parents, educators and CYP about how CYP can be empowered and protected online, and this is an opportunity for industry to listen and consider in their development of digital products and services. There is a need for continued engagement with software designers and digital companies to ensure that children are better protected and empowered and that their rights are taken into consideration in the development of new digital products and services (Donoso et al. , 2016). This is also important to achieve greater transparency about how data are collected, collated and used, especially via apps designed for CYP, with claims that there should be simple opt-out choices for parents (Holloway et al., 2013). CYP need to be empowered to be responsible online, and industry should be encouraged to produce content and tools that are relevant, appropriate and accessible (OECD, 2018). This can be challenging for parents and CYP as they often do not fully understand the broader issues or the terms and conditions. As stated by Betton and Woollard (2019: 177):

> The lengthy and complicated Terms and Conditions found in many mobile applications result in a relationship between the provider and use of the service that are less than clear and transparent. Personalised or targeted advertisements generated by tech companies selling data to marketing companies is common practice and the default business model for companies such as Google and Facebook.

There are examples of multi-stakeholder led initiatives to better protect minors online. For example, the SSNPs (O'Connell et al., 2009) brokered by the European Commission, the CEO Coalition for a Better Internet for Kids – the first industry-led Europe-wide principles in the online safety arena. More recently, the Alliance to Better Protect Minors Online was launched in 2017. The initiative focuses on protection from harmful content, conduct and contact, and seeks to identify possible areas within these three categories that would benefit from a coordinated approach from companies and other stakeholders to overcome them.

Clearly, some effort is being made to consider the role of digital media and CYP mental health and technology companies and their partners arguably are taking this more seriously, although arguably more could be done. We asked Laura Higgins from Roblox, an online game platform, her views on the matter and report her perspective in Box 12.2.

Box 12.2: Expert voice: Laura Higgins, Roblox

What can tech companies do to help safeguard children's mental health?

This is a complex issue but one that is becoming increasingly important. In recent years we have seen some tragic cases of young people exposed to content which is detrimental to their wellbeing, in the worst cases encouraging harmful behaviours such as eating disorders or self-harm. All tech companies have a duty of care for their users; this should have always been a priority and not an afterthought. They should do all they can to prevent serious harm on their platforms, and to provide advice and tools for how to manage lesser harms should they occur.

Creating positive, healthy online environments, removing features that encourage unhealthy behaviours (such as chasing followers or likes) and encouraging empathic communities where people feel safe, are essential for CYP who are still working out the world and their place in it. For many CYP, their online community is a lifeline, they may be looking to meet people with similar issues to themselves, to seek support and advice, or even to escape their day-to-day reality. It is a collective responsibility to ensure that this can happen safely.

While there are some recognised and obvious risks, we need to protect against harmful content, harassment or exploitation, as what affects a young person's mental health can be much more subtle. We need to place ourselves in their world, understand what genuinely happens when they are online, ask what support they need, and then implement this. We need to stop talking for CYP (we don't understand the pressures they face) and start listening instead. Once we understand the breadth of issues, we should use all the tools available to us; these may include technical solutions (text filtering, keyword lists etc.), human moderation and intervention, and education campaigns that support the community, their families and educators. Consider having a specific space on your platform where CYP can find details about relevant support services. Working with a broad range of stakeholders is also essential; if you can, consider having an advisory board including specialists in child safety and mental health (or at least ensure that you can access expert advice when needed), share best practices with other tech companies, and be responsive to the community needs if they change.

Laura Higgins

Director of Community Safety and Digital Civility

Roblox

Some technology companies and some app developers and social media providers are taking steps on their platforms to better protect and assist CYP. We provide an example of such work with the French social networking app Yubo in Box 12.3, as described by Annie Mullins, Yubo's Safety Advisor. In providing this example, we remind you that it is important to consider privacy and security as with any app, and to critically assess the value of any kinds of digital apps as we have encouraged you to do throughout the book.

Box 12.3: Expert voice: Annie Mullins, OBE

Yubo – support, educate and protect

Yubo was founded in 2015 by French engineer graduates whose vision was to connect young people directly beyond the 'likes' and 'scrolling' and saw the need for in-person connections. Anecdotally at least, Yubo's live streaming seems to have been popular with young people, whereby they can connect, talk, have fun and build relationships with each other online. Yubo as a service is designed to be appealing to teenagers and has many challenges to keep them as safe as possible and moderate their behaviour so that 'at risk' behaviours are mitigated.

An investment has been made by Yubo to develop tools in an effort to meet these challenges and it is argued that Yubo is now making an effort to set industry good practice benchmarks with its 'support, educate and protect' strategy.

(Continued)

Sexual behaviour and relationships

Teens are growing up online and are exploring their identity and sexual relationships by testing out themselves and the boundaries of personal freedom. Yubo doesn't want to prevent this but rather to encourage teens to do this safely. For this reason, Yubo has strong community rules, including no nudity or girls being partially clothed, such as girls in their underwear or boys being bare chested. This is enforced in real-time using AI technology to identify anyone in a live stream undressed. The user is notified as quickly as possible by a moderator that this is not acceptable and they are given one minute to comply with the standards or the live stream is terminated. This may seem a strong response but to prevent sexual exploitation it's essential, as many teens on social media platforms find themselves easily entrapped and forced to share explicit sexual images.

Users at risk from self-harm or suicide

Yubo also takes action to identify users at risk from self-harm or suicide, again using AI to identify and intervene to direct users to give the help and support they may need. Yubo works closely with their safety board with teen online experts to draw on their knowledge and expertise to devise strategies to support young people and train moderators. One pilot intervention is to link to NGOs within the app who can provide direct support to them.

Authenticating user identity

A key challenge for all social media services is verifying who users really are to prevent abuse of the service and toxic behaviour. Yubo has entered a partnership with Yoti to use their identity estimation and authentication solutions. Yubo, when discovering suspicious users, will request they undertake Yoti's solution to prove their identity.

Annie Mullins, OBE

Yubo Safety Advisor

Future directions

The rise in digital media and the proliferation of social media are relatively new. This is a rapidly advancing field and one with which research and science have struggled to keep up. Research takes considerable time, effort and funding and the pace at which technology is moving presents researchers with new challenges before they have even begun to address older ones. It is simply the case that the research world has had insufficient time to fully understand the impact of digital and social media, the Internet or technology more broadly. The limited evidence base and the practical, real-world work of practitioners has, however, raised concerns about the engagement of CYP with Internet-enabled devices, the use of smartphones and their reliance on social media for social connectivity. To truly address these concerns, formal research from across the multi-disciplinary spectrum is needed.

An important area for future research is that of inequality, especially inequalities in service and information provision, inequalities in access, and inequalities created by digital media. Interestingly, digital media could be one way in which inequalities in health begin to be addressed.

Addressing inequality through digital media in mental health

There remains a great deal of concern about inequalities in health, and especially in mental health. As discussed, mental health need significantly exceeds what is available. For many, the rising availability of the Internet and the growth of digital technology are part of the solution to tackling the problem. As we have said before, this is because the Internet and digital media can help to deliver mental health information or interventions in an accessible and cost-effective way (Christensen, 2007). In other words, the Internet has been identified as being part of a solution to reach people who may not have traditionally had access to mental health services (King, Spooner & Reid, 2003), and social media can widen access for those who do not want to or cannot access traditional services (Chief Medical Officer, 2013). Furthermore, digital media have changed the way that CYP engage with health care services and the way in which they receive and request information, although we still need more research on how technology might help CYP in challenging contexts (Zinck et al., 2013).

One of the important ways in which digital media have made a difference in mental health care is in reaching groups of CYP who have been more challenging to reach in traditional ways. Those seldom-heard groups may avoid seeking help, may be missed by education or health services and may be more vulnerable to the challenges of providing information, support and treatment. The use of eHealth and mHealth therefore can provide important benefits to these CYP, which may include groups such as those not attending school and those living in poverty (Dunne, Pharm et al., 2017). It is recognised that mHealth has the potential to promote social inclusion for those who are typically marginalised, excluded or geographically isolated (Stephens-Reicher, Metcalf et al., 2011). This is because the use of online systems means that there is nearly universal reach in some areas, and a possibility of 24-hour access to information and/or support with simple methods to update materials (Ellis, Collin et al., 2013).

The use of eHealth and mHealth is also showing promise in majority world countries. Although smartphones still tend not to be affordable by these populations, there is a significant use of text and instant messaging as a means of communication (Chandra et al., 2014), and in India for example, text messaging is the preferred mode of communication (Prasad & Anand, 2012). There are demographic differences in the use of digital devices for health though, as individuals who are older, healthier and more active tend to use the Internet more for health, and there are also ethnic differences with African-American and Hispanic teens more likely to use digital platforms for health information (Wartella et al., 2016). However, in some contexts there are ethical issues such as reminding the user to delete the message chain, issues around consent, and the privacy of minors who seek therapy without the consent of their parents (McGee, 2011).

Issues of inclusion for access to digital health

In managing inequalities in mental health via digital media, there is a related concern regarding inequalities in terms of access to digital media. Digital media can only begin to address inequalities in mental health if it is accessible to all. Currently CYP's access to digital media, and thus by association digital health, is not framed as a 'right'. This is a complicated issue and was explained by Lundy (2020, n.p.) in this way:

> There is no current human right to digital provision or access. However, such access/provision might be necessary to realise other human rights that children have, such as their right to education. In that case, the minimum entitlement would be whatever is necessary to secure the enjoyment of the human right whose imple- mentation is dependent on internet entitlement. Moreover, since rights must be enjoyed without discrimination, children would have an entitlement to the same access as other children, but again only where that is necessary for the realisation of another existing human right.

However, while the picture regarding children's rights is complicated, this connects to wider arguments about inclusion. In the Australian policy context (McDonald, 2011), social inclusion is conceptualised as four key domains of opportunity: the opportunity to

- participate in society through employment and access to services.
- connect with family, friends and the local community.
- deal with personal crises (e.g. ill health).
- be heard.

Social exclusion, on the other hand, is defined as the 'restriction of access to opportunities and [a] limitation of the capabilities required to capitalise on these [opportunities]' (Hayes, Gray, and Edwards, 2008: 6). Social exclusion is not the equivalent of poverty (i.e. inadequate economic resources) or depriva- tion (i.e. an enforced lack of social perceived necessities) (Saunders, Naidoo et al., 2007). Rather, social exclusion is fundamentally about a lack of connected- ness and participation – this includes virtual spaces.

Social exclusion is a useful concept because it can enrich our understanding of social disadvantage, highlighting, for example, the way in which the experi- ence of disadvantage may not only involve financial difficulties but also extend to a sense of disconnection from the broader community. A good example of this is the challenge of reaching rural communities via digital means. This is because many of those in rural communities lack reliable access to high-speed internet (Anderson, 2018b). Social inclusion, when viewed as a series of opportunities, provides a framework for enhancing participation and connectedness, and as such can be seen as a goal to work towards a way of raising the bar and understanding where we want to be and how to get there (Friendly & Lero, 2002).

Recognise the complexity of 'access' when designing information and advice campaigns

Brown and Ormes (2020) argue that free and accessible internet serves the same function as libraries in the past to help promote learning and advancement for people from all economic groups. This is further supported by the Internet Society (2017), who discuss access to the Internet for access to education. The arguments they make are discussed here as equally applicable in equality regarding access to eHealth and raise issues of inclusion. The Internet Society states that access to the Internet is fundamental to supporting better education for all. It can improve the quality of education about mental health in many ways. Access to the Internet, with enough bandwidth, is essential for the development of an information society. Lack of broadband connectivity is preventing widespread use of the Internet in education about mental health and other areas of life in many countries.

Final thoughts

We divided this book into three core sections to provide a narrative of the key areas of work being undertaken in this field. We opened the book with a general section on child development, digital media and mental health as a way of contextualising the core concepts, concerns and practical areas to address. Our second section of the book focused more specifically on the relationship between digital media and mental health in CYP. We paid considerable attention to social media, as this is often subject to much negative rhetoric. In the third section of the book, we distilled the main messages for the book for certain groups including school, parents and mental health practitioners.

The speed at which technology is evolving and the greater availability of digital media to CYP presents both opportunities and risks, and given that the Internet is almost ubiquitous in minority world countries and relatively available in majority world countries, means that this is a significant area for further research and critical discussion. More and more CYP are embracing a range of forms of digital media, especially through the smartphone, and this has impacted on their communication styles, their friendships and their self-expression, and has become fully embedded into family and community structures.

Indeed, we need to move beyond distinctions between on- and offline worlds, as we have shown through the book the boundaries between them are becoming increasingly blurred. As Livingstone (2020, n.p.) wrote:

> As we move into a post-digital world in which simple comparisons of digital and non-digital become implausible, we will need to think differently. Already, and certainly then, it will be important to specify more precisely which dimensions of the digital art or could be of concern. This takes us back to a critical analysis of the digital environment itself, and children's modes of engagement with it.

Alongside these advancements and changes, CYP's mental health has increasingly become a priority and of greater concern to parents, professionals and societies, especially as the prevalence of mental health conditions has risen alongside a greater number of CYP feeling stressed, pressured and generally anxious about life. The connection between the two is arguably overstated and exaggerated, but nonetheless there is a role for digital technology to play, both in terms of tackling the issue and in terms of contributing to the issue, and in this book we have considered this from many different angles.

Natasha Devon has argued that the real cause of the issue society is facing in relation to mental health is not digital media or the Internet, but instead is because of the extreme austerity measures and the cuts to mental health services (Devon, 2018a). In the current climate of COVID-19, in many countries the lack of investment in health care, and specifically in mental health, is now having dire consequences. While technologies can bridge some gaps (e.g. providing opportunities for CYP to communicate with peers and families, providing information about mental health and the virus, and facilitating the continuation of education), we do need to learn lessons from the past. There are many positive ways that they can use digital media to protect their mental health, promote wellbeing and to help them relax and cope with stress. Different groups of CYP are more vulnerable than others, but most can use the Internet and social media in positive ways if they receive appropriate guidance and education, and we need to find ways to maximise this further.

It has been challenging to critically assess the growing evidence in this area as this is often conflicting and confusing for those working with CYP, and equally confusing for parents. In this book we have not treated the positive and negative relationship between digital technology and mental health as a dichotomy but rather as a continuum, seeing the issue from different perspectives and considering the active agents behind the screens. We have provided a practical and interdisciplinary perspective based on real research evidence to try to help you navigate through the minefield of information. We hope you have found it useful and enjoyed the journey.

We close the book and leave you with the expert voice of Valerie Verdoodt to remind you that a balance needs to be found between empowering CYP and promoting their rights online, and protecting them and keeping them safe in the digital world as outlined in Box 12.4.

Box 12.4: Expert voice: Dr Valerie Verdoodt

Empowering and safeguarding CYP

Nowadays, CYP turn to the digital world when they need information or guidance, or when they are struggling and seek emotional support. During the COVID-19 pandemic, downloads of mental health and wellbeing apps soared, offering direct and rapid help for all ages. Such technologies offer great opportunities for the exercise of CYP's rights as awarded to them by the UNCRC. In particular, online therapy can have a positive impact on children's mental health and wellbeing, which ultimately benefits their right to development. In addition, mental health apps are an excellent source of information for CYP, promote awareness and create a community feeling. Unfortunately, the uptake of digital technologies in the context of mental health also raises several important concerns, the most often heard one being the increased collection and use of highly-sensitive personal data. For this reason, mental health apps and other services offering online therapy present important risks to CYP's rights, including their rights to privacy, data protection, freedom of thought and protection from exploitation.

Care workers and organisations can play a crucial role in safeguarding CYP's rights in this context. More specifically, they should help CYP and their parents in balancing the benefits and opportunities for wellbeing with the privacy and commercial risks presented by such apps. When deciding on which apps or services to recommend to CYP and their parents, care workers and organisations should carefully consider the potential impact of the data processing practices on children's rights. They should evaluate the privacy policies of these apps and question what kind of data will be collected through the app: will the app (re)use the data for commercial purposes like advertising or will the data be resold to third parties; how long will the data be stored and so on.

In addition, developers and providers of mental health and wellbeing apps should take up their responsibility for safeguarding CYP's rights to privacy and data protection. In the EU, the General Data Protection Regulation (GDPR) offers specific protection to CYP under the age of 18 years when their personal data are processed, and an additional layer of protection if those data are sensitive, such as health data. Developers and providers of mental health apps to children in the EU must comply with these rules whenever they want to process children's personal data. During the app development phase, they should conduct not only data protection impact assessments, but more broadly children's rights impact assessments, which consider the broad range of rights under the UNCRC and which take into account the voices of children themselves about what they find acceptable data collection, features and safeguards offered by the app.

Dr Valerie Verdoodt

Fellow in Law at the London School of Economics, affiliated postdoctoral researcher at Ghent University and KU Leuven.

REFERENCES

5Rights Foundation (n.d.). From https://5rightsfoundation.com/our-work/child-online-protection/ (accessed 11/2/21).

5Rights Foundation (n.d.) Design of service. From https://5rightsfoundation.com/our-work/design-of-service/ (accessed 31/03/21).

Aarseth, E., Bean, A., Boonen, H., et al. (2017). Scholars' open debate paper on the World Health Organization ICD-11 Gaming Disorder proposal. *Journal of Behavioural Addictions, 6*(3), 267–270.

Abebe, T., & Ofosu-Kusi, Y. (2016). Beyond pluralizing African childhoods: Introduction. *Childhood, 18*(3), 303–316.

Adams, R. (2017). Demanding workload driving young teachers out of the profession. *Guardian*, 15 April. From www.theguardian.com/education/2017/apr/15/demanding-workload-driving-young-teachers-out-of-profession (accessed 11/2/21).

Adams, S., O'Reilly, M., & Karim, K. (2019). Why do teachers need to know about mental health? In C. Cardern (Ed.), *Primary teaching* (pp. 535–552). London: Sage.

Adi, Y., Killoran, A., Janmohamed, K., & Steward-Brown, S. (2007). *Systematic review of the effectiveness of interventions to promote mental wellbeing in children in primary education. Universal Approaches (Non-violence related outcomes).* London: National Institute for Health and Clinical Excellence.

Adler, P. (2006). Technological determinism. In S. Clegg, & J. Bailey (Eds.), *The international encyclopedia of organization studies.* London: Sage.

Ahern, N., & Mechling, B. (2013). Sexting: serious problems for youth. *Journal of Psycho-social Nursing and Mental Health Services, 51*(7), 22–30.

Akhtar, A., & Ward, M. (2020). *Bill Gates and Steve Jobs raised their kids with limited tech-and it should have been a red flag about our own smartphone use.* From www.businessinsider.com/screen-time-limits-bill-gates-steve-jobs-red-flag-2017-10?r = US&IR = T (accessed 2/12/20).

Albeladi, N., & Palmer, E. (2020). The role of parental mediation in the relationship between adolescents' use of social media and family relationships in Saudi Arabia. *Journal of Information Technology Management, 12*(2), 163–183.

Albert, D., Chein, J., & Steinberg, L., (2013). The teenage brain: Peer influences on adolescent decision making. *Current Directions in Psychological Science, 22*(2), 114–120.

Alfano, C., Zakem, A., Costa, N., Taylor, L., & Weems, C. (2009). Sleep problems and their relation to cognitive factors, anxiety, and depressive symptoms in children and adolescents. *Depression and Anxiety, 26*(6), 503–512.

Allan, C. (2018). The mental health crisis is down to government policy, not stigma. From www.theguardian.com/society/2018/oct/16/mental-health-crisis-government-policy-not-stigma (accessed 11/2/21).

Allen, K., Ryan, T., Gray, D., McInerney, D., & Waters, L. (2014). Social media use and social connectedness in adolescents: The positives and the potential pitfalls. *The Australian Educational and Developmental Psychologist, 31*(1), 18–31.

American Psychiatric Association (APA). (2013). *Diagnostic and statistical manual of mental disorders* (5th ed.) (DSM-5). Washington, DC: APA.

Andersen, J. & Blosnich, J. (2013). Disparities in adverse childhood experiences among sexual minority and heterosexual adults: Results from a multi-state probability-based sample. *PloS one, 8*(1), e54691.

Anderson, M. (2018a). A majority of teens have experienced some form of cyberbullying. From www.pewresearch.org/internet/2018/09/27/a-majority-of-teens-have-experienced-some-form-of-cyberbullying/ (accessed 11/12/19).

Anderson, M. (2018b). About a quarter of rural Americans say access to high-speed internet is a major problem. *Pew Research Center*. From www.pewresearch.org/fact-tank/2018/09/10/about-a-quarter-of-rural-americans-say-access-to-high-speed-internet-is-a-major-problem/ (accessed 11/2/21).

Anderson, M., & Jiang, J. (2018a). Teens, social media and technology. From www.pewresearch.org/internet/2018/05/31/teens-social-media-technology-2018/ (accessed 11/2/21).

Anderson, M., & Jiang, J. (2018b). Teens' social media habits and experiences. *Pew Research Center*. From www.pewinternet.org/2018/11/28/teens-social-media-habits-and-experiences/ (accessed 11/2/21).

Anti-Bullying Alliance. (2019). Written evidence for Parliament. From http://data.parliament.uk/writtenevidence/committeeevidence.svc/evidencedocument/science-and-technology-committee/impact-of-social-media-and-screenuse-on-young-peoples-health/written/81132.html (accessed 11/2/21).

Appleby, L., Kapur, N., Shaw, J., Hunt, I. M., Ibrahim, S., Gianatsi, M., Turnbull, P., Rodway, C., Tham, S-G., Burns, J., & Richards, N. (2018). *National confidential inquiry into suicide and safety in mental health. Annual report 2018.* Manchester: University of Manchester.

Ariès P. (1962). *Centuries of childhood* (trans. R. Baldick). New York: Jonathan Cape.

Arseneault, L. (2018). Annual Research Review: The persistent and pervasive impact of being bullied in childhood and adolescence: Implications of policy and practice. *The Journal of Child Psychology and Psychiatry, 59*(4), 405–421.

Asam, A., & Katz, A. (2018). Vulnerable young people and their experience of online risks. *Human Computer Interaction, 33*, 281–230.

Asmundson, G., & Taylor, S. (2020). How health anxiety influences responses to viral outbreaks like COVID-19: What all decision-makers, health authorities, and health care professionals need to know. *Journal of Anxiety Disorders, 71*, 102211.

Australian Bureau of Statistics (ABS). (2014). *Household use of information technology, Australia, 2012–13* (8146.0). Canberra: ABS.

Aven, T., & Renn, O. (2009). On risk defined as an event where the outcome is uncertain. *Journal of Risk Research, 12*(1), 1–11, DOI: 10.1080/13669870802488883

Baggio, S., Starcevic, V., Studer, J., Simon, O., Gainsbury, S. M., Gmel, G., & Billieux, J. (2018). Technology-mediated addictive behaviors constitute a spectrum of related yet distinct conditions: A network perspective. *Psychology of Addictive Behaviors, 32*(5), 564–572.

Bakow, B., & Low, K. (2018). A South African experience: Cultural determinants of Ukuthwasa. *Journal of Cross-Cultural Psychology, 49*, 436–452.

Bandura, A. (1977). *Social learning theory.* Englewood Cliffs, NJ: Prentice Hall.

Bandura, A. (1982). Self-efficacy mechanism in human agency. *American Psychologist, 37*(2), 122–147.

Barnow, S., Schuckit, M., Smith, T. L., Preuss, U., & Danko, G. (2002). The real relationship between the family density of alcoholism and externalizing symptoms among 146 children. *Alcohol and Alcoholism, 37*(4), 383–387.

Barrocas, A., Hankin, B., Young, J., & Abela, J. (2012). Rates of nonsuicidal self-injury in youth: Age, sex, and behavioral methods in a community sample. *Pediatrics, 130*(1), 39–45.

Barry, C., Sidoti, C., Briggs, S., Reiter, S., & Lindsey, R. (2017). Adolescent social media use and mental health from adolescent and parent perspectives. *Journal of Adolescence, 61*, 1–11.

Bartholomew, M., Schoppe-Sullivan, S., Glassman, M., Kamp Dush, C., & Sullivan, J. (2012). New parents' Facebook use at the transition to parenthood. *Family Relations, 61*(3), 455–469.

Bateson, G. (1972). *Steps to an ecology of mind*. New York: Ballantine Books.

Bauman, S., & Lyon. D. (2013). *Liquid surveillance: A conversation*. Cambridge: Polity Press.

Baumrind, D. (1966). Effects of authoritative parental control on child behavior. *Child Development, 37*, 887–907.

Baumrind, D. (1991). The influence of parenting style on adolescent competence and substance use. *The Journal of Early Adolescence, 11*(1), 56–95.

BEAT. (n.d.). The dangers of pro-ana and pro-mia. From www.beateatingdisorders.org.uk/recovery-information/dangers-of-pro-ana-and-pro-mia

Beauregard, T., Özbilgin, M., & Bell, M. (2009). Revisiting the social construction of family in the context of work. *Journal of Managerial Psychology, 24*, 46–65.

Beck, U. (1992). *Risk society: Towards a new modernity*. London: Sage.

Bell, V., Bishop, D., & Przybylski, A. (2015). The debate over digital technology and young people: Needs less shock and more substance. *British Medical Journal, 351*, h3064.

Bello, B., Fatusi, A., Adepoju, O., Maina, B., Kabiru, C. W., Sommer, M., & Mmari, K. (2017). Adolescent and parental reactions to puberty in Nigeria and Kenya: A cross-cultural and intergenerational comparison. *Journal of Adolescent Health, 61*(4), s35-s41.

Benjali, S., Livingstone, S., Nandi, A., & Stoilova, M. (2017). Instrumentalising the digital: Findings from a rapid evidence review of development interventions to support adolescents' engagement with ICTs in low and middle-income countries. *Development in Practice, 28*(3).

Berndt, T. (1979). Developmental changes in conformity to peers and parents. *Developmental Psychology, 15*(6), 608–616.

Berrouiguet, S., Baca-Garcia, E., Brandt, S., Walter, M., & Courtet, P. (2016). Fundamentals for future mobile-health (mHealth): a systematic review of mobile phone and web-based text messaging in mental health. *Journal of Medical Internet Research, 18*(6), e135.

Best, P., Manktelow, R., & Taylor, B. (2014). Online communication, social media and adolescent wellbeing: A systematic narrative review. *Children and Youth Services Review, 41*, 27–36.

Betton, V., & Woollard, J. (2019). *Teen mental health in an online world: Supporting young people around their use of social media, apps gaming, texting and the rest*. London: Jessica Kingsley.

Beyens, I., Pouwels, J., van Driel, I., Keijsers, L., & Valkenburg, P. (2020). *The association between social media use and wellbeing among adolescents: An experience sampling study*. Paper presented at the 70th International Communication Association Conference, Gold Coast, Australia.

Beyth-Marom, R., Austin, L., Fischoff, B., Palmgren, C., & Jacobs-Quadrel, M. (1993). Perceived consequences of risky behavior: Adults and adolescents. *Developmental Psychology, 29*, 549–563.

Biddle, L., Donovan, J., Hawton, K., Kapur, N., & Gunnell, D (2008). Suicide and the internet. *British Medical Journal, 336*, 800.

Billieux, J., Maurage, P., Lopez-Fernandez, O., Juss, D., & Griffiths, M. (2015). Can discovered mobile phone use be considered a behavioral addiction? An update on current evidence and a comprehensive model for future research. *Current Addiction Reports, 2*(2), 156–162.

Bjørnsen, H., Eiletsen, M-E., Ringdal, R., Espnes, G. & Moksnes, U. (2017). Positive mental health literacy: Development and validation of a measure among Norwegian adolescents. *BMC Public Health, 17*, 717–727.

Blakemore, S. (2008). The social brain in adolescence. *Nature Reviews Neuroscience, 9*, 267–277.

Blakemore, S. (2012). Imaging brain development: The adolescent brain. *Neuro-Image, 61*, 397–406.

Blakemore, S. (2018a). *Inventing ourselves: The secret life of the teenage brain*. Doubleday.

Blakemore, S. (2018b). Avoiding social risk in adolescence. *Current Directions in Psychological Science, 27*(2), 116–122.

Bloom, D., Cafiero, E. T., Jané-Llopis, E., Abrahams-Gessel, S., Bloom, L. R., Fathima, S., Feigl, A. B., Gaziano, T., Mowafi, M., Pandya, A., Prettner, K., Rosenberg, L., Seligman, B., Stein, A. Z., & Weinstein, C (2011). *The global economic burden of non-communicable diseases*. Geneva: World Economic Forum.

Blumenfeld, W., & Cooper, R. (2010). LGBT and allied youth responses to cyberbullying: policy implications. *International Journal of Critical Pedagogy, 3*(1), 114–133.

Blumenstyk, G. (2020). Why coronavirus looks like a 'black swan' moment for higher education. *The Chronicle*. From www.chronicle.com/article/Why-Coronavirus-Looks-Like-a/248219 (accessed 11/2/21).

Blum-Ross, A., Donoso, V., Dinh, T., Mascheroni, G., O'Neill, B., Riesmeyer, C., & Stoilova, M. (2018). *Looking forward: Technological and social change in the lives of European children and young people. Report for the ICT Coalition for Children Online*. Brussels: ICT Coalition.

Blum-Ross, A., & Livingstone, S. (2017). 'Sharenting', parent blogging, and the boundaries of the digital self. *Popular Communication, 15*, 2110–2125.

Boardman, J., Dogra, N., & Hindley, P. (2015). Mental health and poverty in the UK – time for change? *British Journal of Psychiatry International, 12*(2), 27–28.

Bone, C., Dugard, P., Vostanis, P., & Dogra, N., (2015) Students' understandings of mental health and their preferred learning platforms. *Journal of Public Mental health, 14*(4), 185–195.

Bonnefoy, J., Morgan, A., Kelly, M., Butt, J., & Bergman, V. (2007). Constructing the evidence base on the social determinants of health: A guide. From www.who.int/social_determinants/knowledge_networks/add_documents/mekn_final_guide_112007.pdf?ua=1 (accessed 11/2/21).

Bor, W., Dean, A., Najman, J., & Hayatbakhsh, R. (2014). Are child and adolescent mental health problems increasing in the 21st century? A systematic review. *Australian and New Zealand Journal of Psychiatry, 48*(7), 606–616.

Bordonaro, L. (2012). Agency does not mean freedom. Cape Verdean street children and the politics of children's agency, *Children's Geographies, 10*(4), 413–426.

Bostik, K., & Everall, R (2006). In my mind I was alone: suicidal adolescents' perceptions of attachment relationships. *International Journal for the Advancement of Counselling, 28*(3), 269–287.

Bowlby, J. (1977). The making and breaking of affectional bonds. *British Journal of Psychiatry, 130*, 201–210.

Boyce, W., & Ellis, B. (2005). Biological sensitivity to context: I. An evolutionary-developmental theory of the origins and functions of stress reactivity. *Development and psychopathology, 17*, 271–301.

boyd, d. (2010). Digital self-harm and other acts of self-harassment. [blog post]. From www.zephoria.org/thoughts/archives/2010/12/07/digital-self-harm-and-other-acts-of-self-harassment.html (accessed 11/2/21).

boyd, d. (2014). *It's complicated: The social lives of networked teens*. London: Yale University Press.

boyd, d. & Ellison, N. (2007). Social network sites: Definition, history, and scholarship, *Journal of Computer-Mediated Communication, 13*(1), 210–230.

boyd, d., & Hargittai, E. (2013). Connected and concerned: variation in parents' online safety concerns. *Policy and Internet, 5*, 245–269.

Boydell, K., Hodgins, M., Pignatiello, A., Teshima, J., Edwards, H., & Willis, D. (2014). Using technology to deliver mental health services to children and youth: A scoping review. *Journal of Canadian Academy of Child and Adolescent Psychiatry, 23*, 87–99.

Bradford, B., & Larson, J. (2009). Peer relationships in adolescence. In R. Lerner, & L. Steinberg (Eds.), *Handbook of adolescent psychology* (pp. 74–103). London: Wiley.

Branson, C., Clemmy, P., & Mukherjee, P. (2013). Text message reminders to improve outpatient therapy attendance among adolescents: A pilot study. *Psychological Services, 10*(3), 298–303.

BrickHouse. (2009). Child locator with wander alerts. From www.brickhousesecurity.com/gps-trackers/child-tracking/ (accessed 11/2/21).

Broadhurst, R. (2019). Child sex abuse images and exploitation materials. In R. Leukfeldt, & T. Holt (Eds.), *Handbook of Cybercrime* (pp. 310–336). London: Routledge.

Bronfenbrenner, U. (1979). Contexts of child rearing: Problems and prospects. *American Psychologist, 34*, 644–850.

Brophy, M., & Holmstrom, R. (2006). The truth hurts: Report of the national inquiry into self-harm among young people. Fact or fiction? London: Mental Health Foundation. From www.mentalhealth.org.uk/publications/truth-hurts-report1 (accessed 11/2/21).

Brosch, A. (2016). When the child is born into the Internet: Sharenting as a growing trend among parents on Facebook. *The New Educational Review, 43*(1), 225–235.

Brown, B., & Marin, P. (2009). *Adolescents and electronic media: Growing up plugged in*. Washington, DC: Child Trends.

Brown, L., & Ormes, S. (2020) Equality of access: An issue paper from the Networked Services Policy Task Group. From www.ukoln.ac.uk/public/earl/issuepapers/equality.html (accessed 11/2/21).

Bruner, J. S. (1960). *The process of education*. Cambridge, MA: Harvard University Press.

Bry, L. J., Chou, T., Miguel, E., & Comer, J. S. (2018). Consumer smartphone apps marketed for child and adolescent anxiety: a systematic review and content analysis. *Behavior therapy, 49*(2), 249–261.

Bucci, S., Schwannauer, M., & Berry, N. (2019). The digital revolution and its impact on mental health care. *Psychology and Psychotherapy: Theory, Research and Practice, 92*(2), 277–297.

Buckingham, D. (2008). Introducing identity. In D. Buckingham (Ed.), *Youth, identity, and digital media*. The John D. & Catherine T. MacArthur Foundation Series on Digital Media and Learning (pp. 1–24). Cambridge, MA: The MIT Press.

Burman, E. (2008). *Deconstructing developmental psychology* (2nd ed.). London: Routledge.

Byrne, J., Kardefelt-Winther, D., Livingstone, S., & Stoilova, M. (2016). *Global Kids Online research synthesis, 2015–2016*. UNICEF Office of Research – Innocenti and London School of Economics and Political Science. Available at www.globalkidsonline.net/synthesis (accessed 10/2/21).

C3P. (2017). *Survivor's survey: Full report*. Winnipeg: Canadian Centre for Child Protection.

Calvert, S. L. (2015). Children and digital media. In M. H. Bornstein, T. Leventhal, & R. M. Lerner (Eds.), *Handbook of child psychology and developmental science: Ecological settings and processes* (pp. 375–415). John Wiley & Sons, Inc.

Calzada, E. J. (2000). *Normative and optimal parenting in Dominican and Puerto Rican mothers of young children.* A dissertation presented to the graduate school of the University of Florida.

Campbell, R., Starkey, F., Holliday, J., Audrey, S., Bloor, M., Parry-Langdon, N., Hughes, R., & Moore, L. (2008). An informal school-based peer-led intervention for smoking prevention in adolescence (ASSIST): A cluster randomised trial. *The Lancet, 371,* 1595–1602.

Carter, E. A., & McGoldrick, M. (1989) *The changing family life cycle: A framework for family therapy* (2nd ed.). New York: Gardner.

Carter, M., Burley, V., Nykjaer, C., & Cade, J. (2013). Adherence to a smartphone application for weight loss compared to website and paper diary: pilot randomized controlled trial. *Journal of Medical Internet Research, 15*(4), e32.

Castells, M. (2013). *Networks of outrage and hope.* Cambridge: Polity Press.

Center for Disease Control and Prevention. (2019). About the CDC-Kaiser ACE study. From www.cdc.gov/violenceprevention/childabuseandneglect/acestudy/about.html (accessed 11/02/21).

Chakroff, J., & Nathanson, A. (2008). Parent and school interventions: Mediation and media literacy. In S. Calvert, & B. Wilson (Eds.), *The handbook of children, media and development* (pp. 552–576). Malden, MA: Blackwell.

Chamorro-Premuzic, T. (2014). Behind the online comments: the psychology of internet trolls. *Guardian,* 18 September. From www.theguardian.com/media-network/media-network-blog/2014/sep/18/psychology-internet-trolls-pewdiepie-youtube-mary-beard (accessed 11/2/21).

Chandra, A., Martino, S., Collins, R., Elliott, M. N., Berry, S. H., Kanouse, D. E., & Miu, A. (2008). Does watching sex on television predict teen pregnancy? Findings from a longitudinal survey of youth. *Pediatrics, 122,* 1047–1054.

Chandra, P., Sowmya, H., Mehrotra, S., & Duggal, M. (2014). 'SMS' for mental health – feasibility and acceptability of using text messages for mental health promotion among young women from urban low-income settings in India. *Asian Journal of Psychiatry, 11,* 59–64.

Chaudron, S., Beutel, M. E., Černikova, M., et al. (2015). *Young children (0–8) and digital technology: A qualitative exploratory study across seven countries.* From http://publications.jrc.ec.europa.eu/repository/handle/JRC93239 (accessed 11/2/21).

Chen, H., Cohen, P., Kasen, S., Johnson, J., Bereson, K., & Gordon, K. (2006). Impact of adolescent mental disorders and physical illnesses on quality of life 17 years later. *Archives of Pediatric and Adolescent Medicine, 160*(1), 93–99.

Chen, J. & Kennedy C. (2005). Cultural variations in children's coping behaviour, TV viewing time, and family functioning. *International Nursing Review, 52*(3), 186–195.

Chen, X., Liu, M., & Li, D. (2000). Parental warmth, control, and indulgence and their relations to adjustment in Chinese children: A longitudinal study. *Journal of Family Psychology, 14*(3), 401–419.

Cherry, E. (2019). *Witness comments to Parliament.* From http://data.parliament.uk/writtenevidence/committeeevidence.svc/evidencedocument/science-and-technology-committee/impact-of-social-media-and-screenuse-on-young-peoples-health/oral/86560.html (accessed 11/2/21).

Chiang, J., Chen, E., & Miller, G. (2018). Midlife self-reported social support as a buffer against premature mortality risks associated with child abuse. *Nature Human Behaviour, 2,* 261–268.

Chief Medical Officer. (2013). Public mental health priorities: investing in the evidence, annual report. From https://assets.publishing.service.gov.uk/government/uploads/system/uploads/attachment_data/file/413196/CMO_web_doc.pdf (accessed 11/2/21).

Child Helpline International. (2019). *Voices of children and young people: Child Helpline data for 2017 and 2018.* From www.childhelplineinternational.org/wp-content/uploads/2019/11/Voices-of-Children-2017-2018-FINAL-Spreads.pdf (accessed 11/2/21).

Child Helpline International (2020). *Voices of children and young people around the world: Child Helpline data for 2019.* From www.childhelplineinternational.org/wp-content/uploads/2020/11/VCYP-2019-Data-Spreads.pdf (accessed 11/2/21).

Childline. (2016). 'It turned out someone did care': Childline Annual Review 2015–16. From https://lfstest.nspxyz.net/globalassets/documents/annual-reports/childline-annual-review-2015-16.pdf (accessed 11/2/21).

Childnet. (2018). Digital resilience: A guide for educators. From www.childnet.com/ufiles/Educator-guidance.pdf (accessed 11/2/21).

Children's Commissioner. (2018). Life in likes: Children's commissioner report into social media use among 8–12-year-olds. From www.childrenscommissioner.gov.uk/report/life-in-likes/ (accessed 11/2/21).

Chomsky, N. (1971). *Chomsky: Selected readings* (edited by J. P. B. Allen and Paul Van Buren). London: Oxford University Press.

Chorpita, B., & Barlow, D. (1998). The development of anxiety: The role of control in the early environment. *Psychological Bulletin, 124*(1), 3–21.

Chou, H., & Edge, N. (2012). They are happier and having better lives than I am *Cyberpsychology, Behavior, and Social Networks, 15*(2), 117–121.

Christensen, H. (2007). Computerised therapy for psychiatric disorders. *Lancet, 370,* 112–113.

Cimbora, D., & McIntosh, D. (2005). Understanding the link between moral emotions and behaviour. In A. Clark (Ed.), *Psychology of moods.* Hauppauge, NY: Nova Science Publishers.

Clarke, B. (2009). Early adolescents' use of social networking sites to maintain friendship and explore identity: Implications for policy. *Policy and Internet, 1*(1), 55–89.

Clarke, D., Usick, R., Sanderson, A., Giles-Smith, L., & Baker, J. (2014). Emergency department staff attitudes towards mental health consumers: A literature review and thematic content analysis. *International Journal of Mental Health Nursing, 23*(3), 273–284.

Clement, S., Schauman, O., Graham, T., Maggioni, F., Evans-Lacko, S., Bezborodovs, N., Morgan, C., Rüsch, N., Brown, J. S. L., & Thornicroft, G. (2015). What is the impact of mental health-related stigma on help-seeking? A systematic review of quantitative and qualitative studies. *Psychological Medicine, 45,* 11–27.

Coleman, S., & Blumler, J. (2009). *The internet and democratic citizenship.* Cambridge: Cambridge University Press.

Collier, K., Coyne, S., Rasmussen, E., Hawkins, A., & Padilla-Walker, L. (2016). Does parental mediation of media influence child outcomes? A meta-analysis on media time, aggression, substance use, and sexual behaviour. *Developmental Psychology, 52*(5), 798–812.

Collins Online Dictionary. (2016). *Sharenting.* From: www.collinsdictionary.com/submission/11762/Sharenting (accessed 11/2/21).

Collishaw, S. (2015). Annual Research Review: Secular trends in child and adolescent mental health. *Journal of Child Psychology and Psychiatry, 56*(3), 370–393.

Committee on the Rights of the Child. (2019). Concept note for a general comment on children's rights in relation to the digital environment. From www.ohchr.org/EN/HRBodies/CRC/Pages/GCChildrensRightsRelationDigitalEnvironment.aspx (accessed 11/2/21).

Compaine, B. M. (2001). *The digital divide: Facing a crisis or creating a myth*. Cambridge, MA: MIT Press.

Connell, S., Lauricella, A., & Wartella, E. (2015). Parental Co-Use of Media Technology with their Young Children in the USA. *Journal of Children and Media, 9*(1), 5–21.

Conway, M. (2012). From al-Zarqawi to al-Awlaki: The emergence and development of an online radical milieu? *CTX: Combating Terrorism Exchange, 2*(4), 12–22.

Cooper, K., Quayle, E., Jonsson, L., & Svedin, C. (2016). Adolescents and self-taken sexual images: A review of the literature. *Computers in Human Behavior, 55*, 706–716.

Corsaro, W. (2011). *The sociology of childhood* (3rd ed.). Thousand Oaks, CA: Pine Forge Press.

Cotton, R. (2019). Using digital technology to design and deliver better mental health services: Perspectives from Australia and the USA. From www.wcmt.org.uk/sites/default/files/report-documents/Cotton%20R%202017%20Final.pdf (accessed 11/2/21).

Couldry, N. (2012). *Media, society, world: Social theory and digital media practice*. Cambridge: Polity Press.

Council of Europe. (2018). *Guidelines to respect, protect and fulfil the rights of the child in the digital environment: Recommendation CM/Rec (2018)7 of the Committee of Ministers* From https://rm.coe.int/guidelines-to-respect-protect-and-fulfil-the-rights-of-the-child-in-th/16808d881a (accessed 11/2/21).

Council on Communications and Media. (2009). Policy statement – Media violence. *Pediatrics, 124*(5), 1495–1503.

Couture, S., & Strong, T. (2004). Turning differences into possibilities: Using discourse analysis to investigate change in therapy with adolescents and their families. *Counselling and Psychotherapy Research, 4*(1), 90–101.

Cowie, H. (2013). Cyberbullying and its impact on young people's emotional health and wellbeing. *The Psychiatrist, 37*, 167–170.

Coyne, S., Stockdale, L., & Summers, K. (2019). Problematic cell phone use, depression, anxiety, and self-regulation: evidence from a three-year longitudinal study from adolescence to emerging adulthood. *Computers in Human Behavior, 96*, 78–84.

Craft, A. (2011). 'Possibility thinking' and digital play in early years settings. From www.teachearlyyears.com/learning-and-development/view/possibility-thinking-digital-play (accessed 11/2/21).

Crane, L., Chester, J., Goddard, L., Henry, L., & Hill, E. (2016). Experiences of autism diagnosis: A survey of over 1000 parents in the United Kingdom. *Autism, 20*(2), 153–162.

Creasy, R., & Corby, F. (2019). Helicopter parents: the real reason British teenagers are so unhappy. *The Conversation*. From https://theconversation.com/helicopter-parents-the-real-reason-british-teenagers-are-so-unhappy-111673 (accessed 11/2/21).

Curtin, S., Warner, M., & Hedegaard, H. (2016). Increase in suicide in the United States, 1999–2014). *NCHS Data Brief, 241*. Hyattsville, MD: National Center for Health Statistics.

d'Haenens, L., Vandoninck, S., & Donoso, V. (2013). How to cope and build online resilence? *EU Kids Online*. From www.eukidsonline.net (accessed 11/2/21).

Dahlberg, L., & Siapera, E. (2007). *Radical democracy and the internet*. Basingstoke: Palgrave Macmillan.

Daine, K., Hawton, K., Singarevelu, V., Stewart, A., Simkin, S., & Montgomery, P. (2013) The power of the web. A systematic review of studies of the influence of the internet on self-harm and suicide in young people. *PLoS oNE, 8*, e77555.

Dallos, R., & Draper, R. (2010). *An introduction to family therapy: Systemic theory and practice* (3rd ed.). Berkshire: Open University Press.

Damjanovic, D., & Dayman, I. (2015). #FOMO leading to higher levels of depression, anxiety for heavy social media users. From www.abc.net.au/news/2015-11-08/well-being-survey-finds-teens-feeling-left-out-on-social-media/6921780 (accessed 11/2/21).

Davidson, J. (2011). Legislation and policy: Protecting young people, sentencing and managing internet sex offenders. In J. Davidson, & P. Gottschalk (Eds.), *Internet child abuse: Current research and policy* (pp. 8–26). Abingdon: Routledge-Cavendish.

Davies, C. (2014). Hannah Smith wrote 'vile' posts to herself before suicide, say police. From www.theguardian.com/uk-news/2014/may/06/hannah-smith-suicide-teenager-cyber-bullying-inquests (accessed 11/2/21).

Davies, C., & Eynon, R. (2013). *Teenagers and technology*. London: Routledge.

Davis, L. (1995). *Enforcing normalcy: Disability, deafness, and the body*. London: Verso.

Day, R., (2017). Anxiety disorders. In N. Dogra, S. Cooper, & B. Lunn (Eds.), *Ten teachers: Psychiatry* (2nd ed.). London: Hodder & Stoughton.

De Bellis, M., Hooper, S., Woolley, D., & Shenk, C. (2010). Demographic, maltreatment, and neurobiological correlates of PTSD symptoms in children and adolescents. *Journal of Pediatric Psychology, 35*(5), 570–577.

Dehue, F., Bolman, C., & Völlink, T. (2008). Cyberbullying: Youngers' experiences and paternal perception. *CyberPsychology & Behavior, 11*(2), 217–223.

Dempsey, A. G., Sulkowski, M. L., Nichols, R., & Storch, E. A. (2009). Differences between peer victimization in cyber and physical settings and associated psychosocial adjustment in early adolescence. *Psychology in the Schools, 46*(10), 962–972.

Department for Digital, Culture, Media and Sport. (2019). Age-verification for online pornography to begin in July. From www.gov.uk/government/news/age-verification-for-online-pornography-to-begin-in-july (accessed 11/2/21).

Department for Education. (2016). *Mental health and behaviour in schools: Departmental advice for school staff*. From www.gov.uk/government/uploads/system/uploads/attachment_data/file/508847/Mental_Health_and_Behaviour_-_advice_for_Schools_160316.pdf (accessed 11/2/21).

Department of Health. (2011). *No health without mental health: A cross-government mental health outcomes strategy for people of all ages*. London: Department of Health.

Devine, P. (2012). A technology enabled journal. *Principal, 91*(3), 14–17.

Devine, P., & Lloyd, K. (2012). Internet use and psychological wellbeing among 10-year-old and 11-year-old children. *Child Care in Practice, 18*(1), 5–22.

Devon, N. (2018a). We need to stop blaming social media for the teenage mental health crisis. *Metro*, 6 August 2018. From: https://metro.co.uk/2018/08/06/we-need-to-stop-blaming-social-media-for-the-teenage-mental-health-crisis-7803618/ (accessed 11/2/21).

Devon, N. (2018b). *Witness statements*. From http://data.parliament.uk/writtenevidence/committeeevidence.svc/evidencedocument/science-and-technology-committee/impact-of-social-media-and-screenuse-on-young-peoples-health/oral/92494.html (accessed 11/2/21).

Didkowsky, N., & Ungar, M. (2016). A social ecological approach to understanding resilience among rural youth. In U. Kumar (ed.), *The Routledge international handbook of psychosocial resilience* (pp. 86–98). London: Routledge.

Dienlin, T., Masur, P., & Trepte, S. (2017). Reinforcement or displacement? The reciprocity of FtF, IM, and SNS communication and their effects on loneliness and life satisfaction. *Journal of Computer-Mediated Communication, 22*, 71–87.

DigiGen (n.d.) Focus: Civic participation. From www.digigen.eu/index.php/civic-participation/ (accessed 10/12/20).

Docrat, S., Lund, C., & Chrisholm, D. (2019). Sustainable financing options for mental health care in South Africa: Findings from a situation analysis and key informant interviews. *International Journal of Mental Health Systems, 13*(4), https://doi.org/10.1186/s13033-019-0260-4

Dodd, J., Saggers, S., & Wildy, H. (2009). Constructing the 'ideal' family for family-centred practice: challenges for delivery. *Disability and Society, 24*(2), 173–186.

Dogra, N. (2010a). Social determinants of mental health disorders in childhood. In D. Bhugra, & C. Morgan (Eds.), *Principles of social psychiatry* (2nd ed.). Oxford: Wiley-Blackwell.

Dogra, N. (2010b). Culture and child psychiatry. In R. Bhattacharya, S. Cross, & D. Bhugra (Eds.), *Clinical topics in cultural psychiatry* (pp. 209–221). London: Royal College of Psychiatrists Press.

Dogra, N. (2015). *Principles of child and adolescent psychiatry, International Encyclopedia of Social and Behavioral Sciences* (2nd ed.). Oxford: Elsevier.

Dogra, N., Frake, C., Bretherton, K., Dwivedi, K., & Sharma, I. (2005). Training CAMHS professionals in developing countries: An Indian case study. *Child and Adolescent Mental Health, 10*(2), 74–79.

Dogra, N., Omigbodun, O., Adedokun, T., Bella, T., Ronzoni, P., & Adesokan, A. (2012). Nigerian secondary school children's knowledge of and attitudes to mental health and illness. *Clinical Child Psychology and Psychiatry, 17*(3), 336–353.

Dogra, N., Parkin, A., Gale, F., & Frake, C. (2017) *A multidisciplinary handbook of child and adolescent mental health for front-line professionals* (3rd ed.). London: Jessica Kingsley.

Dogra, N., Svirydzenka, N., Dugard, P., Singh, S., & Vostanis, P. (2013) The characteristics and rates of mental health problems among Indian and White adolescents in two English cities. *British Journal of Psychiatry, 203*, 44–45.

Dogra, N., Vostanis, P. & Karnik, N. (2018). Child and adolescent psychiatric disorders. In D. Bhugra, & K. Bhui (Eds.), *Textbook of cultural psychiatry* (2nd ed.) (pp. 317–328). Cambridge: Cambridge University Press.

Donker, T., Petrie, K., Proudfoot, J., Clarke, J., Birch, M-R., & Christensen, H. (2013). Smartphones for smarter delivery of mental health programs: A systematic review. *Journal of Med Internet Research, 15*(11), e247.

Donoso, V. (2011). *Assessment of the implementation of the Safer Social Networking Principles for the EU on 14 websites: summary report.* Study commissioned by the European Commission.

Donoso, V., Verdoodt, V., Van Mechelen, M. & Jasmontaite, L. (2016). Faraway, so close: why the digital industry needs scholars and the other way around. *Journal of Children and Media, 10*(2), 200–207.

Donoso, V., Retzmann, N., Joris, W., & d'Haenens, L. (2020). *Digital skills: An inventory of actors and factors.* KU Leuven, Leuven: ySKILLS.

Dorr, A., Kovaric, P., & Doubleday, C. (1989). Parent–child coviewing of television. *Journal of Broadcasting and Electronic Media, 33*, 35–51.

Douglas, T. (2012). Virtual violence: Protecting children from cyberbullying. In S. Livingstone, & T. Palmer (Eds.). *Identifying vulnerable children online and what strategies can help them* (pp. 32–33). London: UK Safer Internet Centre.

Dowling, M., & Rickwood, D. (2014). Experiences of counsellors providing online chat counselling to young people. *Journal of Psychologists and Counsellors in Schools, 24*(2), 183–196.

Drabick, D. A., & Kendall, P. C. (2010). Developmental psychopathology and the diagnosis of mental health problems among youth. *Clinical Psychology, 17*(4), 272–280.

Drury, J. (2003). Adolescent communication with adults in authority. *Journal of Language and Social Psychology, 22*(1), 66–73.

Duckworth, A., Peterson, C., Matthews, M., & Kelly, D. (2007). Grit: Perseverance and passion for long-term goals. *Journal of Personality and Social Psychology, 92*(6), 1087–1101.

Duerager, A., & Livingstone, S. (2012). *How can parents support children's internet safety?* London: EU Kids Online.

Duggan, M., & Smith, A. (2013). *Demographics of key social networking platforms.* Washington, DC: Pew Internet and American Life Project.

Dunne, T., Pharm, L., Avery, S., & Darcy, S. (2017). A review of effective youth engagement strategies for mental health and substance use interventions. *Journal of Adolescent Health, 60*, 487–512.

Durlak, J., Weissberg, R., Dymnicki, A., Taylor, R., & Schellinger, K. (2011). The impact of enhancing students' social and emotional learning: A meta-analysis of school-based universal interventions. *Child Development, 82*, 405–432.

Dwairy, M. (2004). Parenting styles and mental health of Arab gifted adolescents. *Gifted Child Quarterly, 48*(4), 275–286.

Dwairy, M., & Menshar, K. (2006). Parenting style, individuation, and mental health of Egyptian adolescents. *Journal of Adolescence, 29*, 103–117.

Dyson, M., Hartling, L., Shulhan, J., Chrisholm, A., Milne, A., Sundar, P., Scott, S., & Newton, A (2016). A systematic review of social media use to discuss and view deliberate self-harm acts. *PloS One, 11*(5), 0155813.

Edwards, C. (2018a). Social media and mental health: Handbook for parents and teachers. Newark-on-Trent: Trigger Publishing.

Edwards, C. (2018b). *Social media and mental health: Handbook for teens.* Newark-on-Trent: Trigger Publishing.

Ellis, L., Collin, P., Hurley, P., Davenport, T., Burns, J., & Hickie, I. (2013). Young men's attitudes and behaviour in relation to mental health and technology: Implications for the development of online mental health services. *BMC Psychiatry, 13*, Article #119.

Ellis, D., Davidson, B., Shaw, H., & Geyer, K. (2019). Do smartphone usage scales predict behavior? *International Journal of Human-Computer Studies, 130*, 86–92.

Ellison, N., Steinfield, C., & Lampe, C. (2007). The benefits of Facebook 'friends': Social capital and college students' use of online social network sites. *Journal of Computer-Mediated Communication, 12*(4), 1143–1168.

Emejulu, A., & McGregor, C. (2016). Towards a radical digital citizenship in digital education. *Critical Studies in Education, 60*(1), 131–147.

Emsellem, H., Knutson, K., Hillygus, D., Buxton, O., Montgomery-Downs, H., LeBrougeois, M., & Spilsbury, J. (2014). *2014 sleep in America Poll: sleep in the modern family.* Arlington, VA: National Sleep Foundation.

Endicott, J., & Clarke, M. (2014). Nurses in step with the smartphone generation. *Primary Health Care, 24*(8), 20–24.

Englander, E. (2012). *Digital self-harm: Frequency, type, motivations, and outcomes.* From http://webhost.bridgew.edu/marc/DIGITAL%20SELF%20HARM%20report.pdf (accessed 11/2/21).

Englander, E. (2013). *Bullying and cyberbullying: What every educator needs to know.* Cambridge, MA: Harvard Education Press.

Erikson, E. (1968). *Identity: Youth and crisis.* New York: Norton.

European Commission (2008). Europe and the global information society. *Recommendations to the European Council: Conference G7.* From https://op.europa.eu/en/publication-detail/-/publication/44dad16a-937d-4cb3-be07-0022197d9459 (accessed 11/2/21).

Ey, L., & Cupit, C. (2011). Exploring young children's understanding of risks associated with Internet usage and their concepts of management strategies. *Journal of Early Childhood Research, 9*(1), 53–65.

Fairchild, R., Ferng-Kuo, S., Rahmouni, H., & Hardesty, D. (2020). Telehealth increases access to care for children dealing with suicidality depression, and anxiety in rural emergency departments. *Telemedicine Journal E Health, 26*(11), 1353–1362.

Farrugia, L., Grehan, S., & O'Neill, B. (2017). Webwise 2017 parenting survey. From www.webwise.ie/news/webwise-2017-parenting-survey/ (accessed 11/2/21).

Fazel, M., Hoagwood, K., Stephan, S., & Ford, T. (2014). Mental health interventions in schools in high-income countries. *The Lancet Psychiatry, 1*(5), 377–387.

Fergie, G., Hunt, K., & Hilton, S. (2013). What young people want from health-related online resources: A focus group study. *Journal of Youth Studies, 16*, 579–596.

Fergie, G., Hunt, K., & Hilton, S. (2016). Social media as a space for support: Young adults' perspective on producing and consuming user-generated content about diabetes and mental health. *Social Science and Medicine, 170*, 46–54.

Festinger, L., Pepitone, A., & Newcomb, T. (1952). Some consequences of deindividuation in a group. *Journal of Social Psychology, 47*, 382–389.

Fiedorowicz, J., & Chigurupati, R. (2009). The internet in suicide prevention and promotion. In L. Sher, & A. Vilens (Eds.), *Internet and suicide* (pp. 1–12). Hauppauge, NY: Nova Science Publishers.

Finkelhor, D., Ormrod, R., & Turner, H. (2007). Poly-victimization: A neglected component in child victimization. *Child Abuse and Neglect, 31*, 7–26.

Fleschler-Perkin, M., Markham, C., Addy, R., Shegog, R., Thjiel, M., & Tortelero, S. R. (2013). Prevalence and patterns of sexting among ethnic minority urban high school students. *Cyberpsychology, Behavior, and Social Networking, 16*, 454–459.

Flores, A., & James, C. (2013). Morality and ethics behind the screen: Young people's perspectives on digital life. *New Media and Society, 15*(6), 834–85.

Ford, J. D., Wasser, T., & Connor, D. F. (2011). Identifying and determining the symptom severity associated with polyvictimization among psychiatrically impaired children in the outpatient setting. *Child Maltreatment, 16*(3), 216–226. doi: 10.1177/1077559511406109

Ford, T., Edwards, V., Sharkey, S., Ukoumunne, O., Byford, S., Norwich, B., & Logan, S. (2012). Supporting teachers and children in schools: The effectiveness and cost-effectiveness of the Incredible Years teacher classroom management programme in primary school children: A cluster randomised controlled trial, with parallel economic and process evaluations. *BMC Public Health, 12*.

Ford, T., Hamilton, H., Meltzer, H., & Goodman, R. (2008). Predictors of service use for mental health problems among British schoolchildren. *Child and Adolescent Mental Health, 13*(1), 32–40.

Ford, T., & McManus, S. (2020). Prevalence: Are two-fifths of young people really 'abnormal'? *The British Journal of Psychiatry, 216*(1), 58–58.

Ford, T., & Parker, C. (2016). Emotional and behavioural difficulties and mental (ill) health. *Emotional and Behavioural Difficulties 21*(1) 1–7.

Ford, T., Vizard, T., Sadler, K., McManus, S., Goodman, A., Merad, S., Tejerina-Arreal, M., Collinson, D., & the MHCYP Collaboration. (2020). Data resource profile: The Mental Health of Children and Young People Surveys (MHCYP). *International Journal of Epidemiology*, https://doi.org/10.1093/ije/dyz259

Forgays, D., Hyman, I., & Schreiber, J. (2014). Texting everywhere for everything: Gender and age differences in cell phone etiquette and use. *Computers in Human Behavior, 31*, 314–321.

Frau-Meigs, D. (2014) Mediated wellbeing from the perspective of media and communication studies. In A. Ben-Arieh, F. Casas, I. Frønes, & J. E. Korbin (Eds.), *Handbook of child wellbeing. Theories, methods and policies in global perspective* (p. 437).

New York: Springer. doi: 10.1007/978-90-481-9063-8_154, # Springer Science + Business Media Dordrecht.

Freeman, M. (2000). The future of children's rights. *Children and Society, 14,* 277–293.

Friendly, M., & Lero, D. (2002) Social inclusion through early childhood education and care. From https://laidlawfdn.org/assets/wpsosi_2002_june_social-inclusion-for-canadian-children.pdf (accessed 31/3/21).

Frith, E. (2017a). *Access and waiting times in children and young people's mental health services.* London: Education Policy Institute.

Frith, E. (2017b). Social media and children's mental health: A review of the evidence. *Education Policy Institute.* From https://epi.org.uk/wp-content/uploads/2018/01/Social-Media_Mental-Health_EPI-Report.pdf (accessed 11/2/21).

Fuchs, C. (2017). *Social media: A critical introduction* (2nd ed.). London: Sage.

Furber, G., Crago, A., Meehan, K., Sheppard, T., Hooper, K., Abbot, D., Allison, S., & Skene, C. (2011). How adolescents use SMS (Short message service) to micro-coordinate contact with youth mental health outreach services. *Journal of Adolescent Health, 48,* 113–115.

Future of Privacy Forum (FPF) and Family Online Safety Institute (FOSI). (2016). *Kids & the connected home: Privacy in the age of connected dolls, talking dinosaurs, and battling robots.* Washington, DC: FPF & FOSI.

Gabriel, F. (2014). Sexting, selfies and self-harm: Young people, social media and the performance of self-development. *Media International Australia, 151*(1), 104–112.

Garfield, C. (2009). Variation in family composition. In W. Carey, A. Crocker, W. Coleman, E. Elias, & H. Feldman (Eds.), *Developmental-behavioral paediatrics* (4th ed.) (pp. 94–102). London: Elsevier.

Gentile, D., Bailey, K., Bavelier, D., et al., (2017). Internet gaming disorder in children and adolescents. *Pediatrics, 140*(Sppl 2), s81–s85.

George, M., & Odgers, C. (2015). Seven fears and the science of how mobile technologies may be influencing adolescents in the digital age. *Perspectives on Psychological Science, 10*(6), 832–851.

Gerbaudo, P. (2016). Constructing public space. Rousing the Facebook crowd: Digital enthusiasm and emotional contagion in the 2011 protests in Egypt and Spain. *International Journal of Communication, 10*(20), 254–273.

Gibson, K., & Cartwright, C. (2014). Young people's experiences of mobile text counselling: Balancing connection and control. *Children and Youth Services Review, 43,* 96–104.

Gilligan, C. (1982). *In a different voice: Psychological theory and women's development.* Cambridge, MA: Harvard University Press.

Girlguiding. (2019a). Girls' attitudes survey. From www.girlguiding.org.uk/globalassets/docs-and-resources/research-and-campaigns/girls-attitudes-survey-2019.pdf (accessed 11/2/21).

Girlguiding. (2019b). Written evidence to parliament. From http://data.parliament.uk/writtenevidence/committeeevidence.svc/evidencedocument/science-and-technology-committee/impact-of-social-media-and-screenuse-on-young-peoples-health/written/80608.html (accessed 11/2/21).

Glasheen, K., & Campbell, M. (2009). The use of online counselling within an Australian secondary school setting: A practitioner's viewpoint. *Counselling Psychology Review, 24*(2), 42–51.

Glazzard, J., & Mitchell, C. (2018). *Social media and mental health in schools.* St Albans: Critical Publishing.

Glover, A., Karnik, N., Dogra, N., & Vostanis, P. (2018). Child psychiatry across cultures. In D. Bhugra, & K. Bhui (Eds.), *Textbook of Cultural Psychiatry* (2nd ed.). Cambridge. Cambridge University Press.

Goffman, E. (1963). *Stigma: Notes on the management of spoiled identity*. Englewood Cliffs, NJ: Prentice-Hall.

Gonzales, A., & Hancock, J. (2011). Mirror, mirror on my Facebook wall: Effects of exposure to Facebook on self-esteem. *Cyberpsychology, Behavior & Social Networking, 14*(1–2), 79–83.

Goodman, R., Ford, T., Richards, H., Gatward, R., & Meltzer, H. (2000). The development and well-being assessment: Description and initial validation of an integrated assessment of child and adolescent psychopathology. *The Journal of Child Psychology and Psychiatry and Allied Disciplines, 41*(5), 645–655.

Goodman, R., Iervolino, A. C., Collishaw, S., Pickles, A., & Maughan, B. (2007). Seemingly minor changes to a questionnaire can make a big difference to mean scores: A cautionary tale. *Social Psychiatry and Psychiatric Epidemiology, 42*(4), 322–327.

Granic, I., & Lamey, A. (2000). The self-organization of the Internet and changing modes of thought. *New Ideas in Psychology, 18*, 93–107.

Grant, L. (2007). Learning to be part of the knowledge economy: Digital divides and media literacy. From www.nfer.ac.uk/publications/FUTL96/FUTL96.pdf (accessed 11/2/21).

Gray, C., Wilcox, G., & Nordstokke, D. (2017). Teacher mental health, school climate, inclusive education and student learning: A review. *Canadian Psychology/Psychologie Canadienne, 58*(3), 203–210.

Green, J. (1997). Risk and the construction of social identity: Children's talk about accidents. *Sociology of Health and Illness, 19*, 457–479.

Green, J., Howes, F., Waters, E., Maher, E., & Oberklaid, F. (2005). Promoting the social and emotional health of primary school-aged children: Reviewing the evidence base for school-based interventions. *International Journal of Mental Health Promotion, 7*(3), 30–36

Greenberger, E. & Goldberg, W. (1989). Work, parenting, and the socialization of children. *Developmental Psychology, 25*(1), 22–35.

Greenfield, S. (2014). *Mind change: How digital technologies are leaving their mark on our brains*. London: Rider.

Griffiths, M. (1999). Internet addiction. *The Psychologist, 12*, 246–250.

Griffiths, M. (2014). Adolescent trolling in online environments: A brief overview. *Education and Health, 32*(3), 85–87

Griffiths, M. D., Van Rooij, A. J., Kardefelt-Winther, D., et al. (2016). Working towards an international consensus on criteria for assessing Internet Gaming Disorder: A critical commentary on Petry et al. (2014). *Addiction, 111*(1), 167–175.

Gulliver, A., Griffiths, K., & Christensen, H. (2010). Perceived barriers and facilitators to mental health help-seeking in young people: A systematic review. *BMC Psychiatry, 10*, 113–122.

Gunnell, D., Appleby, L., Arensman, E., et al. (2020). Suicide risk and prevention during the COVID-19 pandemic. *Lancet Psychiatry, 7*, 468–471.

Gur, K., Sener, N., Kucuk, L., & Basar, M. (2012). The beliefs of teachers toward mental illness. *Procedia – Social and Behavioral Sciences, 47*, 1146–1152.

Hale, L. & Guan, S. (2015). Screen time and sleep among school-aged children and adolescents: A systematic literature review. *Sleep Med Review, 21*, 50–58.

Hall, G. Stanley. (1904). *Adolescence: Its psychology and its relations to physiology, anthropology, sociology, sex, crime, religion and education*. (Vols *I* & *II*). New York: Appleton.

Hamburger, Y., & Ben-Artzi, E. (2000). The relationship between extraversion and neuroticism and the different use of the internet. *Computers in Human Behavior, 16*(4), 441–449.

Hamm, M., Chisholm, A., Shulhan, J., Milne, A., Scott, S., Given, L., & Hartling, L. (2013). Social media use among patients and caregivers: A scoping review. *BMJ Open*, 3, online.

Hancock, J. T., Liu, X., French, M., Luo, M., & Mieczkowski, H. (2019). Social media use and psychological well-being: A meta-analysis. 69th Annual International Communication Association Conference, Washington, D.C.

Hansson, L., Jormfeldt, H., Svedberg, P., & Svensson, B. (2011). Mental health professionals' attitudes toward people with mental illness: Do they differ from attitudes held by people with mental illness? *International Journal of Social Psychiatry*, 59(1), 48–54.

Hardaker, C. (2013). 'Uh ..... not to be nitpicky ,,,,, but ... the past tense of drag is dragged, not drug.' An overview of trolling strategies. *Journal of Language Aggression and Conflict*, 1(1), 58–86.

Hargittai, E., Schultz, J., & Palfrey, J. (2011). Why parents help their children lie to Facebook about age: Unintended consequences of the Children's Online Privacy Protection Act. *First Monday*, 16, 11.

Harold, G., Acquah, D., Chowdry, H., & Sellers, R. (2016) *What works to enhance inter-parental relationships and improve outcomes for children*. Department for Work and Pensions (DWP), Ad hoc research report 32.

Harold, G., Leve, L., & Sellers, R. (2017). How can genetically-informed research help inform the next generation of interparental and parenting interventions? *Child Development*. ISSN 0009-3920.

Harold, G., & Sellers, R. (2018). Interparental conflict and youth psychopathology: An evidence review and practice focused update. *The Journal of Child Psychology and Psychiatry*, 59(4), 374–402.

Harrison, V., Proudfoot, J., Wee, P., Parker, G., Pavlovich, D., & Manicavasagar, V., (2012). Mobile mental health: Review of the emerging field and proof of concept study. *Journal of Mental Health*, 20(6), 509–524.

Hart, T., & O'Reilly, M. (2017). Written evidence for parliament: Mental health in schools. From http://data.parliament.uk/writtenevidence/committeeevidence.svc/evidencedocument/health-committee/children-and-young-peoples-mental-healththe-role-of-education/written/45582.pdf (accessed 11/2/21).

Hart, T., & O'Reilly, M. (in press). Perspectives on what schools and mental health services can do about bullying of adolescents with severe emotional health conditions. *Pastoral Care in Education*.

Hatzenbuehler, M., Phelan, J., & Link, B. (2013). Stigma as a fundamental cause of population health inequalities. *American Journal of Public Health*, 103(5), 813–821.

Hawkes, N. (2019). CMO report is unable to shed light on impact of screen time and social media on children's health. *British Medical Journal*, 364, l643.

Hawton, K., & Harriss, L. (2007). Deliberate self-harm in young people: Characteristics and subsequent mortality in a 20-year cohort of patients presenting to hospital. *Journal of Clinical Psychiatry*, 68(10), 1574–1583.

Hawton, K., Saunders, K., & O'Connor, R. (2012). Self-harm and suicide in adolescents. *Lancet*, 379, 2373–2382.

Hayes, A., Gray, M. & Edwards, B. (2008). *Social inclusion: Origins, concepts and key themes, AIF Studies*. Canberra: Department of the Prime Minister and Cabinet.

Health Advisory Service Report (1995) *Together we stand: The commissioning, role and management of Child and Adolescent Mental Health Services*. London: HMSO.

Helsper, E., & Eynon, R. (2010). Digital natives: Where is the evidence? *British Educational Research Journal*, 36, 502–520.

Hern, A. (2015). Twitter CEO: We suck at dealing with trolls and abuse. *Guardian*, 5 February. From www.theguardian.com/technology/2015/feb/05/twitter-ceo-we-suck-dealing-with-trolls-abuse (accessed 23/3/21).

Herring, S., Job-Sluder, K., Scheckler, R., & Barab, S. (2002). Searching for safety online: Managing 'trolling' in a feminist forum. *The Information Society*, *18*(5), 371–384.

Herrman, H. (2001). The need for mental health promotion. *Australian and New Zealand Journal of Psychiatry*, *35*, 709–715.

Heyd, T. (2016). Global varieties of English gone digital: Orthographic and semantic variation in digital Nigerian Pidgin, in L Squires, (Ed.), *English in computer-mediated communication: Variation, representation and change*. Berlin: De Gruyter.

Hill, C., Martin, J., Thomson, S., Scott-Ram, N., Penfold, H., & Creswell, C. (2017). Navigating the challenges of digital health innovations: Considerations and solutions in developing online and smartphone-application-based interventions for mental health disorders. *The British Journal of Psychiatry*, *211*, 65–69.

Hinduja, S., & Patchin, J. (2008). Personal information of adolescents on the internet: A quantitative content analysis of MySpace. *Journal of Adolescence*, *31*, 125–146.

Hinduja, S., & Patchin, J. (2009). *Bullying beyond the school yard: Preventing and responding to cyberbullying*. Thousand Oaks, CA: Sage.

Hinduja, S., & Patchin, J. (2010a). Cyberbullying and self-esteem. *Journal of School Health*, *80*(12), 614–621.

Hinduja, S., & Patchin, J. (2010b). Bullying, cyberbullying, and suicide. *Arch Suicide Research*, *14*(3), 206–221.

Hinduja, S., & Patchin, J. (2011). High-tech cruelty. *Educational Leadership*, *68*(5), 48–52.

Hobbs, R. (2010). *Digital and media literacy: A plan of action – a White Paper on the digital and media literacy recommendations of the Knight Commission on the Information Needs of Communities in a Democracy*. Washington, DC: Aspen Institute. From https://files.eric.ed.gov/fulltext/ED523244.pdf (accessed 23/3/21).

Hoekstra, P. (2020). Suicidality in children and adolescents: Lessons to be learned from the COVID-19 crisis. *European Child and Adolescent Psychiatry*, *29*, 737–738.

Hollis, C., Falconer, C., Martin, J., Whittington, C., Stockton, S., Glazebrook, C., & Bethan Davies, E. (2017). Annual research review: Digital health interventions for children and young people with mental health problems – a systematic and meta-review. *Journal of Child Psychology and Psychiatry*, *58*, 474–503.

Holloway, D. (2013). *Digital play: The challenge of researching young children's Internet use*. Proceedings of Australian and New Zealand Communication Association Conference, Melbourne.

Holloway, D., Green, L., & Livingstone, S. (2013). *Zero to eight: Young children and their internet use*. London: EU Kids Online.

Holmes, E., O'Connor, R., Perry, V., et al. (2020). Multidisciplinary research priorities for the COVID-19 pandemic: A call for action for mental health science. *Lancet Psychiatry*, *7*(6), 547–560.

Home Office. (2020). *Domestic abuse: Get help during the coronavirus (COVID-19) outbreak*. From www.gov.uk/government/publications/coronavirus-covid-19-and-domestic-abuse/coronavirus-covid-19-support-for-victims-of-domestic-abuse (accessed 1/5/20).

Hoover, E. (2009). The millennial muddle: how stereotyping students became a thriving industry and a bundle of contradictions. *The Chronicle of Higher Education*, 11.

House of Commons Science and Technology Committee. (2019). *Impact and social media and screen-use on young people's health*. London: House of Commons.

Howard-Jones, P. (2009). Neuroscience, learning and technology (14–19). Coventry: Becta. From https://teenyogafoundation.com/wp-content/uploads/2015/11/2009-Howard-Jones-Neuroscience-Learning-and-Technology-Becta.pdf (accessed 31/3/21).

Huda, M., Jasmi, K., Hehsan, A., Mustari, M., Shahrill, M., Basiron, B., & Gassama, S. (2017). Empowering children with adaptive technology skills: Careful engagement in the digital information age. *International Electronic Journal of Elementary Education, 9*(3), 693–708.

Hudson, K. (2012). Practitioners' views on involving young children in decision-making: Challenges for the children's rights agenda. *Australasian Journal of Early Childhood, 37*(2), 4–9.

Humm, A., Kaminer, D., & Hardy, A. (2018). Social support, violence exposure and mental health among young South African adolescents. *Journal of Child & Adolescent Mental Health, 30*(1), 41–50.

Humphrey, N. (2018). Are the kids alright? Examining the intersection between education and mental health. *Psychology of Education Review, 42*(1), 4–12.

Humphrey, N., & Wiggelsworth, M. (2016). Making the case for universal school-based mental health screening. *Emotional and Behavioural Difficulties, 21*(1), 22–42.

Husain, M., Waheed, W., & Husain, N. (2006). Self-harm in British South Asian women: psychosocial correlates and strategies for prevention. *Ann Gen Psychiatry, 5*(7), 7–14.

Huston, A., Donnerstein, E., Fairchild, H., Wilcox, B., & Fairchild, H. (1992). *Big world, small screen: The role of television in American Society*. Lincoln, NE: University of Nebraska Press.

Innis, H. (2017). *Essays in Canadian economic history* (Edited by M. Q. Innis). Toronto: University of Toronto Press.

International Telecommunication Union (ITU) (2018). Measuring the Information Society report, Volume 1. Geneva, Switzerland: ITU Publications. Available at: www.itu.int/en/ITU-D/Statistics/Documents/publications/misr2018/MISR-2018-Vol-1-E.pdf (accessed 21/4/21).

Internet Matters. (2019). *Deal with it*. From www.internetmatters.org/issues/online-pornography/deal-with-it/ (accessed 11/2/21).

Internet Society. (2017). Consolidation in the internet economy. From www.internetsociety.org/globalinternetreport/ (accessed 11/2/21).

Ito, M., Baumer, S., Bittanti, M., et al. (2010). Introduction. In M. Ito, et al (Eds.), *Hanging out, messing around, and geeking out: Kids living and learning with new media* (pp. 1–28). Cambridge, MA: MIT Press.

James, A. (2009). Agency. In J. Qvortrup, G. Valentine, W. Corsaro, & M. Honig (Eds.), *The Palgrave handbook of childhood studies* (pp. 34–45) Basingstoke: Palgrave.

James, A., & Prout, A. (2015). Introduction. In A. James, & A. Prout (Eds.), *Constructing and reconstructing childhood: Contemporary issues in the sociological study of childhood; classic edition* (pp. 1–5). New York: Routledge.

Jones, L., & Mitchell, K. (2016). Defining and measuring youth digital citizenship. *New Media and Society, 18*(9), 2063–2079.

Jones, L., Mitchell, K., & Walsh, W. (2014a). A content analysis of youth internet safety programs: Are effective prevention strategies being used? *Crimes against Children Research Center*. Durham, NH: University of New Hampshire.

Jones, L., Mitchell, K., & Walsh, W. (2014b). A systematic review of effective youth prevention education: Implications for internet safety education. *Crimes against Children Research Center*. Durham, NH: University of New Hampshire.

Jorm, A. (2012). Mental health literacy: empowering the community to take action or better mental health. *American Psychologist, 67*, 231–243.

Jorm, A. F., Korten, A. E., Jacomb, P. A., Christensen, H., Rodgers, B., & Pollitt, P. (1997). 'Mental health literacy': a survey of the public's ability to recognise mental disorders and their beliefs about the efficacy of treatment. *Medical Journal of Australia, 166*, 182–186.

Kahn, P. (1997). Bayous and jungle rivers: Cross-cultural perspectives in children's environmental moral reasoning. In H. Saltzstein (Ed.), *Culture as a context for moral development* (pp. 23–37). San Francisco, CA: Jossey Bass.

Kamel Boulos, M., Giustini, D., & Wheeler, S. (2016). Instagram and WhatsApp in health and health care: An overview. *Future Internet, 8*(3), 37–51.

Kamel Boulos, M., Wheeler, S., Tavares, C., & Jones, R (2011). How smartphones are changing the face of mobile and participatory health care: An overview with example from eCAALYX. *Biomedicine. Eng, 10*, Online.

Kann, L., Kinchen, S., Shanklin, S., et al. (2014). Youth risk behavior surveillance – United States 2013. *Center for Disease Control and Prevention Morbidity and Mortality Weekly Report, 63*, 1–168.

Kaplan, A., & Haenlein, M. (2010). Users of the world, unite! The challenges and opportunities of social media. *Business Horizons, 53*, 59–68.

Karatzogianni, A., Nguyen, D., & Serafinelli, A. (eds) (2016) *The digital transformation of the public sphere: Conflict, migration, crisis and culture in digital networks*. Basingstoke: Palgrave Macmillan.

Karim, K. (2015). The value of conversation analysis: A child psychiatrist's perspective. In M. O'Reilly, & J. N. Lester (Eds.), *The Palgrave handbook of child mental health: Discourse and conversation studies* (pp. 25–41). Basingstoke: Palgrave MacMillan.

Karim, K., & O'Reilly, M. (2017). *Comment on Public Health England investment in mental health training for schools*. From www2.le.ac.uk/offices/press/think-leicester/health-and-medicine/2017/comment-on-public-health-england-investment-in-mental-health-training-for-schools (accessed 11/2/21).

Katz, A., & Asam, A. (2019). *Vulnerable children in a digital world*. London: Internet matters.org.

Keeley, B., & Little, C. (2017). The state of the world's children 2017. Children in a Digital World: ERIC.

Keenan, T., Evans, S., & Crowley, K. (2016). *An introduction to child development* (3rd ed.). London: Sage.

Kellett, M. (2014). Images of childhood and their influence on research. In A. Clark, R. Flewitt, M. Hammersley, & M. Robb (Eds.), *Understanding research with children and young people* (pp. 15–33). London: Sage.

Kempt, S. (2015). Digital, social and mobile worldwide in 2015. From https://wearesocial.com/uk/special-reports/digital-social-mobile-worldwide-2015 (accessed 11/2/21).

Kessler, R., Amminger, G., Aguilar-Gaxiola, S., Alonso, K., Lee, S., & Ustun, T. (2007). Age of onset of mental disorders: A review of recent literature. *Current Opinion in Psychiatry, 20*, 359–364.

Kessler, R., Avenevoli, S., Costello, E., et al. (2005). Prevalence, persistence, and socio-demographic correlates of DSM-IV disorders in the national comorbidity survey replication adolescent supplement. *Archive of General Psychiatry, 69*, 372–380.

Keyes, C. (2007). Promoting and protecting mental health as flourishing: A complementary strategy for improving national mental health. *American Psychologist, 62*(2), 95–108.

Khosrow-Pour, M. (2018). *Encylopedia of information science and technology* (4th ed.) (pp. 7097–7105). Hershey, PA: IGI Global.

Kickbusch, I. (2008). Health literacy: An essential skill for the twenty-first century. *Health Education, 108*, 101–104.

Kidger, J., Gunnell, D., Biddle, L., Campbell, R., & Donovan., J. (2009). Part and parcel of teaching? Secondary school staff's views on supporting emotional health and wellbeing. *British Educational Research Journal, iFirst Article*, 1–17.

Kim, H., Min, J., Kim, H., & Min, K. (2017). Association between psychological and self-assessed health status and smartphone overuse among Korean college students. *Journal of Mental Health, 28*(1), 11–16.

King, R., Bambling, M., Lloyd, C., Gomurra, R., Smith, S., Reid, W., & Wegner, K. (2006). Online counselling: the motives and experiences of people who choose the Internet instead of face-to-face telephone counselling. *Counselling and Psychotherapy Research, 6*(3), 103–108.

King, R., Spooner, D., & Reid, W. (2003). Online psychotherapy-efficacy and prospects for structured and exploratory approaches. In R. Wootton, et al. (Eds.), *Telepsychiatry and e-mental health*. London: Royal Society of Medicine Press.

Kiyimba, N., & O'Reilly, M. (2016). The value of using discourse and conversation analysis as evidence to inform practice in counselling and therapeutic interactions. In M. O'Reilly, & J. N. Lester (Eds.), *The Palgrave handbook of adult mental health*. (pp. 520–539). Basingstoke: Palgrave.

Kiyimba, N., & O'Reilly, M. (in press). 'Just ask': How to talk to children and young people about self-harm and suicide risk. In M. O'Reilly, & J. N. Lester (Eds.), *Improving communication in mental health settings: Evidence-based recommendations from practitioner-led research*. London: Routledge.

Klaver, K., van Elst, E., & Baart, A. (2014). Demarcation of the ethics of care as a discipline: Discussion article. *Nursing Ethics, 21*(7), 755–765.

Klonsky, E., Glenn, C., Styer, D., Olino, T., & Washburn, J. (2015). The functions of nonsuicidal self-injury: Converging evidence for a two-factor structure. *Child and Adolescent Psychiatry and Mental Health, 9*(1), 44.

Knapp, M., Snell, T., Healey, A., Guglani, S., Evans-Lacko, S., Fernandez, J-L., Howard, M., & Ford, T. (2015). How do child and adolescent mental health problems influence public sector costs? Interindividual variations in a nationally representative British sample. *Journal of Child Psychology and Psychiatry, 56*(6), 667–676.

Kohen, D. (1998). Parenting behaviors: Associated characteristics and child outcomes. *Dissertation Abstracts International: Section B: The Sciences and Engineering, 58*(9-B), 5163.

Kohlberg, L. (1969). *Stages in development of moral thought and action*. New York: Holt.

Korda, H., & Itani, Z. (2013). Harnessing social media for health promotion and behavior change. *Health Promotion Practice, 14*(1), 15–23.

Kotera, Y., Green, P., & Sheffield, D. (2019). Mental health attitudes, self-criticism, compassion and role identity among UK social work students. *The British Journal of Social Work, 49*(2), 351–370.

Koutamis, M., Vossen, H., & Valkenburg P. (2015). Adolescents' comments in social media: Why do adolescents receive negative feedback and who is most at risk? *Computers in Human Behavior, 53*, 486–494.

Kowalski, R., Giumetti, G., Schroeder, A., & Lattanner, M. (2014). Bullying in the digital age: A critical review and meta-analysis of cyberbullying research among youth. *Psychological Bulletin, 140*, 1073–1137.

Krevans, J., & Gibbs, J. C. (1996). Parents' use of inductive discipline: Relations to children's empathy and prosocial behavior. *Child Development, 67*(6), 3263–3277.

Kutcher, S., Wei, Y., Costa, S., Gusmão, R., Skokauskas, N., & Sourander, A. (2016). Enhancing mental health literacy in young people. *European Child and Adolescent Psychiatry, 25*, 567–569.

Kwet, M. (2019). Digital colonialism: US empire and the new imperialism in the Global South. *Race & Class, 60*(4), 3–26.

Lachman, B., Sindermann, C., Sariyska, R., Luo, R., Melchers, M., Becker, B., Cooper, A. J., & Montag, C. (2018). The role of empathy and life satisfaction in internet and smartphone use disorder. *Frontiers in Psychology, 9*, 398.

Lampert, C., & Donoso, V. (2012). Bullying. In S. Livingstone, L. Haddon, A. Goerzig, & A. (Eds.), *Children, risk and safety online: Research and policy challenges in comparative perspective*. Bristol: Policy Press.

Lauricella, A. R., Wartella, E., & Rideout, V. J. (2015). Young children's screen time: The complex role of parent and child factors. *Journal of Applied Developmental Psychology, 36*, 11–17.

Lazard, L. (2017). Sharenting: What is it and are you doing it? From www.open.edu/openlearn/health-sports-psychology/psychology/sharenting-what-it-and-are-you-doing-it (accessed 11/2/21).

Leaver, T. (2015). Born digital? Presence, privacy, and intimate surveillance. In J. Hartley, & W. Qu (Eds.), *Re-orientation: Translingual transcultural transmedia: Studies in narrative, language, identity, and knowledge* (pp. 149–160). Shanghai: Fudan University Press.

Leduc, K., Conway, L., Gomez-Garibello, & Talwar, V. (2018). The influence of participant role, gender, and age in elementary and high-school children's moral justifications of cyberbullying behaviors. *Computers in Human Behavior, 83*, 215–220.

Lemon, J. (2002). Can we call behaviours addictive? *Clinical Psychologist, 3*, 44–49.

Lenhart, A., Ling, R., Campbell, S., & Purcell, R. (2010). *Teens and mobile phones*. Washington, DC: Pew Internet and American Life Project.

Lennon, M. (2018). *Children's mental health briefing*. London: Children's Commissioner.

Lester, D., McSwain, S., & Gunn, J. (2009). Suicide and the Internet: The case of Amanda Todd. *International Journal of Emergency Mental Health, 15*(3), 179–180.

Lester, J. N., & Paulus, T. (2012). Performative acts of autism. *Discourse & Society, 12*(3), 259–273.

Levin, I., & Trost, J. (1992) Understanding the concept of family. *Family Relations, 41*, 348–351.

Levine, D. (2019) Troubling the discourse: Applying Valsiner's Zones to adolescent girls' use of digital technologies. *Technology, Pedagogy and Education, 28*(4), 435–446.

Levine, D., Morton, J., & O'Reilly, M. (2020). Child safety, protection, and safeguarding in the time of COVID-19 in Great Britain: Proposing a conceptual framework. *Child Abuse and Neglect*.

Lewis, S., Mahdy, J., Michal, N., & Arbuthnott, A. (2014). Googling self-injury: the state of health information obtained through online searches for self-injury. *JAMA Pediatrics, 168*(5), 443–449.

Lievens, E. (2011). Risk-reducing regulatory strategies for protecting minors in social networks. *INFO, 13*(6), 43–54.

Link, B., & Phelan, J. (2001). Conceptualizing stigma. *Annual Review of Sociology, 27*, 363–385.

Link, B., Struening, E., Neese-Todd, S., Asmussen, S., & Phelan, J. (2001). The consequences of stigma for the self-esteem of people with mental illnesses. *Psychiatric Services, 52*, 1621–1626.

Litt, E. (2013). Measuring users' internet skills: A review of past assessments and a look toward the future. *New Media & Society, 15*(4), 612–630.

Liu, C., Zhu, Q., Holroyd, K., & Seng, E. (2011). Status and trends of mobile-health applications for iOS devices: A developer's perspective. *Journal of Systems and Software, 84*(11), 2022–2033.

Livingstone, S. (2007). From family television to bedroom culture: Young people's media at home. In E. Devereux (Ed.), *Media studies: Key issues and debates* (pp. 302–321). London: Sage.

Livingstone, S. (2013). Online risk, harm and vulnerability: Reflections on the evidence base for child Internet safety policy. *ZER: Journal of Communication Studies, 18*(35), 13–28. Available at http://eprints.lse.ac.uk/62278/ (accessed 23/3/21).

Livingstone, S. (2019a). From policing screen time to weighing screen use. *The Children's Media Foundation.* From www.thechildrensmediafoundation.org/archives/7165/from-policing-screen-time-to-weighing-screen-use (accessed 11/2/21)

Livingstone, S. (2019b) Rethinking the rights of children for the internet age. From https://blogs.lse.ac.uk/medialse/2019/03/18/rethinking-the-rights-of-children-for-the-internet-age/ (accessed 11/2/21)

Livingstone, S. (2019c) Are the kids alright? *Intermedia, 47*(3), 10–14.

Livingstone, S. (2020). The role of digital technologies in relation to children's well-being: Key questions on theories answered. From https://core-evidence.eu/the-role-of-digital-technologies-in-relation-to-childrens-well-being-key-questions-on-theories-answered/ (accessed 23/3/21).

Livingstone, S. (2021). Children's rights apply in the digital world. *Parenting for a Digital Future,* 24 March. From https://blogs.lse.ac.uk/parenting4digitalfuture/2021/03/24/general-comment-25/ (accessed 31/3/21).

Livingstone, S., & Blum-Ross, A. (2020). *Parenting for a digital future: How hopes and fears about technology shape children's lives.* New York: Oxford University Press.

Livingstone, S., Blum-Ross, A., Pavlick, J., & Ólafsson, K. (2018). *In the digital home, how do parents support their children and who supports them? Parenting for a digital future: Survey Report 1.* London: London School of Economics.

Livingstone, S., Bober, M., & Helsper, E. (2005). *Internet literacy among children and young people: Findings from the UK Children Go Online project.* London: LSE Research Online.

Livingstone, S., Haddon, L., Görzig, A., & Ólafsson, K. (2011). *Risks and safety on the internet: The perspective of European children. Full Findings.* London: EU Kids Online.

Livingstone, S., Haddon, L., Vincent, J., Mascheroni, G., & Òlafsson, K. (2014). Net children go mobile: The UK report: A comparative report with findings from the UK 2010 survey by EU kids online. London: LSE.

Livingstone, S., & Helsper, E. (2008). Parental mediation of children's internet use. *Journal of Broadcasting and Electronic Media, 52*(4), 581–599.

Livingstone, S., Lemish, D., Lim, S., et al. (2017). Global perspectives on children's digital opportunities: An emerging research and policy agenda. *Pediatrics, 140*(Sup. 2).

Livingstone, S., Mascheroni, G., & Staksrud, E. (2015) Developing a framework for researching children's online risks and opportunities in Europe. From http://eprints.lse.ac.uk/64470/1/__lse.ac.uk_storage_LIBRARY_Secondary_libfile_shared_repository_Content_EU%20Kids%20Online_EU%20Kids%20Online_Developing%20framework%20for%20researching_2015.pdf (accessed 11/2/21).

Livingstone, S., & O'Neill, B. (2014). Children's rights online: Challenges, dilemmas, and emerging directions. In S. van der Hof, B. van den Berg, & B. Schermer (Eds.), *Minding minors wandering the web: Regulating online child safety. Information technology and law series (24)* (pp. 19–38). The Hague: Springer with T.M.C. Asser Press.

Livingstone, S., Òlafsson, K., Helsper, E., Lupiáñez-Villanueva, F., Veltri, G., & Folkvord, F. (2017). Maximising opportunities and minimizing risks for children online: The role of digital skills in emerging strategies of parental mediation. *Journal of Communication, 67,* 82–105.

Livingstone, S., & Palmer, T. (2012). *Identifying vulnerable children online and what strategies can help them*. London: UK Safer Internet Centre.

Livingstone, S., & Stoilova, M. (2021). The 4Cs: classifying online risk to children. (CO:RE Short Report Series on Key Topics). Hamburg: Leibniz-Institut für Medienforschung | Hans-Bredow-Institut (HBI); CO:RE – Children Online:Research and Evidence. https://doi.org/10.21241/ssoar.71817

Livingstone, S., & Third, A. (2017). Children and young people's rights in the digital age: An emerging agenda. *New Media & Society, 19*(5), 657–670.

Loades, M., & Mastroyannopoulou, K., (2010). Teachers' recognition of children's mental health problems. *Children and Adolescent Mental Health, 15*(3), 150–156.

Loid, K., Täht, K., & Rozgonjuk, D. (2020). Do pop-up notifications regarding smartphone use decrease screen time, phone checking behavior, and self-reported problematic smartphone use? Evidence from a two-month experimental study. *Computers in Human Behavior, 102*, 22–30.

Lundy, L. (2020). Child rights and their wellbeing. In S. Livingstone (Ed.), The role of digital technologies in relation to children's wellbeing: key questions on theories answered. From https://core-evidence.eu/the-role-of-digital-technologies-in-relation-to-childrens-well-being-key-questions-on-theories-answered/ (accessed 23/3/21).

Lupton, D., & Williamson, N. (2017). The datafied child: The dataveillance of children and implications for their rights. *New Media and Society, 19*(5), 780–794.

Luthar, S., & Ciciolla, L. (2015). Who mothers mommy? Factors that contribute to mothers' wellbeing. *Developmental Psychology, 51*(12), 1812–1823.

Luxton, D., June, J., & Fairall, J. (2012). Social media and suicide: A public health perspective. *American Journal of Public Health, 102*(s2), S195–S200.

Luxton, D., June, J., & Kinn, J. (2011). Technology-based suicide prevention: current applications and future directions. *Telemed J E Health, 17*(1), 50–54.

Ma, L., Phelps, E., Lerner, J., & Lerner, R. (2009). Academic competence for adolescents who bully and are bullied: Findings from the 4-H study of Positive Youth Development. *Journal of Early Adolescence, 29*(6), 862–897.

MacArthur, J., & Gaffney, M. (2001). *Bullied and teased or just another kid? The social experiences of students with disabilities at school*. Wellington: New Zealand Council for Educational Research.

Maccoby, E., & Martin, J. (1983). Socialization in the context of the family: Parent–child interaction. In P. Mussen, & E. Hetherington (Eds.), *Manual of child psychology*, Vol. 4: Social development. (pp. 1–101). New York: Wiley.

Madigan, S., Ly, A., Rash, C., Van Ouytsel, J., & Temple, J. (2018). Prevalence of multiple forms of sexting behavior among youth: A systematic review and meta-analysis. *JAMA Pediatrics, 172*(4), 327–335.

Magliano, J., & Grippo, A. (2015). Why are teen brains designed for risk-taking? Here are four ways parents can reduce the danger. *Psychology today*. From www.psychologytoday.com/us/blog/the-wide-wide-world-psychology/201506/why-are-teen-brains-designed-risk-taking (accessed 11/2/21).

Makela, K., Paavola, T., & Stenman, M. (2010). Development of short message services application for patient-provider communication in clinical psychiatry. *Telemed e-Health, 16*, 827–829.

Mallen, M., & Vogel, D. (2005). Introduction to the major contribution: Counseling psychology and online counseling. *The Counseling Psychologist, 33*, 761–775.

Maltby, J., Day, L., Hatcher, R., et al. (2016). Implicit theories of online trolling: Evidence that attention-seeking conceptions are associated with increased psychological resilience. *British Journal of Psychology, 107*(3), 448–466.

Mandalia, D., Ford, T., Hill, S., Sadler, K., Vizard, T., Goodman, A., Goodman, R., & McManus, S. (2018). *Mental health of children and young people in England, 2017: Services, informal support and education*. London: Health and Social Care Information Centre.

Mann, L., Newton, J., & Innes, J. (1982). A test between deindividuation and emergent norm theories of crowd aggression. *Journal of Personality and Social Psychology, 42*(2), 260–272.

Mann, S., Nolan, J., & Wellman, B. (2003). Sousveillance: Inventing and using wearable computing devices for data collection in surveillance environments. *Surveillance & Society, 1*(3), 331–355.

Mariu, K., Merry, S., Robinson, E., & Watson, P. (2012). Seeking professional help for mental health problems among New Zealand secondary school students. *Clinical Child Psychology and Psychiatry, 17*, 284–297.

Mars, M., & Scott, R. (2016). WhatsApp in clinical practice: A literature review. *Stud Health Technol Information, 231*, 82–90.

Marsh, I., Chan, S., & MacBeth, A. (2018). Self-compassion and psychological distress in adolescents – a meta-analysis. *Mindfulness, 9*(4), 1011–1027.

Marsh, J. (2010). Young children's play in online virtual worlds. *Journal of Early Childhood Research, 8*(1), 23–39.

Marsh, J., Plowman, L., Yamada-Rice, D., et al. (2015). Exploring play and creativity in pre-schoolers' use of apps: Final project report. From www.techandplay.org/reports/TAP_Final_Report.pdf (accessed 11/2/21).

Marshall, P. (2015). Seven-year olds treated for self-harming as number of cases among primary school children rises 10%. From www.itv.com/news/2015-10-13/seven-year-olds-treated-for-self-harming-as-number-of-cases-among-primary-school-children-rises-10/ (accessed 11/2/21).

Martellozzo, E., Monaghan, A., Adler, J.R., Davidson, J., Leyva, R., & Horvath, M. A. H. (2016) *I wasn't sure it was normal to watch it*. London: NSPCC.

Martínez, I., Murgui, S., Garcia, O., & Garcia, F. (2019). Parenting in the digital era: Protective and risk parenting styles for traditional bullying and cyberbullying victimization. *Computers in Human Behavior, 90*, 84–92.

Marwick, A. & boyd, d. (2011) *The drama! Teen conflict, gossip, and bullying in networked publics*. A decade in Internet time: symposium on the dynamics of the Internet and society, September, From http://papers.ssrn.com/sol3/papers.cfm?abstract_id=1926349 (accessed 11/2/21).

Marx, G., & Steeves, V. (2010). From the beginning: Children as subjects and agents of surveillance. *Surveillance and Society, 7*(3/4), 192–230.

Mascheroni, G., & Cuman, A. (2014). *Net children go mobile. Deliverables D6.4 and D5.2*. Milan: Educatt.

Mascheroni, G., & Òlafsson, K. (2014). *Net children go mobile: Risks and opportunities*. Milan: Educatt.

Mason, M., Ola, B., Zaharakis, N., & Zhang, J. (2015). Text messaging interventions for adolescent and young adult substance use: A meta-analysis. *Prevention Science, 16*, 181–188.

Masten, A., & Barnes, A. (2018) Resilience in children: Developmental perspectives. *Children, 5*(7), 98–114.

Masuda, N., Kurahashi, I., & Onari, H. (2013). Suicide ideation of individuals in online social networks. *PLoS ONE, 8*(4), e62262.

Mathiesen, K. (2013). The Internet, children, and privacy: The case against parental monitoring. *Ethics Information Technology, 15*, 263–274.

Matthews, M., Doherty, G., Coyle, D., & Sharry, J. (2008). Designing mobile applications to support mental health interventions. In J. Lumsden (Ed.), *Handbook of research on user interface design and evaluation for mobile technology*, Vols 1 and 2 (pp. 635–656). Hershey, PA: Information Science Reference/IGI Global.

Matthews, T., Danese, A., Wertz, J., Odgers, C., Ambler, A., Mofitt, T., & Arseneault, L. (2016). Social isolation, loneliness and depression in young adulthood: A behavioural genetic analysis. *Social Psychiatry and Psychiatric Epidemiology, 51*, 339–348 (2016).

Mayer, J., & Salovey, P. (1993). The intelligence of emotional intelligence. *Intelligence, 27*, 267–298.

Mbwayo, A., Muthoni, M., Lincoln, K., Kuria, M., & Stoep, A. (2019). Mental health in Kenyan schools: Teachers' perspectives. *Global Social Welfare*, 1–9. 10.1007/s40609-019-00153-4.

McAllister, M. (2003). Multiple meanings of self-harm: A critical review. *International Journal of Mental Health Nursing, 12*(3), 177–185.

McDonald, M. (2011). Social exclusion and social inclusion: Resources for child and family services. From https://aifs.gov.au/cfca/publications/social-exclusion-and-social-inclusion-resources-child

McGee, S. (2011). Mobile contact tracing and counseling for STIs: There's not an app for that. *American Journal of Bioethics, 11*(5), 3–4.

McLoyd, V., Cauce, A., Takeuchi, D., & Wilson, L. (2000). Marital processes and parental socialization in families of color: A decade review of research. *Journal of Marriage and Family Therapy, 62*(4), 1070–1093.

McLuhan, M. (1967). The medium is the massage: An inventory of effects. London: Penguin.

McPake, J., Plowman, L., & Stephen, C. (2013). Pre-school children creating and communicating with digital technologies in the home. *British Journal of Educational Technology, 44*(3), 421–431.

Mehta, N., Croudace, T., & Davies S. (2014). Public mental health: Evidence-based priorities. *The Lancet, 385*, 1472–1475.

Meltzer, H., Gatward, R., Goodman, R., & Ford, T. (2000). *The mental health of children and adolescents in Great Britain*. London: The Stationery Office.

Mental Health Foundation (1999). *Bright futures: Promoting children and young people's mental health*. London: Mental Health Foundation.

Mesch, G. (2009). Parental mediation, online activities, and cyberbullying. *CyberPsychology and Behavior, 12*(4), 387–393.

Messina-Dysert, G. (2016). Rape culture and spiritual violence: Religion, testimony and visions of healing. London: Routledge.

Metzger, M. (2007). Making sense of credibility on the Web: Models for evaluating online information and recommendations for future research. *Journal of the American Society for Information Science and Technology, 58*(13), 2078–2091.

Miles, D. (2011). *Youth protection: Digital citizenship, principles and new resources*. Second Worldwide Cybersecurity Summit, London.

Millard, C., & Wessely, S. (2014). Parity of esteem between mental and physical health. *British Medical Journal, 349*(10), G6821.

Milyavskaya, M., Saffran, M., Hope, N., & Koestner, R. (2018). Fear of missing out: prevalence, dynamics, and consequences of experiencing FOMO. *Motivation and Emotion, 42*(5), 725–737.

Minkkinen, J., Oksanen, A., Kaakinen, M., Keipi, T., & Räsänen, P. (2017). Victimization and exposure to pro-self-harm and pro-suicide websites: A cross-national study. *Suicide and Life-Threatening Behavior, 47*(1), 14–26.

Mlambo-Ngcuka, P. (2013). *Mobile learning facilitated ICT teacher development: Innovation report*. EngD thesis, University of Warwick. From http://wrap.warwick.ac.uk/58641/ (accessed 11/2/21).

Mokomane, Z., Mokhele, T., Mathews, C., & Makoae, M. (2017). Availability and accessibility of public health services for adolescents and young people in South Africa. *Children and Youth Services Review, 74*, 125–132.

Montreuil, M., & Carnevale, F. (2016). A concept analysis of children's agency within the health literature. *Journal of Child Health Care, 20*(4), 503–511.

Moreno, M., Kota, R., Schoohs, S., & Whitehill, J. (2013). The Facebook influence model: A concept mapping approach. *Cyberpsychology, Behavior, and Social Networking, 16*, 504–511.

Moreno, M., Ton, A., Selkie, E., & Evans, Y. (2016). Secret society 123: Understanding the language of self-harm on Instagram. *Journal of Adolescent Health, 58*, 78–84.

Morozov, E. (2011). *The Net Delusion*. New York: Public Affairs.

Morrison, T., Ellis, S., Morrison, M., Bearden, A., & Harriman, R. (2006). Exposure to sexually explicit material and variations in body esteem, genital attitudes, and sexual esteem among a sample of Canadian men. *The Journal of Men's Studies, 14*, 209–222.

Morton, J., & O'Reilly, M. (2019). Mental health, big data and research ethics: Parity of esteem in mental health research from a UK perspective. *Clinical Ethics, 14*(4), 165–172.

Musicaro, R. M., Spinazzola, J., Arvidson, J., et al. (2017). The complexity of adaptation to childhood polyvictimization in youth and young adults: Recommendations for multidisciplinary responders. *Trauma, Violence & Abuse, 20*(1), 81–98.

Nadesan, M. (2008). Constructing autism: A brief genealogy. In M. Osteen (Ed.), *Autism and Representation* (pp. 78–95) New York: Routledge.

Naghieh, A., Montgomery, P., Bonell, C., Thompson, M., & Aber, J. (2015). Organisational interventions for improving wellbeing and reducing work-related stress in teachers (Review). *Cochrane Database of Systematic Reviews 2015*, 4. Art. No.: CD010306.

Nash, V., Adler, J., Horvath, M., Livingstone, S., Marston, C., Owen, G., & Wright, J. (2015). Identifying the routes by which children view pornography online: Implications for future policy-makers seeking to limit viewing. From http://eprints.lse.ac.uk/65450/1/__lse.ac.uk_storage_LIBRARY_Secondary_libfile_shared_repository_Content_Livingstone,%20S_Identifying%20the%20routes_Livingstone_Identifying%20the%20routes_2016.pdf (accessed 22/3/21).

Naslund, J., Aschbrenner, K., Araya, R., Marsch, L., Unützer, Patel, V., & Bartels, S (2017). Digital technology for treating and preventing mental disorders in low-income and middle-income countries: A narrative review of the literature. *The Lancet, Psychiatry, 4*(6), 486–500.

Nathanson, A. (1999). Identifying and explaining the relationship between parental mediation and children's aggression. *Communication Research, 26*(2), 124–143.

National Institute for Health and Care Excellence (NICE). (2013). Self-harm: Quality standard (QS34). From www.nice.org.uk/guidance/qs34 (accessed 22/3/21).

National Institute for Health and Care Excellence (NICE). (2017). *Health app. ChatHealth communication platform in school nursing services*. London: NICE.

NHS. (2017). Anxiety disorders in children. From www.nhs.uk/conditions/anxiety-disorders-in-children/ (accessed 23/3/21).

NHS Digital. (2018). *Mental health of children and young people in England, 2017*: Summary of key findings. From: https://files.digital.nhs.uk/F6/A5706C/MHCYP%20 2017%20Summary.pdf (accessed 23/3/21).

NHS England. (2015). Future in mind. From https://assets.publishing.service.gov.uk/government/uploads/system/uploads/attachment_data/file/414024/Childrens_Mental_Health.pdf (accessed 23/3/21).

Nicholas, J., Oliver, K., Lee, K., & O'Brien, M. (2004). Help-seeking behavior on the Internet: An investigation among Australian adolescents. *Australian e-Journal Advance Mental Health, 3*, 1–8.

Nickel, P. (2006). Vulnerable populations in research: The case of the seriously ill. *Theoretical Medicine and Bioethics, 27*(3), 245–264.

Nikken, P., & Schols, M. (2015). How and why parents' guide the media use of young children. *Journal of Child and Family Studies, 24*(11), 3423–3435.

Nominet Trust (2017). Digital reach: Digital skills for the hardest-to-reach young people. *Nominet*. From https://socialtechtrust.org/wp-content/uploads/2017/07/Online_NT_Digital_Reach_Prospectus_Final.pdf (accessed 25/5/20).

Nordentoft, H., & Kappel, N. (2011). Vulnerable participants in health research: Methodological and ethical challenges. *Journal of Social Work Practice, 25*(3), 365–376.

NSPCC. (2016). What is safeguarding? From https://thecpsu.org.uk/help-advice/introduction-to-safeguarding/what-is-safeguarding/ (accessed 23/3/21).

NSPCC. (2018). How safe are our children? *The most comprehensive overview of child protection in the UK*. London: NSPCC.

NSPCC. (2020). Online pornography. From www.nspcc.org.uk/keeping-children-safe/online-safety/online-porn/ (accessed 23/3/21).

O'Connell, R. (Chair) et al. (2009) Safer social networking principles for the EU. From https://ec.europa.eu/digital-single-market/sites/digital-agenda/files/sn_principles.pdf (accessed 15/12/20).

O'Connor, T. G., & Scott, S. (2007). *Parenting and outcomes for children*. England: Joseph Rowntree Foundation.

O'Keeffe, G., & Clarke-Pearson, K. (2011). Council on Communications and Media: The impact of social media on children, adolescents, and families. *Paediatrics, 127*, 800–804.

O'Reilly, M. (2020). Social media and adolescent mental health: The good, the bad and the ugly. *Journal of Mental Health, 29*(2), 200–206.

O'Reilly, M., Adams, S., Whiteman, N., Hughes, J., Reilly, P., & Dogra, N. (2018). Whose responsibility is adolescent mental health in the UK? The perspectives of key stakeholders. *School Mental Health, 10*, 450–461.

O'Reilly, M., Dogra, N., Hughes, J., Reilly, P., George, R., & Whiteman, N. (2018). Potential of social media in promoting mental health in adolescents. *Health Promotion International, 34*(5), 981–991.

O'Reilly, M., Dogra, N., Whiteman, N., Hughes, J., Eruyar, S., & Reilly, P. (2018). Is social media bad for mental health and wellbeing? Exploring the perspectives of adolescents. *Clinical Child Psychology and Psychiatry, 23*(4), 601–613.

O'Reilly, M., Karim, K., & Kiyimba, N. (2015). Question use in child mental health assessments and the challenges of listening to families. *British Journal of Psychiatry Open, 1*(2), 116–120.

O'Reilly, M., & Lester, J. (2016). Building a case for good parenting in a family therapy systemic environment: Resisting blame and accounting for children's behaviour. *Journal of Family Therapy, 38*(4), 491–511.

O'Reilly, M., Levine, D., & Law, E. (2020). Applying a 'digital ethics of care' philosophy to understand adolescents' sense of responsibility on social media. *Pastoral Care in Education*. https://doi.org/10.1080/02643944.2020.1774635

O'Reilly, M., Ronzoni, P., & Dogra, N. (2013) *Research with Children*. London: Sage.

O'Reilly, M., Svirydzenka, N., Adams, S., & Dogra, N. (2018). Review of mental health promotion in schools. *Social Psychiatry and Psychiatric Epidemiology, 53*(7), 647–662.

O'Reilly, M., Taylor, H., & Vostanis, P. (2009). 'Nuts, schiz, psycho': An exploration of young homeless people's perceptions and dilemmas of defining mental health. *Social Science and Medicine, 68*, 1737–1744.

Odgers, C., & Jensen, M. (2020). Annual Research Review: Adolescent mental health in the digital age: facts, fears, and future directions. *Journal of Child Psychology and Psychiatry, 61*(3), 336–348.

OECD. (2017). *PISA 2015 Results (Volume III): Students' Wellbeing, PISA, OECD Publishing*. Paris: OECD.

OECD. (2018). *Children and young people's mental health in the digital age: Shaping the future*. Paris: OECD.

Ofcom. (2017). Children and parents: Media use and attitudes report. From https://www.ofcom.org.uk/__data/assets/pdf_file/0020/108182/children-parents-media-use-attitudes-2017.pdf (accessed 23/3/21).

Office for National Statistics (2015). Measuring national wellbeing: insights into children's mental health and wellbeing. From www.ons.gov.uk/peoplepopulationandcommunity/wellbeing/articles/measuringnationalwellbeing/2015-10-20 (accessed (23/3/21).

Ofsted. (2014). Inspecting e-safety in schools. From https://static.lgfl.net/lgflNet/downloads/online-safety/LGfL-OS-Ofsted-inspecting-E-Safety-Jan-2014.pdf

Ohler, J. (2011). Character education for the digital age. *Educational Leadership, 68*(5), online.

Orben, A. (2020). Teenagers, screens and social media: A narrative review of reviews and key studies. *Social Psychiatry and Psychiatric Epidemiology, 55*, 407–414.

Orben, A., & Przybylski, A. (2019a). Screens, teens, and psychological wellbeing: evidence from three time-use-diary studies. *Psychological Science, 30*(5), 682–696.

Orben, A., & Przybylski, A. (2019b). The association between adolescent wellbeing and digital technology use. *Nature Human Behaviour, 3*(2), 173–182.

Orben, A., Dienlin, T., & Przybylski, A. (2019). Social media's enduring effect on adolescent life satisfaction. *Proceedings of the National Academy of Sciences of the United States of America, 116*(21), 10226–10228.

Orben, A., Etchells, P. J., & Przybylski, A. (2018). Three problems with the debate around screen time. *Guardian*, 9 August. From www.theguardian.com/science/head-quarters/2018/aug/09/three-problems-with-the-debate-around-screen-time (accessed 23/3/21).

Oswalt, A. (n.d.) Early childhood physical development: Gross and fine motor. From: www.gracepointwellness.org/462-child-development-parenting-early-3-7/article/-12755-early-childhood-physical-development-gross-and-fine-motor-development (accessed 23/3/21).

Oxford English Dictionary. (n.d). FOMO. From www.lexico.com/definition/fomo (accessed 11/2/21).

Oxford English Dictionary. (n.d.). Risk. From https://en.oxforddictionaries.com/definition/risk (accessed 23/3/21).

Padilla-Walker, L., Coyne, S., Fraser, A., Dyer, W., & Yorgason, J. (2012). Parents and adolescents growing up in the digital age: Latent growth curve analysis of proactive media monitoring. *Journal of Adolescence, 35*(5), 1153–1165.

Padmanathan, P., Biddle, L., Carroll, R., Derges, J., Potokar, J., & Gunnell, D. (2018). Suicide and self-harm related internet use. *Crisis, 39*(6), 469–478.

Page, A., Held, K., & Levine, D. (2020). *A project-based approach to primary computing*. Oxford: Oxford University Press.

Palmer, C. (2019). Use of a text messaging service for communication with parents and carers. *Primary Health Care*. doi: 10.7748/phc.e1472

Papatraianou, L., Levine, D., & West, D. (2014). Resilience in the face of cyberbullying: An ecological perspective on young people's experiences of online adversity. *Pastoral Care in Education, 32*, 264–283.

Patchin, J., & Hinduja, S. (2006). Bullies move beyond the schoolyard: A preliminary look at cyberbullying. *Youth Violence and Juvenile Justice, 4*(2), 148–169.

Patchin, J., & Hinduja, S. (2017). Digital self-harm among adolescents. *Journal of Adolescent Health, 61*(6), 761–766.

Patel, V., Saxena, S., Lund, C., et al. (2018). The *Lancet* Commission on global mental health and sustainable development. *Lancet, 392*, 1553–1598.

Patrika, P., & Tseliou, E. (2016). Blame, responsibility, and systemic neutrality: A discourse analysis methodology to the study of family therapy problem talk. *Journal of Family Therapy, 38*(4), 467–490.

Patton, G., Coffey, C., Sawyer, S., et al. (2009). Global patterns of mortality in young people; A systematic analysis of population health data. *Lancet, 374*, 881–892.

Patton, G., Sawyer, S., Santelli, J., et al. (2016). Our future: A *Lancet* commission on adolescent health and wellbeing. *The Lancet, 387*, 2423–2478.

Pavia, L., Cavani, P., Di Blasi, M., & Giordano, C. (2016). Smartphone addiction inventory (SPAI): psychometric properties and confirmatory factor analysis. *Computers in Human Behavior, 63*, 170–178.

Perry, R., Kayekjian, K., Braun, R., Cantu, M., Sheoran, B., & Chung, P. (2012). Adolescents' perspectives on the use of a text messaging service for preventive sexual health promotion. *Journal of Adolescent Health, 51*, 220–225.

Peter, J., & Valkenburg, P. (2008). Adolescents' exposure to sexually explicit internet material, sexual uncertainty, and attitudes toward uncommitted sexual exploration: Is there a link? *Communication Research, 35*, 579–601.

Petterson, T. (2011). The ethics of care: Normative structures and empirical implications. *Health Care Analysis, 19*, 51–64.

Phyfer, J., Burton, P., & Leoschut, L. (2016). Global Kids Online South Africa: Barriers, opportunities and risks. A glimpse into South African children's internet use and online activities. Global Kids Online. In L. Jossel (Ed.), *Centre for justice and crime prevention, South Africa*, Cape Town, South Africa.

Piaget, J. (1932). *The moral judgement of the child*. New York: Harcourt Brace.

Piaget, J. (1936). *Origins of intelligence in the child*. London: Routledge & Kegan Paul.

Pickhardt, C. (2014). Adolescence and risk-taking: Adolescents can't grow without taking risks and exposing themselves to harm. From www.psychologytoday.com/us/blog/surviving-your-childs-adolescence/201407/adolescence-and-risk-taking (accessed 23/3/21).

Pinfold, V., Toulmin, H., Thornicroft, G., Huxley, P., Farmer, P., & Graham, T (2003). Reducing psychiatric stigma and discrimination: Evaluation of educational interventions in UK secondary schools. *British Journal of Psychiatry, 182*(4), 342–346.

Pitchforth, J., Viner, R., & Hargreaves, D. (2016). Trends in mental health and wellbeing among children and young people in the UK: A repeated cross-sectional study, 2000–14. *The Lancet, 388*, 93–93.

Poore, M. (2016). *Using social media in the classroom: A best practice guide* (2nd ed.). London: Sage.

Porter, G., Hampshire, A., Abane, A. Munthali, E., Robson, E., Mashiri, M., & Tanle, A. (2012). Youth, mobility and mobile phones in Africa: Findings from a three-country study. *Information Technology for Development, 18*(2), 145–162.

Prasad, S., & Anand, R. (2012). The use of mobile telephone short message service as a reminder: The effect on patient attendance. *International Dent. Journal, 62*(1), 21–26.

Prensky, M. (2001). Digital natives, digital immigrants. *On the Horizon, 9*(5), 1–6.

Prince, M., Patel, V., Saxena, S., Maj, M., Maselko, J., Phillips, M. R., & Rahman, A. (2007). No health without mental health. *The Lancet, 370*(9590), 859–877.

Prinstein, M. J., Nesi, J., & Telzer, E. H. (2020). Commentary: An updated agenda for the study of digital media use and adolescent development – future directions following Odgers and Jensen (2020). *Journal of Child Psychology and Psychiatry, 61,* 349–352.

Przybylski, A., Murayama, K., DeHaan, C., & Gladwell, V. (2013). Motivational, emotional and behavioral correlates of fear of missing out. *Computers in Human Behavior, 29*(4), 1841–1848.

Przybylski, A., & Weinstein, N. (2017). A large-scale test of the Goldilocks hypothesis: Quantifying the relations between digital screen use and the mental wellbeing of adolescents. *PAS Psychological Science, 28*(2), 204–215.

Public Health England. (2017). Secondary school staff get mental health 'first aid' training. From www.gov.uk/government/news/secondary-school-staff-get-mental-health-first-aid-training (accessed 23/3/21).

Punch, S. (2016). Exploring children's agency across majority and minority world contexts. In F. Esser, M. Baader, T. Betz, & B. Hungerland (Eds.), *Reconceptualising agency and childhood: New perspectives in childhood studies* (pp. 183–196). London: Routledge.

Qvortrup, L. (2006). Understanding new digital media: Medium theory or complexity theory. *European Journal of Communication, 21*(3), 345–356.

Radovic, A., Gmelin, T., Stein, B., & Miller, E. (2017). Depressed adolescents' positive and negative use of social media. *Journal of Adolescence, 55,* 5–15.

Rafla, M., Carson, N., & DeJong, S. (2014). Adolescents and the Internet: What mental health clinicians need to know. *Child and Adolescent Disorders, 16,* 472–482.

Ragnedda, M. (2018). Conceptualizing digital capital. *Telematics and Informatics, 35*(8), 2366–2375.

Rapee, R. (1997). Potential role of childrearing practices in the development of anxiety and depression. *Clinical Psychology Review, 17*(1), 47–67.

Ratele, K. (2019). *The world looks this from here: Thoughts on African psychology.* Johannesburg: Wits University Press.

Ratele, K., Cornell, J., Dlamini, S., Helman, R., Malherbe, N., & Titi, N. (2018). Some basic questions about (a) decolonizing Africa(n)-centred psychology considered. *South African Journal of Psychology, 48*(3), 331–342.

Reid, D., & Reid, F. (2007). Text or talk? Social anxiety, loneliness and divergent preferences for cell phone use. *CyberPsychol Behav, 10*(3), 424–435.

Reid, R. (2019). I invented the term 'sadfishing' so let's talk about what it actually means. From https://graziadaily.co.uk/life/in-the-news/sadfishing/ (accessed 23/3/21).

Reinke, W., Stormont, M., Herman, K., Puri, R., & Goel, N. (2011). Supporting children's mental health in schools: Teachers' perceptions of needs, roles and barriers. *School Psychology Quarterly, 26*(1), 1–13.

Reynolds, D., Stiles, W., Bailer, A., & Hughes, M. (2013). Impact of exchanges and client-therapist alliance in online-text psychotherapy. *Cyberpsychology Behavior Social Network, 16*(5), 370–377.

Riaz, S. (2015). Health apps on the rise, but barriers remain, reveals study. *Mobile World Live.* From www.mobileworldlive.com/apps/news-apps/health-apps-on-the-rise-but-barriers-remain-reveals-study/ (accessed 23/3/21).

Ribble, M. (2017). Digital citizenship: using technology appropriately. From www.digitalcitizenship.net/nine-elements.html (accessed 23/3/21).

Ribble, M., & Bailey, G. (2007). *Digital citizenship in schools.* Washington, DC: International Society for Technology in Education.

Ricciardelli, L., & McCabe, M. (2001). Children's body image concerns and eating disturbance: A review of the literature. *Clinical Psychology Review, 21*(3), 119–123.

Rice, E., Rhoades, H., Winetrobe, H., Sanchez, M., Montoya, J., Plant, A., & Kordic, T (2012). Sexually explicit cell phone messaging associated with sexual risk among adolescents. *Pediatrics, 130*, 667–673.

Rice, L. (2013). It's time for more Lolz NOT trolls. *Vinspitred,* 13 January.

Rideout, V., & Fox, S. (2018). Digital health practices, social media use, and mental wellbeing among teens and young adults in the US. From www.commonsenseme-dia.org/sites/default/files/uploads/research/2018_cs_socialmediasociallife_fullre-port-final-release_2_lowres.pdf (accessed 23/3/21).

Ringeval, F., Schuller, B., Valstar, M., et al. (2019). *AVEC 2019 workshop and challenge: State-of-mind, detecting depression with AI, and cross-cultural affect recognition.* In Proceedings of the 9th International on Audio/Visual Emotion Challenge and Workshop (pp. 3–12).

Rogers, W., & Lange, M. (2013). Rethinking the vulnerability of minority populations in research. *American Journal of Public Health, 103*(12), 2141–2146.

Rogers, W., Mackenzie, C., & Dodds, S. (2012). Why bioethics needs a concept of vulnerability. *International Journal of Feminist Approaches to Bioethics, 5*(2), 11–38.

Romer, D., Reyna, V., & Satterthwhaite, T. (2017). Beyond stereotypes of adolescent risk-taking: Placing the adolescent brain in development context. *Developmental Cognitive Neuroscience, 27*, 19–34.

Rose, D., Thornicroft, G., Pinfold, V., & Kassam, A. (2007). 250 labels used to stigmatise people with mental illness. *BMC Health Services Research, 7*, 97–104.

Rothi, D. M., Leavey, G., & Best, R. (2008). On the front-line: Teachers as active observers of pupils' mental health. *Teaching and Teacher Education, 24*, 1217–1231.

Rowling, L. (2009). Strengthening 'school' in school mental health promotion. *Health Education, 109*(4), 357–368.

Royal College of Psychiatrists, (2020). Coping with stress: For young people. From: www.rcpsych.ac.uk/mental-health/parents-and-young-people/young-people/coping-with-stress-for-young-people (accessed 14/4/20).

Royal Society for Public Health (RSPH). (2017). *#StatusofMind: Social media and young people's mental health and wellbeing.* From https://www.rsph.org.uk/static/uploaded/d125b27c-0b62-41c5-a2c0155a8887cd01.pdf (accessed (23/3/21).

Royal Society for Public Health (RSPH). (2019). *#New Filters to manage the impact of social media on young people's mental health and wellbeing.* London: RSPH.

Rubin, K. (1994). Editorial: From family to peer group: Relations between relationship systems. *Social Development, 3*(3), iii–viii.

Ruof, M. (2004). Vulnerability, vulnerable populations, and policy. *Kennedy Institute of Ethics Journal, 14*(4), 411–425.

Rüsch, N., Corrigan, P., Wassel, A., Michales, P., Larson, J., Oleschewski, M., Ilkniss, S., & Batia, K. (2009). Self-stigma, group identification, perceived legitimacy of discrimination and mental health service use. *British Journal of Psychiatry, 195*, 551–552.

Rutter, M. (2007). Resilience, competence and coping. *Child Abuse and Neglect, 31*, 205–209.

Saarni, C. (2011). Emotional development in childhood. In the *Encylopedia of Early Childhood Development.* From www.child-encyclopedia.com/emotions/according-experts/emotional-development-childhood (accessed 23/3/21).

Sadler, K., Vizard, T., Ford, T., Goodman, A., & Goodman, R., (2018). *Mental health of children and young people in England, 2017.* London: Mental Health Foundation.

Salter, M. (2013). *Organised sexual abuse.* London: Glasshouse/Routledge.

Sanders, J., Munford, R., Liebenberg, L., & Ungar, M. (2017). Peer paradox: The tensions that peer relationships raise for vulnerable youth. *Child & Family Social Work, 22*(1), 3–14.

Sands, N. (2004). Mental health triage nursing: An Australian perspective. *Journal of Psychiatric Mental Health Nursing, 11*, 150–155.

Sarriera, J., Abs, D., Casa, F., & Bedin, L. (2012). Relations between media, perceived social support and personal wellbeing in adolescence. *Social Indic Res, 106*, 545–561.

Saunders, P., Naidoo, Y., & Griffiths, M., with the assistance of Davidson, P. (ACOSS), Hampshire, A. (Mission Australia), Taylor, J. (Brotherhood of St Laurence), Bellamy, J., & King, S. (Anglicare, Diocese of Sydney) (2007). *Towards New Indicators of Disadvantage: deprivation and social exclusion in Australia.* Sydney: Social Policy Research Centre, University of New South Wales.

Schachaf, P., & Hara, N. (2010). Beyond vandalism: Wikipedia trolls. *Journal of information Science, 36*(3), 357–370.

Schön, D. (1983). *The reflective practitioner.* New York: Basic Books.

Schuller, B. W. (2018). Speech emotion recognition: two decades in a nutshell, benchmarks, and ongoing trends. *Communications of the ACM, 61*(5), 90–99.

Scott, D., Crossin, R., Ogeil, R., Smith, K., & Lubman, D. (2018). Exploring harms experienced by children aged 7–11 using ambulance attendance data: A 6-year comparison with adolescents aged 12–17. *International Journal of Environmental Research and Public Health, 15*, 1385–1398.

Scott, H., Gardani, M., Blello, S., & Woods, H. (2016). *Social media use, fear of missing out and sleep outcomes in adolescents.* Conference: 23rd Congress of the European Sleep Research Society, Bologna.

Scott, H., & Woods, H. (2018). Fear of missing out and sleep: Cognitive behavioural factors in adolescents' night-time social media use. *Journal of Adolescence, 68*, 61–65.

Seabrook, E., Kern, M., & Rickard, N. (2016). Social networking sites, depression, and anxiety: A systematic review. *JMIR Mental Health, 3*, e50.

Seko, Y., Kidd, S., Wiljer, D., & McKenzie, K. (2014). Youth mental health interventions via mobile phone: A scoping review. *Cyberpsychology, Behavior, and Social Networking, 17*, 591–602.

Selwyn, N. (2009). The digital native – myth and reality. *Aslib Proceedings, 61*(4), 364–379.

Sethi, A. (2007). Domestic sex trafficking of Aboriginal girls in Canada: Issues and implications. *The First Peoples Child & Family Review, 3*(3), 57–71.

Shanley, D., Reid, G., & Evans, B. (2008). How parents seek help for children with mental health problems. *Adm Policy Mental Health, 35*, 135–146.

Shatte, A., Hutchinson, D., & Teague, S. (2019). Machine learning in mental health: A scoping review of methods and applications. *Psychological Medicine, 49*, 1426–1448.

Shaw, D., Sandy, P., & Gesondheid, S. (2016). Mental health nurses' attitudes toward self-harm: Curricular implications. *Health, 21*, 406–414.

Sherman, L., Greenfield, P., Hernandez, L., & Dapretto, M. (2018). Peer influence via Instagram: Effects on brain and behavior in adolescence and young adulthood. *Child Development, 89*, 37–47.

Shivayogi, P. (2013). Vulnerable populations and methods for their safeguard. *Perspectives Clinical Research, 4*(1), 53–57.

Skinner, B. F. (1966). *Contingencies of reinforcement.* New York: Appleton-Century-Crofts.

Simm, R., Roen, K., & Daiches, A. (2008). Educational professional's experiences of self-harm in primary school children: 'You don't really believe it unless you see it'. *Oxford Review Education, 34*, 253–269.

Simm, R., Roen, K., & Daiches, A. (2010). Primary school children and self-harm: The emotional impact upon education professionals, and their understandings of why children self-harm and how this is managed. *Oxford Review of Education, 36*(6), 677–692.

Simmons, R. (2014). The secret language of girls on Instagram. From http://time.com/3559340/instagram-tween-girls/ (accessed 11/2/21).

Sims, H., Sanghara, H., Hayes, D., Wandiebe, S., Finch, M., Jakobsen, H., Tsakanikos, E., Okocha, C. I., & Kravariti, E. (2012). Text message reminders of appointments: a pilot intervention at four community mental health clinics in London. *Psychiatric Services (Washington, D.C), 63*(2), 161–168.

Sims-Schouten, W. (2017). 'Mental health first aid training' in schools is a sticking-plaster solution. From https://theconversation.com/mental-health-first-aid-training-in-schools-is-a-sticking-plaster-solution-80166 (accessed 23/3/21).

Sinclair, R. (2020). Online sexual exploitation of children in the Philippines: Analysis and recommendations for governments, industry, and civil society. International Justice Mission, the US Department of State Office to Monitor and Combat Trafficking in Persons and the Philippine Inter-Agency Council Against Trafficking.

Singh, I. (2004). Doing their jobs: Mothering with Ritalin in a culture of mother-blame. *Social Science and Medicine, 59*, 1193–1205.

Singletary, J., Bartle, C., Svirydzenka, N., Suter-Giogini, N., Cashmore, A., & Dogra, N. (2015). Adolescents' perceptions of mental and physical health in the context of general wellbeing. *Health Education Journal, 74*(3), 257–269.

Sirkko, R., Kyrönlampi, T., & Puroila, A-M. (2019). Children's agency: opportunities and constraints. *International Journal of Early Childhood, 51*, 282–300.

Sladek, M., Salk, R., & Engeln, R. (2018). Negative body talk measures for Asian, Latina (o), and white women and men: Measurement equivalence and associations with ethnic-racial identity. *Body Image, 25*, 66–77.

Slote, M. (2007). *Ethics of care and empathy.* London: Routledge.

Smahel, D., Machackova, H., Mascheroni, G., Dedkova, L., Staksrud, E., Ólafsson, K., Livingstone, S., & Hasebrink, U. (2020). EU Kids Online 2020: Survey results from 19 countries. *EU Kids Online.* doi: 10.21953/lse.47fdeqj01ofo

Smahelova, M., Juhová, D., Cermak, I., & Smahel, D. (2017). Mediation of young children's digital technology use: The parents' perspective. *Cyberpsychology: Journal of Psychosocial Research on Cyberspace, 11*(3). doi:10.5817/cp2017-3-4.

Smetaniuik, P. (2014). A preliminary investigation into the prevalence and prediction of problematic cell phone use. *Journal of Behavioral Addictions, 3*, 41–53.

Smith, C., & Carlson, B. (1997). Stress, coping, and resilience in children and youth. *Social Service Review, 71*, 231–256.

Sowell, E., Peterson, B., Thompson, P., Welcome, S., Henkenius, A., & Toga, A. (2003). Mapping cortical change across the human life span. *Nature Neuroscience, 6*(3), 309–15.

Spinazzola, J., Habib, M., Knoverek, A., Arvidson, J., Nisenbaum, J., Wentworth, R., & Pond, A. (2013). The heart of the matter: Complex trauma in child welfare. *Child Welfare 360°,* Special Issue: *Trauma-Informed Child Welfare Practice,* 8–9, Winter edition.

Stafford, V., Hutchby, I., Karim, K., & O'Reilly, M. (2016). 'Why are you here?' Seeking children's accounts of their presentation to CAMHS. *Clinical Child Psychology and Psychiatry, 21*(1), 3–18.

Staksrud, E., & Lobe, B. (2010). Evaluation of the implementation of the Safer Social Networking Principles for the EU, Part 1: general report. Study commissioned by the European Commission.

Stald, G., Green, L., Barbovski, M., Haddon, L., Mascheroni, G., Sagvari, B., Scifo, B., & Tsaliki, L. (2014). *Online on the mobile: Internet use on smartphones and associated risks among youth in Europe.* London: EU Kids Online, LSE.

Steinberg, L. (2008). A social neuroscience perspective on adolescent risk taking. *Developmental Review, 28*, 78–106.

Steinberg, L. (2010). A dual systems model of adolescent risk-taking. *Developmental Psychobiology, 52*, 216–224.

Steinberg, L., Icenogle, G., Shulman, E., et al. (2017). Around the world, adolescence is a time of heightened sensation seeking and immature self-regulation. *Developmental Science*, doi:10.1111/desc.12532

Steinberg, S. B. (2017). Sharenting: Children's privacy in the age of social media, 66 Emory, L. J. 839. From http://scholarship.law.ufl.edu/cgi/viewcontent.cgi?article=1796&context=facultypub (accessed 11/2/21).

Stephen, R., & Edmonds, R. (2018). *Briefing 53: Social media, young people and mental health*. London: Centre for Mental Health.

Stephens-Reicher, J., Metcalf, A., Blanchard, M., Mangan, C., & Burns, J. (2011). Reaching the hard-to-reach: How information communication technologies can reach young people at greater risk of mental health difficulties. *Australasian Psychiatry, 19*(Suppl 1), s58-s61.

Stettler, N. M., & Katz, L. F. (2017). Minority stress, emotion regulation, and the parenting of sexual-minority youth. *Journal of GLBT Family Studies, 13*(4), 380–400.

Stoewen, D. (2017). Dimensions of wellness: Change your habits, change your life. *Canadian Veterinary Journal, 58*(8), 861–862.

Stratton, P. (2010). *The evidence base of systematic family and couples' therapies*. London: The Association for Family Therapy & Systemic Practice.

Strong, T., & Sesma-Vazquez, M. (2015). Discourses on children's mental health: A critical review. In M. O'Reilly, & J. N. Lester (Eds.), *Handbook of Child Mental Health*. Basingstoke: Palgrave McMillan.

Sturgeon, S. (2007). Promoting mental health as an essential aspect of health promotion. *Health Promotion International, 21*(S1), 36–41.

Summerhurst, C., Wammes, M., Arcaro, J., & Osuch, E. (2018). Embracing technology: Use of text messaging with adolescent outpatients at a mood and anxiety program. *Social Work in Mental Health, 16*(3), 337–345.

Susman, J. (1994). Disability, stigma and deviance. *Social Science and Medicine, 38*, 15–22.

Svirydzenka, N., Aitken, J., & Dogra, N. (2016). Research and partnerships with schools. *Social Psychiatry and Psychiatric Epidemiology, 51*, 1203–1209.

Swartz, L. (1998). *Culture and mental health: A Southern African view*. Cape Town: Oxford University Press.

Swire-Thompson, B., & Lazer, D. (2020). Public health and online misinformation: Challenges and recommendations. *Annual Review of Public Health, 41*, 433–451.

Syed-Abdul, S., Fernandez-Luque, L., Jian, W-S., et al., (2013). Misleading health-related information promoted through video-based social media: Anorexia on YouTube. *Journal of Medical Internet Research, 15*(2), e30 – online.

Symons, K., Ponnet, K., Walgrave, M., & Heirman, W. (2017). A qualitative study into parental mediation of adolescents' internet use. *Computers in Human Behavior, 73*, 423–432.

Tamburrino, I., Getanda, E., O'Reilly, M., & Vostanis, P. (2020). 'Everybody's responsibility': Conceptualisation of youth mental health in Kenya. *Journal of Child Health Care, 4*(1), 5–18.

Tanaka, M., Wekerle, C., Schmuck, M. L., Paglia-Boak, A., & The MAP Research Team (2011). The linkages among child maltreatment, adolescent mental health, and self-compassion in child welfare adolescents. *Child Abuse & Neglect, 35*, 887–898.

Terras, M. & Ramsay, J. (2016). Family digital literacy practices and children's mobile phone use. *Frontiers in Psychology*, Article 23, online.

Terras, M., Yousaf, F., & Ramsay, J. (2016). 'The relationship between parent and child digital technology use,' in Proceedings of the British Psychological Society Annual Conference, Nottingham.

Teufel, M., Hofer, E., Junne, F., Sauer, H., Zipfel, S., & Giel, K (2013). A comparative analysis of anorexia nervosa groups on Facebook. *Eating and Weight Disorders – Studies on Anorexia, Bulimia and Obesity, 18*(4), 413–420.

Thacker, S., & Griffiths, M. D. (2012). An exploratory study of trolling in online video gaming. *International Journal of Cyber Behaviour, Psychology and Learning, 2*(4), 17–33.

Thapar, A., & Harold, G. (2014). Why is there such a mismatch between traditional heritability estimates and molecular genetic findings for behavioural traits? *Journal of Child Psychology and Psychiatry, 55*(10), 1088–1091.

The Academy of Medical Sciences. (2018). Challenges and priorities for global mental health in the sustainable development goals (SDG) era. London: The Academy of Medical Sciences.

The Alan Turing Institute. (2019). AI for precision mental health: Producing AI tools than can personalise mental health profiles and advance the precision of early diagnosis and subsequent treatment. From www.turing.ac.uk/research/research-projects/ai-precision-mental-health (accessed 11/2/21).

The Health Foundation. (2014) Improving mental health services: it's everybody's business. From www.health.org.uk/newsletter-feature/improving-mental-health-services-it%E2%80%99s-everybody%E2%80%99s-business (accessed 11/2/21).

The Key. (2017) State of Education Survey Report 2017: Rising to the challenge examining the pressures of schools and how they are responding. From https://view.joomag.com/state-of-education-report-2017/0676372001494577623 (accessed 11/2/21).

Theron, L. (2016). Toward a culturally and contextually sensitive understanding of resilience: Privileging the voices of black, South African young people. *Journal of Adolescent Research, 31*, 635–670.

Theron, L. C., Levine, D., & Ungar, M. (2020). African emerging adult resilience: Insights from a sample of township youth. *Emerging Adulthood.* https://doi.org/10.1177/2167696820940077

Theron, L., Liebenberg, L., & Ungar, M. (Eds.). (2015) *Youth resilience and culture.* The Hague: Springer.H

Thomas, R. M. (2000). *Comparing theories of child development* (5th ed.). Belmont, CA: Wadsworth/Thomson Learning.

Thompson, R. (1991). Emotional regulation and emotional development. *Educational Psychology Review, 3*, 269–307.

Thornicroft, G. (2006). *Shunned: Discrimination against people with mental illness.* Oxford: Oxford University Press.

Thorson, K. (2012). What does it mean to be a good citizen? Citizenship vocabularies as resources for action. *The Annals of the American Academy of Political and Social Science, 644*, 70–85.

Tierney, S. (2007). The dangers and draw of online communication: Pro-anorexia websites and their implications for users, practitioners, and researchers. *Eating Disorders, 14*(3), 181–190.

Tomm, K., Wulff, D., St. George, S., & Strong, T. (Eds.) (2014). *Patterns of interpersonal interactions: Inviting relational understandings for therapeutic change.* New York: Routledge.

Topocco, N., Riper, H., Araya, R., et al. (2017). Attitudes toward digital treatment for depression: A European stakeholder survey. *Internet Interventions, 8*, 1–9.

Townsend, E. (2019). Time to take self-harm in young people seriously. *The Lancet: Psychiatry, 6*, 279–280.

Trnka, S. (2016). Digital care: Agency and temporality in young people's use of health apps. *Engaging Science, Technology and Society, 2,* 248–265.

Tronto, J. (2005). An ethic of care. In A. Cudd, & R. O. Andreasen (Eds.), *Feminist theory: A philosophical anthology* (pp. 251–263). Oxford: Blackwell.

Turkle, S. (2011). Alone together: Why we expect more from technology and less from each other. New York: Basic Books.

Turner, S. G. (2001). Resilience and social work practice: Three case studies. *Families in Society, 82*(5), 441–448.

Twenge, J., Joiner, T., Rogers, M., & Martin, G. (2018). Increases in depressive symptoms, suicide-related outcomes, and suicide rates among US adolescents after 2010 and links to increased new media and screen time. *Clinical Psychological Science, 6,* 3–17.

Uhlhaas, P., & Torous, J. (2019). Digital tools for youth mental health. *npj Digital Medicine, 2,* 204. From www.nature.com/articles/s41746-019-0181-2

UK Safer Internet Centre. (2018). Digital friendships: The role of technology in young people's relationships. UK Safer Internet Centre.

Underwood, M., & Ehrenreich, S. (2017). The power and pain of adolescents' digital communication: Cyber victimization and the perils of lurking. *American Psychologist, 2,* 144–158.

UNESCO. (2013). *Global Media and Information Literacy (MIL): Assessment Framework: Country Readiness and Competencies.* Paris: UNESCO. From http://unesdoc.unesco.org/images/0022/002246/224655e.pdf (accessed 11/2/21).

Ungar, M. (Ed.). (2005). *Handbook for working with children and youth: Pathways to resilience across cultures and contexts.* London: Sage.

Ungar, M. (2011). The social ecology of resilience: Addressing contextual and cultural ambiguity of a nascent construct. *American Journal of Orthopsychiatry, 81,* 1–17.

Ungar, M. (2019). Designing resilience research: Using multiple methods to investigate risk exposure, promotive and protective processes, and contextually relevant outcomes for children and youth. *Child Abuse and Neglect, 96.* doi: https://doi.org/10.1016/j.chiabu.2019.104098

Ungar, M., & Liebenberg, L. (2011). Assessing resilience across cultures using mixed methods: Construction of the child and youth resilience measure. *Journal of Mixed Methods Research, 5*(2), 126–149.

UNICEF. (n.d). What is the Convention on the Rights of the Child? From www.unicef.org/child-rights-convention/what-is-the-convention (accessed 11/2/21).

UNICEF. (1989). Summary of the UNCRC made for children. From www.unicef.org.uk (accessed 11/2/21).

United Nations. (1989). *Conventions on the Rights of the Child.* New York: UN.

United Nations Convention on the Rights of the Child (2021). General comment No. 25 (2021) on children's rights in relation to the digital environment. From https://tbinternet.ohchr.org/_layouts/15/treatybodyexternal/Download.aspx?symbolno=CRC/C/GC/25&Lang=en (accessed 31/3/21).

Vaillancourt, K., Cowan, K., & Skalsk, A. (2016). *Providing mental health services within a multi-tiered system of supports.* Silver Spring, MD: National Association of School Nurses.

Valcke, M., Bonte, S., De Wever, B., & Rots, I. (2010). Internet parenting styles and the impact on Internet use of primary school children. *Computers and Education, 55*(2), 454–464.

Valkenburg, P., & Peter, J. (2007). Preadolescents' and adolescents' online communication and their closeness to friends. *Developmental Psychology, 43,* 267–277.

Valkenburg, P., & Peter, J. (2009). Social consequences of the internet for adolescents: a decade of research. *Current Directions in Psychological Science, 18*(1), 1–5.

Valkenburg, P., & Peter, J., (2013). The differential susceptibility to media effects model. *Journal of Communication, 7,* 197–215.

Valkenburg, P. M., & Piotrowski, J. T. (2017). *Plugged In: How media attract and affect youth.* London: Yale University Press.

Valkenburg, P. M., Piotrowski, J. T., Hermanns, J., & de Leeuw, R. (2013). Development and validation of the perceived parental mediation scale: A self-determination perspective. *Human Communication Research, 39*(4), 445–469.

Valsiner, J. (1997). *Culture and the development of children's action: A theory of human development.* Chichester: Wiley.

Van Breda, A. (2017). The youth ecological-resilience scale: A partial validation. *Research on Social Work Practice, 27,* 248–257.

Van Breda, A. (2018). A critical review of resilience theory and its relevance for social work. *Social Work, 54*(1), online.

van Deursen, A., Helsper, E. J., & Eynon, R. (2015). Development and validation of the Internet skills scale (ISS). *Information, Communication & Society, 19*(6), 804–823.

Van Dijk, J. (2006). Digital divide: Research, achievements and shortcomings. *Poetics, 34,* 221–235.

van Driel, I., Pouwels, J., Beyens, I., Keijsers, L., & Valkenburg, P. (2019). *Posting, scrolling, chatting, and snapping: Youth (14–15) and social media in 2019.* From www.project-awesome.nl/images/Posting-scrolling-chatting-and-snapping.pdf (accessed 11/2/21).

Van Geel, M., Vedder, P., & Tanlion, J. (2014). Relationship between peer victimization, cyberbullying, and suicide in children and adolescents. *JAMA Pediatrics, 168,* 435–442.

Van Ouytsel, J., Van Gool, E., Walrave, M., Ponnet, K., & Peeters, E. (2017). Sexting: Adolescents' perceptions of the applications used for, motives for, and consequences of sexting. *Journal of Youth Studies, 20*(4), 446–470.

van Rooij, A., Ferguson, C., van de Mheen, D., & Schoenmakers, T. (2017). Time to abandon Internet addiction? Predicting problematic internet, game, and social media use from psychosocial wellbeing and application use. *Clinical Neuropsychiatry, 14*(1), 113–121.

Vanden Abeele, M. (2020). Digital wellbeing as a dynamic construct. From https://doi.org/10.31219/osf.io/ymtaf. Available: https://osf.io/ymtaf/ (accessed 11/2/21).

Vaterlaus, J., Beckert, T., Tulane, S., & Bird, C. (2014). They always ask what I'm doing and who I'm talking to: Parental mediation of adolescent interactive technology use. *Marriage and Family Review, 50*(8), 691–713.

Verhulst, F., Achenbach, T., van der Ende, J., et al. (2003). Comparisons of problems reported by youths from seven countries. *American Journal of Psychiatry, 160,* 1479–1485.

Viner, R., Aswathikutty-Gireesh, A., Stiglic, N., Hudson, L., Goddings, A., Ward, J., & Nicholls, D. E. (2019). Roles of cyberbullying, sleep, and physical activity in mediating the effects of social media use on mental health and wellbeing among young people in England: A secondary analysis of longitudinal data. *The Lancet: Child and Adolescent Health, 3*(10), 685–696.

Vogel, E., Rose, J., Roberts, L., & Eckles, K. (2014). Social comparison: Social media, and self-esteem. *Psychol. Pop. Media Cult, 3,* 206–222.

Vygotsky, L. (1978). Mind in Society: The development of higher psychological processes. Cambridge, MA: Harvard University Press.

Waasdorp, T., & Bradshaw, C. (2014). The overlap between cyberbullying and traditional bullying. *Journal of Adolescent Health, 56,* 483–488.

Wall, J. (2008). Human rights in light of childhood. *International Journal of Children's Rights, 16,* 523–543.

Wallace, J. (2010). Mental health and stigma in the medical profession. *Health, 16*(1), 3–18.

Walsh, S., White, K., & Young, R. (2008). Over-connected? A qualitative exploration of the relationship between Australian youth and their mobile phones. *Journal of Adolescence, 31*, 77–92.

Walters, K. L., Evans-Campbell, T., Simoni, J. M., Ronquillo, T., & Bhuyan, R. (2006). 'My spirit in my heart', identity experiences and challenges among American Indian two-spirit women. *Journal of Lesbian Studies, 10*(1–2), 125–149.

Wang, M., & Degol, J. (2016). School climate: A review of the construct, measurement, and impact on student outcomes. *Educational Psychology Review, 28*(2), 315–352.

Wartella, E., Rideout, V., Montague, H., Beaudoin-Ryan, L., & Lauricella, A. (2016). Teens, health and technology: A national survey. *Media and Communication, 4*(3), 13–23.

Weare, K. (2000). *Promoting mental, emotional and social health: A whole–school approach.* London: Routledge.

Weare, K., & Nind, M. (2011). Mental health promotion and problem prevention in schools: What does the evidence say? *Health Promotion International, 26*(S1), i29–i69.

Weerasekera, P. (1996) *Multi-perspective case formulation: A step towards treatment integration.* Malabar: Krieger.

Wegmann, E., & Brand, M. (2016). Internet-communication disorder: It's a matter of social aspects, coping, and internet-use expectancies. *Frontiers in Psychology, 7,* online.

Weinstein, E., & Selman, R. (2014). Digital stress: Adolescents' personal accounts. *New Media and Society, 8*(3), 391–409.

Weist, M., & Murray, M. (2008). Advancing school mental health promotion globally. *Health Promotion, 1*(sup1), 2–12.

Weller, C. (2017). Bill Gates and Steve Jobs raised their kids tech free – and it should've been a red flag. From www.independent.co.uk/life-style/gadgets-and-tech/bill-gates-and-steve-jobs-raised-their-kids-techfree-and-it-shouldve-been-a-red-flag-a8017136.html (accessed 11/2/21).

Werner, E. E. (2001). *Through the eyes of innocents.* New York: Basic Books.

Westheimer, J., & Kahne, J. (2004). Educating the good citizen: political choices and pedagogical goals. *Political Science and Politics, 37*, 241–247.

Whiteford, H., Degenhardt, L., Rehm, J., et al. (2013). Global burden of disease attributable to mental and substance use disorders: Findings from the Global Burden of Disease Study, 2010. *The Lancet, 382*(9904), 1575–1586.

Whitlock, J., Powers, J., & Eckenrode, J. (2006). The virtual cutting edge: The Internet and adolescent self-injury. *Developmental Psychology, 42*, 407–417.

Willard, N. (2006). Cyberbullying and cyberthreats: Effectively managing Internet use risks in schools. From www.cforks.org/Downloads/cyber_bullying.pdf (accessed 11/2/21).

Willard, N. (2007). Educator's guide to cyberbullying and cyberthreats. From www.cyberbully.org/cyberbully/docs/cbteducator.pdf (accessed 7/6/20).

Williams, A., & Merten, M. (2011). iFamily: Internet and social media technology in the family context. *Family and Consumer Science Research Journal, 40*, 15–170.

Williams, J. (2011). The effect on young people of suicide reports in the media. *Mental Health Practice, 14*, 34–36.

Williams, R., & Salmon, G. (2002). Collaboration in commissioning and delivering child and adolescent mental health services. *Current Opinion in Psychiatry, 15*, 349–353.

Wilson, J., Peebles, R., Hardy, K., & Litt, I. (2006). Surfing for thinness: A pilot study of pro-eating disorder Web site usage in adolescents with eating disorders. *Pediatrics, 118*(6), 31635–e1643.

Wind, T., Rijkeboer, M., Andersson, G., & Riper, H. (2020). The COVID-19 pandemic: The 'black swan' for mental health care and a turning point for e-health. *Internet Interventions, 20*, 100317.

Wolak, J., Mitchell, K., & Finkelhor, D. (2006). *Online victimization: 5 years later (No. 07–05–025)*. Alexandria, VA: National Center for Missing & Exploited Children.

Woods, H., & Scott, H. (2016). #Sleepyteens: Social media use in adolescence is associated with poor sleep quality, anxiety, depression and low self-esteem. *Journal of Adolescence, 51*, 41–49.

World Health Organization. (n.d). *Mental health: Suicide prevention*. Geneva: WHO.

World Health Organization. (2004). *Promoting mental health: Concepts, emerging evidence, practice (Summary report)*. Geneva, WHO.

World Health Organization. (2005a). Mental health: Facing the challenges, building solutions. Report from the WHO European Ministerial Conference. Copenhagen: WHO Regional Office for Europe.

World Health Organization. (2005b). *Human resources and training in mental health*. Geneva: WHO.

World Health Organization. (2011). mHealth: New horizons for health through mobile technologies. Geneva: WHO.

World Health Organization. (2013). *Mental Health Action Plan 2013–2020*. Geneva: WHO.

World Health Organization. (2014a). *Mental Health: A State of Wellbeing*. Geneva: WHO.

World Health Organization. (2014b). *Preventing suicide: A global imperative*. Geneva: WHO.

World Health Organization. (2016). *Mental health: Strengthening our response*. Geneva: WHO.

World Health Organization. (2018a). *Adolescent pregnancy*. Geneva: WHO.

World Health Organization. (2018b). The ICD-11 International Classification of Diseases: The global standard for diagnostic health information. Geneva: WHO.

World Health Organization. (2018c). *Mental health atlas, 2017*. Geneva: WHO.

World Health Organization. (2019). Maternal and child mental health. From www.who.int/mental_health/maternal-child/en/ (accessed 11/2/21).

World Health Organization and the Calouste Gulbenkian Foundation. (2014). *Social determinants of mental health*. Geneva: WHO.

Wright, M., Masten, A., & Narayan, A. (2013). Resilience processes in development: Four waves of research on positive adaptation in the context of adversity. In S. Goldstein, & R. B. Brooks (Eds.), *Handbook of resilience in children* (pp. 15–37). New York: Springer Science + Business Media.

Yardi, S., & Bruckman, A. (2011). *Social and technical challenges in parenting teens' social media use*. In Proceedings of the SIGCHI Conference on Human Factors in computing systems (pp. 3237–3246).

Yau, J., & Reich, S. (2017). Are the qualities of adolescents' offline friendships present in digital interactions? *Adolescent Research Review, 3*(3), 339–355.

Ybarra, M., & Mitchell, K. (2005). Exposure to internet pornography among children and adolescents: A national survey. *Cyberpsychology and Behavior, 8*(5), 473–486.

Yip, K-S. (2006). Self-reflective practice: A note of caution. *British Journal of Social Work, 36*, 777–788.

Young Minds. (2016). Resilience for the digital world: Research into children and young people's social and emotional wellbeing online. From https://youngminds.org.uk/media/1490/resilience_for_the_digital_world.pdf (accessed 11/2/21).

Young Minds (2018) 'Kids in Crisis' Documentary on CAMHS. As retrieved 27th May 2020 from https://youngminds.org.uk/blog/kids-in-crisis-documentary-on-camhs/ (accessed 11/2/21).

Young Minds. (2019) Anxiety. From https://youngminds.org.uk/find-help/conditions/anxiety/#what-is-anxiety? (accessed 11/2/21).

Young, D. (2014). A 21st-century model for teaching digital citizenship. *Educational Horizons, February*, 9–12.

Young, J. C. (2019). The new knowledge politics of digital colonialism. *Environment and Planning A: Economy and Space, 51*(7), 1424–1441.

Young, K. S. (2005). An empirical examination of client attitudes towards online counselling. *Cyberpsychology Behavior, 8*, 172–177.

Yu, M., & Baxter, J. (2016). Australian children's screen time and participation in extracurricular activities. *LSAC annual statistical report*. From https://growingupinaustralia.gov.au/research-findings/annual-statistical-report-2015/australian-childrens-screen-time-and-participation-extracurricular (accessed 11/2/21).

Zahradnik, M., Stewart, S., O'Connor, R. M., Stevens, D., Ungar, M., & Wekerle, C. (2009). Resilience moderates the relationship between exposure to violence and posttraumatic re-experiencing in Mi'kmaq youth. *International Journal of Mental Health and Addiction, 8*, 408–420.

Zaman, B., & Nouwen, M. (2016). Parental controls: Advice for parents, researchers and industry. *EU Kids Online*. From eprints.lse.ac.uk/65388/1/__lse.ac.uk_storage_LIBRARY_Secondary_libfile_shared_repository_Content_EU Kids Online_EU_Kids_Online_Parental controls short report_2016.pdf (accessed 11/2/21).

Zetterqvist, M. (2015). The DSM-5 diagnosis of nonsuicidal self-injury disorder: A review of the empirical literature. *Child and Adolescent Psychiatry and Mental Health, 9*, 31–44.

Ziebland, S., & Wyke, S. (2012). Health and illness in a connected world: How might sharing experiences on the internet affect people's health? *Milbank Quarterly, 90*, 219–249.

Zimmerman, P., & Iwanski, A. (2014). Emotion regulation from early adolescence to emerging adulthood and middle adulthood: Age differences, gender differences, and emotion specific developmental variations. *International Journal of Behavioral Development, 38*, 182–194.

Zinck, E., McGrath, P., Fairholm, J., Contursi, M., Mushquash, C., Forshner, A., & Ungar, M. (2013). *Using technology to provide support to children and youth in challenging contexts*. Halifax: CYCC Network.

Zuboff, S. (2015). Big other: surveillance capitalism and the prospects of an information civilization. *Journal of Information Technology, 30*(1), 75–89.

Zuckerman, E. (2013). *Rewire: Digital cosmopolitans in the age of connection*. Vancouver: Norton.

INDEX